Pastoral Quechua

History, Languages, and Cultures of the Spanish and Portuguese Worlds

This interdisciplinary series promotes scholarship in studies on Iberian cultures and contacts from the premodern and early modern periods.

RECENT TITLES IN THE SERIES

The Jesuit and the Incas: The Extraordinary Life of Padre Blas Valera, S.J. (2003)
Sabine Hyland

Upholding Justice: Society, State, and the Penal System in Quito (1650–1750) (2004)
Tamar Herzog

Conflict and Coexistence: Archbishop Rodrigo and the Muslims and Jews of Medieval Spain (2004)
Lucy K. Pick

The Origins of Mexican Catholicism: Nahua Rituals and the Christian Sacraments in Sixteenth-Century Mexico (2004)
Osvaldo F. Pardo

Missionary Tropics: The Catholic Frontier in India (16th–17th Centuries) (2005)
Ines G. Županov

Jews, Christian Society, and Royal Power in Medieval Barcelona (2006)
Ella Klein

How the Incas Built Their Heartland: State Formation and Innovation of Imperial Strategies in the Sacred Valley, Peru (2006)
R. Alan Covey

Pastoral Quechua: The History of Christian Translation in Colonial Peru, 1550–1650 (2007)
Alan Durston

Pastoral Quechua

The History of Christian Translation in Colonial Peru, 1550–1650

ALAN DURSTON

University of Notre Dame Press

Notre Dame, Indiana

Notre Dame, Indiana 46556
www.undpress.nd.edu

Designed by Wendy McMillen
Set in 11.3/13.4 Centaur MT by EM Studio
Printed on 55# Nature's Recycle paper in the U.S.A. by Versa Press, Inc.

Library of Congress Cataloging-in-Publication Data

Durston, Alan, 1970–
Pastoral Quechua : the history of Christian translation in colonial Peru, 1550–1650 / Alan Durston.
p. cm. — (History, languages, and cultures of the Spanish and Portuguese worlds)
Includes bibliographical references and index.
ISBN-13: 978-0-268-02591-5 (pbk. : alk. paper)
ISBN-10: 0-268-02591-6 (pbk. : alk. paper)
1. Quechua language—Peru—History. 2. Quechua language—Peru—Religious aspects. 3. Indians of South America—Missions—Peru. 4. Catholic Church—Missions—Peru. 5. Peru—Languages—Political aspects. 6. Peru—History—1548–1820. I. Title.
PM6301.D87 2007
498'.3230985—dc22
2007025517

This book printed on recycled paper.

For Maju

Contents

Acknowledgments ix

Transcription, Translation, and Citation Norms xii

Map xiv

Introduction 1

Chapter 1 Background 25

PART I. HISTORY

Chapter 2 Diversity and Experimentation—1550s and 1560s 53

Chapter 3 Reform and Standardization—1570s and 1580s 76

Chapter 4 The *Questione della Lingua* and the Politics of Vernacular Competence (1570s–1640s) 105

Chapter 5 The Heyday of Pastoral Quechua (1590s–1640s) 137

PART II. TEXTS

Chapter 6 Pastoral Quechua Linguistics 181

Chapter 7 Text, Genre, and Poetics 221

Chapter 8 God, Christ, and Mary in the Andes 246

Chapter 9 Performance and Contextualization 271

Conclusion 303

Glossary 316

Notes 319

Pastoral Quechua Works 357

Bibliography 359

Index 381

Acknowledgments

It is a pleasure and a relief to be able to thank the people who made this book possible. First mention goes to my dissertation committee at the University of Chicago. Jean Comaroff provided both theoretical guidance and administrative help at various key phases of the project, as did Michael Silverstein, whose teaching contributed much to my understanding of the topic. I was also blessed with the guidance and support of two outstanding scholars of the colonial Andes: Tom Cummins and Bruce Mannheim. During the dissertation writing process, Manuela Carneiro da Cunha and Danilyn Rutherford encouraged me to think about key problems and helped me to see the implications of my research more clearly. I should also mention the ongoing stimulus I have received from my friends and teachers in Santiago, Chile, where I carried out my early graduate work and first acquired an interest in the colonial Andes, especially Patricio Cisterna Alvarado, Jorge Hidalgo Lehuedé, and José Luis Martínez Cereceda.

The main phase of research in 2000–2002 was supported by grants from the United States Department of Education (Doctoral Dissertation Research Abroad or Fulbright-Hays Fellowship), the National Science Foundation (Dissertation Improvement Grant, Award 0075898), and the Wenner-Gren Foundation for Anthropological Research (Small Grant for Dissertation Research, number 6743). Briefer stages of research were aided by grants from the Division of the Social Sciences and the Department of Anthropology of the University of Chicago, and from the Program for Cultural Cooperation between Spain's Ministry of Education, Culture and Sports and U.S. Universities. Finally, the dissertation writing process was greatly facilitated by a Mark Hanna Watkins Dissertation Write-Up Fellowship (2002–3) from the Department of Anthropology of the University of Chicago. I am extremely grateful to all of these institutions for their generosity.

I am indebted to many people who in different ways aided my research in Peru. The Pontificia Universidad Católica del Perú, where I was *investigador afiliado* first in the Faculty of Social Sciences, and then in that of Humanities, provided institutional backing, library resources, and a forum to present my research. In particular, I am grateful for the encouragement and guidance provided by Professors Rodolfo Cerrón-Palomino and Marco Curatola, both of the Facultad de Humanidades. I also frequented the Instituto Francés de Estudios Andinos, where I benefited from conversations with César Itier and Gerald Taylor. My research would have been impossible without the help, often above and beyond the call of duty, of many archivists and librarians in Lima. I would especially like to thank Laura Gutiérrez Arbulú and Melecio Tineo Morón at the Archivo Histórico Arzobispal de Lima, Elinos Caravasis and his colleagues at the Sala de Investigadores de la Biblioteca Nacional del Perú, Lothar Busse and Fernando López at the Archivo del Cabildo Metropolitano de Lima, Ana María Vega at the Archivo de San Francisco de Lima, and Father José Luis Mejía at the Archivo de Santo Domingo de Lima.

Sabine MacCormack played a key role in the passage from dissertation to book by taking the project under her wing as the first in her series "History, Languages, and Cultures of the Spanish and Portuguese Worlds" to be published by the University of Notre Dame Press. Sabine also contributed the photograph that graces the front cover of this book. I am grateful to everyone at the University of Notre Dame Press for their enthusiasm and flexibility, especially Rebecca DeBoer, who copyedited the manuscript with great acuity, and Barbara Hanrahan. The anonymous readers provided a wealth of general and specific suggestions that were very helpful in the revisions. These were made possible by a postdoctoral fellowship at the Erasmus Institute of the University of Notre Dame in 2005–6, which also provided an ideal environment for writing and reflection.

Among my less tangible debts, one of the greatest is to the pioneers of the young field of Quechua historical linguistics and general language history, in particular Rodolfo Cerrón-Palomino, César Itier, Bruce Mannheim, Gerald Taylor, and Alfredo Torero. My research was only possible because of their painstaking and insufficiently recognized work, which has achieved exemplary syntheses of historical, anthropological, and linguistic concerns. I am equally indebted to my Quechua teachers, both professional instructors—in particular Gina Maldonado (at the Centro de Estudios Andinos "Bartolomé de Las Casas") and Clodoaldo Soto (at the University of Illinois at Urbana-Champaign)—and the numerous people who had the patience to chat with me in different parts of Peru, especially my hosts in Sarhua, Ayacucho.

The entire process was made much easier by the support and encouragement of my parents, Riet Delsing and John Durston, both researchers themselves. Finally, this book is dedicated to Maju Tavera for her love, understanding, and patience.

Transcription, Translation, and Citation Norms

Quechua texts are presented in their original form, with the exception of abbreviations, which have been completed. Isolated Quechua terms are represented with the standardized orthography of the Third Lima Council (1582–1583), but for specific segments (phonemes and suffixes), or when a more accurate transcription of a word is required, I use the modern phonological alphabet between forward slashes (see Mannheim 1991: 235–238 on the current official orthography for Southern Peruvian Quechua). However, I only represent glottalized and aspirate stops (for example, /k'/, /kh/, /p'/, /ph/ . . .) when citing from a specific text or author whose original orthography distinguishes these segments from the plain forms (/k/, /p/ . . .). Brackets ({ }) are used for orthographic units. Verb stems are represented with a hyphen to indicate that they must be followed by one or more suffixes (e.g., *cuya-* 'to have compassion' or 'to love'), but not noun stems (e.g., *huasi* 'house'). For the sake of consistency and ease of reading, the following modifications have been made to Spanish texts: punctuation and case have been modernized; abbreviations have been completed; {y}, {i}, {u}, and {v} are used as in modern Spanish; and word-initial {rr} is changed to {r}. All Spanish names have been fully modernized unless they appear in a direct quotation.

When quoting Quechua or Spanish texts for their content, a translation is provided in the main text and the original appears in an endnote, unless the quotation is very brief, in which case it is sometimes omitted or follows directly on the translation. When the formal properties of a text are at stake, the original is presented in the main text, followed by a translation. When quoting verse, I have tried to provide a line-for-line translation, but this has frequently not been possible because of the differences in word and sentence structure between Quechua and English.

Citations of primary documents from archives or published document collections are provided in endnotes. The notation "f." indicates that a manuscript or printed work is numbered only on the recto or front of each leaf, as distinct from regular page numbering; "v." indicates the verso side—e.g., "f. 23v." means the verso side of the twenty-third numbered folio.

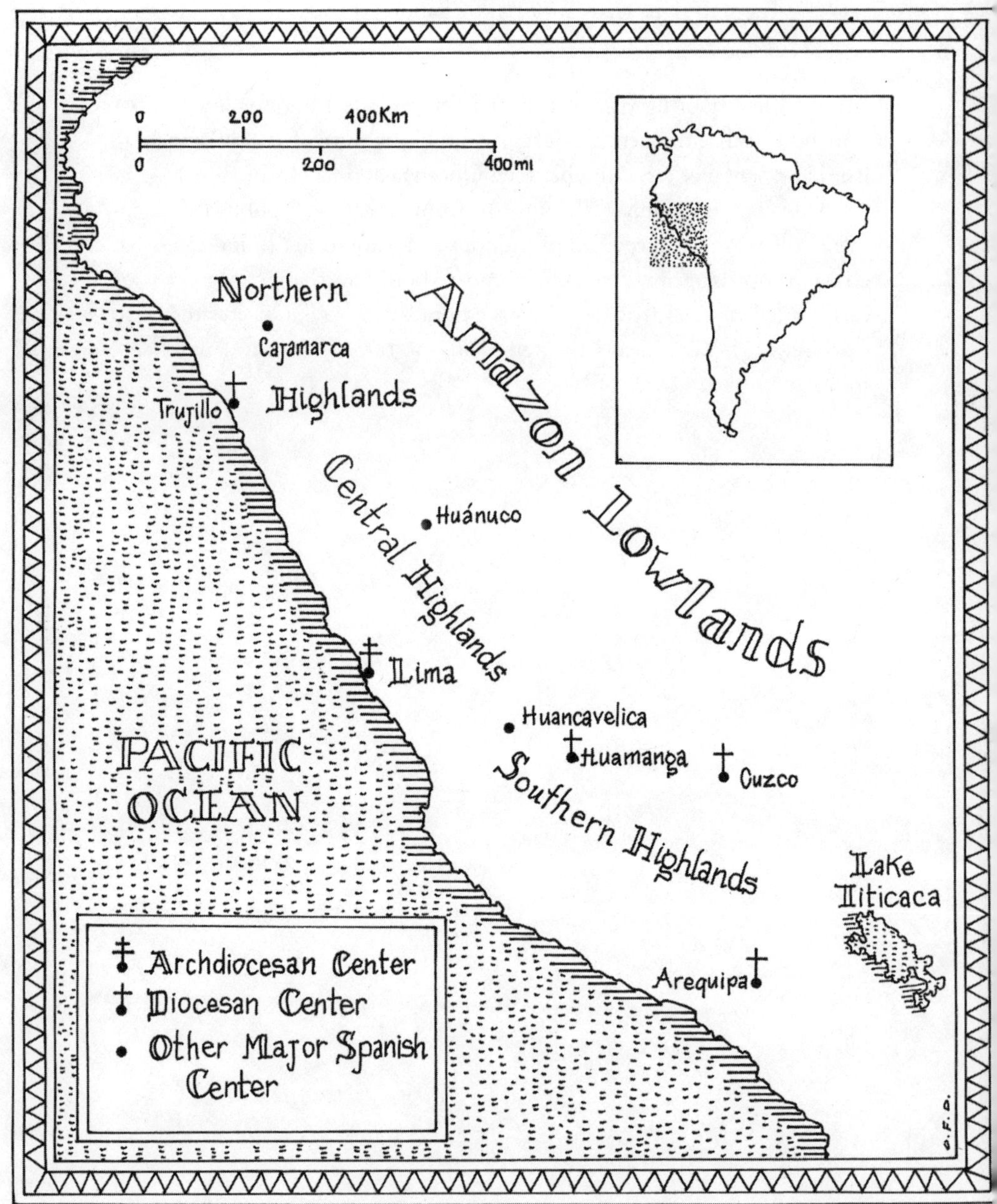

Main Spanish Centers of Colonial Peru

Pastoral Quechua

Introduction

The systematic appropriation of indigenous languages for missionary and pastoral uses was one of the most telling features of Spanish colonialism in the Americas. It is also one of the least understood today, a topic that tends to fall through the cracks between history, anthropology, and linguistics. In its everyday sense, the term "translation" does not convey the full dimensions of the process, which ranged from the selection and development of the appropriate language varieties for use in a given area to the imposition of performance systems for inculcating entire Christian literatures in these languages. Missionary translation in this broader sense was a key instrument of colonialism—interethnic relations were established and mediated by conversion, which in turn worked through, and was epitomized by, translation (Rafael 1993 [1988]). Translation itself can be understood as a way of establishing relations—often hierarchical ones—between languages, and thus between cultures and groups of people (Benjamin 1968 [1955]). The translation activities of the Spanish church in Latin America are a privileged window onto the divergent projects and ideologies vis-à-vis Indian Christianity that emerged within the colonial establishment. These activities are recorded in a mass of extant texts that make up the bulk, if not the totality, of the historical literature of many Amerindian languages. Such texts, which include liturgical and devotional genres as well as strictly catechetical ones, are particularly abundant in the languages of Mesoamerica and the Andes, the focal areas of the Spanish empire.

Quechua is no exception. A family of closely related languages and dialects, it is more widely spoken today than any other comparable Amerindian group—there are an estimated eight to ten million Quechua speakers, living mostly in Bolivia, Ecuador, and Peru.[1] Quechua is also heavily stigmatized, and most of these speakers are either subsistence farmers or rural immigrants in the cities who have little choice but to rapidly discard it for the dominant language, Spanish. Its role as a medium of written communication ranges from very limited to nil. The subjugated condition of Quechua is starkest in Peru, which of the three Andean nations concentrates the largest number of speakers and the greatest variety of forms of Quechua (cf. Mannheim 1991: 80–109). In short, Quechua is the language of the poor and marginal in a poor and marginal part of the world. In the aftermath of the conquest, however, it was of strategic importance for Spanish imperial interests, being widely spoken in an area characterized by immense mineral wealth (primarily silver) and a dense, sedentary native population that had been administratively unified under the Inca empire.

Accordingly, Quechua became the prime object of language study and translation in Spanish South America, particularly during the heyday of official interest in vernacular projects, which stretched from the mid-sixteenth to the mid-seventeenth century. About a dozen volumes featuring Quechua sermons, catechisms, prayers, hymns, and other genres are known to have survived from this period, all written by Spanish priests for use in Indian parishes. The church's efforts did not, however, accommodate the internal diversity of the Quechua language family. The corpus comes in its entirety from what is now highland and coastal Peru, and is not fully representative of the diversity even of this area—instead, description, codification, and translation focused overwhelmingly on the Quechua of the southern highlands, particularly a written standard based on the variety of Cuzco, the Inca capital.

The Christian literature in Quechua is little known even among specialists in the colonial Andes. Scholars of Quechua have traditionally used Christian texts mostly as linguistic witnesses—it is only in the past decade or so that Quechuists such as Rodolfo Cerrón-Palomino (1997), César Itier (1995a, 1995b), Bruce Mannheim (1998a, 2002), and Gerald Taylor (2001a, 2001b, 2002, 2003) have begun to approach them as objects of study in their own right. At the same time, historians of Christianity in the Andes, especially Juan Carlos Estenssoro Fuchs (2003) and Sabine MacCormack (1985, 1994), have been paying serious attention to the Quechua texts written by the Peruvian clergy. However, the two fields of research have remained separate, and the formal characteristics of the extant literature have not been explored systematically in relation to the historical contexts that produced them. Much the same could be said of research on other parts of the Spanish empire, not to mention early-modern missionary enterprises in general.[2] Even the rich historical and anthropological literature on Christian conversion in Africa and South Asia in the nineteenth and twentieth centuries rarely places linguistic and textual practices at center stage.[3]

This book seeks to help fill these gaps by telling the story of how the church in Peru developed and promoted what I call pastoral Quechua—the Christian "language" or register in Quechua. I prefer this label to more obvious ones such as "missionary Quechua" because the overwhelming bulk of the corpus was intended for use in fully organized parishes in areas that had been under Christian control for generations.[4] I examine the extant texts as instances of systematic efforts to "incarnate" Christianity in Quechua, and explore how Spanish colonial ideologies and strategies are reflected in their ways of rendering Christian categories and terms, in their dialectology, and in their use of poetic resources. Conversely, I ask what these apparent minutiae contributed to the construction of an Andean Christianity and of certain types of relationships between Spaniards and Indians in Peru. While I speak of "pastoral Quechua" in the singular, much of my research has been directed at charting diversity and change at different levels—e.g., in the Christian terminology employed—and at tying them to splits and shifts within the church and the colonial regime as a whole. The tightness of the relation between even the most minute formal characteristics of a text and broad historical processes is most apparent when one focuses on variation and its motives. In particular, I examine variability in the pastoral Quechua corpus in relation to an orthodox standard established via a set of official catechetical texts published by the Third Lima Council (1582–83), which have left a lasting imprint on Christian discourse in Quechua up to the present day.

This book is based on the assumption, which I hope to demonstrate, that the pastoral Quechua literature carries implications that go far beyond the strictly linguistic or philological. Christian writing in Quechua was one of the front lines of Spanish colonialism in the Andes, an activity in which Spanish aims and intentions were confronted in very direct and precise ways with the language and culture of conquered peoples. Pastoral Quechua texts are strategic witnesses to colonial interactions and power relations because they enacted them—they are not post facto commentaries or rationalizations. Key issues in the study of colonialism, such as religious hybridity or syncretism, are analyzable with an empirical precision in these texts that is not often possible in other kinds of sources. I will attempt to show that the pastoral Quechua literature not only is illuminated by its historical contexts, but in turn illuminates them and even contributed towards their construction.

Some comment on the terms "language" and "translation" may help to further explain my approach. Beyond the generic, deindividuated sense of "language" as the activity of verbal communication in general, two basic meanings are involved here: "language" in the ordinary sense of a linguistic variety, as when one speaks of Italian or Japanese as "languages" (the default meaning); and "language" in the sense of a register or mode of expression associated with a specific practice, profession, institution, discipline, ideology, etc., as when one speaks of "legal language" or the "language of scholasticism." In Mikhail Bakhtin's words, the first is "[language] in the sense of a system of elementary forms (linguistic symbols) guaranteeing a *minimum* level of comprehension in practical communication" and the second "[language] conceived as ideologically saturated, language as a world view, even as a concrete opinion, insuring a *maximum* of mutual understanding in all the spheres of ideological life" (Bakhtin 1981: 271). While in Spanish the two are conveniently distinguished as *lengua* and *lenguaje,* respectively, there is unfortunately no such lexical distinction in English.

A "language" in the second of the two senses is a heterogeneous "bundle" of different elements: styles, vocabularies, and tropes; textual genres and media; performance conventions and contexts; as well as a discursive and ideological order (sets of topics, modes of argumentation, etc.). Languages in the first sense are certainly more characterizable entities—their basic structural workings can be defined with some precision at levels such as grammar and phonology. However, identifying them and discerning their boundaries is not as straightforward as may appear. Languages tend to exist in a continuum of variation where it is hard to say where one begins and the other ends. The study of linguistic variation is one of the least developed branches of linguistics—that of synchronic (geographical or social) as opposed to historical variation is known as "dialectology," a term that is something of a misnomer as it presumes clear boundaries between languages. In practice, the ways in which people distinguish, classify, and hierarchize linguistic varieties has little to do with their structural characteristics, and everything to do with the groups that speak them, and how they in turn are perceived—a point expressed in the well-worn adage "a language is a dialect with an army and a navy" (cf. Irvine and Gal 2000).

Quechua provides an excellent example of the problems involved in identifying and discerning "languages" in the first of the two senses outlined above: even though there is very limited or no intelligibility between some varieties, it is popularly regarded as a single language—a fact reflected in the absence of names for different varieties other than the purely geographical designations used by linguists. This perception results from the fact that for over four hundred years Spanish has been the dominant language throughout the Andes, and from a lack of correspondence between important divisions within the Quechua language family and political units. On the other hand, these same facts have meant that homogenous, clearly bounded varieties have not developed, as happened with many European languages due to nation-state formation. One of the central questions of this book is how the Spanish perceived and dealt with the diversity presented by "Quechua," a question examined both through what they had to say on the subject and through the dialectology of the Quechua texts they wrote.

Only a small fraction of the pastoral Quechua corpus consists of direct translations of canonical texts. Rendering such texts into any vernacular language was a highly restricted activity in the Catholic church during the period of this study. More commonly, an ad-hoc Spanish text would be written specifically for translation—often fairly loose translation—into Quechua. Many texts were originally composed in Quechua. It might seem, then, that "translation" is not the best label for the activity studied here. However, if translation is approached as a program, practice, or set of norms rather than as a singular act of transference (cf. Hermans 2002), it makes little difference whether a given text is a direct translation or has more generic models. Even those texts that were originally composed in Quechua followed European genre conventions very closely, as well as striving to reproduce Christian discourses. A broader definition of translation that takes this issue into account can be formulated more or less as follows: translation is the process of recreating a "language" (in the second of the two senses) in a new linguistic variety ("language" in the first sense).[5]

This focus on translation as a process of transposing a "language" rather than a set of individual texts seems particularly appropriate to pastoral Quechua. Since few canonical texts were translated, and a policy was soon established not to allow variant translations of key texts such as the basic prayers, questions concerning text-to-text relations, such as the literal-versus-free translation paradigm, never became very prominent. Instead, debate and disagreement focused on how to render key terms, on stylistic issues, and on the appropriateness of different varieties of Quechua as Christian media. Perhaps unexpectedly, the reader will not find in this book much in the way of one-to-one comparison of originals and translations, or, to use the translation studies terminology, "source" texts and "target" texts.[6] Far more attention is paid to relations *among* translations (or target texts). As translation theorist Theo Hermans points out, "[a]ll translations bounce off existing translations." In other words, translation "gestures not just to a given source text but just as much, obediently or defiantly, to prevailing norms and modes of translating" (2002: 15, 16), a principle that is amply illustrated in this book.

The purpose of my research has been to develop a holistic understanding of Christian translation into Quechua as a practice extending both before and beyond the establishment of a written text. This involves different levels of analysis. A first level concerns the identification of the appropriate linguistic variety to be used—as will be seen, the church required the use of a single, standard variety which had to be selected and, to some extent, created. A further level of translation practice involves the role or scope of Quechua as a Christian medium in relation to Latin and Spanish—the question of what particular texts, genres, and styles of religious speech were to be reproduced in Quechua. Such questions logically precede more obvious issues in translation practice, also studied here, such as the development of lexical forms to play the role of "untranslatable" Christian terms such as "God," "church," "baptism," etc. Particular attention is paid to terminological disagreements, as they were tied to one of the key ideological rifts that developed within the church in Peru—the degree to which an author-translator was open to using existing religious vocabulary depended on his evaluation of pre-conquest religion as a whole and its relationship to Christianity. The role Andean religious terms and categories were given in pastoral Quechua is a central question for this book. Finally, the analysis extends to the issues of transmission and (intended) reception via liturgical and catechetical performances in the Indian parishes, the question being how various levels of context were supplied for texts that now reach us as isolated fragments. The issue of contextualization—how the church sought to control perceptions of and interactions with the pastoral texts—was of particular importance because of the radical differences between source and target cultures.

The fact that this study combines close analysis of a corpus of texts with an examination of their broad historical contexts has made it difficult to organize into a neat series of thematically or chronologically defined chapters. Instead, I have chosen to divide it into two qualitatively distinct parts preceded by a background chapter. Part I (chapters 2–5) provides a narrative history of the pastoral literature in Quechua and, more broadly, of the pastoral regime in the Andes. Discussion of the language of the texts is kept to a minimum in these chapters, which focus on presenting the literature in its broad outlines and institutional and ideological contexts, while also detailing the particular histories of texts and authors. Part II consists of four chapters dealing directly with the pastoral literature in its linguistic, textual, and performative aspects. This structure results in some overlap and repetition, but I have found it to be the most effective way of combining the historical and linguistic/textual themes and information.

Chapter 1 sets the background for the rest of the book, discussing the development of the colonial system in Peru and of Spanish colonial linguistic ideologies and policies, and drawing the outlines of the linguistic landscape of the Andes at the time of the conquest. The next two chapters survey the development of pastoral Quechua and of the pastoral regime in general during a phase of diversity and experimentation in the 1550s and 1560s (chapter 2) and a period of reform and consolidation in the 1570s and 1580s that culminated in the Third Lima Council (chapter 3). Chapter 4 deals with the politics of linguistic selection (i.e., the question of what language[s] to use in missionary and pastoral contexts) and clerical language training from the 1570s up to the middle of the seventeenth century. Chapter 5 doubles back to the 1590s to survey the general development of pastoral Quechua writing in the wake of the Third Lima Council, continuing until a sudden drop around 1650.

The first two chapters of part II provide a synchronic survey of the pastoral Quechua literature in its formal characteristics: chapter 6 deals with grammar, dialectology, and Christian terminology, while chapter 7 discusses the kinds of texts and genres that are present in the corpus and their poetic resources (tropes and textual figures). Chapter 8 focuses on the use of Andean religious categories, images, and motifs in the creation of a deliberately syncretic Catholic-Andean iconography surrounding the figures of God, Christ, and Mary that is in evidence in the work of specific author-translators. This chapter examines the types of dialogue between Christian and Andean religious traditions that these author-translators sought to establish. Chapter 9 deals with the issue of contextualization. First, it provides an overall description of the organization of catechesis and liturgy in the Indian parishes in order to determine how and for what purposes specific texts were performed. Second, it discusses the mechanisms that were intended to orient and control the ways in which Indians engaged the texts, focusing on the implicit metalanguages present in performance practices, in the formal organization of the texts, and in certain aspects of Quechua grammar.

The only portions of the book that may be difficult to read without some knowledge of Quechua and/or descriptive linguistics are parts of chapter 6 and the final section of chapter 9. Readers interested in following the details of the arguments made there can consult Bruce Mannheim's *The Language of the Inka Since the European Invasion* (1991)—which apart from its other contributions has very useful appendices clarifying technical issues—and the sections on Quechua in Willem Adelaar and Pieter Muysken's *The Languages of the Andes* (2004). The standard reference work in Spanish is Rodolfo Cerrón-Palomino's exhaustive *Lingüística quechua* (1987). These books provide in-depth treatment of topics in Quechua grammar, phonology, dialectology, and historical linguistics that are only mentioned here in passing.

Themes

This book draws on a variety of distinct traditions of scholarship without fitting squarely into any particular one. Although it is, most obviously, a piece of historical research, it began as a dissertation in sociocultural anthropology and is especially indebted to themes and concepts from linguistic anthropology. My hope is that it will appeal to all those interested in colonialism, religious conversion, and the language-society relation in historical perspective. As a way of situating the book in broader frames of reference, I highlight three interdisciplinary areas of research that are of special relevance to it: (1) the social history of language, (2) translation studies, and (3) the history/anthropology of religious accommodation and syncretism.

The Social History of Language

The "new cultural history"—the historiography focused on the production of meaning as the basis of social life that developed in the 1980s—is often identified with a "linguistic turn" (cf. Eley 2005). However, the expression is a misleading one in that this historiography has paid very limited attention to language in the first of the two senses outlined above. Hence the importance of the calls by Peter Burke (1993, 2004), a cultural historian of early modern Europe, for a "social history of language" drawing on linguistic anthropology and sociolinguistics to study the relations between historical processes and the development, distribution, and use of languages.

As the orientation of Burke's surveys suggests, a (or perhaps *the*) central task for a social history of language is the study of linguistic perceptions and policies and their relation to actual language use. The most prominent examples of this sort of research concern the relation between nationalism and processes of linguistic standardization, unification, and purification in the nineteenth and twentieth centuries (e.g., Anderson 1991 [1983]). However, all societies are linguistically diverse, and no society is indifferent to this diversity: all interpret and manage it in particular ways. There may be disagreement regarding when one can speak of outright language *planning*, but it is clear that explicit linguistic debates and policies can be found much earlier than the nineteenth century—in sixteenth- and seventeenth-century Europe and its overseas colonies, for instance. They are not necessarily located in the state or based on political programs—all sorts of historical processes and institutions involve the *questione della lingua* in some form (see Bloomer ed. 2004). In the early modern context, religious schism and reform come to mind immediately. Not only is the management of linguistic diversity an important historical practice in its own right, it also reflects and mediates a variety of other domains.

The social history of language has much in common with the study of language ideologies, a growing field in linguistic anthropology (cf. Kroskrity ed. 2000; Schieffelin, Woolard, and Kroskrity eds. 1998). The concept of language ideology refers to largely implicit, socially held understandings of the nature and appropriate use of language in general, and, differentially, of particular languages. It involves the ways in which languages are classified, hierarchized, and related to social groups. The notion that there is, or should be, a correspondence or isomorphism between nation-state and language is an example of a particularly pervasive modern linguistic ideology. A related but much older linguistic-ideological notion holds that the essential characteristics of groups of people (e.g., civility, barbarism) are reflected in the languages they speak; in this sense, Judith Irvine and Susan Gal speak of "iconicity" as one of a set of widespread cognitive or semiotic procedures in the classification and valorization of languages (Irvine and Gal 2000).

The agenda of a social history of language is especially relevant to colonial contexts, where linguistic differences are unusually prominent and laden with inequalities. Translation practice would also seem to be a particularly fruitful field for its application, especially for the opportunities it presents to combine the study of linguistic policies and ideologies with that of actual language use. As a form of language use necessarily involving at least two different languages, translation is a uniquely deliberate and pregnant one. This is particularly the case with large-scale translation programs between previously separate cultural traditions. The many choices translators must make in such cases, starting with which particular linguistic variety to use and what texts or genres to translate, are determined by often tacit understandings and policies regarding the relative status and potentials of the languages and cultures involved. Once enshrined in actual texts and performances, these choices in turn serve to consolidate, reproduce, and naturalize such understandings and policies.

Translation

The historical study of translation has been going on independently for some time within translation studies, a discipline that has grown under the aegis of modern language departments. Translation studies is distinguished from the vast, primarily applied literature on translation by its concern for the contexts and effects of historical translation activities. One prominent line that developed in the early stages of translation studies during the 1970s and 1980s sought to monitor the roles that translated literatures assume in the "literary systems" of target languages and cultures, and to establish fixed correlations between variations in the organization of such literary systems and translation practices (e.g., Toury 1995; cf. Gentzler

2001, chapters 4 and 5). This literature made an important break with a previous reductionist focus on the relation between source text and target text, and emphasized the need to study translation in terms of broad programs involving entire literatures rather than isolated texts. The earlier concern with fidelity and appropriateness was tempered in light of evidence that the norms that define what is faithful and what is appropriate vary historically and culturally. At the same time, however, much of this literature was marred by an excessively typological and rule-bound focus.

Under the influence of poststructuralism and postcolonialism in the 1980s and 1990s, translation studies developed a heightened sensitivity to the political implications of translation activity. In particular, postcolonial translation studies has dealt with the issues involved in translation between Third World/colonized languages and First World/colonialist languages. Very much in line with the postmodern critique in anthropology, postcolonial translation scholars have essentially been concerned with understanding and counteracting the power effects underlying translation from colonized into colonialist languages. Translation is understood as an instrument of cultural representation and control that reaffirms colonial preconceptions and stereotypes of the Other, and neutralizes and domesticates foreign cultures (cf. Basnett and Trivedi eds. 1999; Simon and St-Pierre eds. 2000; and Tymoczko and Gentzler eds. 2002).

The reader will quickly notice, however, that the translation studies literature does not figure prominently in this book. With some exceptions, I have not found translation studies theory particularly applicable to the issues surrounding pastoral Quechua. First of all, translation studies has focused on literary translation, with very limited attention to religious languages, whose translation presents unique problems. Religious traditions of the dogmatic, revealed type tend to impose strict limits on the translation of canonical texts in order to guarantee the role of ritual specialists as well as the distinctive, sacral character of the texts themselves. Similar limitations apply at the level of religious terminology, such as terms for deities and institutions; translators often prefer to leave them untouched by introducing them as loan words instead of searching for a risky equivalent in the target language and culture. Religious translation programs usually involve a tension between the need to translate in order to fulfill missionary or pastoral mandates and the fear that translation will lead to corruption and betrayal, and such tensions have not been dealt with systematically in translation studies.

A second problem is that translation studies has focused overwhelmingly on translations carried out by members of the target culture—i.e., translators who translate foreign works into their native language, as is usually the case in literary translation. This could be called "endogenous translation" in opposition to "exogenous translation," where the translators are members of the source culture and seek to introduce their own texts and textual traditions into a foreign language and culture. There are, of course, many instances where the distinction does not apply—e.g., if the translator is bi- or multicultural, or if the source and target languages share a common sociocultural context. Often enough, however, translation activities are quite clearly classifiable as either endogenous or exogenous, particularly in the increasingly monolingual modern world and, historically, in colonial contexts. It could be suggested that "internal" translators have a tendency to produce translations that maximize continuity with the traditions of the target language, whereas "external" ones are more likely to emphasize fidelity to the source language and produce translations that involve greater transformations of target norms. This may not always be the case—indeed, the opposite could occur—but whenever the endogenous-exogenous distinction is applicable, it would seem to have major consequences for what is translated and how.

Even though it is clear that a substantial portion of all historical translation activity has been of the exogenous variety, translation studies have focused so overwhelmingly on endogenous translation that the terms "source text" and "foreign text" have become virtually synonymous. A similar slant is apparent in anthropology: when anthropologists deal with translation, they tend to do so in the reflexive mode—it is their own endogenous acts of translation with which they are concerned.[7] Little if any attention is given to the exogenous acts of translation carried out by anthropologists, as when they have to explain themselves and their research projects to their hosts. As a product of translation that is both religious and exogenous, pastoral Quechua belongs to a class of less-studied translation programs and it is a very large and historically important class. It thus has the potential to modify or broaden understandings of how translation works, and to what effect.

Accommodation and Syncretism

Whether the author-translators wanted it or not, the story of pastoral Quechua is one of contact and interaction between religious and cultural traditions that had developed in complete isolation from one another. Christian conversion strategies have historically involved forms of religious adaptation or accommodation whose modern expression (post–Second Vatican Council) is inculturation theology, which proclaims the need for Christianity to be expressed through the values, ideologies, and symbols of particular cultures. Accommodation is a two-way street: Christianity is adapted to a specific cultural context, but local categories and forms are themselves radically transformed through contact with Christianity. Translation is, of course, a key aspect of accommodation, but should not be identified with it too closely—accommodation does not necessarily involve translation, and, as will be seen, translation is not necessarily accommodationist.

How far the give-and-take of accommodation can be allowed to go before essential elements of Christianity are lost or corrupted has been a highly controversial issue for the Catholic Church up to the present day. The forms, extent, and purposes of accommodation have varied widely. The main canonical locus is in Gregory the Great's instructions for Augustine of Canterbury in 601, advising that the pagan temples of Anglo-Saxon England be adapted for use as churches and that the practice of slaughtering cattle in their festivities be allowed to continue on Christian feastdays.[8] Accommodation appears here as an expediency to make the transition to Christianity less abrupt—certain aspects of the local religion are assimilated into Christianity not because they are judged to have any intrinsic value, but because they are judged harmless or regarded as lesser evils. Modern inculturation theology contemplates more profound and radical forms of adaptation grounded in a valorization of cultural diversity and a belief that all cultures are in essence compatible with Christianity (e.g., Shorter 1988). Even in the absence of modern ideologies of multiculturalism or cultural relativism, accommodation programs in the past have also been inspired, and justified, by a belief in the presence of the "seeds of the faith" in the culture being evangelized.

On the broad stage of early modern Catholic expansion overseas, the Spanish church in Peru does not stand out for the boldness of its accommodationist practices. In the contemporary mission fields of India and China, accommodation was taken to lengths that caused open conflict within the church. During the late sixteenth and early seventeenth centuries, Jesuit missionaries carried out systematic modifications of the liturgy in order to accommodate native social norms and sensibilities, resulting in the prolonged Chinese and Malabar (Tamil) Rites controversies, which were eventually resolved in favor of orthodoxy by papal commissions (*Catholic Encyclopedia,* "Malabar rites" and "Matteo Ricci;" cf. Županov 1999). Jesuits throughout South and East Asia dressed, acted, and to some extent lived like natives, something which would have been inconceivable in the Andes. In Peru, as elsewhere in the Americas, the *need* for accommodation was obviated by full military conquest and the destruction of native political and religious institutions. The *viability* of accommodation was compromised by the fact that the most influential Spanish commentators, such as the Jesuit José de Acosta, saw major shortcomings and deficiencies in Andean society and culture. For all their achievements, the Incas were thought to be very far from attaining the same level of civility and rationality as the Chinese and Japanese, which meant that their customs were less compatible with natural and divine law (cf. Pagden 1986).

Missionary and pastoral practices in the Americas were thus characterized more by a *tabula rasa* or "clean slate" approach than by accommodation, and this is very much apparent in the development of pastoral Quechua. One might object that translation is itself an act of accommodation, but it can be carried out in ways that minimize interaction between Christianity and the religious traditions associated with the target language. A recent (2001) post-inculturationist Vatican instruction on liturgical translation advises that key terms be "translated" with loan words and neologisms instead of the native categories that most seem to approximate them, even if the result is initially unfamiliar (not to say unintelligible) for the target audience.[9] This approach is apparent even in the way Latin was adopted as the language of Western Christianity in the fourth century—the translators of the liturgy made heavy use of Greek loan words and Latin neologisms that became a permanent part of the Latin of the Catholic Church, while existing Latin terms which were fairly close equivalents of the Greek terms were often excluded precisely because they were *religious* terms and thus carried the danger of "contamination" from pagan associations (Mohrmann 1957: 54–55).

Similar principles were applied in the development of the standard or canonical forms of pastoral Quechua, especially as represented in the catechetical volumes of the Third Lima Council. However, the scholarship on the early church in Peru has shown that there were ongoing debates regarding the compatibility of Andean religious traditions with Christianity that had direct consequences for missionary and pastoral practices, including translation (Estenssoro Fuchs 2003; MacCormack 1985, 1991, 1994). A few author-translators engaged in often daring accommodationist practices, deliberately, if implicitly, provoking identifications between Christian and Andean religious entities and categories through the use of key terms and motifs. A central concern of this book is thus to distinguish the more from the less accommodationist translation programs, and to work out their contrasting motivations and implications.

The topic of missionary accommodation can be considered a subset of the study of syncretism, even if the term is a controversial one. From a missiological point of view, syncretism is accommodation or inculturation run amok—religious traditions are merged to the point where essential features of the Christian message are lost. The term is also unpopular in academic discourse, particularly in anthropology, where it is felt that it presumes the existence of pure, uncontaminated cultural traditions and forms that can be distinguished from syncretic ones. Notwithstanding these reservations, there have been calls for an anthropology of syncretism that would be "concerned with competing discourses over mixture," or "metasyncretic" discourses—in other words, "the commentary, and registered perceptions of actors as to whether almagamation has occurred and whether this is good or bad" (Stewart 1999: 58, cf. Stewart and Shaw 1994). One thus avoids the problem of determining whether a specific form is syncretic or not (just about anything can be considered syncretic from one perspective or another), to focus instead on syncretism as a category guiding the production and interpretation of texts (broadly understood), even if the term itself is not employed and there is no explicit discussion of the subject.

Accommodation can be considered a key "metasyncretic discourse," one that deliberately produces syncretism instead of merely commenting on it. It is not a fruitless exercise to distinguish "the native" from "the Christian" in, say, the imagery of a Quechua hymn when it is apparent that it was written (and perhaps meant to be interpreted) in precisely these terms. The author-translators certainly worked with such oppositions in mind, and some attempted to bridge them in very precise and deliberate ways. Exactly how and why they did so is an issue of some importance from the perspective both of the cultural politics of colonialism and of Andean cultural history in general (see especially chapter 8).

Scope

This is a book about Spanish colonial uses of Quechua. The issue of native response is not dealt with directly—it is addressed only from the perspective of the clerical authors, whose translation practices were naturally oriented by their understandings of audience response. My decision to limit the book's scope in this respect stems both from the belief that native response is a distinct (though not separate) topic requiring full treatment in its own right, and from the fragmentary nature of the relevant sources. A first place to look for native reactions to, or reinterpretations of, Christian discourse would be in Christian texts of native authorship. However, pastoral Quechua is the product of an overwhelmingly exogenous translation program: the extant texts are almost all, as far as one can tell, the work of priests, and Indians were excluded from the priesthood.[10] Most of these priests were *criollos,* Spaniards born in Peru who were often native speakers of Quechua. We know a few of them to have been mestizos, but mestizos who were raised and educated in Spanish contexts. It is possible that some of the author-translators worked closely with native collaborators, but there are almost no references to such collaboration. In general, very few Quechua texts of native authorship have survived, in contrast to the wealth of sources available to Mesoamericanists. Nor is there much in the way of archival sources that might bear testimony to indigenous responses. Although there are abundant references to indigenous appropriations of Christian images, sacraments, and institutions in the "extirpation of idolatries" trials, which were directed at eradicating the clandestine practice of native cults (see Mills 1997), the appropriation of Christian *language* is not so well documented.

Similarly, the broader question of how pastoral Quechua impacted Andean culture and society in the short and long term is only dealt with tangentially. Frank Salomon has pointed to issues such as the effects of the introduction of a standardized, written form of Quechua on the development of indigenous discourses and forms of historical memory (1994: 231). The literature on colonial indigenous writing has often made note of the very prominent influence of pastoral language (e.g., Adorno 1986; Duviols 1993; Itier 1993 and 2005; Salomon 1991), although it has sometimes been hampered by the lack of a more precise understanding of the characteristics and development of the pastoral literature in Quechua. One of the purposes of this book is to aid future research in these directions.

The chronological and geographical limits of this study are fairly clear-cut. I use 1550 as a symbolic date for the period when a missionary/pastoral regime first began to develop in a more or less centralized and systematic way after the upheaval that followed on the conquest in 1532. Furthermore, the oldest extant pastoral Quechua texts date to around 1550 (see chapter 2). For reasons which will be discussed in chapter 5, the colonial regime all but abandoned its vernacular project around the middle of the seventeenth century, when there was a dramatic decline in the production of new pastoral Quechua texts. The 1550–1650 period can be considered both formative and classical in relation to the late colonial and republican production. The standard established by the Third Lima Council for basic Christian terms and expressions has remained stable, as have its translations of the basic prayers, which are still used universally, if with the appropriate dialectal modifications. Later authors of Christian texts come nowhere near Luis Jerónimo de Oré, Juan Pérez Bocanegra, Francisco de Avila, and other writers of this period in the extent and sophistication of their writings. Above all, their texts stand out because they were the product of a large-scale translation program that for a time involved the entire colonial establishment. By comparison, subsequent efforts have been limited and derivatory.

Defining my geographical area of research as "Peru" is, of course, an anachronism, but the southern and northern frontiers of the modern nation-state (the Peru-Chile frontier at Tacna excepted) roughly approximate important colonial jurisdictions within the Viceroyalty of Peru (i.e., Spanish South America)—in particular the *audiencia* of Lima.[11] I concentrate on the coastal and highland areas of what is now central and southern Peru—the archdiocese of Lima and the dioceses of Cuzco, Huamanga (modern Ayacucho), and (to a lesser degree) Arequipa as they existed in the seventeenth century. All of the known pastoral Quechua literature comes from this area. Of the thirteen individuals we know to have authored or translated important extant works, only two were from Spain, and they spent their careers in Peru. The rest were all natives of Spanish towns in Peru, with the exception of Pablo de Prado, a Jesuit from La Paz, and he seems to have spent all of his adult life in Peru. Most of the published works were printed in Lima, and all seem to have been written in Peru.

I have not dealt systematically with the colonial diocese of Trujillo (now northern Peru), which was subject to the archdiocese of Lima and contained Quechua-speaking populations. This is because no pastoral Quechua texts can be linked to this area, which was characterized by a significant presence of non-Quechua languages such as Mochica and Culli. Similarly, my decision not to deal at all with Bolivia (colonial Charcas) and Ecuador (colonial Quito) reflects the absence of relevant texts from these areas.[12] They were also distinct jurisdictionally from what is now Peru—in the seventeenth century Charcas was a separate archdiocese and audiencia, while Quito, the seat of a separate audiencia, was subject ecclesiastically to an archdiocese based in Bogotá. There can be little doubt that many of the Quechua texts studied here were also employed in the parishes of Bolivia and Ecuador, but I have not researched this topic myself and there is not much in the way of a relevant secondary literature to work from. It should be a priority of future historical research on Quechua language and culture to work across the modern and colonial boundaries.

Sources

The pastoral Quechua corpus is modest in size compared to equivalent literatures in some of the other major vernacular languages of the Spanish empire—the corpus of pastoral texts in Nahuatl, for instance, is several times larger.[13] For precisely this reason, the Quechua material is susceptible to study within the frame of a single research project. I am not, of course, claiming to have dealt thoroughly with the entire corpus—in particular, I have paid much closer attention to texts intended for public or private performance by Indians, such as prayers and hymns, than to sermons, which quantitatively make up the bulk of the corpus. However, addressing the questions outlined above to all of the known extant works has been essential both for contextualizing individual translation programs and for discerning the full range of variation in the literature.

A broad distinction between catechetical and liturgical genres may be useful to introduce the reader to the types of texts I address. While catechesis is a pedagogical activity, the liturgy brings participants directly into relation with God and the saints (see Stapper 1935 [1931] for a survey of the Catholic liturgy and its history). In its strict sense, the term "liturgy" refers to the official public services of the mass, canonical hours, and sacraments, but I will be using it somewhat more broadly to include formal and regular acts of public worship in general. The liturgy is usually distinguished from the private devotions (such as the rosary, which is performed on an individual basis), which can be considered a third category of texts, although they are patterned on the liturgy. One of the key differences between catechetical and liturgical texts is that the former by definition tend to be translatable, whereas the translation of liturgical texts (in particular those that are specific to the mass, canonical hours, and sacraments) is problematic. The catechesis/liturgy distinction is not a hard-and-fast one, however—individual texts can serve both catechetical and liturgical purposes depending on the performance context.

Catechetical and liturgical genres and practices were not entirely stable throughout the period of this study, the early part of which straddles the transformations of the Counter-Reformation or Catholic Reformation. Nonetheless, certain generalizations can be made about Spanish colonial practice. The fundamentals for catechetical instruction were provided by brief compilations of basic canonical texts that were intended for memorization and generally included the basic prayers (the Pater Noster, Credo, Ave Maria, and Salve Regina), the Articles of the Faith, and the Ten Commandments. These compilations were know as *cartillas* and often doubled as basic literacy primers. The cartillas, also called *doctrinas cristianas,* were complemented by catechisms—concise and systematic expositions of basic doctrines and texts in question-answer format. Like the cartillas, catechisms were intended for memorization, or in any case for repetitive recitation. The book genre commonly referred to as the "catechism" typically contained a cartilla and one or more catechisms proper. Another key catechetical text was the sermon, to which the laity were intended to have a primarily passive relation. Sermons were often published in book-length compilations or *sermonarios,* of which there were two main types: the thematic sermonario, which was organized on a doctrinal basis, and the liturgical sermonario, in which each sermon was intended to be read on a specific date of the liturgical calendar and contained a paraphrase of, and commentary on, the Gospel passage read in that day's mass. While the Quechua cartillas consisted of translations of canonical texts, most Quechua catechisms and sermons were translations of Spanish texts composed in Peru for Indian audiences.

The formal Catholic liturgy is contained in three main books: the missal (for the mass), the ritual (for the administration of the sacraments), and the breviary (for the canonical hours). All three books were undergoing a process of standardization in the aftermath of the Council of Trent, but there was still a considerable amount of variability in their content and organization. The archdioceses of Toledo and Seville, for instance, each had their own rituals, which were also used throughout Spanish America and were only gradually superseded by the Tridentine Roman Ritual. Neither the mass nor the canonical hours were translated into Quechua systematically, and although there were Peruvian rituals, they only provided Quechua versions of some of the sacramental texts. Rituals often contained a *confesionario,* a list of questions to be asked by the priest in confession. Peruvian confesionarios often went into extraordinary detail in their typification of the sins most commonly committed by native Andeans. In addition to translating fragments of the official liturgy, the author-translators also wrote a variety of new Quechua texts of a liturgical or devotional character, in particular hymns, litanies, and prayers. Pastoral Quechua books often combined liturgical and sacramental texts—for instance, Juan Pérez Bocanegra's well-known *Ritual formulario* (Brief Ritual) of 1631 contains catechisms and a collection of prayers and hymns as well as a ritual proper. The proportion of Quechua text in these books ranges from under 10 percent to slightly under half. The preliminary texts, headings, indexes, and the like are always in Spanish, and the Quechua texts are usually accompanied by Spanish versions.

The Quechua grammars and dictionaries, while not an object of study in themselves, have been taken into account as supplements to the main source base of pastoral texts. Apart from the short pastoral texts that many of them contain, these linguistic works are important because they were written as aids for priests who would be using Quechua in pastoral contexts, and they directly complement the pastoral literature per se. While no linguistic work can be regarded as a neutral description of a language, these grammars and dictionaries are perhaps more clearly programmatic than is usually the case, in that they were instruments for defining the "correct" Quechua for pastoral use at dialectal, orthographic, and terminological levels. Some of the most important author-translators also wrote grammars and dictionaries (which unfortunately have been lost), and it is clear that the extant grammars and dictionaries are part and parcel of specific translation programs.

I have not studied the five extant colonial Quechua plays as examples of pastoral Quechua, although four of them, *El hijo pródigo, El robo de Proserpina y sueño de Endimión, El pobre más rico,* and *Usca Paucar,* are examples of a tradition of vernacular religious drama that developed in Cuzco during the seventeenth century (the first two plays are *autos sacramentales* that were probably performed as part of the Corpus Christi celebrations).[14] This exclusion is partly for chronological reasons, since the earliest of these four plays date to the very end of the period of this study, if at all.[15] Moreover, these plays are, strictly speaking, neither catechetical nor liturgical in nature. César Itier has argued that religious plays such as *El pobre más rico* and *Usca Paucar* are not instances of a *teatro de evangelización* and should be seen instead as moral exhortations directed at audiences that were considered to already have a solid Christian background (Itier 1995c).[16] It has also been suggested that the intended audience was not "Indian" at all, and that the plays were composed by and for the bilingual criollo elite of Cuzco, which would have cultivated Quechua literature as part of an identity politics (Mannheim 1991: 70–74).[17]

The dozen volumes of pastoral works that have been analyzed are the remains of a much larger literature. I have had access to all of the known printed books from this period, but there are references to numerous works that were never published and of which no manuscript copies are known to have survived.[18] In fact, only two pastoral Quechua manuscripts from the period of this study are known to scholars today (D. Molina [1649] and Castromonte [ca. 1650]; for the latter, see also Durston 2002).[19] The loss of a significant portion of the original literature creates obstacles for defining change and variability and interpreting the features of specific texts. It seems likely that the lost manuscript literature was more diverse than the printed literature because it was not subject to the approval process necessary for publishing a book. Furthermore, among the missing manuscripts are important early works, without which it is difficult to get a clear picture of the initial development of pastoral Quechua. Equally problematic is the uneven chronological distribution of the different genres. For instance, most of the liturgical literature dates from what I call the postcouncil period (ca. 1590–1640), but none of the sermonarios written during this time have survived. This makes charting chronological changes in translation practices more difficult, because genre-for-genre comparisons across different periods cannot always be made. I have attempted to navigate these gaps in different ways. To begin with, they are often significant in themselves. The unequal distribution of genres reflects changing understandings of what needed to be available in Quechua. Even when we know that a specific gap is due to problems of conservation, some significance can still be attributed to it—conservation is very much a function of printing, and which texts made it to the presses was not a matter of chance. Most importantly, my analysis of what the extant texts tell us in terms of general tendencies and changes in translation practices is always correlated with political, ideological, and institutional developments that are documented elsewhere.

Four main types of Spanish-language texts have provided information on the broader contexts of pastoral Quechua, on performance practices, and on the individual histories of texts and authors: (1) chronicles and treatises, (2) letters and reports, (3) legislation, and (4) administrative documents. The chronicles of the Incas and the Spanish conquest, as well as those of the religious orders, contain scattered but often valuable information on missionary and pastoral practices, though it is extremely rare for them to discuss specific texts. Treatises such as José de Acosta's *De procuranda indorum salute* (On obtaining the salvation of the Indians, 1577), a theoretical work on the conversion of the Indians of Peru, are essential for understanding the ideological currents and interpretations of native languages and cultures that guided translation.

Letters and reports were written by pastoral agents, ranging from parish priests to archbishops, to their superiors. Perhaps the best-known example of this type of document is the missionary letter, a peculiarly Jesuit genre that was produced in great abundance and detail during this period. These reports were collected and anthologized in the *cartas annuas,* which were sent to the Jesuit leadership in Rome on a yearly basis. While the secular and mendicant clergy did not write regular pastoral reports, their superiors (bishops and provincials) did correspond with each other and with the crown. Legislation relevant to the development of pastoral Quechua is concentrated in the Peruvian councils and synods. However, as a result of the *patronato real* arrangement that gave the crown control over the secular church in the Indies, royal legislation is also of relevance, as are the letters and reports sent by viceroys and other royal officials to Spain.

The administrative category comprises documents produced in the day-to-day running of the parishes, including the parish priests' titles and certificates of language competence, various sorts of litigation (often initiated by Indian parishioners against their priests), and administrative inspections (*visitas*) carried out on behalf of the bishop. A particularly important administrative genre is the *información de oficio* (also known as *probanza de méritos*), an extensive biographical file that accompanied petitions for promotion sent to the crown. These files go into great detail and often include transcriptions of earlier texts related to the priest's activities in

Indian parishes. Administrative documents illuminate the general institutional milieu in which the author-translators, most of whom were parish priests, were trained and worked, as well as the workings of the parishes themselves. They also provide key biographical information on many individual author-translators.

There are major gaps in the serial documentation (letters/reports and administrative documents)—only some periods, areas, and institutions are well represented in the archives. As regards the secular church, the archive of the archdiocese of Lima (AAL) has fairly complete series starting around 1600, and is complemented by the archive of the Lima cathedral chapter (ACML), which contains important sixteenth-century records. However, there are no equivalent series for the dioceses of Cuzco, Huamanga, and Arequipa—important records have been lost, especially in Cuzco, and others remain off-limits to most researchers.[20] Most mendicant archives remain closed, and those that are accessible contain only a tiny fraction of the documentation that the orders must have produced in running their parishes.[21] As for the Jesuit order, few early records remain in Peru as a result of the expulsion in 1767, but an important collection of reports and letters held in different archives, including the famous cartas annuas, has been published in the eight Peruvian volumes of the *Monumenta Missionum* series.[22] Fortunately, the Archivo General de Indias in Seville (AGI), the central archive of the Spanish empire, holds a mass of letters and informaciones de oficio by both secular and regular clergy from every area and period that do much to fill these gaps.

A final methodological issue concerns the paucity and opacity of explicit statements concerning linguistic and translation policies, which often went unremarked or were glossed over in terms of "correct" or "proper" usage. There is a sharp contrast here with the sources available to students of nineteenth- and twentieth-century missionization, both Catholic and Protestant, in Asia and Africa. In the writings of the later missionary translators one often finds an explicit recognition of the fact that they were creating new languages through dialectal standardization and the semantic transformation of the lexicon, as well as discussions that explicitly weigh alternative translation practices and their implications.[23] The contrast can be attributed to basic changes in the perception of language that occurred between the sixteenth and nineteenth centuries. Since purely conventional understandings of language had not yet prevailed, the agents studied here seem to have regarded the activity of creating pastoral Quechua as one of purification and "reduction" to order rather than engineering—Anthony Pagden has remarked on the prevalence among sixteenth-century linguists of Amerindian languages of the belief that they were "restoring" them to a more pristine state (1986: 181). There was also a sense that translation was divinely guaranteed through the authoritative mediation of the church (Rafael 1993 [1988]). Because of these naturalizing assumptions, the concrete strategies and perceptions that guided translation practice have to be teased out through the examination of the Quechua texts themselves and the archival reconstruction of their historical contexts. Both records are incomplete and ambiguous, but they reinforce each other on key points.

Chapter 1

Background

Pastoral Quechua developed from the confluence of disparate cultural, political, and linguistic histories. My outline of this background begins with a brief account of the organization of church and crown in colonial Peru as it concerned the indigenous population, discussing some of the changes that occurred during the period of this study. In the next section I shift my focus to sixteenth-century Europe, specifically the language ideologies and policies associated with the rise of vernaculars and with the processes of religious reform that are characteristic of the period. The final two sections are dedicated to the complex linguistic landscape of the Andes. A discussion of the modern dialectology of the Quechua language family serves as an introduction to current interpretations of the geographical and social distribution of Quechua on the eve of the Spanish conquest. I also emphasize that Quechua was merely the most widespread of a number of language families that were just as well established in what is now Peru. Finally, I provide an overview of Spanish perceptions of the Andean languages and of the impact of colonial rule on these languages.

Church, Crown, and Conversion

In very broad terms, the administrative system that had congealed by the late sixteenth century was organized around two overlapping dualities (imperfect ones, as will be seen): lay versus ecclesiastical, and Spanish versus Indian. As regards the first duality, colonial Peru was ruled by parallel administrative structures: royal officialdom and the ecclesiastical hierarchy. Both were centered in Lima, which was the seat of a viceroy who held sway over all of Spanish South America; of an audiencia or royal court whose jurisdiction corresponded roughly to modern Peru (excluding the Amazon basin); and of an archdiocese, which throughout the sixteenth century was the primate see of the continent. (In the early seventeenth century archdioceses were also established in La Plata [Sucre, Bolivia] and Bogotá.) A separate diocese had existed in Cuzco since 1536, and additional ones (at Arequipa, Huamanga, and Trujillo) were set up within the territory of the audiencia in the early seventeenth century.[1]

Matters on the ecclesiastical side were complicated, first, by the presence of the regular clergy—that is, the mendicant orders (Dominicans, Franciscans, Augustinians, and Mercedarians) and the Jesuits (who arrived last, in 1568). These orders were more or less independent from the secular (i.e., diocesan) prelates and established their own administrative hierarchies based in Lima.[2] The mendicants were the first to have a presence in the area, and early conversion efforts were almost exclusively their work. In fact, many bishops were regulars, including the first archbishop of Lima, the Dominican Jerónimo de Loayza (1543–75). This did not prevent rivalry and conflict between the dioceses and the orders, which were particularly rife when a see was occupied by a secular cleric (as would be the case in the archdiocese of Lima after Loayza) or was being run by the cathedral chapter. The fact that the mendicants administered many Indian parishes, even though this was in principle the task of the secular clergy, was the main bone of contention.

A further complication concerns the lack of separation of lay and ecclesiastical hierarchies: as a result of its powers of royal patronage in the Americas, the crown exercised considerable control over all secular church appointments, from the archdioceses down to the parishes. The crown's ecclesiastical and pastoral policies were transmitted to bishops and archbishops in the form of direct orders that sometimes conflicted with and superseded papal bulls and briefs. Furthermore, viceroys and audiencias had considerable jurisdiction over ecclesiastical matters: the former had the final say in assigning benefices (including parishes), and the latter was the highest court for certain kinds of ecclesiastical cases. The crown's control over the regular clergy was nowhere near as complete as over the secular clergy, but the former's very presence in the colonies and control over parishes depended on royal approval.

The second duality, Spanish versus Indian, is expressed in the vision of colonial society as two legally, institutionally, and spatially separate "republics"—the *república de españoles* and the *república de indios.* The patchwork of polities and ethnicities that had formed the Inca empire was subsumed under the homogenizing legal category of "Indian," which entailed a set of obligations (particularly a head tax and corvée labor) and some protections against the depredations of non-Indians.[3] While there was initially some debate regarding the viability and convenience of maintaining the larger polities and their traditional leadership, and these polities certainly did not disappear overnight, the Spanish opted for breaking them down into small, territorially discreet units based in *pueblos de indios*—nucleated villages with a mixed political system of Spanish-style municipal officials and hereditary *curacas* or chiefs, who were subject to Spanish provincial governors (*corregidores*). The application of the "two republics" logic was thus severely limited—Indian self-rule was restricted to the local level, and there was no Indian clergy. Indian parishes, known as *doctrinas*, were run by Spanish priests (*doctrineros*) appointed by the local bishop or, in the case of parishes in mendicant hands, by superiors within the order.

The ambiguities surrounding the separate-but-unequal status of Indians in colonial society have everything to do with how their transition to Christianity was perceived by the Spanish. The concept of conversion as an individual epiphany, a moment of total transformation, does not appear very often with reference to Indians in the colonial sources. What separated the Christian from the pagan Indian was the sacrament of baptism, and except at the very beginning of the period of this study, most Indians were baptized at birth. Baptism was the beginning of an arduous and gradual process through which the individual Indian and the Indian "nation" as a whole were infused with the effective contents of Christianity through doctrinal instruction and the power of the sacraments. The immediate goal was to make the Indians *Christian enough* for them to attain salvation, and what exactly this involved was open to debate. Regardless of the attainments of individual Christian Indians, Indian Christianity was always suspect—particularly of relapse into "idolatry"—and permanently in need of reinforcement. Estenssoro Fuchs (2001) argues that during the period of this study the recognition of full Christianity among the Indians was constantly deferred because it would have undermined the category of Indian itself, and thus the basis of colonial society. It was necessary to always find new faults in Indian Christianity, and new remedies for these faults.

The Indian ministry was a central part of the mandate of every colonial institution, and greater prominence in this ministry equaled greater prestige and power in colonial society as a whole, as well as control over

Indian resources and labor. There was continuous disagreement and conflict over pastoral jurisdictions, especially between the secular church and the mendicant orders. These rivalries carried over into language policy and translation, in that competing institutions justified their claims by their ability to minister to the Indians in the vernacular. The mendicants in particular were unwilling to toe the lines drawn by the secular church and the crown in these matters, if only because pastoral ministry was an essential aspect of their mission, which they were loath to submit to an external authority.

The constitution of a stable missionary and pastoral regime can easily take on the appearance of a continuous and incremental process. It is not until the middle of the sixteenth century that one can speak of systematic, centralized efforts and policies; the 1530s and 1540s were a time of upheaval taken up first by the different phases of the conquest itself and then by fighting among conquistador factions. The process of consolidation culminated in the 1570s and 1580s, when a definitive set of pastoral institutions and practices was developed thanks to the efforts of Viceroy Francisco de Toledo (1569–81), Archbishop (later Saint) Toribio Alfonso de Mogrovejo (1581–1606), and the Third Lima Council (1582–83). While Toledo, in particular, put the church in Peru on a stable administrative footing, especially regarding parish organization, the Third Lima Council provided its basic legislative core and produced a printed corpus of official catechetical texts in Spanish, Quechua, and Aymara versions.

There is some truth to the view that the changes that occurred during the second half of the sixteenth century reflect the colonial regime's process of "getting its act together." However, such an account would ignore the crucial fact that the sixteenth century was a time of great transformations in the Catholic world as a whole, especially as regards translation and pastoral policies. The practices of the 1550s and 1560s appear fundamentally different from later ones, and not merely because of their incipiency and variability. Sabine MacCormack has argued for a radical shift from models of conversion based on persuasion and accommodation to more intolerant and coercive practices later in the sixteenth century. MacCormack notes, for example, that the 1560 Quechua grammar and dictionary of the Dominican Domingo de Santo Tomás suggested the use of Quechua terms to translate key Christian concepts where Spanish loan words would later be used by the Third Lima Council (MacCormack 1985: 449). The process is summed up as follows: "By the late sixteenth century, missionary Christianity had . . . crystallized into a rigid and self-contained body of doctrine impermeable to any influence from Andean religion. Quechua terminology used to describe Christian concepts had been carefully eliminated from dictionaries, catechisms, and manuals of preaching to Indians, and the same purist attitude defined all other aspects of Christian life in the Andes" (ibid.: 456).

This shift has been further explored by Estenssoro Fuchs, who distinguishes a *primera evangelización* (first evangelization) that was at its height during the 1550s and 1560s from a reform period that set in during the 1570s and 1580s in implementation of the policies of the Council of Trent (1545–63) and, more broadly, of the Counter-Reformation. The primera evangelización was characterized by pastoral practices that were more diverse and flexible and less focused on formal catechesis, by very limited administration of sacraments other than baptism, and by a greater openness to the appropriation of native cultural forms and religious terminology. It was brought to an end by a wide-ranging uniformization program that implemented the Counter-Reformation's narrower orthodoxy and its demands for full catechetical instruction and a complete sacramental regime for all Christians (Estenssoro Fuchs 2003).

The differences between the primera evangelización and post-reform practices can, to a considerable degree, be identified with those between medieval Western Christianity and modern, post-Tridentine Catholicism. The Tridentine reforms implemented key practices that today seem constitutive of Catholicism, such as the centering of the religious life of the laity in the parish and the regular administration of the sacraments—in fact, it was only at this point that the sacraments of confession and marriage acquired their modern forms. Above all, the reforms sought to do away with the rampant diversity of the way Christianity was practiced and to impose common norms and central authority (particularly that of the episcopal hierarchy) over both clergy and laity.[4] As in much of Europe, these reforms were achieved in Peru through a combination of more stringent legislation, the publication of standard versions of key texts, and political muscle obtained through alliances with the state. And as in Europe, reformed Catholicism in Peru made full use of printing: the press was introduced in 1584 specifically for the publication of the Third Lima Council's catechetical corpus, and without it the ensuing campaign of both textual and linguistic standardization would hardly have been possible. As will be seen in chapter 3, the Third Council's preference for print was such that it banned manuscript copies of its own catechetical texts. By contrast, the vernacular texts of the primera evangelización had circulated in manuscript form.

The pastoral regime established during the 1570s and 1580s remained in force through the mid-seventeenth century. The most important institutional process in the wake of the Third Lima Council was the rise of the secular church, which acted with increasing independence from royal officials—after the late sixteenth century, direct intervention by viceroys and audiencia judges in ecclesiastical matters declined. The bishops also began to challenge the autonomy of the mendicant orders, although not always successfully. Mogrovejo carried out a series of wide-ranging visitas or administrative inspections of his archdiocese during the 1590s, implementing the new pastoral system and regularizing the administrative framework. Additionally, he held several diocesan synods whose decrees were collected in a 1613 synod held by Mogrovejo's successor. Starting around the time of Mogrovejo's death in 1606, three new dioceses were created. The northern Peruvian coast and highlands were separated from the archdiocese of Lima and a new see established in the coastal town of Trujillo. Two further dioceses were dismembered from that of Cuzco, one based in Huamanga (modern Ayacucho) and the other in Arequipa.

Archbishop Bartolomé Lobo Guerrero (1609–22) had headed the Inquisition in Mexico before coming to Peru and brought a new, more punitive style of pastoral administration. It is surely no coincidence that at the time of his arrival alarms began to sound over the clandestine survival of native cults in the highland parishes of the archdiocese, particularly as a result of the investigations of the enterprising secular cleric Francisco de Avila, who publicized his discoveries in an *auto de fe* held in Lima in 1609. "Idolatry" became one of the primary concerns of the secular church in the archdiocese of Lima throughout the seventeenth century—formal extirpation campaigns were carried out by ecclesiastical judges who combed highland parishes for infractions and prosecuted the guilty, and a whole generation of clerics made their careers as experts in detecting, uprooting, and refuting "idolatry" (see especially Duviols 1977a [1971] and Mills 1997). Interestingly, the extirpation boom never really caught on in the other Peruvian dioceses—the bishops of Cuzco, Huamanga, and Arequipa refer to the issue, but do not seem to have been seriously concerned about it. Extirpation in the archdiocese of Lima became a cyclical process: there was only sporadic activity under archbishops Gonzalo de Campo

(1625–26) and Fernando Arias de Ugarte (1630–38), but Pedro de Villagómez (1641–71) got the extirpation machine moving again on an even greater scale.

There appears to have been a parallel ebb and flow in the production, or at least printing, of pastoral texts during the first half of the seventeenth century. Several Quechua and Aymara grammars and dictionaries, and reeditions of the Third Council texts appeared during the first two decades of the century. There was almost no printing of works in or about Quechua during the 1620s and 1630s (with one important exception in 1631). While Archbishop Arias de Ugarte strongly promoted vernacular training among the clergy, no pastoral or linguistic texts were approved for publication during his tenure. The revival came under Villagómez, who mounted a wide-ranging extirpation campaign in 1649 in which he placed special emphasis on "preventive" anti-idolatry catechesis and preaching in Quechua. That same year he published a lengthy pastoral letter to the priests of Peru instructing them on anti-idolatry methods, which was distributed jointly with a new Quechua sermonario. Pastoral Quechua writing and publishing reached an all-time high in the late 1640s, coinciding with the new extirpation campaigns. However, concern over idolatry should not be seen as the motor behind pastoral translation in the seventeenth century. The works of the first forty years of the century have no clear connection to extirpation at all, and even those of the late 1640s cannot all be regarded as offshoots of, or preparations for, Villagómez's campaigns. Instead, the author-translators seem to have exploited periods of intensified official interest in the Indian ministry to get their works published.

Language and Religious Reform in Early Modern Europe

Spanish colonial policies vis-à-vis Quechua need to be examined in the light of contemporary European developments in two main areas: linguistic ideologies and policies, and religious reform and reaction. As regards the first area, Burke speaks of a "discovery of language" in early modern Europe—a heightened interest in linguistic variation and change, and in the differing qualities and potentials of languages (2004: 15–42). The spread of humanism, with its emphasis on the need to restore Latin to its classical purity, was a major part of this new awareness. The fifteenth and sixteenth centuries were also a time when the rise of the vernaculars as written languages was accelerating and becoming more visible, as witnessed by their codification in grammars, the first of which was Antonio de Nebrija's *Gramática de la lengua castellana* (Salamanca, 1492). As Nebrija explained in his prologue, the need for such a work was twofold. First, it would serve to fix or stabilize the Spanish (or Castilian) language at what Nebrija believed to be its stage of greatest perfection, protecting it from the ravages of time and making it a worthy medium for history and letters, as Latin and Greek had been thanks to grammatical regulation. Second, Spanish was to become a language of empire, and the grammar was necessary for Castile's new subjects to learn it (Nebrija 1992 [1492]: II 13–17). While other vernaculars may not have had the same imperial aspirations—at least, not yet—their rise was also a question of standardization: a particular variety or dialect would acquire special prestige, and a standard written form would then develop via grammatical description and widespread use in print. As Burke puts it, "vernaculars won the battle with Latin by ceasing to be vernaculars, by creating a sort of 'authorized version' of language that was distant from colloquial speech" (2004: 90).

The early modern rise of the vernaculars should not be confused with that of national languages. The Herderian principle of the isomorphism of language and nation-state belongs to the nineteenth and twentieth centuries (Burke 2004: 160–172). Nonetheless, it is clear that a loose identification between peoples or "nations" and languages was developing, and that there was a growing belief in the virtues of linguistic uniformity—the trend towards standardization is a witness to this. The rise of the vernaculars was often associated with that of centralizing states—this was most clearly the case in Spain, where the fortunes of Spanish flourished alongside those of the crown of Castile, as Nebrija suggested.

The implications of these developments for the treatment of Indian languages in the Spanish empire can be read in different ways. The promotion and cultivation of Spanish as a literary language with expressive powers on a par with those of Latin could serve as a charter for the status of Amerindian languages as "new vernaculars" that could be studied, codified, and written. Indeed, Nebrija's grammar served as a model for the first grammar of Quechua, published only sixty-eight years later in Valladolid (Cerrón-Palomino 1995a; Torero 1997). On the other hand, the growing prestige of Spanish could also justify the eradication of Indian languages. The homogenizing tendencies in early modern language ideologies and the rise of a "people-language" identification could also cut both ways. Combined with the perception of all "Indians" as a single republic, they justified the promotion of *a* native vernacular at the expense of other dialects and languages. However, the incomplete and subordinate character of the república de indios, in particular the fact that it relied on Spanish priests and magistrates, would be used as an argument for Hispanization in the seventeenth century. Perhaps the clearest effect of the particular "language culture" of sixteenth-century Europe was the very hierarchical and discriminating way in which Indian languages were perceived—there was a tendency to seek out the best, purest, and most correct languages and language varieties. This was partly a practical response to the great diversity encountered, but the specific ways in which languages were ranked, praised or vilified, and subjected to processes of written standardization reflect contemporary discourses and policies vis-à-vis the European vernaculars, particularly the highly competitive environment in which the vernaculars vied against each other and against Latin.

The other story that needs to be told here is that of religious translation policies and the effect that the religious upheavals of the sixteenth century had on them. Movements of reform and renewal had been developing in Spain for some time before the Reformation, among them the Christian humanism championed by Erasmus of Rotterdam, which emphasized the need both for the learned to study the Bible in the original Hebrew and Greek and for the people to have direct access to it in the vernacular (Bataillon 1950 [1937]). The promotion of humanist language studies in Spain is exemplified in the new university of Alcalá de Henares and its polyglot edition of the Bible (1514–17), the first to allow the direct comparison of the Hebrew and Greek originals with the Vulgate (ibid.: I 12–51).[5] While full vernacular translations of the Bible had been frowned upon in Spain since the late fifteenth century (Andrés 1976: I 322), selections of biblical and Patristic texts and portions of the canonical hours in Spanish continued to be common in the early sixteenth century (Bataillon 1950 [1937]: I 51–56).

This same period also witnessed important missionary experiments with the Muslim population of Granada, under Christian rule since 1492, which anticipated what would be done in Mesoamerica and the Andes. Hernando de Talavera, who became archbishop of Granada in 1496, promoted Arabic languages studies and the publication of linguistic and catechetical works for the clergy (Bataillon 1950 [1937]: I 68–69). Talavera even went as far as reforming the liturgy to use it as an instrument of conversion, promoting the use of the vernacular (perhaps Arabic as well as Spanish) for the biblical readings of the mass, and of *villancicos,* or vernacular religious songs, in the canonical hours (Hauf i Valls 2001: 232–236; Illari 2001: 152).[6] Talavera's policies, which were directed at gradual, voluntary conversions, were soon superseded by forced baptisms and, decades later, by the wholesale expulsion of the *moriscos*, the population of recent Muslim descent that had formally accepted Christianity. Talavera's linguistic and liturgical adaptations would find more fertile ground in the Americas, among less controversial and threatening populations.

The Counter-Reformation naturally had major consequences for religious translation, and these consequences were not necessarily repressive in character. Admittedly, the translation of canonical texts, and of the Bible in particular, became highly problematic. There were three main reasons for this: (1) translation was one of the main demands of the Reformation; (2) translation put canonical texts in the hands of people who, from the perspective of the church, had not been properly trained to interpret them; and (3) new translations undermined the authority of traditional ones, in particular the Vulgate. While the Council of Trent did not prohibit vernacular Bibles, as is often claimed, it did declare the Vulgate to be the "authentic" version (Council of Trent 1941 [1545–1563]: 18). In reaction against Protestant demands for the vernacularization of the liturgy, the council also ordered that the mass be said in Latin (ibid.: 148). As one of the council's theologians put it, citing Origen, "the word of God, even though not understood, produces fruit, provided it is received with faith" (Marco 1961: 119).

At the same time, however, the Council of Trent established the obligation of bishops and parish priests to preach in the vernacular. In the course of the mass itself, especially on Sundays and feast days, pastors were to explain the biblical readings and the nature of the eucharist to the people (Council of Trent 1941 [1545–1563]: 148). More generally, they were obligated to explain the "efficacy and use" of the sacraments in the vernacular and to expound the "divine commands and the maxims of salvation" on all feast days (ibid.: 197–198). One of the central objectives of the Council of Trent and the Counter-Reformation in general was to raise the level of religious instruction among the laity as a whole, and this very clearly involved the use of the vernacular as a catechetical medium.

The Counter-Reformation was also a movement for the standardization of church dogma and liturgy, uniformity being seen as an essential prerequisite for the maintenance of orthodoxy. This demand was most clearly expressed in the production of new or reformed compilations of doctrinal and liturgical texts in the years following the Council of Trent. First came the Roman Catechism or Catechism of Pius V, a handbook of Catholic doctrine intended for parish priests, in 1566; it was followed by a reformed breviary (1568) and missal (1570) designed to standardize the liturgy of the canonical hours and of the mass; and by the *Rituale Romanum*, the Tridentine ritual, which appeared belatedly in 1614. The demands for the standardization of pastoral texts one finds in the Lima provincial councils, and which were implemented by the Third Council, should be seen in the light of this broader process.

The reforming zeal of the Spanish crown often went beyond that of the papacy itself, especially during the reign of Phillip II, which spanned most of the second half of the sixteenth century. In 1551 the Spanish Inquisition instituted an outright ban of Spanish translations of the Bible (cf. Rodríguez 1998, chapter 3), and the 1559 Index extended the ban to books containing translations of brief texts, especially the collections of Epistle and Gospel readings from the missal (Bataillon 1950 [1937] I: 54). A project for translating the Roman Catechism into Spanish backed by Pius V himself was vetoed by the Inquisition in 1570 on the grounds that the theological depth of the catechism made it unsuitable for popular consumption (Rodríguez 1998). Ironically, the first Spanish translation of the Roman Catechism to be published was part of a bilingual Spanish-Nahuatl edition printed in Mexico in 1723 (ibid.: 15). The trial of the Franciscan mystic Luis de León is probably the best-known example of the repression of translation activities in Counter-Reformation Spain: León was imprisoned for five years by the Inquisition beginning in 1572, not on any doctrinal grounds but because of his Spanish translation of the Song of Songs and his humanist philological approach to the Bible, which were seen as undermining the authority of the Vulgate (Zamora 1988: 28–36). Phillip II's dedication to the Counter-Reformation principles of textual uniformity and orthodoxy is exemplified in his ban on all editions of the reformed missal and breviary that were printed out of his domains, as it was believed that foreign editions contained modifications deliberately introduced by heretics during the printing process.[7]

These restrictions give us some idea of the climate in which pastoral Quechua developed during the second half of the sixteenth century—if religious translation into the tongue of the conquerors was so suspect, what could be said of the languages of the vanquished? Translation, however, was as necessary as it was dangerous. Henry Kamen emphasizes the "dual obligation" to use both the vernaculars and Latin in Counter-Reformation Spain and points to a boom in the publication of catechetical and devotional texts in Catalan and Basque, as well as Spanish, beginning in the 1560s (Kamen 1993: 347, 363–364). The late sixteenth century was the heyday of Spanish religious literature, with the mystical and devotional writings of Teresa de Avila, Juan de la Cruz, and Luis de Granada, among others. However, there continued to be debate regarding the appropriateness of writing on these subjects in Spanish, which many regarded as dangerous for the laity (Andrés 1976: II 570–576).

These contradictory tendencies are very much in evidence in colonial language policies in the Americas. For much of the sixteenth and seventeenth centuries the crown was strongly inclined towards a Hispanization policy: a series of *cédulas* or royal decrees required all Indians to learn Spanish on the grounds that Indian languages lacked the terms necessary for expressing Christian doctrine. However, the crown also repeatedly ordered the clergy to learn Indian languages and instruct their parishioners in the local vernacular, and such orders could be issued almost simultaneously with the Hispanization decrees (Solano 1991). The Council of Trent appears to have been a crucial turning point for crown policy, since it produced a clear statement on the obligations of parish priests to communicate with their parishioners in the local language. While the crown had reacted strongly in the 1550s against attempts to officialize the pastoral use of Nahuatl in Mexico, and ordered that Indians learn Spanish as the essential step towards Christianization, cédulas from the 1560s onwards established the need for instruction in the vernacular (ibid.: 47–55).[8]

On the other hand, the stringent controls on translation implemented in Spain beginning in the mid-sixteenth century had immediate effects in the colonies, where there was a reaction against what was seen as unbridled translation activity. The First Mexican Council of 1555 prohibited the circulation and copying of manuscript pastoral texts, especially sermons, among Indians, and set more stringent standards for the examination of pastoral translations by ecclesiastical authorities to prevent doctrinal errors (Sell 1993: 121–122). In 1559 judicial proceedings were initiated by the archdiocese of Mexico against the Franciscan Maturino Gilberti for his 1559 Tarascan catechism, which allegedly contained heretical propositions of a Protestant bent. The proceedings dragged on until Gilberti was exonerated in 1576 by (ironically) the newly-arrived Inquisition—which did, however, express concern over the extensive religious literature that was circulating in indigenous languages, especially the existence of translations of biblical texts (Fernández del Castillo ed. 1982 [1914]: 4–37, 81–85).

Quechua and the Andean Languages

The Spanish encountered in the Andes a linguistic landscape of great complexity, which they interpreted and transformed in accordance with the preconceptions they brought with them from Europe. As a result, this landscape is very hard to reconstruct today. However, extraordinary progress has been made over the past forty years by a handful of scholars working on Andean historical linguistics, in particular by overcoming a set of misconceptions common even in academic circles. Above all, there is a deeply entrenched narrative according to which Quechua—considered the Andean language *par excellence*—originated in Cuzco, spread widely as the lingua franca of the Inca empire, and subsequently degenerated into various local "dialects," maintaining its original purity only in Cuzco itself. This perception is, to a large degree, a result of the development of pastoral Quechua in the late sixteenth and early seventeenth centuries, particularly the canonization of a Cuzco-based dialectal standard as the only form of Quechua suited to be a written vehicle of Christianity. In parallel fashion, historical writings from this period—particularly those of the hugely influential mestizo chronicler "Inca" Garcilaso de la Vega—focused attention on Cuzco as the source of all that was good and noble in Andean culture (cf. Cerrón-Palomino 1987: 324–327; Mannheim 1991: 9–10).

Most professional Quechua scholars now hold that Cuzco Quechua, which can be considered a dialect of what Mannheim (1991) calls "Southern Peruvian Quechua," has no particular claim to primordiality within what is in reality a language family. All modern varieties of Quechua are characterized by a very regular agglutinative morphology in which grammatical relations are expressed by different classes of suffixes and share an extensive lexicon of common origin. However, significant variation in the form of many suffixes as well as in phonology and prosody drastically reduces intelligibility between some varieties.[9] The most successful classificatory scheme for the modern varieties, developed independently by Gary Parker and Alfredo Torero in the 1960s, proposed two main branches or groups of languages and dialects (Parker 1963; Torero 1964, 1974). One branch, termed "Quechua B" by Parker and "Quechua I" in Torero's more widely used terminology, is spoken in a continuous area in the central Peruvian highlands—mainly the modern provinces (*departamentos*) of Ancash, Huánuco, Pasco, and Junín. Branch "A," or "II," includes the varieties spoken both to the south (southern Peru and Bolivia) and north (northern Peru and Ecuador) of the "Quechua I" area. The southern border between Quechua I and Quechua II corresponds roughly to the modern administrative boundary between the provinces of Junín (Quechua I) and Huancavelica (Quechua II). In Torero's classification each branch is subdivided into lettered sub-branches—the southern Peruvian and Bolivian varieties, for instance, are included in sub-branch "II-C."

This model has its gray areas, and there is disagreement over the classification of several "transitional" or "mixed" varieties. Peter Landerman (1991) argues that the criteria for defining the Bolivian, Ecuadorian, and southern and northern Peruvian varieties as a single group in opposition to the central Peruvian varieties (which in Landerman's view do form a clear group) are insufficient. Instead, Landerman proposes a simpler, non-genetic classification based on four geographical areas: "Southern" (including the southern Peruvian and Bolivian varieties), "Central" (Torero's branch I), "Northern Peruvian," and "Northern" (Ecuadorian). For the purpose of discussing the dialectology of the pastoral Quechua corpus I will use the categories "Central Quechua" and "Southern Quechua," adapted from Landerman's scheme, to refer to the colonial ancestors of Torero's "I" and "II-C," respectively. I should specify, however, that in speaking of "Southern Quechua" I will not be including the Bolivian varieties because of the lack of early information on them, and because their historical relation to the Quechua spoken in southern Peru remains unclear. "Southern Quechua" as used here is thus equivalent to Mannheim's "Southern Peruvian Quechua" (Mannheim 1991: 4–16). I have chosen to use these categories not because I am opposed to Torero's classification, but because it is unnecessarily complex for present purposes.

Since almost all colonial texts are in Southern Quechua, it is necessary to discuss the modern dialectology of this group in more detail (see Mannheim 1991 for the most in-depth linguistic and historical treatment of the subject). The modern provinces of Huancavelica, Ayacucho, Apurímac, Cuzco, Puno, and parts of Arequipa are today predominantly Quechua-speaking, and the varieties employed in this area are quite uniform by comparison to those of the central Peruvian area—they can be considered a single language in terms of intelligibility. However, they are usually divided by dialectological surveys into two main blocks named after the main urban centers of each area: Cuzco (or Cuzco-Collao), spoken in the provinces of Cuzco, Puno, Arequipa and the western half of Apurímac, and Ayacucho (or Ayacucho-Chanca), spoken in Ayacucho, Huancavelica, and the eastern half of Apurímac. The Cuzco varieties are characterized by the presence of glottalized and aspirate stops in addition to plain stops, glottalization and aspiration being absent from the Ayacucho varieties and from most of the language family as a whole. Mannheim (1991) argues that they were acquired long before the Spanish conquest through prolonged contact with Aymara. Cuzco Quechua has also undergone a process of lenition or fricativization of syllable-final stops, which was consummated in the eighteenth century—the change did not affect Ayacucho Quechua, which retains the syllable-final stops. Finally, there are a number of lexical and a few minor morphological differences—in these cases, the Ayacucho form is usually closer to the Central one (Ayacucho Quechua is geographically sandwiched between Central Quechua and Cuzco Quechua).

As Itier warns, the modern dialectological map of Peru cannot be simplistically projected back to the time of the conquest (2000b: 47). However, certain general conclusions can be drawn from it. The first historical implication of modern dialectological research is that the traditional, Cuzco-centric narrative of the origin and spread of Quechua is untenable. Both the historical and archeological evidence indicates that the Inca expansion beyond the Cuzco region took place during the second half of the fifteenth century and the first three decades of the sixteenth century (Bauer 1992: 48). If Quechua had indeed spread with the Inca expansion, as Latin did with the Roman empire, the modern dialectological scene could not be so diverse. The distance between the main branches of the Quechua family tree is such that the original dispersion must have occurred over a much longer period of time, and perhaps in several phases. While the Ayacucho-Cuzco split within Southern Quechua is of uncertain chronology, the Central-Southern split probably goes back centuries before the Inca expansion. Additionally, the fact that dialectal variation is unusually dense in the central Peruvian highlands (the Central Quechua–speaking area) suggests that the presence of Quechua there is older than in other parts of the Andes (cf. Torero 1974; Cerrón-Palomino 1987: 327–338; Mannheim 1991: 9–10).

Admittedly, there are fairly specific testimonies in the Spanish chronicle literature to the effect that the Incas imposed their language—usually referred to as the *lengua del Cuzco*—on the peoples they conquered (e.g., Cieza de León 1985 [n.d.]: 92; Garcilaso 1945 [1609]: II 88–89, 91–92 [citing Blas Valera]). These statements need to be understood in the context of early modern European preconceptions concerning the relation between language and empire (Burke 2004: 22). It was only to be expected that the Incas imposed Quechua, because this is what imperial peoples do. On the other hand, there is some agreement among linguists today that the Incas employed a specific variety of Quechua as a lingua franca for communication among elites throughout the empire, and this lingua franca may have been the basis for the Spanish observations on Inca linguistic imperialism. As Mannheim puts it, "the Inka lingua franca was a thin overlay over a language family that was already spread widely and diversely across the central Andes" (Mannheim 1991: 9).

A number of Quechua scholars, beginning with Alfredo Torero, have argued that the Inca lingua franca was not the Quechua of the Cuzco region but was based instead on that of the central coast of Peru, a variety of which is represented in the oldest linguistic description of a Quechua language, published by Domingo de Santo Tomás in 1560. This variety, which is now extinct, was similar to Southern Quechua but had several phonological peculiarities, a different prosodic system, and a number of lexical items usually associated with Central Quechua. There are chronicle references to the effect that the Incas selected coastal Quechua, specifically the variety of Chincha, as the medium of imperial communication. This choice would have been motivated by the oft-ignored importance of the central Peruvian coast, which was rich, densely populated, and strategically placed as a north-south corridor. While the Spanish initially appropriated the coastal lingua franca, interest soon shifted to the Quechua of the southern highlands, and the coastal varieties rapidly lost importance and eventually disappeared (Cerrón-Palomino 1987: 327–328, 1988, 1989, 1995a; Taylor 2000d [1985]: 36–38; Torero 1974: 96, 132–133).[10]

It is also argued that at the time of the conquest, languages and language groups other than Quechua were far more numerous and prominent than they are today, and on this point the evidence is overwhelming. Except for some tiny pockets in Yauyos (in the highlands close to Lima) where two languages related to Aymara are still spoken, no indigenous language other than Quechua persists today in highland and coastal Peru north of the Titicaca basin. But as the vestiges in Yauyos suggest, Aymara and a set of closely related languages (the "Aymara," "Jaqi," or "Aru" language family) were once spoken throughout central and southern Peru and have been in long-term interaction with the Quechua languages (Adelaar and Muysken 2004: 259–319; Cerrón-Palomino 1999, 2000). The relation between the Aymara and Quechua language families is one of the most debated issues in Andean linguistics. The similarities between them are extensive and profound at all levels, but the question of whether Quechua and Aymara had a common origin remains unresolved (Cerrón-Palomino 1994, 2000; Mannheim 1991: 53–60). Puquina, a third, apparently unrelated language or language family, was widely spoken in southern Peru and the Bolivian altiplano at the time of the conquest and for much of the colonial period, although it is now extinct. What is now northern Peru—the colonial diocese of Trujillo—was particularly diverse: Mochica (or Yunga) and a variety of other languages were spoken on the coast, while Culli was an important language in the highlands, coexisting with varieties of Quechua. The last vestiges of Puquina, Mochica, and Culli appear to have vanished in the nineteenth or early twentieth centuries (cf. Adelaar and Muysken 2004: 319–392; Cerrón-Palomino 1995b; Torero 1987, 2002).

The territorial, ethnic, and social distribution of the Andean languages at the time of the conquest was highly complex. Bruce Mannheim's analysis of the "social ecology of language contact" in the pre-Hispanic Andes points to a non-correspondence between language, territory, and polity (Mannheim 1991: 31–60). In particular, the tendency for social groups to occupy territory in a discontinuous fashion (in order to have access to agricultural lands in different ecological zones), added to the Inca practice of transplanting groups over vast distances, resulted in an intricate linguistic landscape. Polities tended to be multilingual in at least two different ways. In many cases, an intrusive ethnic group coexisted with a local, subordinate group that spoke another language and was also differentiated socioeconomically. Another form of multilingualism involved the coexistence of a lingua franca (usually a form of Quechua or Aymara) spoken by elites with a local language spoken by the general population—Spanish missionaries and administrators thus classified Andean languages into two groups: *lenguas generales* (widely spoken languages) and *lenguas particulares* or *lenguas maternas* (more localized languages) (ibid.: 34, 43–47, 51). Mannheim also suggests that in the Andes "languages have moved across populations" (ibid.: 52): in any given area, historical and toponymic evidence points to multiple linguistic strata, which can often be attributed to language shift, the result of a combination of rampant multilingualism and changing relations of power over time.[11]

The Incas themselves may be the best illustration of multilingualism and linguistic fluidity in the pre-Hispanic Andes. Rodolfo Cerrón-Palomino has argued that Cuzco was a predominantly Aymara-speaking area that was Quechuaized at a relatively late date. He also suggests that the Inca ethnic group, who were mythologically identified with the area around Lake Titicaca, were originally Puquina speakers who assimilated Aymara when they moved into the Cuzco region (Cerrón-Palomino 1999).[12] Quechua would have acquired greater importance for the Incas as their influence spread west and northwest, into areas that were predominantly Quechua-speaking—the form of Quechua they adopted as an imperial lingua franca was thus not that spoken in Cuzco, but the variety of their important new subjects on the central coast. For the Incas, language was not the proverbial "handmaiden of empire" it was for the Spaniards—instead, they adapted to and exploited the linguistic situations they encountered.

Quechua and Spanish Rule

The Andean languages presented problems for the Spanish colonists that were both conceptual and practical—problems of classification, evaluation, ranking, selection, and appropriation. Sixteenth- and seventeenth-century Spanish thinkers employed two main explanatory models for dealing with new languages: a genetic or Platonic model, which focused on the origins of languages and was based on the assumption that all ultimately proceeded from God, and a conventional or Aristotelian model, in which languages were understood as reflections of the societies that spoke them (cf. Burke 2004: 21; Pagden 1986: 127–128). It was widely accepted that Adam and Eve had spoken a divine language—usually thought to have been Hebrew—and that seventy-two additional languages had been "infused" by God into different groups of people at the tower of Babel as a punishment for humanity's arrogance. Evaluating or classifying a language from this perspective involved establishing whether it was one of the original seventy-two, and if not, which one it derived from. Even though the multiplication of tongues at Babel was in principle a punishment, these seventy-two languages were of direct divine creation, so a special prestige was associated with them.[13] The notion that language reflects society did not necessarily contradict these Bible-based genetic accounts because of the concept of linguistic change—languages could be degraded or perfected over time, according to who spoke them. Both explanatory models were strongly hierarchical and value-laden, in tone with the competitive character of linguistic debates in Europe—languages were either closer to or farther from a divine origin, and embodied greater or less civility and sophistication.

Most negative arguments concerning the Andean languages were conventionalist—they saw reflected in these languages the barbaric state of Andean societies. One such argument concerned not the characteristics of specific languages, but their large number. America in general and the Andes in particular were, as José de Acosta put it, a "forest of language" in which each valley seemed to have its own, and different languages were spoken by the same groups. This confusion of tongues was regarded as both cause and effect of the barbarism of the Indians, barbarism being defined essentially by the inability to communicate (Pagden 1986: 180). Specific Andean languages, including even the most esteemed forms of Quechua, were often condemned for their "short vocabulary," meaning not only that they lacked the terms necessary for expressing Christian doctrines, but also that they were missing all the abstract categories that were considered essential for philosophical discourse. In view of the very precise relation that was thought to exist between language, understood as lexicon, and what we would call culture, the absence of a term indicated the absence of the concept itself (ibid.: 180–181, 185).

The apologists who responded to these negative evaluations drew on both genetic and conventionalist arguments. The prologue of Santo Tomás's 1560 Quechua grammar, addressed to Phillip II, contains a much-cited panegyric of the Quechua language which argues that it embodied the civility of Inca society. Santo Tomás was a follower of his correligionary Bartolomé de Las Casas and an advocate of indigenous economic and political rights, and he argued that the qualities of Quechua were proof that the Indians of Peru deserved better treatment and greater autonomy. These qualities included an extensive lexicon whose terms were "convenient" with the things they signified, and an orderly grammar that conformed to the "rules and precepts" of Latin. Santo Tomás went on to claim that essential similarities between Quechua and both Spanish and Latin were a sign of God's will that Quechua and its speakers be incorporated into the Spanish empire (Santo Tomás 1995 [1560]: 8–9). Beyond the political arguments that Santo Tomás was seeking to make—the Incas belonged in the Spanish empire, but deserved a place of respect—he was also drawing on the topos of the praise of language, so popular in the Europe of the rising vernaculars (Burke 2004: 65).

Other apologists for Quechua preferred a genetic approach, linking it to Bible-based accounts of the origins of languages—genetic arguments were especially effective for establishing the viability of Quechua as a vehicle for Christianity. Although the point does not seem to have been made explicitly, it stood to reason that a language that came from God must have some residue of its divine origin, and could be made to return to it. One particularly widespread argument held that Quechua derived from Hebrew—a reflection of the persistent but far from universal belief that the Indians of Peru were one of the Lost Tribes of Israel. One of the earliest proponents of the Hebraic origin theory was the Dominican Francisco de la Cruz, who claimed in the 1570s that he knew of many words of Hebrew origin in the Quechua language through divine revelation—in particular, he pointed to the alleged fact that both languages used a suffix *-i* as the first-person possessive (Abril Castelló and Abril Stoffels eds. 1996–1997: II 1223–1224, I 556). In 1607 another Dominican named Gregorio García published a book titled *Origen de los indios de el nuevo mundo e indias occidentales* (The Origin of the Indians of the New World and Western Indies), which was dedicated to the Hebraic origin hypothesis and also presented linguistic evidence, including the purported similarity in the first-person possessive (García 1607: 300). Linking Quechua to Hebrew had major implications for the treatment of the language and its speakers—Hebrew was, after all, the first language, the language that was closest to God.

An alternative genetic approach was to identify Quechua as one of the seventy-two languages of Babel. This argument was made by Fernando de Avendaño, a canon of the Lima cathedral and extirpator of idolatries, in a Spanish-Quechua sermonario published in 1649. Avendaño's ninth sermon is dedicated to rebutting an alleged native denial of the common origins of mankind based on linguistic diversity. He explains that linguistic diversity was created by God, who infused the builders of the Tower of Babel with seventy-two new languages in addition to Hebrew, which had until then been spoken by all mankind. He went on to suggest that both Quechua and Aymara were among these seventy-two languages that had been created by God, whereas other Andean languages (among which he mentions Mochica and Puquina) were derivative:

> [W]hile I cannot state with certainty that the language of the Inca [Quechua] and the Aymara language were among the seventy-two root languages that God taught [at the Tower of Babel], it seems to me nonetheless that the Inca could not have invented a language as beautiful and complex as Latin, and so I say that the language of the Inca and the Aymara language were not entirely invented in this land, but rather that God taught them to the grandchildren of Noah, and that one of Noah's families spoke in the language of the Inca, and another in the Aymara language, or that they derived from the Latin language, because they are very similar in their artifice, and that the other languages there are in this land are the daughters of these seventy-two root languages . . .[14]

Avendaño's immediate objective in making this argument was to link the Indians of Peru to universal history. But there were other implications too—the pastoral use of Quechua and Aymara was justified by identifying them as root languages in opposition to the other Andean tongues, which were derivative and not of (immediate) divine origin. Avendaño was also establishing their viability as Christian languages. If they were not among the original seventy-two created by God, then they must have derived from Latin, the language of the church.

The transformations produced in the linguistic landscape of the Andes by Spanish colonialism can best be summed up in terms of homogenization: the fluid diversity of the pre-Hispanic period was replaced by a monolithic hierarchy which opposed Spaniards to Indians (see Mannheim 1991: 60–79). The decline of linguistic diversity in the Andes since the Spanish conquest is indisputable—several languages or language families have disappeared entirely (Puquina, Mochica, and Culli top the list). However, their demise is poorly understood and not easily tied to specific colonial policies or processes, since in most cases these languages continued to be spoken into the republican period.

As much as the spread of Spanish, the colonial emphasis on minimizing the number of indigenous languages used in missionary/pastoral contexts is often seen as the culprit behind the decline in linguistic diversity. As well as being a matter of expedience, this emphasis resulted from the hierarchical and value-laden way in which languages were classified: not all the Andean languages could be paragons of civility, and not all could have derived from Hebrew or Latin. The Aymara spoken in the Titicaca basin and the Bolivian altiplano acquired the status of a colonial standard in that area, and there is a significant pastoral literature in it—the catechetical texts of the Third Lima Council were published in parallel Quechua and Aymara versions. However, the colonial regime's investment in Aymara paled by comparison to its dedication to Quechua, certainly within what is now Peru. The early focus on Quechua was to some extent inevitable—Quechua was by far the most widely-spoken language family of the Andes, and Spanish observers identified it automatically with the Inca empire. The problem was, of course, *which* Quechua.

At first efforts focused on the coastal lingua franca discussed above, but during the 1570s and 1580s attention shifted to the varieties of the southern Peruvian highlands, particularly the Cuzco region (Cerrón-Palomino 1988, 1992; Torero 1974: 188–189). Beginning with the Third Lima Council's publications, pastoral Quechua texts were written in the same highly standardized variety of Southern Quechua. Although there has been some debate as to the precise nature and origins of this variety, I will argue, following Cerrón-Palomino and Mannheim, that it was a written standard based on the Quechua of the Cuzco area (Cerrón-Palomino 1988: 138, 1997: 86; Mannheim 1991: 66–67). This variety was used in pastoral contexts throughout the area and time period of this study, and it also acquired a certain currency among the indigenous elites, who used it for nonreligious written communication (see below), and perhaps also among the colonial lay administration.

I will be using the term "Standard Colonial Quechua" as a label for this variety. It is often referred to as "lengua general" in the modern scholarship on Quechua, but this use of the term is problematic. In colonial Peru *la lengua general* was most often a shorthand for Quechua in general. In some instances it can be seen to refer specifically to "correct" Quechua as opposed to nonstandard varieties (cf. Itier 2000b; Taylor 2000d [1985]; Torero 1995), but colonial sources are generally neither careful nor consistent in distinguishing varieties of Quechua, which was regarded as a single language. It is often hard to establish the precise meaning and scope of "lengua general" and other terms such as *lengua del inca* (or *inga*) and *lengua del Cuzco*. When the ambiguity seems especially significant, I reproduce the original terms used in the colonial sources instead of translating them into my own terminology and thus giving them a fixed and possibly incorrect meaning.

It can be suggested that colonial economic processes as well as religious ones had a homogenizing effect. Itier has proposed a bold new model according to which the relative homogeneity and wide geographical spread of modern Southern Quechua is the result of processes of koinéization or linguistic unification accompanying the development of a powerful economic circuit based on mining in the second half of the sixteenth century (Itier 2000b, 2001). The silver mines at Potosí were the motor of this circuit, which extended northwest through the Titicaca basin, Cuzco, Huamanga, and the mercury mines of Huancavelica to Lima. The indigenous population was drawn into the circuit by the infamous *mitas,* the drafts that provided labor for the mines, and by their involvement, voluntary or involuntary, in interregional trade. In particular, Itier emphasizes the growth of a class of urban Indians in Spanish cities like Potosí, Cuzco, and Huamanga, and the frequency of the interactions between Indians from different areas during their stays in these urban centers. These processes would have resulted in a widespread process of convergence and homogenization, and in a sense created Southern Quechua, or at least contributed significantly to its expansion. In particular, Itier suggests that much of the area where the Ayacucho-type varieties are spoken today was originally Central Quechua speaking and was "Southernized" as a result of these processes (Itier 2001: 64–67). He also proposes that Standard Colonial Quechua as codified by the Third Lima Council was based on the Cuzco variant of the developing Southern koiné, or Cuzco Quechua as affected by these processes of convergence or unification (Itier, personal communication).

It stands to reason that the commercial links and labor movements produced by mining had linguistic consequences—they probably contributed to the spread of Quechua at the expense of other languages, as the colonial sources cited by Itier state. However, there is little evidence as yet to support the radical and swift effects in terms of the development of the Southern Quechua space that Itier suggests.[15] More precise correlations would have to be established between economic and administrative developments on the one hand and linguistic ones on the other. From a chronological perspective, it seems implausible that the process of homogenization or koiné development occurred rapidly enough to be reflected in the Third Council works, especially since the trade and labor draft circuit Itier refers to only developed in the 1570s, as a result of Viceroy Francisco de Toledo's reforms (see chapters 3 and 4). I find it easier to believe that the Southern Quechua area has been relatively stable since pre-conquest times, and that the main effect of the rise of the mining circuit was to give an existing dialectal block greater prominence in colonial designs, as Alfredo Torero has argued (Torero 1974: 188, 1995: 14).

As for the long-term consequences of the promotion of Standard Colonial Quechua by the church, there is no concrete evidence that it resulted in any significant linguistic change or language shift. Colonial authorities in the audiencia of Lima did want Quechua to replace other languages and language families, but it is not clear that they were pushing the Southern standard onto speakers of other varieties—the colonial legislation is difficult to interpret in this respect because of the ambiguity and variability of the terms used to designate languages. The situation that developed locally as a result of pastoral monolingualism can be characterized as one of diglossia: the population as a whole may have memorized prayers and listened to sermons in Standard Colonial Quechua, but this did not mean that they spoke it—only the elite would have needed to acquire any degree of active competence. The internal diversity of Quechua does not seem to have been greatly affected except for the disappearance of coastal Quechua, which was due to a more severe demographic collapse of the indigenous population and a larger Spanish and African presence on the coast. It is possible, however, that pastoral monolingualism contributed to the retreat of non-Quechua languages.

The effects of Standard Colonial Quechua on the development of Quechua literacy are indisputable. Pastoral writing was the fount of Quechua literacy and contributed to its period of greatest florescence. On the other hand, it constrained its development by providing a single, monolithic dialectal and orthographic model: Quechua literacy was ipso facto Standard Colonial Quechua literacy. Native Andeans did not adopt the use of alphabetic writing as quickly or as thoroughly as Nahuas, Mayas, Mixtecs, and other Mesoamerican peoples, but beginning around 1600, and continuing for much of the seventeenth century, literacy in Quechua seems to have become fairly common or at least unexceptional among the native elite (Durston n.d.). As Itier has argued, the widespread availability of models for writing Quechua as a result of the publication of the Third Lima Council pastoral corpus provided an essential boost to native literacy (Itier 1992b: 2). The Huarochirí Manuscript, a book-length account of the religious narratives and cult practices of the province of Huarochirí written around 1600, is the most famous Quechua text of native authorship (Salomon and Urioste eds. 1991 [n.d.]; Taylor ed. 1999 [1987, n.d.]). Numerous brief Quechua texts are contained in the Spanish-language chronicles of Felipe Guaman Poma de Ayala (Guaman Poma de Ayala 1980 [1615]) and Juan de Santacruz Pachacuti Yamqui Salcamaygua (Pachacuti Yamqui Salcamaygua 1993 [n.d.]), who also wrote in the early seventeenth century. Most tellingly, at least a dozen Quechua documents or small series of documents written by Indians for legal-administrative purposes or for private correspondence between 1597 and 1679 have been discovered (Durston 2003, n.d.). All of these texts can be broadly identified as Standard Colonial Quechua, even though many of them hail from Central Quechua–speaking areas.

In present-day Peru, however, Quechua literacy is almost nonexistent, and Quechua has no real presence in print media. How the original development of Quechua literacy in the sixteenth and seventeenth centuries relates to the current situation is a subject for future debate. As mentioned above, colonial pastoral translation is at the root of the persisting myth of the primacy of Cuzco Quechua, and this myth has arguably had very negative repercussions for the linguistic self-esteem of the vast majority of Quechua speakers, and for their willingness and ability to express themselves in writing. On the other hand, proponents of bilingual education and general language revitalization have argued that the use of a standard would greatly facilitate the task of producing educational materials as well as written communication between speakers of different varieties. It has even been suggested that Standard Colonial Quechua could be resurrected to play this role, at least among Southern Quechua speakers. It has the advantage of not being identifiable with any specific modern variety (it no longer resembles Cuzco Quechua very closely because of the historical changes discussed above) and of being represented in an extensive literature and in numerous grammatical and lexicographical works (Taylor 1992: 182–183; cf. Cerrón-Palomino 1992: 231). While Standard Colonial Quechua can be said to have died after the middle of the seventeenth century, it has had a surprisingly long afterlife.

PART I

History

Chapter 2

Diversity and Experimentation—1550s and 1560s

One possible starting point for a narrative of the development of pastoral Quechua would be November 16, 1532—the date of the infamous encounter between Francisco Pizarro and the Inca sovereign Atahuallpa, which resulted in Atahuallpa's capture and the massacre of his retinue. While accounts of the events vary, there is some agreement that Atahuallpa was addressed a sermon of sorts by Vicente de Valverde, the Dominican friar who accompanied Pizarro, that was somehow translated into some form of Quechua by an interpreter identified as an Indian youth whom the Spaniards dubbed Felipillo ("little Phillip") (cf. MacCormack 1989; Seed 1991). However, such episodes of oral, *in situ* translation or interpretation belong to the prehistory of pastoral Quechua—spontaneous efforts by mostly Indian interpreters that were probably never recorded in writing. It was only in the late 1540s and early 1550s that concerted translation programs began to develop, and that crown and church officials began to exercise some measure of centralized control over pastoral and linguistic policies. The conquest of the Inca empire was not truly secured until 1537, when Atahuallpa's half brother and successor Manco retreated into the jungles east of the Andes after a failed attempt to recover Cuzco. There followed a period of civil war among the Spanish themselves—rival conquistador bands, pro- and anti-crown factions—that continued throughout the 1540s (see Hemming 1970).

The study of what Estenssoro Fuchs calls the primera evangelización is drastically limited by the sources. Our only direct window on the translation practices of the time is provided by Santo Tomás's Quechua grammar and dictionary (both published in Valladolid in 1560), which contain two brief texts. The primera evangelización worked through manuscript texts, when it worked through texts at all, and sadly none of these manuscripts have survived. Additionally, there is very little in the way of administrative documentation or detailed reports on missionary and pastoral activities, so research has to rely heavily on legislation and other prescriptive texts. As early as 1545, Archbishop Loayza issued a set of preliminary missionary/pastoral guidelines titled *Instrucción de la orden que se a de tener en la doctrina de los naturales* (Guidelines on how to instruct the natives in [Christian] doctrine), and he later presided over the First and Second Lima Councils (1551–52 and 1567–68), whose decrees contain more detailed instructions. There are also letters, most of them from high-level functionaries rather than agents "in the field," and occasional references to missionary and pastoral activities in the chronicle literature. When these scattered sources are brought together, it becomes clear that the pre-reform period was distinguished by a logic of its own, as much as by its incipient character.

Early Ecclesiastical Jurisdictions and Directives

At the time of the First Lima Council, only a very incipient system of missionary and pastoral jurisdictions was in place. The council's decrees speak vaguely of the *provincia* as the basic unit—probably an extensive area that corresponded to the civil *corregimiento* territories. Many provincias were assigned to one of the mendicant orders, whose organization made them more mobile than secular clergy. The order in question was to establish a convent in the main settlement of the provincia and use it as a base from which other population centers could be visited for purposes of catechesis and sacramentation (Vargas Ugarte ed. 1951–1954: I 24). In areas which were under the control of the secular clergy, each priest was to set up his headquarters in the main settlement (*pueblo*) of his district (*distrito*) and work permanently with the population of this settlement and its surrounding territory (*comarca*). He was to congregate the population of the main *pueblo* for catechesis sessions at least twice a week, and on Sundays and feast days he was to gather the population of the surrounding *comarca*. As for more distant settlements in the *distrito*, the priest was to visit them at least twice a year (Vargas Ugarte ed. 1951–1954: I 33). Again, there is little sense of the dimensions of the territories and populations involved, and they probably varied, although lone secular priests must have been given smaller areas to work with than mendicant convents with several friars.

There was as yet no talk of Indian *parishes,* but rather of setting up a network of centers or bases from which the missionaries or pastors—know as *doctrineros* 'teachers of doctrine'—would work outwards. There was no attempt to impose a system in which each person was under the jurisdiction of a specific parish priest who required him or her to attend mass and receive the sacraments on a regular basis. Colonial occupation and knowledge of the territory was as yet too thin—the area was too vast, and settlement patterns too dispersed and intricate for a true parish system to be established. Such a system only became possible after the resettlement campaigns of the 1570s, which segmented the pre-conquest ethnic and territorial formations into small, territorially continuous units in which the population was congregated ("reduced") to a single Spanish-style settlement. However, it could also be argued that a true parish system was not envisioned by the First Council because in Europe itself such a thing only became a common reality after the Council of Trent.[1]

Catechesis consisted of the memorization of the basic prayers (the Credo or Apostle's Creed, Pater Noster, and Ave Maria), the Ten Commandments, and the other elements known collectively as the cartilla, and instruction via *pláticas,* or brief, simple sermons, which both the 1545 *Instrucción* of Loayza and the council decrees sought to standardize. Indians were also to hear mass on Sundays—the *Instrucción* had ordered that after the Offertory the priest should recite the Credo, Pater Noster, and Ave Maria aloud so that the Indians who were present could recite them too, and preach the commandments and articles of the faith (Vargas Ugarte ed. 1951–1954: II 147–148). These decrees do not specify what language was to be used, and there is evidence that catechesis was carried out largely in Spanish and Latin during this period (Estenssoro Fuchs 2003: 50–51). The council did, however, authorize the use of a specific Quechua version of the cartilla and some accompanying *coloquios,* apparently brief sermons (see p. 67 below). In 1551 Loayza founded a chaplaincy known as "the chaplaincy of the [Indian] language" (*capellanía de la lengua*), which provided a stipend for a secular cleric or friar who knew "the language of the Indians" (probably the coastal Quechua lingua franca) and would preach to them in the Lima cathedral every Sunday and feast day.[2] In spite of this initiative, vernacular language training among the clergy did not become widespread until the 1570s and 1580s.

The First Council's decrees on sacramentation reflect a situation in which much of the Andean population was still formally pagan. Prebaptismal catechesis was a concern, because Indians were still being baptized in adulthood—for an Indian who was eight years or older to be baptized, he or she had to be taught the Pater Noster, the Credo, the Ave Maria, and the Ten Commandments and other basic doctrinal elements over a period of thirty days (Vargas Ugarte ed. 1951–1954: I 9–10). Several decrees deal with the pagans (*infieles*) who lived among baptized Indians, and it was ordered that someone be posted at the church door during mass to prevent them from entering (ibid.: I 14). Since the Christianity of even baptized and catechized Indians was very incipient, it was determined that only the sacraments of baptism, confession, and marriage could be administered to Indians on a regular basis. Indian communion required a special license from the bishop (ibid.: I 15). Because of a shortage of qualified priests, Indians were obligated to make confession only once a year, during Lent—at this time bishops were to send priests who were *lenguas* (i.e., familiar with an indigenous language) to areas where the local priests were not (ibid.: I 19). Another issue that arose with Indians who had only recently become Christian concerned the sacrament of marriage. Decree 15 determined that native marriages were valid under natural law, and had only to be "rectified" via the sacrament, in spite of the fact that Andean marriage practices permitted matches between close relatives, especially among nobles. The council even went to the extreme of allowing marriages between siblings, which if properly constituted in Andean terms (*según sus ritos y costumbres*) were to be recognized, pending papal approval (ibid.: I 17).

The late 1560s, and the Second Lima Council in particular, were to some extent a prelude to the reforms of the 1570s and 1580s. Both royal officials and prelates were taking stock of what had been achieved during the first generation of Spanish rule in Peru, and alarms sounded over the lack of instruction among formally Christian Indians, the persistence of "idolatry," and even movements of military resistance. In the mid-1560s clergymen in the diocese of Cuzco claimed to have discovered and extirpated a religious movement know as *taqui oncoy* ('dancing/singing sickness') that was aimed at destroying the Spanish presence in Peru and restoring the cult of the *huacas,* or Andean deities (cf. Stern 1993 [1982]: 51–71).[3] In 1565 the president of the Lima audiencia, Lope García de Castro, claimed in a letter to the king that the archbishop and the heads of the orders had admitted that out of three hundred thousand baptized Indians, only forty (!)

were truly Christian. He also warned that the Indians were on the verge of revolt.[4] Another audiencia official, Gregorio González de Cuenca, carried out a visita of the northern provinces of the archdiocese of Lima in 1566 and 1567 and noted that few Indians confessed or understood catechetical instruction because the priests did not know their languages. He recommended that vernacular competence be required of all priests who worked among Indians, and that a true parish system be set up.[5] Cuenca seems to have been the first royal official to insist on the importance of vernacular instruction.

All this coincided with the official reception of the decrees of the Council of Trent in Lima in October of 1565.[6] In 1567–68 the Second Lima Council was held to apply the Tridentine decrees in Spanish South America. Interestingly, while the original decrees of the previous council had been in Spanish, those of the Second Lima Council were issued in Latin, perhaps reflecting a greater will to conform to the universal norms of the church.[7] Another evident change is the greater attention to Indian "idolatry," which had been only a passing concern in the First Council. Everyday customs, such as burial rites and even hairstyles, were denounced for their pagan content and prohibited (Vargas Ugarte ed. 1951–1954: I 205–212). Another major innovation was the attempt to impose the Tridentine concept of the parish—a clearly defined territory and group of people assigned to a specific priest—as the basic institution for the conversion and pastoral care of Indians (ibid.: I 193–195). The parish system was essential for the implementation of Tridentine standards of instruction and sacramentation, which required that priests be able to monitor and keep records on individual parishioners. Each parish was thus limited demographically to four hundred heads of household (ibid.: I 194).

In fulfillment of the Council of Trent, priests were required to administer Easter communion and viaticum to those who had acquired some understanding of the eucharist (Vargas Ugarte ed. 1951–1954: I 186–187), a major change with respect to the First Council, and extreme unction was to be made available to all (ibid.: I 193). The council also instituted Wednesday and Friday *doctrina* or catechesis sessions and Sunday and feast day sermons (ibid.: I 200–202). Finally, it instituted the Tridentine requirement of knowledge of the vernacular for priests of Indian parishes, ordering that those who were negligent in learning Quechua were to lose a third of their stipends (ibid.: I 240–241). However, the immediate impact of the decrees of the Second Lima Council seems to have been limited, and it did not become the definitive expression of Counter-Reformation Catholicism in the Andes—the primera evangelización was effectively brought to an end by the cumulative effect of the reforms of Viceroy Toledo in the 1570s and the Third Lima Council in the early 1580s, as will be seen in the next chapter.

The Primera Evangelización: Liturgy and Accommodation

Estenssoro Fuch's portrayal of the primera evangelización emphasizes three main features which contrast sharply with the post-reform period (2003, chapters 1 and 2). First, conversion practices were more diverse and flexible due to the relative independence of the different agents involved, especially the mendicant orders. Second, there was a tendency to downplay the need for Indians to assimilate the full range of doctrines or receive sacraments other than baptism, with greater emphasis on participation in the liturgy and on the use of nonverbal media, especially music. Third, there was a greater openness to the adaptation of native Andean religious forms to Christian contexts.

Of the features noted by Estenssoro, it is the liturgical orientation of the primera evangelización that is expressed most clearly in the sources. The Franciscans in particular systematically trained Indian boys as musicians to perform in the mass and the canonical hours in their convents. When in 1563 an audiencia judge ordered them to release the boys who were serving in their convents or to pay for their services, the Franciscans protested that they were being trained to serve as acolytes, recite the canonical hours, sing in the choir, and play flutes and other musical instruments for the liturgy. Their services not only improved the splendor of the liturgy, but were necessary for the conversion of the Indian population as a whole, since Indians were deemed to be especially fond of music—*aficionados a música.*[8]

The Augustinian chronicler Antonio de la Calancha reveals a similar emphasis on Indian participation in the liturgy in his order during this same period. According to Calancha, Augustinian missionaries of the 1550s and 1560s were instructed to teach Indians liturgical music as a means of inculcating "respect, love and devotion" for church feasts and doctrines (Calancha 1974–1982 [1638]: 811). Calancha described early Augustinian pastoral activity in Huamachuco as being centered on the liturgy: the evening Angelus prayer (which commemorates the Incarnation of Christ) was performed every day and masses were sung throughout the week for the souls in purgatory (on Mondays), to the eucharist (Thursdays), and to the Virgin (Saturdays). Sundays and feast days were celebrated with elaborate processions (ibid.: 883–884). The secular clergy did not stay far behind. In the early 1560s Luis de Olvera, priest of the province of Parinacochas, had no less than thirty local boys singing the hours of the Virgin every day in the province's main church, a practice more common in cathedrals than in parish churches.[9]

This emphasis on the liturgy as the key instrument of Christianization was not a new one. In the late thirteenth century a Franciscan missionary in Peking ransomed 150 children to train them in the performance of the canonical hours, and claimed that their singing made a positive impression on the khan. It appears that the texts were sung in the Mongol language, into which the Franciscans had translated the psalms and were planning to translate the entire Latin liturgy (Marco 1961: 55–58). However, there are no references to the translation of Latin texts from the mass or the canonical hours into Quechua during the primera evangelización. There clearly was some expectation that exposure to the Latin liturgy would "bear fruit," just as it was believed to do among Europeans who did not know Latin. The benefits of participation in the liturgy were also seen at musical and dramaturgical levels. The Indians' love for church music is a commonplace in the colonial sources—they were also perceived as having an unusual capacity to learn European music. This love of music was a counterpart to the Indians' alleged difficulties in the exercise of their rational faculties—they were thought to be more susceptible to the sensory and the emotional than to logic.

An important and unexpected source on the primera evangelización that illustrates many of the other features pointed to by Estenssoro Fuchs has been found in the records of the Inquisition trial of Francisco de la Cruz, one of the most prominent Dominicans in Peru (Abril Castelló ed. 1992; Abril Castelló and Abril Stoffels eds. 1996–1997). De la Cruz came to Peru in 1561, was posted as priest of Pomata on the shores of Lake Titicaca, and went on to become prior of the convent of Chuquisaca and president of the University of San Marcos in Lima, which was then under Dominican control. In 1572 he was arrested by the newly arrived Inquisition and was burnt at the stake in 1578. De la Cruz was accused of organizing a millenarian cult in Lima that predicted the imminent destruction of

Christendom in Europe and the establishment of a new, pure church in Peru under his leadership on the eve of the Apocalypse. De la Cruz's heresies were indeed quite radical, but Estenssoro Fuchs has stressed that he should not be seen as an isolated case, and that many of the less spectacular views recorded in his trial are representative of models for the creation of an Andean Christianity that characterized the pre-reform period. His trial also exemplifies the repression of these models that occurred in the 1570s (Estenssoro Fuchs 2003: 184–188).

De la Cruz claimed to know through divine revelation that the Indians of Peru were descendants of the lost tribes of Israel—as evidence for the link he mentioned several apparent similarities between Quechua and Hebrew words (Abril Castelló and Abril Stoffels eds. 1996–1997: I 555–559). God had deprived them of the full use of their rational faculties in order to maintain them in a state of innocence, thus preparing them for a full conversion. They had to be introduced to Christianity in a gradual fashion, and should not be required to assimilate the more difficult dogmas such as the Trinity or the Incarnation, or to confess—a general belief in the existence of a creator God was sufficient for their salvation (Abril Castelló ed. 1992: 628–631; Abril Castelló and Abril Stoffels eds. 1996–1997: II 1327, 958). Nor were Indians to be forced to live in Spanish-style communities and under Spanish law because this would only infect them with the sins of avarice and pride that were characteristic of Europeans—he even claimed that because of their ancestry Indians should observe the laws of Moses rather than those of Spain (Abril Castelló ed. 1992: 850; Abril Castelló and Abril Stoffels eds. 1996–1997: II 1213, 1328). De la Cruz criticized the Second Lima Council for (allegedly) prohibiting the performance of *taquis* or native song-dance genres (from Quechua /taki/ 'song') and of funerary and initiation rites, claiming that these were not necessarily idolatrous and that the prohibition was alienating the Indians from Christianity. Many Indian *costumbres* were in fact derived from Jewish ones, and, in any case, the church had long allowed the Christian adaptation of pagan rites and festivals among newly converted peoples (Abril Castelló and Abril Stoffels eds. 1996–1997: I 638–642).

Although he was a Dominican, de la Cruz's pastoral program is strongly reminiscent of the millenarianism of early Franciscan missionaries in Mexico such as Jerónimo de Mendieta. De la Cruz shared Mendieta's belief that the Indians were ideal converts because of their natural humility and innocence, and that the Primitive Church would be reestablished in the New World (Phelan 1970 [1950]). He also shared Mendieta's isolationism—the belief that Spanish social customs and institutions, known generically as *policía,* should not be imposed on the Indians. On the other hand, de la Cruz's argument that Indians should not be required to assimilate the full range of Christian dogmas seems to have been characteristic of early Dominican missionary projects in Peru. Estenssoro Fuchs notes that the catechetical texts that have survived from this period, most of which are associated with the Dominican order, share a common emphasis on a broad Christian narrative and anthropology and coincide in the omission of what would later be regarded as key doctrines that were essential for salvation (Estenssoro Fuchs 2003, chapter 1).

One of the most striking features of Francisco de la Cruz's pastoral program was his favorable perception of the taquis and his willingness to adapt what he referred to as "dances without idolatry" (*bailes sin idolatría*) to Christian uses. He stated that during his tenure as priest of Pomata he had treated the taquis as analogous to the secular dances used by Christians to celebrate Corpus Christi and Christmas, and allowed their performance on the condition that the songs spoke of "natural things" (*cosas naturales*) and "past things" (*cosas pasadas*) and were not dedicated to the huacas. Some of these taquis had an explicitly Christian content, containing statements such as "there is only one God," "we should not worship the huacas," and "God feeds us" (Abril Castelló and Abril Stoffels eds. 1996–1997: I 638–642).

De la Cruz recalled that when a leading curaca, or native lord, of Pomata died, he had initially attempted to implement the Second Council's prohibition of a form of public mourning, which he phrased as "they should not be allowed to weep for their dead through the streets"—the original decree used the term *ululare* ('to howl' or 'to wail') (Vargas Ugarte ed. 1951–1954: I 209–210). When he noticed that the prohibition was distressful for his parishioners, he allowed the mourning ritual to be performed in litany style with responses: "he changed that weeping into a litany chant in such a way that the choir boys from the school went in procession, separated into pairs and singing in the language of the Indians: 'St. Mary' or 'St. Peter,' etc. And all would answer, weeping in their language: 'pray for him and for us.'"[10] It appears that de la Cruz's Christianization of the mourning ritual involved adapting a native song style by inserting Christian invocations and having them recited in responsorial fashion. The taqui in question was probably of the *haraui* genre: the term *ululare* used in the conciliar prohibition makes one think of the falsetto that characterizes the modern /harawi/ style, and the gloss for haraui provided by the Jesuit linguist Diego González Holguín in his 1608 dictionary matches the use described by de la Cruz: "Songs about the deeds of others or the memory of absent loved ones, and of love and affections, and now they are used as devout and spiritual songs" (González Holguín 1989 [1952, 1608]: 152).[11]

De la Cruz's efforts to adapt Andean taquis for Christian uses were not unique. In fact, they seem to have been quite mainstream for the time. The original decrees of the Second Lima Council contain no outright ban on taquis, and one decree explicitly allowed for the continued use of indigenous rites for harvest and planting time—which must have included taquis—as long as they were performed *in honorem Dei*, which is exactly what de la Cruz was attempting to do (Vargas Ugarte ed. 1951–1954: I 209; cf. Estenssoro Fuchs 1992: 364). As Carolyn Dean notes, at this time the Spanish "distinguished between the means of celebration and the object being celebrated . . . [and] divorced Andean festive forms from Andean religious beliefs" (Dean 1999: 15). The most detailed references concerning Christian uses of taquis during this period concern Corpus Christi, a major Catholic festival celebrating the eucharist that, very appropriately, coincided with harvest time in the Andes (late May and early June). Corpus Christi was an especially apt ground for the incorporation of taquis, as it had traditionally involved representations of religious "others" (ibid.: 7–14).

The earliest detailed account of Corpus Christi taquis in Peru comes from a Jesuit mission report describing the celebrations held in Huarochirí, in the highlands above Lima, under the order's supervision in 1570. This episode should not be considered representative of Jesuit policies, which will be discussed in the following chapter—it belongs to the very early stages of the order in Peru (it arrived in 1568), and the report describes a practice that was already in existence. As part of the Corpus Christi procession, several indigenous dances were performed in honor of the eucharist, and "[t]he most unusual of these dances was that of the nobles who are called Incas, and the most noble one among them sang the very soulful lyrics, which were of four syllables each verse. And the Spaniards and priests who were there suddenly noticed that the lyrics contained very good epithets for Our Lord. And when asked where they took them from, they said that the same epithets they had given to the sun and to their king in their antiquity they now turned into praise for Jesus Christ, using the content of the sermons they had heard."[12] The author of the report does not tell us exactly what native genres were performed in the celebrations, but the reference to a dance in which nobles sang epithets that had originally been addressed to the sun deity and the Inca sovereign is reminiscent of the *haylli*, another taqui genre. In contrast to the haraui, the haylli was a triumphal taqui performed in both military and agricultural contexts. According to Garcilaso de la Vega, hayllis were sung "in praise of the sun and of their kings" (*en loor del sol y de sus reyes*), a description that matches that of the Jesuit report (Garcilaso 1945 [1609]: II 228–229; cf. González Holguín 1989 [1952, 1608]: 157).

Garcilaso himself left a much-cited account of a Corpus Christi haylli, explicitly identified as such. Although writing in Spain around the turn of the sixteenth century, Garcilaso had spent his childhood in Cuzco, and his account refers to a Corpus Christi celebration he witnessed there as a schoolboy in 1550 or 1551: "Eight of my fellow mestizo schoolmates came out dressed as Indians, each with a foot plow in his hands, and performed in the procession the song and *haylli* of the Indians, with the entire choir [of the cathedral] helping them sing the chorus, to the great contentment of the Spaniards and the utmost joy of the Indians, seeing that the Spaniards solemnized the feast of our lord God (whom they call Pachacamac, which means 'he who gives life to the universe') with their [the Indians'] songs and dances."[13] Garcilaso specifies that the song was a *chanzoneta* (a vernacular religious genre similar to the villancico) composed for organ music by the cathedral's choir master in imitation of a haylli.

In analyzing this haylli-chanzoneta Estenssoro Fuchs argues that it was not an instrument of conversion, but rather a form of commentary on the relation between Inca religion and Christianity: "we are confronted by a phenomenon that seeks to be the reverse of syncretism, that is founded on a disjunction . . . If the ancient haylli had to subsist, it was not in order to preserve its ancient meaning, but in order to reveal its hidden 'true meaning,' to become a premonition of Catholicism . . . [it] acts as an interpretive cue, demanding an effort of exegesis, forcing a resemantization."[14] The term "disjunction" is borrowed from art historian Erwin Panofsky, who uses it to designate a mechanism whereby viewers are stimulated to find a Christian meaning in a pagan sign—to carry out an *interpretatio christiana*.

In other words, this is a mode of accommodation that is not intended as a means of transmitting a Christian message in a form more easily assimilated by an originally non-Christian audience. Instead, attention is drawn to the contrast between the Christian and the native elements, which are brought together in a surprising way—the Indians (probably Inca nobility) who witnessed the Corpus Christi haylli-chanzoneta were overjoyed, Garcilaso tells us, to see the Spanish using their songs and dances to praise God. This surprise leads to a reflection, not on Christianity itself, but on how native things relate to it. The performers, who were sons of conquistadors and Inca women and were being educated as Spanish noblemen in the cathedral school, were in Indian garb, which they would not normally have worn—the indigenous forms (music, foot-plows, dress) were exhibited in an almost folklorizing way (Estenssoro Fuchs 2003: 151). The whole performance was an expression of the principle that native forms of worship were pleasing to God and had a place in the liturgy, and that an Indian, or rather, Inca Christianity was possible. Garcilaso reinforced this principle with a linguistic counterpart by mentioning, in an apparently off-hand fashion, that the Indians called God *Pachacamac*, the point being that if there was a Quechua word for God, the Indians must have had some knowledge of God before the arrival of the Spaniards (cf. Estenssoro Fuchs 2003: 150–152).

The concept of disjunction does not seem applicable to Francisco de la Cruz's adaptation of a funerary song in Pomata or to the Corpus Christi taquis witnessed by the Jesuits in Huarochirí, which on the surface are very similar to Garcilaso's haylli-chanzoneta. Disjunction requires an audience with a solid Christian background, as would have been the case with the young Garcilaso and his classmates from the cathedral school—one has to be Christian in order to carry out an *interpretatio christiana*. Unlike Cuzco, a major center of Spanish settlement, Pomata and Huarochirí were purely Indian towns, and thus missionary frontiers. Accommodation here conforms to the familiar paradigms: the objective is to ease the transition to Christianity among people who are considered still essentially pagan by allowing a certain amount of continuity with pre-Christian rites. The indigenous forms are allowed to remain, to blend in and serve as a sort of bridge. These cases correspond to what Estenssoro Fuchs calls "syncretism" as opposed to "disjunction," although I would rephrase the distinction in terms of "conjunctive" versus "disjunctive" syncretism/accommodation. I will return to this issue in chapter 8, which examines the use of Andean religious categories and motifs in the Quechua liturgy.

The reform of the pastoral regime that began in the late 1560s was partly a campaign to purify the liturgy of taquis. The Counter-Reformation in general was characterized by an effort to establish clearer boundaries between the sacred and the secular—for instance, secular songs and instruments were banned from the Corpus Christi liturgy in Spain (Kamen 1993: 183–185). The Second Lima Council forbade passion plays during Holy Week and vernacular religious songs during Corpus Christi (*motetes et versus* in the Latin version, *letras* in the Spanish version) unless they were authorized by the bishop (Vargas Ugarte ed. 1951–1954: I 120, 229). It also expressed intense concern over the continuation of the huaca cults under the guise of the Christian liturgy, especially during Corpus Christi, when idols were reportedly hidden in the litters used for carrying the statues of the saints (ibid.: I 203–204).[15] In some respects, however, the Second Lima Council reflected the practices of the primera evangelización, as witnessed by its tolerance for certain indigenous "rites." As a result, the Third Lima Council was compelled to modify its content in the official Spanish version it produced, omitting accommodationist suggestions and adding an outright ban of taquis (Estenssoro Fuchs 1992: 363–364, 367, 383).

The accommodationist practices of the primera evangelización should be seen in the context of contemporary understandings of Andean religion as expressed in the chronicle literature, particularly the belief that it had important monotheistic and even outright Christian elements. It was widely held that Peru had been visited by an apostle, usually identified as Thomas, and that although his teachings had been lost, certain elements remained embedded in the pagan religion (Duviols 1977a [1971]: 55–70; MacCormack 1991: 312–316). De la Cruz's Jewish origin hypothesis was quite common and had important consequences for conversion practices. Regardless of whether the Indians were literally considered to be Jews, they were persistently compared to them, and Indian cultures and their relation to Christianity were seen through the lens of the Old Testament and its relation to the New. Estenssoro Fuchs argues that the exegetical habit of reading the Old Testament for prefigurations or "types" of Christian revelation was applied to Andean religious forms and practices, thus justifying their use in Christian contexts (Estenssoro Fuchs 2003: 155). Louise Burkhart makes a similar point in discussing mendicant conversion programs among the Nahuas: "If the Old Testament is a type for the New Testament, and the pre-conversion Indians are placed symbolically in an Old Testament world (which was, after all, a world of temples, sacrifices, prophets, wars of conquest, kings and priests), then pre-conversion culture can act as a type for Indian Christianity" (Burkhart 1988: 240).

Another form of argument that retroactively Christianized Andean religion focused on the workings of natural reason among the Indians as a *praeparatio evangelica*: as MacCormack puts it, "God was known not thanks to a unique and lapidary revelation; He was discovered, rather, in a series of steps, resulting in a gradually growing acquaintance" (1991: 213). Bartolomé de Las Casas stated that the Incas, specifically the Inca sovereign Inca Yupanqui, also known as Pachacuti, had come to believe in the existence of a single creator God under the name "Viracocha" through natural reason (ibid.: 216; Zamora 1988: 101). Juan de Betanzos, a layman who settled in Cuzco and married a widow of Atahuallpa, went out of his way in a chronicle of the Incas written in the 1550s to present them as monotheists. Among other things, he claimed that the name Viracocha was the direct equivalent of Spanish *Dios,* translated a prayer in which Inca Yupanqui addressed Viracocha as "lord God who made me and gave me the being of man" (*Señor Dios que me hiciste y diste ser de hombre*), and quoted a Quechua sentence affirming the resurrection of the flesh at the end of time (Betanzos 1987 [1557]: 78, 32, 101).

There has been much debate among modern scholars about the nature of Viracocha and his true role in pre-Hispanic religion (Demarest 1981; Szemiñski 1997; Urbano 1991)—the Spanish sources are notoriously contradictory (MacCormack 1991: 350). The very etymology of the term is obscure: it can be read as the Quechua noun phrase /wira qucha/ 'lake of fat,' but Betanzos vehemently denied this interpretation, saying simply "it does not mean that, rather, it properly means 'God'" (*no quiere decir aquello sino propiamente 'Dios'*) (Betanzos 1987 [1557]: 78). The balance of the evidence suggests that Viracocha was a pan-Andean culture hero known under several different names who aided the establishment of human societies by conveying key technologies (especially agricultural ones), rather than a creator god. In some accounts there were several Viracochas, or at least avatars of the main one. It is possible that "Viracocha" was in fact a generic term for certain types of entities rather than a proper name, which would explain why it was applied to the Spanish invaders. It seems unlikely that anything approximating the Western concept of the universe as the product of a divine creation *ex nihilo* existed in native cosmology.[16] Spanish accounts of Viracocha as a supreme, remote creator god would thus reflect an automatic assimilation of Andean religious categories and narratives to Judeo-Christian ones, and/or a deliberate effort to establish equivalencies between Inca religion and Christianity, as a result of which Viracocha was selected to "play the role" of the Inca creator god (Duviols 1977b, 1993; Itier 1993; Urbano 1981).

The First Pastoral Texts in Quechua

Language acquisition and translation efforts in Peru seem to have focused from the start on varieties of Quechua. The earliest Christian texts in Quechua on which we have specific information were written in the 1540s by Betanzos, who stated that he spent six years of his youth translating a *doctrina cristiana* (probably a cartilla) and composing two dictionaries, a series of *coloquios* (brief sermons, also known as *pláticas*), and a confesionario. Betanzos, who must have had an exceptional knowledge of Quechua for a Spaniard at that time, appears to have been commissioned by the crown to write these texts (Betanzos 1987 [1557]: 7; cf. Hamilton 1996). Although they have disappeared, it can be surmised from his statement on the meaning of the name Viracocha (quoted above) that Betanzos used it to designate God in them. This is of some importance, since no extant Quechua text refers to God with any term other than the Spanish loan word *Dios*. In fact, it could be suggested that Betanzos's interpretations of Inca religion developed as a result of his translation activities—that is, his search for a Quechua name for God, which he found in Viracocha, may have in turn inspired his conviction that the Incas were monotheists. It also seems likely that his texts were written in the Inca lingua franca variety, which is apparent in the Quechua words and phrases cited in his chronicle, rather than in the Cuzco variety of Southern Quechua.

Betanzos was not the only Spaniard writing Christian texts in Andean languages in the 1540s. Loayza's 1545 *Instrucción* mentions the existence of "some cartillas in the languages of the natives" but prohibits their use under pain of excommunication, on the grounds that they had not been examined for their orthodoxy and faithfulness to Spanish or Latin originals. The cartilla was to be learned in Spanish or Latin. However, the *Instrucción* also authorized the use of "certain sermons that have been written in their language" (*ciertos coloquios o pláticas que están hechos en su lengua*), and stated that the vernacular cartillas were to be studied by a committee of experts who would develop a single authorized version (Vargas Ugarte ed. 1951–1954: II 142). Loayza's *Instrucción* warned that extreme caution had to exercised in Indian catechesis because any errors would, when corrected, give Indians the impression that Christian doctrine was variable (ibid.: II 142). The first decree of the First Lima Council expanded on this principle, requiring that all Indians be taught "the same things and in the same style and language" (*una misma cosa y en un mismo estilo y lengua*) (ibid.: I 7). A similar concern would be expressed by the Second and Third Lima Councils: changes and variations in catechetical texts were to be avoided at all cost because they would lead Indians to believe that they corresponded to changes and variations in the doctrines themselves. In all three councils, the key issue was the stability or uniformity of the translations, more than their accuracy and intelligibility. The obsession with uniformity can be associated with the contemporary doctrinal struggles in Europe, but may also be explained in terms of a need to transmit Western conceptions of religious doctrine, of Truth and Error, to cultures whose forms of religious thought were essentially pluralistic and nondogmatic.

The official cartilla promised in the 1545 *Instrucción* was apparently in existence at the time of the First Lima Council, although the relevant decree is unclear on this point: "the common prayers Pater Noster, Ave Maria, Credo, the Commandments and the Works of Mercy, Articles of the Faith, etc., should be in our Spanish language, in accordance with the cartilla which has been ordered by this council. And because in these kingdoms of Peru there is one language that is in more general use among the natives, in which a cartilla and certain coloquios that explain it have been written, we allow that this [version of the cartilla] be used, and no other."[17] The injunction that the basic prayers and other components of the cartilla be in Spanish apparently meant that this, rather than Latin, was to be the language of reference for catechetical instruction. The next sentence authorized the use of a specific Quechua translation and of a set of coloquios or brief sermons that explicated it.

Little is known about these early texts—they were never published and no copies have been discovered. The First Lima Council never carried much authority, and its approval of the Quechua cartilla and coloquios had been lukewarm in the first place. Most witnesses to catechesis in the 1550s and 1560s either claim that it was carried out primarily in Spanish and Latin, or that pastoral agents were allowed to catechize in Quechua as they saw fit.[18] The cartilla and coloquios were almost certainly the work of Dominicans—Domingo de Santo Tomás was active around this time, and Loayza himself was a Dominican. According to a much later Dominican chronicle, a May 1551 royal cédula granted the Dominicans a large sum of money as a reward for their pastoral efforts, which included translating the *doctrina christiana* into the "language of the Indians" (Meléndez 1681–1682: I 209–210). This text was almost certainly a Quechua cartilla, and was probably the very text recommended by the council—the decree quoted above makes clear that the Quechua cartilla and coloquios were not commissioned by the council, but simply approved by it.

In spite of the absence of direct information on the texts authorized by the First Lima Council, much can be inferred from Domingo de Santo Tomás's dictionary and grammar. Santo Tomás arrived in Peru in 1540, not long after the conquest, and was prior of the Dominican convent in Lima from 1545 to 1548. He participated in the First Council as the official representative of his order, and was elected its provincial in 1553. He carried out most of his missionary work in coastal valleys to the north and south of Lima, and probably also in the valley of Lima itself, which still had a large indigenous population. In 1555 he returned to Spain, which means that his grammar and dictionary were prepared before that date. Santo Tomás obtained royal patronage for his works: they were printed by the king's printer, and the crown paid for 1,583 copies (of each book?) so that the author could take them to Peru.[19]

Santo Tomás's books contain two complete texts, which are presented as samples of the language he was describing: the Confiteor, or General Confession prayer, at the beginning of the dictionary, and the *Plática para todos los indios,* a sermon, plática, or coloquio containing a brief history of creation that was appended to the grammar (Santo Tomás 1951 [1560]: 18; 1995 [1560]: 172–179). Additionally, the grammar quotes fragments of the Credo and the Ave Maria to exemplify how theological terms and expressions which had no equivalents in Quechua could be translated with paraphrases (1995 [1560]: 92). The Quechua versions of the Confiteor, Credo, and Ave Maria used by Santo Tomás were probably those of the cartilla approved by the council—it seems unlikely that, as a prominent Dominican, he would have flouted the council's ban on other cartillas in a printed work intended for wide distribution. It also seems nearly certain that he was one of the translators of the official Quechua cartilla. The *Plática para todos los indios* can be matched point for point with the outlines of catechetical contents contained in Loayza's 1545 *Instrucción* and in the decrees of the First Lima Council, which suggests that it was one of the pláticas or coloquios approved by the council.[20]

Since no other Christian texts in Quechua are available from this period, the only way to characterize them is by comparison with the Third Lima Council corpus, which constitutes the historical standard for pastoral Quechua (Third Lima Council 1985a [1584], 1985b [1585], and 1985c

[1585]). A first point of comparison is dialectal: as mentioned in chapter 1, Santo Tomás's linguistic works are of special importance because they record an extinct form of Quechua spoken on the central coast, which is also believed to have been the source of the Inca lingua franca. There are also significant terminological differences. Santo Tomás's texts employ a number of Quechua neologisms and adapted terms,[21] which the Third Lima Council translators would later replace systematically with loan words, among them the terms for "saint," "confession," "soul," and "virgin" (Estenssoro Fuchs 2003: 84–114; cf. MacCormack 1985; Taylor 2001b). One striking example of the terminological differences is provided by Santo Tomás's dictionary, where the term *çupay,* which in all later texts means simply 'devil,' is proposed as a neutral designation for angels as well as devils, distinguished with the qualifiers *alli* 'good' and *mana alli* 'bad' (Santo Tomás 1951 [1960]: 40).

In Estenssoro Fuchs's view, the terminological practices suggested in Santo Tomás's dictionary are more daring than those used in the Quechua texts, which leads him to the conclusion that the translations of the Confiteor and the *Plática para todos los indios* were not Santo Tomás's work, and that they represent later and more conservative translation practices—in particular, he points to the fact that the term *çupay* is not applied to the angels in the *Plática* (Estenssoro Fuchs 2003: 100, 103–105). However, lexicographic description and writing official pastoral texts are two very different activities—Santo Tomás could simply have exercised greater caution in the latter. Regardless of whether he participated in the translation of these texts, he clearly regarded them as good exemplifications of the principles laid out in his linguistic work. On a side note, the Quechua glosses that Santo Tomás provided for Christian terms in the Spanish-Quechua section of his dictionary are not necessarily representative of, or proposals for, actual translation practice—they can be understood as just that, glosses. As in other dictionaries, the Christian glosses provided for Quechua terms in the Quechua-Spanish section are more indicative, since they deal with (in principle, at least) actually occurring terms.

It can be argued that Santo Tomás's preference for Quechua terms as opposed to loan words reflects a belief in the commensurability of Christian and native religious concepts and institutions. Santo Tomás was a supporter of Bartolomé de Las Casas and shared his tendency to see an innate Christian potential in Indian cultures—as mentioned, the prologue to his grammar contains an apology for Andean society, whose civility was said to be reflected in the orderliness of Quechua grammar (Santo Tomás 1995 [1560]: 8–9). Greater recourse to Quechua terms may also reflect the nature of Santo Tomás's catechetical program. The *Plática* reveals a concern for transmitting a general anthropology and cosmology rather than concrete doctrines, an approach that can be related to contemporary arguments that all that was necessary for Indians to be saved was a general understanding of the existence of a creator God and of the difference between Good and Evil. This generality of contents would have made the use of Quechua paraphrases and neologisms as opposed to loan words more feasible—standards of terminological precision were simply lower than in post-reform catechesis.

While the Second Lima Council gave a significant impulse to vernacular instruction, its policy regarding the First Council texts is unclear. Indians were to memorize the cartilla "in Spanish and also in their own language," but there is no indication of what Quechua version of the cartilla is referred to (Vargas Ugarte ed. 1951–1954: I 175). The council stressed the need for a standard catechism for Indians, but its development was postponed in light of the announcement by the Council of Trent of a "universal catechism" which would provide the basis for any definitive Peruvian catechism (the Tridentine Roman Catechism had in fact been published in 1566 but apparently had not yet reached Peru) (ibid.: I 160–161). In the meantime, the council delegated the task of producing official catechisms to the diocesan level, instructing each bishop to develop one for his diocese that was to be approved or corrected in a diocesan synod (ibid.: I 161). The council also ordered a confesionario to be written, presumably in Quechua, by a team of experts who were familiar both with the language and with the sins which Indians tended to commit (ibid.: I 185). It is not known whether this confesionario was ever completed.

The emphasis on catechisms in the Second Lima Council marks a significant change with respect to earlier policies, apparently as a result of the influence of the Council of Trent. There is no reference to catechisms in the First Lima Council—instead, instruction worked through the cartilla texts and short sermons (coloquios or pláticas) whose contents appear to have been very general, if one can judge from Santo Tomás's plática. It was only in the late 1560s and 1570s that the use of catechisms came to be regarded as essential, reflecting the growing emphasis on the full comprehension of a wide range of doctrines. Another shift is reflected in the Second Council's call for a confesionario, which stands in contrast to the scant attention generally given to the sacrament of confession during the primera evangelización.

Pastoral Quechua Texts in Cuzco, 1560s and 1570s

In addition to the information that can be gleaned from the First and Second Lima Councils and from the works of Santo Tomás, which mainly concerns translation activities in the archdiocese and city of Lima, there are important testimonies on the development of independent projects in Cuzco. Betanzos's efforts in the 1540s seem to have initiated, or formed part of, a distinctive translation tradition associated with the city of Cuzco and its diocese. As early as 1567, before the completion of the Second Lima Council, titles issued by the bishop or cathedral chapter of Cuzco to new parish priests instructed them to catechize their parishioners with official Quechua texts referred to as "the cartilla, sermon, and catechism written in the lengua general of this diocese," or some similar phrase.[22] It appears that the diocese of Cuzco was running ahead of the archdiocese of Lima in the development of pastoral texts in Quechua—there is no evidence that Lima ever had an official Quechua catechism prior to the Third Lima Council. Starting around 1574, parish titles speak of a cartilla and catechism that had been recently revised and were accompanied by a Spanish translation.[23] References to the revised versions appear shortly after the beginning of Sebastián de Lartaun's ten-year episcopate in 1573, but they were the work of a team commissioned by the cathedral chapter while it was still running the diocese during the interim following the death of the previous bishop.

Information on the revision process is provided by a single manuscript source: the 1574 información de oficio of Melchor del Aguila, a Spanish-born secular priest who was a member of the team. Del Aguila was described in the introductory petition as "one of the most erudite and accomplished clerics, very learned and able in the lengua general of the Inca, and in that language he has written a cartilla and catechism to catechize the natives with proper and legitimate idioms and terms, of which great fruit has resulted and will result."[24] However, the questionnaire of the información makes clear that del Aguila was part of a team named by the chapter to revise rather than rewrite the texts. He is referred to as "one of those charged with modifying the Christian cartilla and catechism with which the natives are taught and with perfecting and giving it more congruity of terms and words."[25] These references suggest that the previous versions of the cartilla and catechism were considered unsatisfactory either for dialectal reasons or for terminological ones, or perhaps both.

Del Aguila's role continued after these modifications had been completed: "the most illustrious dean and chapter of this holy church [entrusted him] with polishing it all and writing it with proper and natural characters and with the orthography of the lengua general, and completing it with points and strokes, and finally translating it all into Spanish so that the cartilla and catechism in the lengua general of the Indians and in our language could go together, as they do now, and thus Christian doctrine is taught in this fashion."[26] After the team had revised the diocesan cartilla and catechism, then, del Aguila proceeded to transcribe them using a new orthographic system which apparently employed some form of diacritics (*puntos y rasgos*). It can be surmised that the novel elements of this orthography were designed to represent glottalized and aspirate stops, which are characteristic of Cuzco Quechua and have no equivalents in European languages. It is also significant that del Aguila translated the Quechua texts into Spanish, which indicates that the catechism was originally composed in Quechua.

Most interestingly, the información goes on to state that certain clergymen formally objected to the new versions before Viceroy Toledo during his visit to Cuzco in the early 1570s—one witness mentions an Augustinian friar as the main objector—and that del Aguila successfully refuted the objections in a public debate.[27] The información does not provide details on the debate, but it does explain that as a result of del Aguila's defense, "what had been done in the said cartilla and catechism was considered apt in the lengua general of the Indians and Catholic and appropriate" (*lo hecho en la dicha cartilla y catheçismo [quedó] por congruo en la lengua general de los yndios y por cathólico y açertado*).[28] This indicates that the criticisms had been aimed both at the dialectal appropriateness of the texts and at their orthodoxy. It seems likely that terminological disagreements were at the heart of the conflict. The mention of an Augustinian as one of the critics is significant: the diocese was probably attempting to impose the use of the new texts, which would have produced conflicts with the mendicant orders.

Controversy continued to dog Cuzco's pastoral corpus. In 1583 Bishop Lartaun was accused before the Third Lima Council by the Cuzco *cabildo* or town council of committing a series of irregularities and abuses, among them the imposition of a Latin cartilla which Indians were incapable of learning but was being sold at six pesos a copy.[29] Lartaun's representative before the council replied that the cartilla in question was in fact a Quechua cartilla that had been translated under the bishop's supervision with the participation of the best Quechua experts of Peru—secular clerics, friars, Jesuits, and even mestizos and Indians. Parish priests were indeed being charged four pesos per manuscript copy, but this only covered the copying expenses.[30] For the second time in a decade the diocesan Quechua corpus had undergone a formal revision or retranslation.

Cuzco was clearly an important center for Quechua studies and a hotbed of debate on translation. One of the main protagonists of these debates was the secular cleric Cristóbal de Molina, priest of one of the Indian parishes of the city and one of the most respected lenguas of his time. In the 1570s he held a position as the official, salaried preacher to the Indians of the city, preaching in Quechua in front of the cathedral every Sunday and feast day.[31] It is more than likely that Molina was a member of the team that revised the cartilla and catechism—as a witness in del Aguila's información, he stated that he had been present when del Aguila transcribed the texts into the new orthography, and that he too had defended the new versions when they came under attack.[32] Guaman Poma apparently heard Molina preach in Cuzco, and quoted him decades later in a section of his chronicle where he gathered excerpts from sermons in Quechua (Guaman Poma de Ayala 1980 [1615]: 576–582; cf. Taylor 1999). Most of these quotes are satires of priests who spoke Quechua poorly or used the pulpit to intimidate their parishioners, but Guaman Poma presented Molina admiringly as a *gran lenguaraz* (profficient lengua). The brief text, whose phrasing is very ambiguous, is unusual for its highly metaphorical and visual presentation of Christ, God, and the Trinity, comparing them to the sun and moon, and to flowers (Guaman Poma de Ayala 1980 [1615]: 581). It is not clear that this text can be considered representative of Molina's actual style of preaching, but the possibility is tantalizing.

Molina is best known today as the author of the *Relación de las fábulas y ritos de los ingas,* an account of Inca state religion that he completed around 1575 and dedicated to Bishop Lartaun. This work is very much in the tradition of Betanzos and Las Casas in its presentation of the Inca state cult as centered on a creator God and its claims that Inca Yupanqui acquired a knowledge of God through natural reason. It also contains fourteen short prayers in Quechua—twelve addressed to Viracocha and the remaining two to the earth deity Pachamama—which were allegedly recited by the Inca sovereign and the high priests during the most important festivities of the Inca calendar (C. Molina 1989 [1575]: 81–96, 123–125). This is the second oldest corpus of Quechua texts after those of Domingo de Santo Tomás. Eleven of the twelve prayers to Viracocha appear in Molina's account of the Citua festival, which had been originally organized by Inca Yupanqui (ibid.: 58–62, 73–96). Molina refers to the Citua festival as a *pasqua* ('pasch') and describes a rite in which the officiants ate a mixture of maize and blood of sacrificed llamas or alpacas in terms very reminiscent of Christian communion. The prayers contain formal elements and epithets that can be considered pre-Hispanic, but they also address Viracocha as the one who created man and the universe through speech. In the first prayer, for instance, Viracocha is referred to as "[he] who made [people] by saying 'let there be man, let there be woman'" (*cari cachon huarmi cachon nispa llutac rurac*) (ibid.: 81). The other prayers contain similar epithets. The Quechua texts were garbled by the copyist of the extant version of Molina's *Relación,* but they seem closer dialectally to the Third Council texts, which were modeled on Cuzco Quechua, than to those of Santo Tomás.

Very similar prayers are featured in the early-seventeenth-century chronicles of Guaman Poma and Pachacuti Yamqui and (in a Spanish version) in the prologue to an important pastoral Quechua work, the *Symbolo catholico indiano* (1598) of Luis Jerónimo de Oré (Guaman Poma de Ayala 1980 [1615]: 45; Pachacuti Yamqui Salcamaygua 1993 [n.d.]: 200–201; Oré 1992 [1598]: 157–158). It has been argued—in most detail with respect to Pachacuti Yamqui's prayers (Duviols 1993; Itier 1993)—that these texts are missionary fabrications which took elements from authentic pre-Hispanic prayers or songs and fused them with Christian content.[33] These "pseudo-Inca" prayers could even be considered pastoral texts. They served a double purpose as historical proofs of the worship of a creator God by the Incas and as models for the use of Inca religious terminology in Christian contexts. Indeed, a few pastoral texts from the post–Third Council period apply some of the clearly autochthonous epithets used in these prayers directly to God (see chapter 8). Molina's connection to Cuzco's pastoral Quechua corpus as revised in the early 1570s raises the possibility that it contained similar adaptations.

Chapter 3

Reform and Standardization—1570s and 1580s

The reforms that brought the primera evangelización to an end can be characterized in terms of the imposition of Counter-Reformation norms for standardized, universal catechesis and sacramentation. At the same time, the crown was struggling to make effective the authority that the patronato real gave it over the church. There was no contradiction between these two processes—in fact, pastoral reformation and standardization would never have been possible without royal intervention. The reform period in colonial Peru was inaugurated by two key events at the end of the 1560s. One was the beginning, in 1569, of Viceroy Francisco de Toledo's administration, which was responsible for most of the institutional changes that made the new pastoral regime possible. More than any other individual, Toledo was at the heart of the religious reform process. The arrival of the Society of Jesus the previous year was another major component, as the Jesuits brought with them a familiarity with and commitment to the new standards and procedures. As newcomers in an already established missionary field, they were particularly critical of existing practices and eager to start anew. Both set the stage for the Third Lima Council and its corpus of pastoral texts, which are the main concern of this chapter.

Toledo's Reforms

Francisco de Toledo is best known for carrying out the resettlement or *reducción* program and for organizing a system of labor drafts—the infamous *mitas*—for the mines of Potosí and Huancavelica, two vast administrative achievements that had a profound and lasting impact on Andean society. He is regarded as the creator of the civil administrative system of colonial Peru, while the equivalent role in ecclesiastical matters is attributed to Archbishop Toribio Alfonso Mogrovejo, who arrived after the end of Toledo's term. Although Mogrovejo's importance is undeniable, this division of labor is inexact. Toledo was specifically ordered to investigate and reform pastoral practices, a matter in which the crown had not yet intervened systematically.[1] He was the direct instrument of Phillip II's intense interest in ecclesiastical affairs and was granted absolute powers to carry out reforms in the church as well as in civil government. He had been Phillip II's representative in the 1566 Spanish provincial council of Toledo, where his task was to push through the reforms of the Council of Trent in the face of the resistance of the Spanish clergy (Nalle 1992: 40). The fact that he had been entrusted with such a task shows that Toledo, although a layman, was well versed in ecclesiastical matters and completely dedicated to the Counter-Reformation program.

Toledo's main achievement in the realm of civil government, the reducción program, was inseparable from his pastoral reforms. Reducción was the forceful congregation of the native population into large nucleated villages—*pueblos de indios*—each of which was to hold about four hundred heads of household, precisely the population established by the Second Lima Council for Indian parishes. Reducción went hand in hand with, and made possible, the creation of a network of parishes, such that (at least in principle) every family resided in a pueblo which was also the seat of a parish with a resident priest (in practice, many of the new pueblos were annexes of a larger pueblo that was the parish seat).[2] As part of the reducción process Toledo created hundreds of new parishes, and appointed parish priests at will for much of his government.[3]

Reducción produced wide-ranging changes in the nature of Andean Christianity and in the Peruvian church. The network of parishes and pueblos made it possible to keep track of individual Indians and their sacramental lives. It also made universal catechesis a reality. A sacristan and a variable number of parish sheriffs (*fiscales* or *alguaciles de doctrina*), cantors, and musicians were established for each pueblo to aid the priest in his various duties—in return they received exemption from the head tax or *tributo* and from labor services (no small advantage).[4] The reducción program is often characterized as a failure because the new towns lost most of their population over the decades that followed as a result of migration to smaller settlements and to other jurisdictions (cf. Wightman 1990, chapter 1). However, this assessment should not obscure the fact that the reducción program and the institutions it created had an enormous and long-lasting effect on Indian society. It seems likely that for much of the period of this study a significant proportion of the population lived in reducción pueblos, which continued to be very prominent in local society even when they lost most of their original inhabitants (Mumford 2004: 259–271).

Another secular reform with pastoral implications, though less direct ones, was Toledo's campaign to delegitimize the remnants of the Inca elite and deprive the indigenous nobility of any influence above the strictly local level of the pueblos he was creating. A first step was the destruction of the neo-Inca state of Vilcabamba and the capture and execution of Tupac Amaru, the last independent Inca sovereign, in 1571–72. This act was accompanied by a historiographic campaign to debunk favorable accounts of the Inca empire, which could be used to challenge the legitimacy of Spanish rule in the Andes. A series of judicial informaciones were produced, allegedly using one hundred of the oldest indigenous witnesses, to prove that the Inca sovereigns had been tyrants rather than legitimate kings, and the works of Bartolomé de Las Casas were banned from circulation in Peru (Mumford 2004: 243–244; Pérez Fernández 1986: 459f.).

As for strictly ecclesiastical matters, Toledo's reforms involved substantial transformations in the clergy. First, he applied the principles of the patronato real arrangement, especially the viceroy's final say in the appointment of parish priests, as well as the Tridentine requirement that they reside in their parishes. These policies brought him into conflict with the mendicant orders in particular. The principle of in-parish residence was especially problematic for mendicants, who preferred to live together in convents located in the larger pueblos. Toledo also complained to Phillip II that they opposed reducción itself, even though it made the fulfillment of their pastoral duties much easier, because reducción facilitated supervision of parish priests as well as parishioners.[5] By and large, Toledo was successful at greatly reducing the power and autonomy of the orders, and the Dominicans were particularly affected. They lost control of the University of San Marcos in Lima (and thus of the education of the criollo clergy) and of their most important Indian province—Chucuito, on Lake Titicaca, where Toledo accused the Dominicans of exploiting their parishioners and neglecting their pastoral duties (Urbano 1987). The trial and execution for heresy of Francisco de la Cruz must also have been a serious blow.

Second, it was under Toledo that the principle of obligatory vernacular instruction for priests of Indian parishes finally began to be enforced. In 1570 Toledo informed the king that most priests still relied on interpreters to carry out their duties, and needed counter-interpreters (*contralenguas*) to ensure the reliability of the translations—in other words, a second interpreter was used to monitor the first one's translations.[6] In 1571 Archbishop Loayza founded a Quechua teaching chair at the Lima cathedral, motivated by the problems that rose from the use of interpreters: apart from the fact that interpreters generated errors that were very difficult to detect and correct, they were to blame for the much-feared variability in the expression of Christian doctrines.[7] In 1578 the crown ordered Loayza not to appoint priests who did not know Quechua to Indian parishes, noting that many of his appointees attempted to fulfill the requirement merely by memorizing a few words from a confesionario.[8]

In the late 1570s Toledo established a Quechua chair with wide-ranging powers at the University of San Marcos. He made the Quechua course obligatory for the *bachiller* and *licenciado* degrees, instructed the prelates not to ordain clergymen who had not studied Quechua, and warned clerics that those who had taken the course would be preferred in all appointments. Furthermore, all priests already appointed to Indian parishes in the audiencia of Lima were to be examined by the university chair within a specific period of time, and would be removed from their posts if they failed the exam. Toledo's interest in empowering the chair was such that he made personal appearances at the lectures.[9] The chair was given the royal seal of approval in a 1580 cédula, which dictated that no cleric could be ordained or assigned an Indian parish in the territory of the audiencia without a certificate from the chair stating that he knew Quechua and had followed the course for at least a year.[10] It might seem that the initiative in ensuring the vernacular training of the clergy originally came from the secular church, as the cathedral chair was established several years before the royal chair at the university began to function. However, it is more likely that Loayza's decision had been spurred on by Toledo's demands for vernacular competence among the clergy. Loayza may have been trying to preempt the crown's language training and examination program, which would inevitably become an instrument for crown officials to exercise even greater control over the parish clergy.

A third aspect of the reformation of the clergy in which Toledo had a hand was the exclusion of mestizos, a policy which was in direct contradiction with the principle of vernacular competence. The issue is tied to the *limpieza de sangre* or purity of blood norms that had excluded people of Jewish ancestry from the clergy and other professions in Spain since the fifteenth century, the rationale being that individuals inherited their basic moral and even religious dispositions from their parents. Prior to Toledo's arrival, all of the mendicant orders, with the exception of the Mercedarians, had policies against the ordination of mestizos, but it seems to have been common practice among the secular clergy. Although the First and Second Lima Councils had been very clear on the exclusion of Indians, there is no reference to mestizos (Hyland 1994: 2, 202). In 1576 and 1577 Pope Gregory XIII issued decrees authorizing the ordination of mestizos and persons born out of wedlock (most mestizos in Peru were illegitimate) on the grounds that their knowledge of the local languages made them indispensable for the evangelization. However, soon afterwards Phillip II ordered the bishop of Cuzco (in 1577) and the archbishop of Lima (in 1578) to refrain for the time being from ordaining mestizos (ibid.: 213).[11] Toledo wrote to the king on this issue in 1579, supporting the cédula and denying the validity of the grounds for admitting mestizos. He argued that a bad priest who knows the vernacular will do more damage than a bad priest who does not and has to work through an interpreter, the premise being that mestizos generally made bad priests.[12] It is not clear what inspired the crown to oppose the ordination of mestizos so strenuously at this particular time and in direct contradiction to the desires of Gregory XIII (the ban was later repealed). It is possible that Phillip II's opinion on the matter was swayed by Toledo's hostility towards mestizos. As will be seen, the debate continued into the 1580s, particularly within the Jesuit order.

Finally, one of the least known legacies of Toledo's government was a concrete program for the creation of standard vernacular catechetical materials, something which would not be achieved until the Third Lima Council. Archbishop Mogrovejo is naturally seen as the driving force in this process, but in 1583 Juan de Balboa, Quechua chair at the University of San Marcos and head of the Quechua translation team of the Third Council, would remember Toledo as the originator of the program.[13] In 1571 Toledo had informed the king that the bishops were making no real effort at standardization and that each secular cleric or friar could write his own catechism if he wanted to. He argued that in spite of the problem of linguistic diversity a single catechism had to be imposed.[14] By 1572 he had developed a plan according to which a Spanish catechism prepared in Spain would be translated by the best lenguas congregated in a provincial council, taking great care to define the most appropriate terms and phrases—*se examinen mucho el frasis y naturaleza de vocablos*. The translation was to be made into a variety of Quechua which, Toledo claimed, had been widely imposed by the Incas. This translation would then be printed in Mexico or Spain and a large number of copies brought back to Peru, thus reducing the risk of modifications that could produce doctrinal errors.[15] Although the Third Lima Council did not follow these proposals in all respects—the Spanish originals were written ad hoc in Peru, and the printing was also done locally—the similarity between what Toledo proposed and what was eventually done is clear. In Toledo's view the need for uniformity also extended to performance practices—the "ceremonies" of catechesis, the mass, and the administration of the sacraments. This was especially important because the Indians were, as he put it, "extremely fond of ceremonies and visible things" (*en estremo amigos de ceremonias y desto visible*)—that is, they focused too much on the external aspects of the rites and thought that different gods were being venerated when they were performed differently.[16]

The Jesuits

The Jesuit conversion strategy contrasted sharply with the existing practices of the secular and mendicant clergy in Peru. Most obviously, the Jesuits took permanent charge of only two parishes—Juli on lake Titicaca and Santiago del Cercado on the outskirts of Lima. In accordance with their role as "shock troops" of the church, they specialized in mobile missions in which pairs of highly trained priests worked for days or weeks at a time in a wide area, catechizing, preaching, confessing, and administering other sacraments as necessary. As outlined in José de Acosta's *De procuranda indorum salute* (1984–1987 [1577]), Jesuit catechesis focused on the transmission of a full range of doctrinal contents while also developing pedagogical strategies for different levels of understanding (*entendimiento*) among the Indian population.

Participation in the traditional liturgy was not a central part of this program—instead, Jesuit missionaries focused on producing highly choreographed catechetical performances in which the population of a pueblo walked in processions through the plaza and streets while reciting the cartilla and catechism. Native segmentary units—moieties and *ayllus* (the sub- or supra-moiety unit)—were taken advantage of: individuals were summoned to performance by these groupings, which were also used in the organization of the performance itself—ayllus and moieties would be assigned roles such as reciting the questions or answers of a catechism.[17] Another important catechetical instrument was the use of Quechua songs referred to as *cantares, cantarcicos, coplas,* or *motetes.*[18] All of the references seem to involve European musical genres; the 1570 Jesuit account of the performance of taquis in Corpus Christi festivities in Huarochirí cannot be considered representative of Jesuit practice, but rather was characteristic of the primera evangelización (Estenssoro Fuchs 1994: 78–79). Compared to liturgical hymns, these songs were probably simpler, more accessible vernacular genres. Unfortunately, no texts are known to have survived. All this may sound similar to what the mendicants had been doing for the previous twenty years or so, but there are key differences. The mendicants recruited Indians into the existing liturgy, while the Jesuits designed ad hoc exercises that were tailored to transmit catechetical contents to their charges. This difference was partly a matter of conversion strategy, but also a matter of logistical necessity—the Jesuits usually had to do their work quickly and independently of the liturgical calendar.[19]

The order was also characterized by an intense concern for vernacular competence and translation. Acosta's *De procuranda indorum salute* made the argument at length, citing scriptural loci such as the Pentecostal gift of tongues and attacking the use of interpreters. Acosta emphasized that the standards that prospective priests of Indian parishes had to set themselves were high, mentioning that many priests believed that it was sufficient to understand only a few words from a confession in order to give absolution. He duly warned such priests that this was admissible only in deathbed confessions (J. Acosta 1984–1987 [1577]: II 47–82). The first Jesuits destined for Peru were studying Quechua in Seville months before embarking, presumably from Santo Tomás's works, which had been published in Valladolid seven years earlier.[20] By 1569 Jesuits in Lima had already translated a catechism into some form of Quechua.[21]

The first and second Jesuit provincial congregations, both held in Cuzco in 1576, developed an ambitious program for producing vernacular catechetical texts. The first congregation ordered that two catechisms, a brief one intended for memorization and a longer one for more in-depth instruction, as well as a cartilla and a confesionario, be translated into both

Quechua and Aymara.[22] The second congregation instructed Alonso de Barzana to complete a brief catechism, a confesionario, and a grammar in Quechua and Aymara that he was working on and ordered that they be printed—further catechisms and dictionaries were left for a later date.[23] Barzana was the leading lengua of the first generation of Jesuits in Peru; in 1576 he held the preaching chaplaincy at the cathedral of Lima,[24] a clear testimony to the zeal with which the Jesuits went about becoming expert lenguas. The combination of vernacular texts that the order was producing in the mid-1570s—a cartilla, short and long catechisms, a confesionario, and linguistic works to accompany them—is very reminiscent of the Third Lima Council corpus.

The Jesuits have a reputation for being progressive or pro-indigenous, which they were in the sense that they believed that being Christian meant much the same thing for an Indian as it did for a Spaniard. They promoted Indian communion at a time when the general policy was to allow it only in exceptional cases, and they invested considerably in the training of native elites and in the formation of cadres of Indian assistants who could act independently. At the same time, however, the Jesuits in Peru imposed a narrower and more dogmatic Catholicism which allowed little leeway for the development of specifically Andean forms of Christianity. While the first Jesuit mission reports contain some indications of accommodationist tendencies, it seems clear that the dominant trend in the order during its early period in Peru was to react against the accommodationism of the primera evangelización. Sabine Hyland has argued that a hardening of Jesuit attitudes towards native Andeans and Andean culture resulting from early disappointments in the field is reflected in a radical change in policy on the ordination of mestizos—while the first Jesuits in Peru actively sought out mestizo novices, particularly for their knowledge of Indian languages, they stopped admitting them in 1576, and the 1582 provincial congregation voted for a definitive ban (Hyland 1994).

As Estenssoro Fuchs and MacCormack have noted, *De procuranda indorum salute* and Acosta's other major work, *Historia natural y moral del nuevo mundo* (Natural and Moral History of the New World, 1590) are filled with criticisms of what he considered to be the misguided and superficial primera evangelización (Estenssoro Fuchs 2003: 188–193; MacCormack 1994: 94). Acosta persistently discredited the two key historical claims that had underwritten accommodationist practices: Jewish origin and proto-evangelization by an apostle (Estenssoro Fuchs 2003: 191). More generally, Acosta's understanding of Inca culture and religion was very different from that of Cristóbal de Molina, Betanzos, or Las Casas. Inca mores, rites, and laws are described as being "very far from correct reason and the practices of the human species" and filled with "monstrous deviations" (J. Acosta 1984–1987 [1577]: I 65). While he stated in his *Historia* that native Andeans had acquired some knowledge of the existence of a creator God whom they knew as Viracocha, Pachacamac, or Pachayachachic (J. Acosta 1987 [1590]: 314), Acosta also claimed that Inca monotheism was very limited in nature and that none of the New World languages had a true name for God: "if we want to find a word that corresponds to 'God' in an Indian language, such as *Deus* in Latin, *Theos* in Greek, *El* in Hebrew, and *Alá* in Arabic, it will not be found in the language of Cuzco nor in that of Mexico [Nahuatl] . . . which shows us what a limited knowledge they had of God, since they cannot even name him but with our [Spanish] word."[25] This statement directly contradicts earlier opinions on the subject, especially those of Betanzos, who claimed that Viracocha properly meant "God" (Betanzos 1987 [1557]: 78).

Acosta interpreted similarities between Christianity and native religion pointed to by earlier writers, such as the existence of forms of confession and communion among the Incas, as inventions of the Devil, who sought to have himself worshipped in the same way as God (cf. Estenssoro Fuchs 2001 on this *simia Dei* motif). He claimed that the existence of these demonic parodies could actually facilitate conversion—the introduction of the Christian sacrament of confession, in particular, was made easier by the fact that Indians were already in the habit of confessing a certain kind of sin (J. Acosta 1987 [1590]: 311–387; J. Acosta 1984–1987 [1577]: II 425–429). However, this did not mean that the existing religious forms and practices could themselves be adapted to Christianity; he saw the study of native religion primarily as an instrument for extirpating it (J. Acosta 1986 [1590]: 387). Acosta's anti-accommodationist approach is expressed in his injunction that Christian terms be routinely translated with loan words, as would indeed be done in the Third Lima Council texts: "one should not worry too much if the terms 'faith,' 'cross,' 'angel,' 'virginity,' 'marriage,' and many others cannot be translated well and with propriety into the language of the Indians. They could be taken from Spanish and appropriated, which is something that any prudent *simiyachac*, which is how the teacher of the Indian language is called, already tends to put into practice."[26] Interestingly, Acosta's Latin text exemplified the principle of lexical borrowing by rather unnecessarily using the Quechua term *simiyachac* ('knower of language[s]') for 'language instructor.'

Acosta also argued at length against the contemporary claims that a general knowledge of God based on natural reason was sufficient for salvation (J. Acosta 1984–1987 [1577]: II 187–241). His insistence that salvation required at least an acquaintance with the full range of basic doctrines doubtlessly reflects the orthodoxy of the time, but the fact that he considered it necessary to argue this point in detail is indicative of the frequency of the contrary view—namely, that God could not have allowed countless generations of Indians to be damned when they had no possible means of receiving Christianity. Acosta's arguments shored up Toledo's historiographic campaign to present the Incas as illegitimate tyrants, since they implied that the Incas had all been damned—the notion that a knowledge of God based on natural reason had been attained by the Incas, combined with the belief that such a knowledge was sufficient for salvation, obviously carried undesirable political implications.

If in Peru the Jesuits played the role of guardians of orthodoxy vis-à-vis their mendicant predecessors, this relation was inverted in the Asian missionary fields. There, the Jesuits were the first to arrive and carried the principle of accommodation to extraordinary lengths, while the mendicants who followed on their heels denounced them for compromising the faith (Županov 2005: 22). Such a radical divergence within the same, highly centralized order can be explained by differences in political context (all-out conquest versus largely commercial penetration). It could also be argued that late arrivals in a mission field, regardless of what order they belonged to, tended to react conservatively to the practices of their predecessors. Differences of "national" origin in the missionary ranks were another factor. The Jesuit missions in India, China, and Japan, while under Portuguese jurisdiction, included many priests from other countries, especially Italy. The main proponents of missionary accommodation—most notably Matteo Ricci (in China), Roberto Nobili (in India), and Alessandro Valignano (in Japan)—were Italians who often came into conflict with their more conservative Portuguese brethren. The Jesuit order in Peru was overwhelmingly Spanish, and Spaniards tended to pursue more uncompromising missionary strategies, perhaps because of cultural and educational differences, but most obviously because they were directly identified with the colonial power. The importance of "national" origin is exemplified by the famous Aymaraist Ludovico Bertonio, one of a handful of Italian Jesuits who worked in Peru, and the only one who became prominent in missionary/pastoral work. As well as being an exceptionally prolific linguist and translator, he encouraged his Indian assistants to produce their own translations of Christian texts, something which no other priest in the Andes is known to have done (see the prologues to Bertonio 1984 [1612] and Bertonio 1612).

The Third Lima Council and Its Texts

The preface to the Spanish version of the decrees of the Third Lima Council makes clear that they were to be the definitive charter of the Peruvian church (Vargas Ugarte ed. 1951–1954: I 314–321).[27] A third council had been sought throughout Toledo's government, but its execution had been delayed first by Archbishop Loayza's old age and then by his death. Things finally got under way in 1581 with the simultaneous arrival of a new viceroy—Martín Enrríquez, formerly viceroy of New Spain—and a new archbishop, Toribio Alfonso Mogrovejo. The council was inaugurated in March 1582 and dragged on until October 1583, witnessing (and perhaps hastening) the deaths of two bishops and of the viceroy himself. It succeeded in congregating the bishops of Cuzco, Quito, La Plata (Sucre), Rio de la Plata (Buenos Aires), Tucumán, Santiago de Chile, and La Imperial (Concepción, Chile), sees which had been represented in the previous councils by delegates, or not at all. Precisely because it was a full house, this was an exceptionally stormy council, whose sessions were halted for an entire year by lawsuits among the bishops, especially Mogrovejo and Lartaun. The fact that the council reached a successful conclusion and achieved key reforms should not be attributed to a consensus among the participants, but rather to the efforts of a small sector of ecclesiastics who were in tune with the desires of the crown, and thus had the full backing of royal officialdom in Lima: Mogrovejo himself, and the Jesuits, who set the doctrinal and pastoral tone of the council (Vargas Ugarte ed. 1951–1954: III 54–113). Toledo's understanding of what needed to be done, especially regarding the standardization of catechetical materials, also had a major effect on the direction taken.

One of the first tasks of the council was to determine what was to become of the existing conciliar decrees. The First Lima Council was declared invalid on the grounds that it had not assembled a quorum of bishops, but the Second Council was to continue in full force. One of the most significant achievements of the Third Council was the implementation of the Second Council's pastoral regime. In future, all parish priests were required to have copies of the decrees of both councils, which together formed the basic legislative corpus of the Andean church (Vargas Ugarte ed. 1951–1954: I 315, 322–323). It seems likely that the version of the Second Council decrees to be used was the Spanish summary produced by the Third Council, which contains important additions and omissions.

The Third Council went beyond the Second Council in imposing stringent and detailed norms for catechesis and sacramentation. It made the first clear and firm statement on the clergy's obligation to instruct parishioners in their native language(s)—*Hispanicus hispanice, Indus indice*—and ordered that Indians no longer be required to learn the cartilla in Latin (Vargas Ugarte ed. 1951–1954: I 325). Confessors were now under the obligation to understand each individual sin uttered in an indigenous language, and the Second Council's commands that priests administer viaticum and prepare their charges for Easter communion, which apparently had been widely disregarded, were repeated (ibid.: I 329–331). The fact that reducción had already been achieved was certainly a significant factor in allowing the Third Council to require a more complete sacramental regime. The Second Council's limit of four hundred heads of household per parish priest was reduced to three hundred. Pueblos de indios that were much larger than this limit were to be divided between two priests, and those significantly smaller than two hundred were to be enlarged or merged with other parishes (ibid.: I 348).

The council decrees make no reference to one of the most controversial issues brought before it—the royal ban on the ordination of mestizos. In October 1582 a group of mestizos, with backing from some members of the clergy, presented a petition asking the council to make a statement in their favor. Their main argument was that mestizos were the key to the success of conversion efforts because of their knowledge of Indian languages—especially Indian languages other than Quechua, which they alone knew because these languages were not being taught. A series of informaciones were presented late in 1583 to substantiate the mestizos' claims, placing special emphasis on the contributions mestizos had already made as translators of the Third Council's pastoral texts into Quechua and Aymara. The petitioners succeeded in obtaining a formal opinion from the council stating that those mestizos who had begun the ordination process should be allowed to complete it, and a papal brief by Gregory XIII authorizing the ordination of mestizos was included in an official summary of canon law privileges and dispensations granted to the Indians by different popes.[28] Significantly, however, the council did not address the issue in its decrees, and when the summary of the privileges of the Indians was published in the 1585 *Confessionario para los curas de indios*, Gregory XIII's decree was replaced by an entirely different text at the express command of Archbishop Mogrovejo (Third Lima Council 1985b [1585]: 312–313). The issue was rendered moot in 1588, when the crown reversed its policy in a cédula instructing all bishops and archbishops of the Indies to ordain qualified mestizos (Hyland 1994: 229; cf. Recopilación 1987 [1681]: I 32). Nonetheless, the crown appears to have remained hostile to the ordination of mestizos, and the orders—with the exception of the Mercedarians—continued their policy of exclusion (Hyland 1994: 229–230).

The most important result of the Third Lima Council, for present purposes at least, was the creation of an official corpus of catechetical texts. Two Spanish catechisms (short and long) structured around the contents of the cartilla were composed at the council's behest, probably by Acosta, the council's leading theologian, and their use was made obligatory throughout the "province" (the archdiocese of Lima and the suffragan dioceses, which at that moment covered all of Spanish South America). The council then had these catechisms and the cartilla translated into a form of Quechua referred to as *la lengua del Cuzco* and into Aymara, and the resulting trilingual set of texts was printed in book form in 1584 under the title *Doctrina christiana y catecismo para instruccion de los indios . . .* (Cartilla and Catechism for the Instruction of the Indians . . . , quarto, 182 pages) (Vargas Ugarte ed. 1951–1954: I 323).[29] Two additional texts were mentioned in the council's decrees: a confesionario and an exhortation to be read to dying Indians (ibid.: I 372, 374). Along with some additional texts concerning confession and matrimony, they were published in 1585 under the title *Confessionario para los curas de indios . . .* (Confesionario for the Priests of Indians . . . , quarto, 142 pages). A third book—a trilingual sermonario titled *Tercero cathecismo y exposicion de la doctrina christiana por sermones . . .* (Third Catechism and Exposition of Christian Doctrine through Sermons . . . , quarto, 446 pages)—appeared a few months after the *Confessionario*. All three books were printed in Lima under Jesuit supervision by the Piamontese printer Antonio Ricardo (Third Lima Council 1985a [1584], 1985b [1585], 1985c [1585]). Unlike the *Doctrina christiana y catecismo*, neither the *Confessionario* nor the *Tercero cathecismo* were of obligatory use, although priests of Indian parishes were required to have copies of them (Third Lima Council 1985b [1585]: 202, 1985c [1585]: 360).

The council, backed by the audiencia, made the use of the Aymara and Quechua versions of the cartilla and catechisms contained in the *Doctrina christiana y catecismo* obligatory for the instruction of Indians in these two languages. The use of all other Quechua or Aymara cartillas, translations of the Third Council catechisms, and basic catechetical texts in general, was prohibited (Third Lima Council 1985a [1584]: 8–18). While bishops were instructed to have the cartilla and catechisms translated into other languages, as was indeed done with Mochica, Puquina, and Guarani (cf. Durán 1982: 203–206), Quechua and Aymara varieties other than those used in the council's translations did not qualify as distinct languages. The council admitted that its translations were not necessarily perfect, but variants were nonetheless not to be allowed: "Although there may be things that perhaps could be said better in another way (for it is inevitable that there always be different opinions in these matters of translation) . . . it has been judged, and it is, less inconvenient to tolerate some imperfections that the translation might have than to allow variety and discord, as the Catholic church has wisely ordered with regard to translations of Holy Scripture."[30]

The *Doctrina christiana y catecismo,* centerpiece of the Third Council's pastoral corpus, contains the following elements: (1) the cartilla or *doctrina cristiana,*[31] (2) a brief, simplified catechism *para los rudos y ocupados* (for the less intelligent or very busy); (3) a plática summarizing the main points of Christian doctrine; and (4) the *catecismo mayor,* which is divided into four parts dealing with the Credo, the Sacraments, the Ten Commandments, and the Pater Noster. The catechisms are in a question-answer format in which the questions are attributed to the priest. A letter from the council which prefaces the book specified, however, that the catechisms were intended to be memorized and both questions and answers were to be recited by Indians during catechetical exercises or whenever the opportunity arose (Third Lima Council 1985a [1584]: 13–14). The *Epístola del concilio* also explained that the catechisms were based on the 1566 Roman Catechism, known as the catechism of Pius V (ibid.: 13), but this was true only as far as their general contents and organization were concerned (especially the four-part division of the *Catecismo mayor*).[32] At the end of the book is a document titled *Annotaciones, o scolios, sobre la traducción de la Doctrina christiana, y Catecismo en las lenguas Quichua, y Aymara* (Notes on the Translation of the Cartilla and Catechism into the Quechua and Aymara Languages), which deals with specific terminological, dialectal, and orthographic aspects of the texts that required explanation. There are separate sections on the Quechua and Aymara translations, each followed by a short glossary of key terms in each language (ibid.: 167–187).

The *Confessionario para los curas de indios* can almost be considered a small ritual of sorts, as it consists of texts intended to aid parish priests in the administration of the sacraments of confession and matrimony, and of the last rites, although it did not include actual sacramental offices. The confesionario proper and accompanying exhortations against sin are followed by three documents in Spanish enumerating the most common Andean "rites and superstitions." These small treatises on Inca and local religion were inserted so that confessors could ask more detailed questions on sins of idolatry. Then come two exhortations (brief and long versions) to be read to the dying, and a litany for praying for their souls. This *pro morientes* section is followed by the summary of papal privileges and dispensations mentioned earlier, which has no vernacular versions. Finally, there are two texts in trilingual version dealing with the sacrament of marriage: a sermon explaining the canonical marriage restrictions and a text for publishing the bans.

The *Tercero cathecismo y exposicion de la doctrina christiana por sermones* consists of thirty sermons, each addressing a specific doctrinal issue. Its prologue explains that while the catechisms were designed for Indians to learn (i.e., memorize) the main points of Christian doctrine, the sermons were to be read by the priest to *persuade* the Indians that they were true. Its odd title emphasized its complementary role in relation to the brief and long catechisms of the *Doctrina christiana,* while obscuring the fact that it was actually a sermonario, something which the council had not authorized. The sermonario's title page states that it had been written "in accordance with the provisions of the holy provincial council of Lima" (*conforme a lo que en el Sancto Concilio Provincial de Lima se proveyó*), rather than "by the authority of the provincial council" (*por autoridad del Sancto Concilio Provincial de Lima*), as happens in the other two volumes.

Since there are no references in the Third Council decrees to a sermonario, nor to some of the texts included in the *Confessionario,* one might ask to what degree all three volumes can be considered a product of the council. Nonetheless, they were widely regarded as such, and it is clear that they do form a set. Mogrovejo's 1585 synod ordered parish priests to have printed copies of "the catechism, sermons, and confesionario made by order of the holy provincial council of 1583" (Torres ed. 1970: 46). Everything indicates that they were the work of the same team of author(s) and translators, and they all have the same dimensions, format, fonts, decorative elements, and cover designs. Most importantly, they all conform to the same doctrinal program and are completely uniform in their language, at least as far as the Quechua translations are concerned.

The Quechua texts of the Third Council corpus had their linguistic complement in a single-volume Quechua grammar and dictionary published at the press of Antonio Ricardo in 1586—the anonymous *Arte y vocabulario en la lengua general del Peru llamada quichua, y en la lengua española . . .* (Grammar and Dictionary in the Lengua General of Peru called Quichua and in the Spanish Language . . .), which was probably the work of the Jesuit Alonso de Barzana.[33] This book is the first extant description of a Southern Quechua variety and remained the standard linguistic work for much of the colonial perod, essentially condemning Santo Tomás's works to oblivion. It underwent three reeditions (essentially reprints) in the early seventeenth century (Seville 1603, and Lima 1604 and 1614)—an exceptional record for a colonial Quechua work.[34] However, its relation to the Third Lima Council and the three-volume pastoral set is unclear. There are no references to grammars or dictionaries in the Third Council decrees or in any of the pastoral texts themselves, and the *Arte y vocabulario,* though printed by Antonio Ricardo the year after the *Confessionario* and *Tercero cathecismo,* has different typographical features. However, both the printer and the author of the *Arte y vocabulario* declared in their prefaces that it was intended to aid priests in the use of the Third Council catechisms, confesionario, and sermonario (Anonymous 1603 [1586]: n.p.n.), and there is a clear consonance between it and the linguistic appendix of the *Doctrina christiana y catecismo.* The *Arte y vocabulario* even used some of the Third Council translations as examples of correct Quechua.[35]

The three-volume set, complemented by the *Arte y vocabulario,* was a formidable pastoral tool intended as the complete and definitive basis for the instruction and sacramentation of native Andeans. The Jesuit imprint on the corpus is clear. It has a strong focus on instruction in a complete range of basic doctrines, with an emphasis on the Trinity, the Incarnation, the Fall and Redemption, and the punishment of evil. The selection of texts mirrors the calls made by Acosta (repeating the instructions of the first and second Jesuit provincial congregations) for both a short and a long catechism—one for memorization and the other for in-depth instruction—accompanied by a confesionario that detailed the most habitual sins among Indians and a text for the wedding bans (J. Acosta 1984–1987 [1577]: II 293). The pedagogical discourse emphasizing the essentially rational but still infantile intellectual condition of the Indians that was so characteristic of the Jesuits, and Acosta especially, is very much present in the Spanish prologues, especially the prologue of the sermonario.

The Third Council greatly broadened pastoral Quechua by carrying out a large-scale translation program which made a substantial new corpus of texts widely available, but it also limited it by making these texts obligatory and exclusive, and by establishing a canonical standard for Christian discourse in Quechua. The council made clear that the requirement that parish priests instruct Indians with the official texts should not prevent them from further explaining the doctrines contained in these texts in their own words (Third Lima Council 1985a [1584]: 17). A model had to be established for all future Christian utterances in Quechua—in fact, the *Doctrina christiana y catecismo* served as one for the slightly later *Tercero cathecismo*. The latter's prologue states that while some of the original translators were not available to translate the sermons, their absence was not a problem "because the main terms are the same as in the catechism [i.e., the *Doctrina christiana y catecismo*]" (*pues los principales términos son los mismos del catecismo*) (Third Lima Council 1985c [1585]: 360). The expression *principales términos* refers to the basic Christian terminology, which was one of the main things the council sought to regulate.

For a model to function as such, it has to be internally consistent: the standardization campaign expressed in the Third Council corpus involved not only exclusivity—that is, the requirement that *only* these texts be used for certain purposes—but also internal uniformity. In fact, the Quechua texts of the Third Council are unusually homogeneous terminologically, dialectally, and orthographically; a study of the Spanish originals would probably show that these are less uniform than their Quechua translations.[36] This uniformity served both to control the interpretation of the texts and to ensure their imitability.

At a terminological level, the main characteristic of the Third Council standard was its heavy reliance on Spanish loan words as opposed to Quechua neologisms or adapted terms. The search for Quechua terms for Christian categories and institutions had generated intense controversy, so the council's translators opted for avoiding them entirely, except in a few cases where a Quechua word had already acquired wide currency and its use seemed relatively harmless, as occurred with *hucha* 'sin,' *supay* 'devil,' and *mucha-* 'to worship.' Another basic concern of the council was that there be a single term (or at most a pair of synonyms) rather than a variable paraphrase for each key Christian concept, and that its use be absolutely consistent. As well as being an instrument of control and orthodoxy, the unicity or monovalence sought here is clearly related to the fact that catechetical instruction was to be far more detailed and extensive than it had been previously, and thus required greater terminological precision and stability.

The Third Council Quechua texts also established Standard Colonial Quechua as the dialectal model for all subsequent Christian discourse. What exactly Standard Colonial Quechua was, how it developed, and why other varieties were excluded from the pastoral literature are questions that will be discussed in chapters 4 and 6. For now, suffice it to say that it was a highly standardized form of the Quechua of the Cuzco area, and was thus noticeably different from the coastal variety used by Santo Tomás. The linguistic appendix of the *Doctrina christiana y catecismo* claims that the translators had attempted to produce texts which would be intelligible throughout the Quechua-speaking world, but it also contains a lengthy indictment of the Quechua spoken by the *Chinchaysuyos*, a term derived from the name of the northwestern quarter of the Inca empire (Chinchaysuyu) which designated the inhabitants of most of what is now highland and coastal Peru as well as Ecuador (cf. D'Altroy 2002: 87–89). In other words, all forms of Quechua except those of the southern Peruvian highlands and (apparently) modern Bolivia were considered inadequate as vehicles for Christian doctrine. The appendix even provides a list of lexical, phonological, and grammatical forms—most of which would now be considered characteristic of Central Quechua—that exemplified the "imperfection and barbarity" with which Quechua was spoken to the west and north of Cuzco (Third Lima Council 1985a [1584]: 167–168). While the dictionary of the 1586 *Arte y vocabulario* contains many distinctively Central terms, they are always marked with the notation *(chin.)*—for "Chinchaysuyo"—to indicate that they were not proper Quechua. Furthermore, these terms only appear in the Quechua-Spanish section, indicating that priests should be capable of recognizing but not using them.

The Third Council texts followed a clear norm at stylistic as well as dialectal and terminological levels. The prologue of the *Tercero cathecismo* explained that the correct way of preaching to the Indians was to use a "plain, simple, clear, and brief style" (*modo . . . llano, senzillo, claro y breve*), mixed in with a few simple similes or analogies and frequent exhortations and exclamations which would appeal to their emotional nature (Indians, like women, were thought to be more easily convinced by *affectos* than by *razones*) (Third Lima Council 1985c [1585]: 355–356). The prologue criticizes contemporary preachers who were going over the heads of their audiences by preaching to the Indians as if they were educated Spaniards: "they preach to the Indians about complicated topics or in an elevated style, as if they were preaching in some court or university, and instead of doing good they do great harm, because they obfuscate and confuse the limited and underdeveloped intellects of the Indians."[37] Preachers were to avoid both excessive complexity in the exposition of Christian doctrine and figurative styles of speech, referred to as *lenguaje exquisito* and *términos affectados* (ibid.: 355). A precious glimpse of the kind of preaching style decried here is provided by Guaman Poma's quotation from a sermon by Cristóbal de Molina mentioned in chapter 2, in which a play of associations is established between the Trinity and the shining of the sun and moon and the blooming of flowers.

The demand for an *estilo llano* or "plain style" is associated with the restricted range of genres produced by the Third Council, and especially with its emphasis on catechetical at the expense of liturgical discourse. While there are commentaries on certain aspects of the liturgy in the council's catechisms and sermons, there are no translations of texts from the canonical hours, mass, or sacramental liturgies, and no hymns or songs of any kind. The *Confessionario para los curas de indios* contains guidelines for administering the sacraments of confession and matrimony and for the last rites, but, as noted earlier provides no actual sacramental forms or offices in any language. The council's translators did indeed establish what would eventually become the canonical Quechua and Aymara versions of the baptismal form, but hid them in the catechism on the sacraments instead of presenting them explicitly as such (Third Lima Council 1985a [1584]: 112). Even though the council had insisted on the need to prepare Indians for communion, the three-volume set does not provide specific instructions or any of the prayers traditionally used in preparation for communion.

Sermon 29 of the *Tercero cathecismo* discusses the uses and meanings of the Pater Noster, Ave Maria, and Confiteor prayers and gives instructions for making the sign of the cross and taking holy water, but sums up the rest of the liturgy as follows: "The holy church, inspired by the Holy Spirit, has many other very beautiful and wonderful things, songs, psalms, offices, prayers, blessings, and sacred clothing and ceremonies with great harmony and order, and these are all things filled with mystery so that we may honor and serve our great God with the soul and with the body. But for you, my children, it is sufficient for now that you know well what I have said [i.e., the previous commentary on the common prayers and basic devotional gestures]."[38] Interestingly, the Quechua translation of this passage differs in content from the Spanish original. There is no attempt to translate the concept of "mystery," and instead of telling Indians that they need not concern themselves with the broader liturgy, it simply reads: "My children, cherish these things I have said [about the liturgy]" (*Churiicuna camcunaca cay cay ñiscaycunacta soncoyquichicpi chasquiichic*) (Third Lima Council 1985c [1585]: 731). This divergence suggests a disagreement between the author(s) and translators of the sermonario regarding Indian participation in the liturgy, a disagreement that was probably widespread.

The nonliturgical bent of the Third Council corpus was partly motivated by contemporary restrictions on the translation of canonical texts, especially the biblical texts which were so frequent in the mass and canonical hours. The sermon cited above makes clear that there was also a concern that the liturgy, and liturgical texts in particular, were too complex and obscure for Indians, who were only able to assimilate an *estilo llano* void of metaphor, implicit textual references, and "mysteries." There may have been an Erasmian-like concern that Indians would become too involved in the "exterior" (formal and routinized) aspects of the liturgy. The Jesuit missionary style, with its scant attention to the formal liturgy, must have been a factor, too, considering the enormous influence the Society of Jesus exercised in the council.

However, a few exceptions to this pattern should be noted. The exhortations to the dying in the *pro morientes* section of the *Confessionario* were intended to provide a vernacular substitute for, or complement to, the offices of the last rites (including viaticum, or deathbed communion, and extreme unction). The texts of the exhortations include lengthy utterances, presented as the speech of the dying person, whose content is very similar to that of the protestations of the faith, which were part of the last rites (Third Lima Council 1985b [1585]: 285–303). They are followed by a litany for the dying, the most important properly liturgical text in the Third Council corpus (ibid.: 304–309). No reference was made to it in the council's decrees, but it was among the texts approved in manuscript form by the bishops while the council was still in course, so it was not an afterthought. It seems out of context in relation to the rest of the corpus, and no explanatory comments are provided.

An important commentary on this litany is provided by Franciscus Haroldus, the editor of a compilation of Mogrovejo's councils and synods, published in Rome in 1673 as part of the canonization process, which provides annotated Latin translations of some of the texts of the three-volume set. Haroldus explained that the litany from the *Confessionario*, referred to as "litanies for the commendation of the soul for the Peruvian Indians," was an adaptation of a traditional Latin litany (Haroldus 1673: 121). The council probably felt free to present an adaptation of this text because of the nature of the litany genre. Since a litany was essentially a string of invocations and petitions which could be omitted without transforming the nature of the text, variations on specific litanies could be made quite freely.

Haroldus's notes explain the criteria behind the modifications to the original litany. For example, he says that the epithet "father of the heavens" (*pater de coelis*) was changed to "heavenly father" (*pater coelestis*)—*padre celestial* rather than *padre de los cielos* in the Spanish original[39]—because the Andean tradition of worshipping heavenly bodies made the traditional epithet problematic. In other words, it was thought that the expression *pater de coelis* would lead Indians to understand that "the heavens" were literally God's children, and thus gods too. This concern for preventing indigenous misinterpretations of Christian terms and categories is in evidence throughout the Third Council corpus, especially in its preference for loan words. Haroldus also claims that the council added the names of the angels Michael, Gabriel, and Raphael specifically in order to stimulate the cult of the angels among Indians; and that the names of the Old Testament patriarchs Abel and Abraham were omitted in light of the danger that their invocation would lead Indians to believe that salvation was possible outside the church (Haroldus 1673: 121–122). This last omission is particularly significant given the earlier debates regarding the requirements for the salvation of the Indians, and appears to be a pointed reaction against some of the tenets of the primera evangelización—especially as represented by Francisco de la Cruz, who not only claimed that salvation without believing in a full range of basic doctrines was possible for the Indians, but was also convinced that they were Jews.[40]

The Development and Enforcement of the Third Council Corpus

It is surprisingly difficult to find information on the author(s) and translators of the Third Council texts.[41] None are named in the printed books, and there was clearly an effort to stifle opposition to the texts by separating them from the individuals who produced them—they are presented simply as the work of the council. While the names of the translators do appear in some of the council's official documents, these documents never name the author(s) of the Spanish originals of the catechisms, confesionario, sermons, and other texts. The council presented the catechisms as the work of a team (Third Lima Council 1985a [1584]: 13), but the prologue of the *Tercero cathecismo* implies that both sermons and catechisms were written by a single person (Third Lima Council 1985c [1585]: 358). José de Acosta has traditionally been identified as the main author. The evidence is not conclusive, but Jesuit sources contain fairly precise statements to this effect, and certain thematic emphases apparent in the catechisms match Acosta's catechetical program as outlined in *De procuranda indorum salute* (Bartra 1967: 361; Durán 1982: 239–249).[42]

We know the identities of the Quechua translators thanks to a single manuscript source: the volume of certified originals of the Third Council decrees held in the archive of the Lima cathedral chapter (the Archivo del Cabildo Metropolitano de Lima), which includes the Quechua texts later printed in the *Doctrina christiana y catecismo* as well as the exhortations and litany for the dying published in the *Confessionario para los curas de indios*, all signed by both translators and bishops. I cite this volume as "Third Lima Council 1583" and will refer to it as the ACML volume. A total of ten secular clerics, Jesuits, and friars signed the Quechua texts, but only four signed as translators (the rest simply approved the translations).[43] The Quechua team that translated the texts of the *Doctrina christiana y catecismo* was composed of three secular clerics—Juan de Balboa (a canon at the Lima cathedral), Alonso Martínez (a canon at the Cuzco cathedral), and Francisco Carrasco (also associated with the Cuzco cathedral)—and one Jesuit, Bartolomé de Santiago. Francisco Carrasco, a native of Cuzco, and Bartolomé de Santiago, of Arequipa, were mestizos, sons of conquistadors and Indian women (Bartra 1967: 365). Significantly, both Carrasco and Santiago also participated in the Aymara translation,[44] and were clearly native speakers of Quechua and Aymara. Carrasco was illegitimate as well as mestizo—precisely the sort of person who was finding it increasingly difficult to enter the priesthood at this time.[45] Six additional priests signed off on the translations of the cartilla and catechisms: the Augustinian Juan de Almaraz, the Dominican Pedro Bedón, the Mercedarians Alonso Díaz and Lorenzo González, and the Jesuits Blas Valera and Martín de Soto.

The Quechua versions of the *pro morientes* texts were signed only by Martínez, Carrasco, and Santiago, and by the bishops (Third Lima Council 1583: f. 68–68v). The ACML volume contains no reference to the sermons, but the preface of the *Tercero cathecismo* states that they were translated by only some of the members of the original group, because the rest had had to take care of other business (Third Lima Council 1985c (1584): 360). However, this statement applies to both Quechua and Aymara translators, so it does not tell us if one or more of the original team of Quechua translators were absent.

The translation team is striking both for the predominance of secular clerics and for the absence of the most renowned lenguas of the time. Franciscan sources claim that Luis Jerónimo de Oré, perhaps the most famous of all Quechua lenguas for works published in 1598 and 1607, was one of the translators, but his name is nowhere to be found and his participation is highly unlikely (see chapter 5). Given the legendary and highly secretive nature of the Third Council translations, references to a person's participation must be taken with a grain of salt. Another name that is outstanding in its absence is that of Alonso de Barzana, the most accomplished Jesuit linguist of his time and translator of the pastoral texts commissioned by the first Jesuit congregations in 1576, which appear to have served as models for the Third Council corpus. Finally, Sabine Hyland's book on the mestizo Jesuit Blas Valera states that he was one of the Quechua translators, but the ultimate source for this assertion is the ACML volume itself, where it is clear that his role was limited to approving the translations. Hyland's claim that a conflict developed between Acosta and Valera regarding translation practices also seems unfounded (Hyland 2003: 63–64, 171).

The absence of mendicants on the translation team can only be understood in the light of the previous decade or so of reforms, and exemplifies the degree to which the Tridentine standardization process had resulted in the marginalization of the mendicant orders. Four mendicants (an Augustinian, a Dominican, and two Mercedarians) did indeed approve the translations, along with two additional Jesuits, collectively referred to in one of the prefaces of the *Doctrina christiana y catecismo* as "the best masters of the language that could be brought together" (Third Lima Council 1985a [1584]: 17). As far as the mendicant approvers are concerned, I have found independent references only to Alonso Díaz, a mestizo Mercedarian whom Toledo in 1575 made parish priest of the Indian servants or *yanaconas* attached to the Mercedarian convent of Arequipa (Hyland 1994: 250). It seems likely that the approvals were merely a rubber stamp obtained to give the translations an aura of consensus by having the main orders represented, although (oddly) no Franciscan signatures were obtained.

There is not much to go on when it comes to understanding how the translation team worked. One of the prefaces of the *Doctrina christiana y catecismo* explains that the translations were made "with no small labor, because of the great difficulty there is in explaining such difficult and novel things to the Indians, and after having conferred extensively, consulting different writings, and everything that could aid a good translation."[46] Juan de Balboa was the official head of the team—his signature appears in first place in the certifications of the cartilla and catechisms (followed by Martínez's, Santiago's, and finally Carrasco's), and the team was said to have worked out of Balboa's home in Lima (Bartra 1967: 364).[47] In a March 1583 letter to the king, Balboa came close to saying that the job had been assigned to him alone (Bartra 1967: 362), but it seems likely that he acted in a supervisory capacity. As a native of Lima he was probably not very familiar with the form of Quechua used, and his signature is absent from the translation of the *pro morientes* texts. His official prominence can be attributed to the fact that he was both the university Quechua chair and a canon at the Lima cathedral, and thus represented both crown and church. Alonso Martínez, second in rank after Balboa because he was a canon at the Cuzco cathedral and had been the first Quechua chair of the Lima cathedral, was Spanish-born but had come to Peru in his early teens. He had been a parish priest in Huaylas, a Central Quechua–speaking area, during the 1560s, and a canon in Cuzco since 1575 or 1576.[48]

It seems more than likely that the two mestizos, Carrasco and Santiago, bore the brunt of the translation work, as the 1583 información on the contributions of mestizo priests states.[49] Esteban de Villalón, a Cuzco canon who testified in Carrasco's información, claimed that his opinion on matters of translation into both Quechua and Aymara had more weight than that of any other member of the translation team.[50] Cristóbal de Molina, who also testified, added that Carrasco was an excellent Quechua grammarian who knew how to explain the language "by the rules and precepts of grammar."[51] Carrasco arrived as part of Sebastián de Lartaun's entourage and had worked closely with him as an interpreter and preacher. Santiago must also have had a decisive role: he was the only Jesuit on the team, and his order exercised significant influence over the production of the pastoral corpus from start to finish. He does not figure very prominently in the Jesuit annals, probably because he was mestizo, but he was clearly valued for his abilities as a lengua. After his death in Potosí he received an obituary in the 1589 carta annua which mentioned that he had earned the sobriquet *misqui simi* ('sweet mouth/speech') for the beauty of his Quechua and Aymara sermons.[52]

As for the time frame in which the corpus was completed, the preface to the Third Council's decrees states that the catechisms were composed and translated during a one-year hiatus in the sessions which ended on August 15, 1583 (Vargas Ugarte ed. 1951–1954: I 317). In fact, the Quechua versions of the cartilla and catechisms were finished by July 27.[53] A clean copy was then made by one of the official scribes of the council, who clearly did not know Quechua, and this copy (henceforth to be known as "the original") was then signed by translators, approvers, and by the bishops gathered in the council on August 13 (Third Lima Council 1583: f. 63v–64v). The same was done with the Quechua versions of the exhortations and litany for the dying, which were signed on September 17 and 23 (ibid.: f. 68–68v). The originals and translations of the confesionario and sermonario were approved several months after the end of the council by Archbishop Mogrovejo, on May 18 and July 23, 1584, respectively (Third Lima Council 1985b [1585]: 197, 1985c [1585]: 349). This is a very rapid turnover, especially in the case of the catechisms. Clearly, there was considerable pressure to complete the work as quickly as possible—the contents of the *Doctrina christiana y catecismo* in particular needed to be finished in time to be approved by the council. The publication process was also very fast considering the obstacles encountered (there was as yet no printing in all of South America) and the high editorial and typographical quality of the finished products.

On September 30, 1583, the council had written to the king asking for authorization to print the cartilla and catechism on the grounds that errors would occur if the texts were copied by hand, and that even the smallest variations could have dire consequences. The printing had to be done in Lima because there were no proofreaders capable of reading the Quechua and Aymara texts in Mexico or Spain.[54] Almost a year later, on August 12, 1584, the audiencia of Lima anticipated the king's response and issued a decree authorizing Antonio Ricardo, who had recently come to Lima from Mexico expressly for this purpose, to print the catechism, confesionario, and *pro morientes* texts. The printing was to be carried out in the

Jesuit college of Lima and supervised by two of the translators (presumably one for each language), by the Jesuit provincial Juan de Atienza, and by José de Acosta. Each printed copy had to be signed either by Atienza or Acosta in certification that it was true to the original held in the Lima cathedral archive. The decree also ordered all ecclesiastical authorities to ensure that priests of Indian parishes all had copies of these texts and instructed their parishioners by them alone (Third Lima Council 1985a [1584]: 8–11). The printing of the *Doctrina christiana y catecismo* was carried out that same year according to the imprint. The *Confessionario* was available in print by mid-1585,[55] and the *Tercero cathecismo* appeared late in the year (both bear the imprint 1585). Extant copies of all three volumes bear the signature of Acosta or Atienza on the title page, along with the manuscript note "it matches the original" (*concuerda con el original*) (Rivet and Créqui-Montfort 1951: 4–16).[56]

Acosta and his colleagues seem to have monopolized the whole editorial process as well as the printing. They probably had an especially large role in developing the sermonario, and they even seem to have corrected and adapted the "originals" of the *Doctrina christiana y catecismo* prior to the printing. A comparison of the Quechua texts in the ACML volume with the printed versions reveals dozens of small differences. The scribe who made the "original" copy did not know Quechua and committed numerous errors, some of which he erased and corrected and others not—the ACML volume versions omit letters, syllables, and words, run words together, and so on. Most of the changes are fairly transparent corrections of copy errors, but others are true modifications: there are some relatively minor orthographic changes, and at least one question-answer pair was entirely rephrased to make it more explicit.[57]

Printing not only made the Third Council corpus widely available, it also made it easy to distinguish between the legitimate copies of the texts and those that had been modified. By mid-1585 numerous manuscript copies of the *Doctrina christiana y catecismo* and *Confessionario* were in circulation, and archdiocesan and audiencia authorities reacted by banning them and ordering parish priests to use only printed copies. The July 1585 Lima synod pointed to "errors that may result from the copying," extending the prohibition to the as yet unpublished sermonario.[58] An October 22 audiencia decree that was included in the *Tercero cathecismo* suggests that the modifications were intentional, stating that in making the manuscript copies "certain persons try to change the translation [into Quechua and Aymara of the Third Council texts]" (*algunas personas tratan de inovar la dicha traducción*). This contravened the Third Council's desire "that the instruction of the natives . . . be uniform, without allowing variation even in a single syllable, because of the great damage that resulted from it not having been done this way in the past."[59] The decree orders corregidores to confiscate and destroy all manuscript copies of the Third Council texts "before the damage is done," and to ensure that the printed texts were followed to the letter, without even the smallest modifications: "they must be used in printed, not manuscript copies, without innovating, amending or interpreting them beyond what is there [in the printed copies] . . . you must inform yourselves in particular as to whether catechesis is done in all of your jurisdiction using the said translation, without changing a single syllable." Those priests who did not comply were to have their stipends withheld until they did.[60]

The audiencia's heavy-handed demand for observance of the council's texts, which twice repeats the ban on modifying the translations even by "a single syllable," reflects both the premium placed on uniformity by the crown as well as certain sectors of the church, and a certain amount of alarm at how the texts had been received. One can only imagine the impact they must have had as they arrived in parishes where the basic prayers were said in a completely different translation, or where dialectal differences or the heavy reliance on loan words rendered the conciliar translations incomprehensible. The secular clergy, at least, could not afford to simply disregard the orders of council, archbishop, and audiencia, and in any case the conciliar texts were a magnificent pastoral resource. The solution was thus to adapt the texts by transcribing with the necessary modifications. It may never become clear exactly what modifications were being made, but they were probably of at least two different types: dialectal adaptations to make the texts more intelligible among populations not familiar with Cuzco Quechua, or, more broadly, Southern Quechua; and terminological adaptations—changes in the way key terms were rendered.

Outright resistance to the Third Council texts was strongest in institutions not directly subject to the archdiocese of Lima. The 1591 synod of the diocese of Cuzco noted that there had been "some negligence" in the implementation of the Third Council's demand that all priests have copies of its texts, and it established a fine for those who did not use them once large numbers of copies became available—*quando ay copia del dicho cathecismo, confessionario y sermones* (Lassegue-Moleres 1987: 41). Although the synod seems to point to a distribution problem, it can be suggested that the delay was due to the fact that the diocese had been using its own Quechua cartilla and catechism for years, and that the transition to the Third Council texts was a slow and difficult one. More overt resistance came from the mendicant orders, who clearly did not feel bound by the council. The mendicants' qualifications as pastoral agents were central to their identity and the main justification for their presence in Peru, and yet they were being required to use a corpus of pastoral texts in whose production they had not participated. In 1592 Mogrovejo asked the king to issue a cédula that would bring the mendicants into line in this respect.[61] That same year the Dominican provincial chapter ordered parish priests to obtain and study (although apparently not to use) the Third Council texts (Meléndez 1681–1682: I 13). In 1598 Mogrovejo informed the pope that mendicant parish priests were still not using them.[62] To my knowledge no cédula was ever issued compelling the mendicant orders to toe the line, but it is clear that joint pressure from the crown and the secular church obtained some measure of acceptance of the Third Council cartilla and catechisms, at least. The books of the Franciscans Luis Jerónimo de Oré (1598 and 1607) and Diego de Molina (1649)—the only mendicant works of any significance to have survived from after the Third Council—followed the conciliar model quite closely at dialectal and terminological levels, and used the conciliar versions of the cartilla texts. Balboa's successor as university Quechua chair, Juan Martínez, was an Augustinian and a champion of the Third Council standard.

The canonical character of the Third Council corpus was kept alive for decades by diocesan legislation and visitas and by a series of partial reeditions. The Spanish and Quechua texts of the *Doctrina christiana y catecismo* were reprinted in Rome in 1603, and that same year the *Confessionario* was printed in Seville—all, apparently, under the auspices of the Jesuit Diego de Torres Bollo (not to be confused with Diego de Torres Rubio, the contemporary Jesuit linguist), the province's representative in Spain. A further edition of the Spanish-Quechua cartilla and catechisms was published in 1613, this time in Lima. Portions of the cartilla and catechisms appeared in several compilations of pastoral texts, such as those of Luis Jerónimo de Oré (1598 and 1607) and the Jesuit Pablo de Prado (1641), not to mention dozens of works from the eighteenth, nineteenth, and twentieth centuries.

In 1649 the secular cleric Fernando de Avendaño published a sermonario that included ten sermons from the *Tercero cathecismo*. One of the clearest testimonies to the enduring status of the Third Council texts is the Sixth Lima Council's decision to reprint the entire *Tercero cathecismo* in 1773. The Third Council's Quechua translations of the common prayers are still in use all over the Andes, if with some dialectal adaptations, and current Christian terms and expressions bear the imprint of its brand of pastoral Quechua.

Chapter 4

The *Questione della Lingua* and the Politics of Vernacular Competence (1570s–1640s)

At this point it becomes necessary to interrupt my general narrative of the development of pastoral and translation practices to focus on the Peruvian church's *questione della lingua,* broadly understood to include issues such as what indigenous language(s) to use, how specialized or inclusive the vernacular project ought to be, and even whether to use indigenous languages at all. My central concern here is the development of Standard Colonial Quechua: I ask why it acquired such prominence, to what degree it excluded the formal use of other varieties of Quechua and of non-Quechua languages, and how it stood up against the challenge of Hispanization proposals. Special attention is given to policies and administrative practices concerning the linguistic competence of the clergy, an area where the *questione della lingua* acquired particular prominence. The primera evangelización is dealt with only briefly here because of the lack of information, so my account begins with the reforms of the 1570s and 1580s, carrying on into the mid-seventeenth century. The development of the Quechua literature and of general pastoral discourses and strategies from the 1590s through 1640s is discussed in the next chapter, which picks up the narrative where it was left off in chapter 3.

The Rise of Standard Colonial Quechua

With the exception of the prayers recorded by Cristóbal de Molina, the Quechua texts that have survived from before the Third Council can be identified either with coastal Quechua or with a lingua franca variety that was in wide use before the conquest and during the first decades of Spanish rule and that seems to have been of coastal origin (see chapter 6 for the linguistic details). At the same time, there is no evidence of an attempt to codify a single standard variety during this period. In the prologue to his grammar, Santo Tomás described what he knew as *la lengua general* as "the language . . . that was used and is used throughout the realm of that great lord called Guaynacapa [Huayna Capac]," but volunteered no opinion regarding the point of origin of the language or where it was spoken most correctly, questions that later linguists and translators would consider very important (Santo Tomás 1995 [1560]: 9). When Santo Tomás discussed the problem of dialectal variation he did not distinguish between correct and incorrect forms. His dictionary in particular often records alternative lexical forms without indicating that one form was to be preferred over the other. Instead, variability is understood as a "common and widespread defect in all the peoples and languages of the world" (*defecto común y general en todas las naciones y lenguas del mundo*), and the variation in Quechua is compared with the differences in the way natives of Portugal, Spain, and France pronounce Latin words, each adapting the language to their mother tongue (ibid.: 18).

The evidence suggests that during the 1550s and 1560s and to some extent into the 1570s, missionary and pastoral agents were free to produce vernacular texts with the dialectal characteristics they considered most apt for their specific audience. The diocese of Cuzco was developing its own independent translation program, and went to the trouble of designing an orthography that reflected local phonological characteristics that were not shared with the Inca lingua franca. An Augustinian text from around 1560 states that the order's missionaries in Huamachuco (in the northern highlands) produced a catechism and cartilla in the local language—probably Culli (Castro de Trelles ed. 1992 [ca. 1560]: 45; cf. Adelaar and Muysken 2004: 401). If so, this would be the first and the last known reference to Christian texts in Culli.

The shift that occurred during the 1570s and 1580s was characterized both by a demand for dialectal uniformity in pastoral discourse and by a turn towards the Quechua of the southern highlands, in particular that of Cuzco. Linguistic evidence supporting the view that Standard Colonial Quechua was based on the Quechua of Cuzco will be presented in chapter 6. Nonlinguistic evidence can be found in the biographies of the Third Council translation team: I have argued that the brunt of the work was done by the two mestizos—Francisco Carrasco, who was a native of Cuzco and spent all his life there, and Bartolomé de Santiago, who was from Arequipa, an area whose modern varieties are very close to those of Cuzco. Santiago had also been a member of the first Jesuit missionary team in Cuzco during the early 1570s, when he was in his early twenties. Juan de Balboa was a native of Lima and thus would have been more familiar with the coastal varieties privileged during the 1550s and 1560s, but he probably acted in a supervisory capacity or as a figurehead. Alonso Martínez was Spanish-born and seems to have first acquired Quechua in Huaylas during the 1560s, but he had been a canon in the Cuzco cathedral since 1575 or 1576 and had thus been exposed to Cuzco Quechua for several years by the time of the Third Council.

However, Standard Colonial Quechua should not be identified too closely with Cuzco Quechua. Rather, the forms of Quechua spoken in the Cuzco region provided the basis for the development of the standard. Most subsequent pastoral Quechua texts followed this standard quite closely, and even those that diverged from it in some significant respect show its influence in others. As will be seen in the next section, clerical language training was carried out almost exclusively in this variety. Standard Colonial Quechua acquired wide currency as the language not only of vernacular Christianity, but also of written communication in general—it was used in legal and administrative contexts for writing petitions and drawing up titles to land and office (although never on the scale apparent for some Mesoamerican languages) and, above all, for personal correspondence (Durston 2003; Itier 1991, 1992b; Taylor 2000b [1995], 2000d [1985]). While this "mundane" Quechua literature is far from uniform, all the extant texts reflect the council's dialectal and orthographic standard. Texts written by speakers from the central highlands often contain Central Quechua elements, but there is still a visible effort to follow the conciliar norm.[1]

The dialectal homogeneity of the Quechua literature of this period reflects a true standardization campaign, one which resulted in a dramatic marginalization both of non-Quechua languages and of the non-Southern varieties of Quechua. The fact that the conciliar corpus included Aymara translations should not obscure this fact. The Aymara texts were intended primarily for use in the Charcas area (modern Bolivia), which was heavily Aymara-speaking. For the rest of the colonial period only a handful of Aymara texts made it to the Lima presses. The Third Lima Council had provided for the use of languages unrelated to Quechua or Aymara, and ordered that the cartilla and catechisms be translated into these languages. This policy was carried out to some extent with Mochica and Puquina, but with the exception of a 1644 Mochica grammar, no book dedicated to an Andean language other than Quechua and Aymara was ever printed. Most significantly, no chairs for teaching languages other than Quechua were ever founded in the audiencia of Lima, and the university Quechua chair was initially given the task of examining the vernacular competence of all applicants for Indian parishes in the entire audiencia. An even greater marginalization was applied to non-Southern varieties of Quechua. The Third Council did not provide for further translations of its pastoral corpus into such varieties—in fact, it specifically forbade them.

The narrow focus of language training and translation efforts created serious obstacles for missionary and pastoral communication. Luis López, one of the first Jesuits to explore the mission field in Peru (and who would later be tried and exiled by the Inquisition) warned his superiors in 1570 that it was necessary for the Jesuits to learn the *lenguas particulares* or *lenguas maternas* as well as the "lengua general," which in this context probably referred specifically to the Inca lingua franca: "it is necessary to know the lengua general of the Indians and the local language of each district in order to confess them, because [in the "lengua general"] one can only discuss very general things with the women and the lower status men, and if one is to discuss specifics it can only be done in the local language of each district."[2] The "lengua general" was widely understood, but its intelligibility decreased as one moved down the social scale. Learning the *lenguas particulares* was an absolute necessity if the Jesuits were to fulfill their pastoral mission.

The difficulties are exemplified in two Jesuit mission reports from Huarochirí, a highland area close to the city of Lima. After a 1576 mission, the polyglot Barzana wrote that he had been unable to communicate with a substantial part of the population, particularly women, and that he had relied on a curaca who translated the substance of his preaching into the local language(s). These languages were almost certainly varieties of Quechua and Aymara (there is no record of other languages in this area), but Barzana was unable to understand or be understood even though he was familiar with both Quechua and Aymara as they were spoken in the southern highlands.[3] In 1609, a generation later, Jesuit missionaries in the same area were unable to confess local women who had *pretended* to understand the "lengua general" in order to receive the sacrament, knowing that they would not be able to communicate with the Jesuits in any other language—in this case, "lengua general" probably referred specifically to Standard Colonial Quechua. They had memorized a few sentences but were unable to answer any questions, and ultimately had to confess via an interpreter (Taylor 1987: 95).

Did colonial authorities attempt to resolve these problems by imposing Standard Colonial Quechua, or Southern Quechua more generally, on the indigenous population as a whole? Toledo's 1575 decrees for the newly created pueblos de indios ordered that the *lengua del inga* be spoken by all on the grounds that it would facilitate catechesis.[4] Toledo's policy was questioned by his successor, Martín Enrríquez, who informed the king in 1582 that Quechua chairs were not sufficient for the language training of the clergy, and suggested that parish priests be assigned permanently to their parishes as a way of forcing them to learn the local language.[5] Enrríquez's successor, Fernando de Torres y Portugal or Conde del Villar, however, espoused Toledo's solution to the problem of linguistic diversity—to force the entire native population to speak the "lengua general."[6] Similar demands were repeated by the archdiocese of Lima during the first half of the seventeenth century (e.g., Lima Synods 1987: 44). The question is whether expressions like "lengua del inga" or "lengua general" referred specifically to Standard Colonial Quechua, to Southern Quechua more generally, or simply to any form of Quechua. Colonial authorities would certainly have preferred Indians who spoke other languages to learn "proper" Quechua of the sort used in pastoral writing, but having Central Quechua–speaking parishioners was still much preferable to having parishioners who spoke no Quechua at all.

In any case, there is no evidence of Central Quechua–speaking populations being "Southernized" linguistically as a result of colonial policies. Instead, it seems more likely that situations of diglossia developed in which the elite, particularly those who were literate and held parish posts, acquired Standard Colonial Quechua while the rest of the population did little more than memorize texts and perhaps develop a passive competence—more or less as Romance-language speakers in Europe did with church Latin. However, there must have been some degree of language mixing, at least in certain contexts—when Central Quechua–speaking elites wrote Standard Colonial Quechua it was often with considerable Central interference, especially at the lexical level. Standard Colonial Quechua was essentially a written medium that was manifested orally through text-based performances. It is not at all clear that it ever spread as a true spoken language, independently of pastoral writing. As a final note on the question of language shift, I should stress that I have found no evidence of actual efforts on the ground to impose Standard Colonial Quechua or any other form of Quechua as a language of everyday communication.

The sources are silent on the rationale behind the changes that occurred in colonial language policy between Santo Tomás's day and the Third Council, but some inferences can be made. Two main problems are involved here: first, the motives for the increasing standardization or specialization of translation and language training efforts at a time when greater institutional resources and control of the terrain could have led to a diversification; and second, the motives for the focus on Southern Quechua, and Cuzco Quechua specifically.

As for the first question, the specialization of the colonial vernacular project can be explained by a variety of both practical and ideological concerns. Given the higher standards for orthodoxy and uniformity in the Counter-Reformation context, keeping control of several translation programs rather than just one or two would have required a vast effort from the colonial regime. In each case, a new "lengua general," in the sense of a literary codification of a chosen prestige variety, would have had to be created. The task of monitoring indigenous uses of Christian discourse would be made much easier if this discourse could be restricted to a single linguistic variety. The avoidance, if not outright prohibition, of translation into different forms of Quechua can also be attributed to a fear of producing variant translations: if the same texts were available in closely related languages, there was a danger that key terms and expressions would "migrate" from one language to another, leading to the much-feared diversity.

Finally, the standardization process can be related to the establishment of the Jesuit order in Peru. The Jesuits exercised extraordinary influence, thanks to their relatively good relations with Viceroy Toledo and the key role they played in the Third Council. Due to their institutional structure the Jesuits had a strong vested interest in the specialization of translation and language training efforts. One of the distinguishing characteristics of the Jesuit order was its tendency to keep its members concentrated in large urban colleges, from which they set out on periodic missions, instead of posting them for long periods of time in specific parishes. Furthermore, the order tended to move its members around from one college (i.e., Spanish town) to another instead of letting them remain in a single area, a practice considered necessary for the upkeep of moral and intellectual standards. The order thus *required* the existence of a single standard in order to maintain its missionary style and esprit de corps. Luis López's call for missionaries to be posted permanently in specific areas so that they might learn the local languages never seems to have been taken seriously. As Johannes Fabian puts it with regard to the development of colonial language policies in the Belgian Congo during the early twentieth century, "the analysis of a linguistic situation was bent to fit political decisions anticipated or already taken" (1986: 41). Questions of linguistic intelligibility, similarity, and difference being particularly subject to ideological distortion, the isolated reports that a knowledge of a single variety of Quechua was not sufficient to fulfill pastoral duties probably fell on deaf ears, and the Jesuit annals from Peru are silent on the problem of instruction in languages other than Southern Quechua and the Aymara of the altiplano.[7]

To explain the growing focus on Southern Quechua in the 1570s and 1580s, Alfredo Torero has pointed to major demographic and economic changes in the Andean region. First of all, the demographic collapse and rapid Hispanization of the coastal population and the disappearance of the old contexts of elite interaction greatly undermined the viability of the old lingua franca of the Inca empire as a "vehicular language" (Torero 1995: 15). It could also be suggested that the 1570s and 1580s correspond to the period when the generations of Indians that had reached adulthood before the conquest were disappearing. Second, Torero points to the development of the mining economy during the 1570s, primarily as a result of the creation of the *mita*, or labor draft system, as a key motive for the fixation on Southern Quechua (Torero 1974: 188, 1995: 14). This circuit had its southern pole in the silver mines of Potosí (present-day Bolivia), an area where a variety of Quechua closely related to that of Cuzco is spoken today. The axis of commercial and labor flows ran in a northwesterly direction from Potosí through the Titicaca basin, Cuzco, Huamanga, and on to the mercury mines of Huancavelica, which today mark the northern limit of the Southern Quechua–speaking area.[8]

In other words, an area dominated by speakers of Southern Quechua and of Aymara acquired paramount importance in colonial designs during the 1570s.[9] Not only did Southern Quechua become more useful as an administrative vehicle, but the crown made the pastoral care of populations subject to the mining mitas a top priority for ethical reasons—the formal justification for Spanish rule in the Andes and for the appropriation of

Indian labor for mining and other enterprises was that Indians would receive salvation in return. Additional explanations should be sought for the specific focus on Cuzco Quechua within the Southern dialectal block. Once again, developments within the Jesuit order are suggestive. The Jesuits headed for Cuzco soon after their arrival and embarked on an intensive missionary program among the Inca nobility, making Cuzco their prime missionary site in Peru. The first and second provincial congregations were both held in Cuzco in 1576, and the most important early Jesuit lenguas—Alonso de Barzana, Bartolomé de Santiago, and Blas Valera—were active in Cuzco during this period.[10] The Jesuits, who were probably attracted to Cuzco by their elite-oriented pastoral strategy, clearly had a hand in exalting and codifying Cuzco Quechua.

However, the key factors behind the fixation on Cuzco Quechua and the increasing specialization of the vernacular project should be sought in contemporary language ideologies, particularly understandings of the relation between language and community and perceptions of linguistic change and diversification as processes of degradation (cf. Woolard 2002). If Quechua was the language of the Inca empire, it could be assumed that it maintained its pure or correct form at its point of origin, which was necessarily the empire's capital, Cuzco (Cerrón-Palomino 1995a: li). Quechua was thus perceived as a cloth that was whole at the center but had become tattered at the edges.

This rationale should be understood in relation to the contemporary processes of legitimization and codification of the European vernaculars, which involved defining specific varieties associated with urban centers of power and learning as the appropriate vehicles of formal and literate expression, on a par with Latin. As the Huamanga-born Franciscan Luis Jerónimo de Oré would put it in a major work published in 1598: "the city of Cuzco is the Athens of the Quechua language . . . because there it is spoken with all the rigor and elegance that can be imagined, as Ionic [Greek] in Athens, Latin in Rome, and Spanish in Toledo."[11] An urban-rural opposition was clearly at work here, in that Cuzco Quechua was identified with the only great "city" of the Andean world, while the Quechua of the "Chinchaysuyos" was considered "rustic" (Third Lima Council 1985a [1584]: 168).

The historical narrative supporting the fixation on Cuzco Quechua is expressed most clearly in the writings of Blas Valera, as quoted by Garcilaso. According to Valera, the "lengua general" had spread far and wide from its home in Cuzco by means of colonies of Cuzco natives settled by the Inca sovereigns in the newly conquered areas. It provided a providential medium for the spread of Christianity, just as Latin had in the territories of the Roman empire, even though at present it was spoken so "corruptly" in many areas that is seemed a different language (*casi parece otra lengua diferente*) (Blas Valera in Garcilaso 1945 [1609]: II 91–92). Valera attributed extraordinary qualities to the "lengua general," especially as it was spoken by the Incas. All Indians who learned it were ennobled and their intelligence enhanced, and thus became more fit to learn Christian doctrine, but it was "the Incas of Cuzco, who speak [Quechua] more elegantly and urbanely, [who] receive the evangelical doctrine in the mind and in the heart with more efficacy and profit" (*los Incas del Cozco, que la hablan más elegante y más cortesanamente, reciben la doctrina evangélica en el entendimiento y en el coraçón con más eficacia y más utilidad*) (ibid.: II 94–95). The efficacy attributed to Cuzco Quechua—and to Quechua in general, insofar as it had not diverged significantly from its original form—stemmed from its (mis)identification with the Incas. Regarded as the language of an elite, it was considered especially apt as a vehicle for lofty concepts.

The rise of Standard Colonial Quechua provides textbook examples of how linguistic perceptions and policies are predetermined by ideological tendencies and mechanisms of control. In particular, it exemplifies the three semiotic processes of "iconization," "erasure," and "fractal recursivity" which Judith Irvine and Susan Gal identify in the ways colonial regimes interpret and seek to transform situations of linguistic diversity (Irvine and Gal 2000: 37–39). Iconization—the identification of the qualities associated with a group of people in their language—is most evident in the glorification of Cuzco Quechua as an "elegant" and "urbane" language and the condemnation of the Quechua of the Chinchaysuyos for, in the words of the Third Council translators, its "coarse words" (*vocablos . . . algo toscos*) and its "sing-song [characteristic] of rustic and uncivilized people" (*sonsonete de rústicos y agenos de policía*) (Third Lima Council 1985a [1584]: 167–168). These characterizations also exemplify the principle of fractal recursivity—the application of the same opposition at different levels of a classificatory system. In this case, some indigenous languages are contrasted to others in the same way that indigenous languages in general are contrasted to Spanish or Latin, as the uncivil to the civil. Finally, the workings of the principle of erasure are obvious both in the total or relative neglect of non-Quechua languages, and in the perception of non-Southern

Quechua varieties as corrupt dialects rather than closely related languages. The exaltation of the Incas and their (presumptive) language served as a convenient justification for these erasures and for the standardization of Christian discourse in Quechua, which in turn contributed to greater clerical control over it.

The Vernacular Competence System

Although initially there were calls for the clergy to learn indigenous languages by residing for extended periods of time in specific parishes, the language teaching system that was actually instituted consisted of classroom instruction based on written texts. With some exceptions that are discussed in the next section, there was also an overwhelming focus on Standard Colonial Quechua. A network of salaried teaching and examination posts was set up, the most important teaching posts being the cathedral and university chairs in Lima. The occupant of the latter was also, at least initially, examiner of all priests who applied for Indian parishes in the audiencia. Soon, however, the Jesuits and the mendicant orders had their own Quechua chairs (although very little is known about the internal language training systems of the orders), and each diocese set up its own examination system.

The vernacular competence system affected the careers of a large part of the Peruvian clergy—probably the majority, since Indian parishes were by far the most abundant and accessible positions. In order to be assigned to an Indian parish, and in some cases just to be ordained, a cleric had to present a license certifying that his linguistic competence was sufficient. Criollo secular clerics were often ordained *a título de la lengua*—on account of their knowledge of "the language"—after they had presented the requisite license. This exempted them from the obligation to demonstrate that they had the financial means to maintain themselves, as it was presumed that they would make a living as parish priests, and made it possible for criollos (and probably many mestizos too) who lacked independent means to have clerical careers. Even after a priest was assigned to a parish his language skills were under constant scrutiny. Diocesan visitadores routinely questioned Indian parishioners regarding their priest's competence in this respect during their tours of inspection. When Indian parishioners sued their priests for abuse or failure to carry out their duties—which, fortunately for modern historians, they did with great frequency—one of the standard accusations or *capítulos* was that they lacked the necessary knowledge of *la lengua*.

Precisely because of its pervasiveness, the teaching and examination system was highly contested. The power to train and examine parish priests was a strategic and controversial one, caught up in a variety of institutional, ideological, and personal struggles. The first recorded disputes concern the powers of the Lima university chair, a post that was under the direct control of the crown. As established by Toledo and the 1580 cédula that confirmed his arrangements, this chair was also the official examiner for the entire audiencia, and taking his course was a requirement for both ordination and receiving an Indian parish. This highly centralized Quechua training and examination program faced stiff resistance from the church, and it was never really implemented. In 1583 the bishops congregated in the Third Lima Council wrote to the king asking him to revoke the 1580 cédula and allow language examinations to be carried out at the diocesan level,[12] and one of the council's decrees ordered the appointment of diocesan examiners (*examinadores sinodales*) to evaluate applicants for Indian parishes (Vargas Ugarte ed. 1951–1954: I 368). In 1584 an audiencia decree allowed examinations for parishes in the diocese of Cuzco to be carried out in the city of Cuzco rather than in Lima, and named an official examiner.[13]

Six days before the bishops gathered in the Third Lima Council petitioned for the language examination process to be carried out at the diocesan level, Juan de Balboa, the university chair, wrote to the king explaining that this was precisely what Viceroy Toledo, the creator of the system, had wanted to avoid. If the bishops controlled language examination, argued Balboa, they would simply use it as an instrument for appointing clergymen who had won their favor for reasons other than language expertise. The clergy would then lose one of their primary motivations for learning Quechua. Most interestingly, Balboa claimed that the Third Council's efforts to standardize vernacular catechesis would be of no avail if the examinations were left in the hands of each bishop.[14] In 1586 he obtained a decree from Viceroy Conde del Villar ordering enforcement of the 1580 cédula and declaring that parish priests were not using the Third Council texts because they were not being taught and vetted by Balboa.[15]

The impracticality of having the clergy of the entire audiencia examined in Lima eventually won the day: by 1588 Conde del Villar had revoked his earlier decree along with the 1580 cédula and allowed language examinations to be carried out by local clergy in cities other than Lima. He also suggested that the corregidores of the main Spanish cities should name the examiners, apparently as a way of maintaining royal control over them. Among the reasons Conde del Villar mentioned for the revocation was the fact (which apparently had only recently come to his attention) that clergymen who took Balboa's course did not actually learn to speak and understand Quechua.[16] If following Balboa's course did not qualify one for carrying out pastoral duties in Quechua, there was no reason why doing so should be a requirement for ordination or for applying for a parish. Balboa's argument that the universal use of the Third Council texts would only be achieved if he alone taught and examined future parish priests was also questionable—the Third Council itself had favored examination at the diocesan level.

A language licensing system had been established in Cuzco at a fairly early date. The earliest licenses I have found were issued around 1580 by Cristóbal de Molina, who had been named *examinador general en la lengua del inga* by both Toledo and Bishop Lartaun.[17] Molina had held the cathedral's preachership since the early 1570s. By 1591 another prominent lengua, Canon Alonso Martínez, had been named *examinador* by the bishop and the viceroy, and he continued to occupy the post until 1596 at least. Alonso Martínez also succeeded Molina as the cathedral preacher, and three or four thousand Indians were said to gather from the urban parishes of Cuzco every Sunday and feast day to hear his sermon.[18] In the late 1590s Bishop Antonio de la Raya transferred licensing functions in the diocese to the Jesuit college of Cuzco, which was to be responsible for teaching Quechua as well. The preaching appointment that had been held by Alonso Martínez and Cristóbal de Molina was also transferred to the Jesuits.[19] However, Jesuit control of language licensing in the diocese of Cuzco only lasted for a few years. By 1602 Juan Pérez Bocanegra, a Cuzqueño secular cleric who was one of the most expert lenguas of his time and would publish a major pastoral Quechua work in 1631, was examining would-be priests of Indian parishes. Pérez Bocanegra continued to act as *examinador sinodal* until 1617 at least, examining priests in their knowledge of Aymara and Latin as well as Quechua.[20] In 1627 we find Pedro Arias de Saavedra, priest of the parish of the Indian hospital, exercising the function of *examinador general de la lengua de los indios,* often jointly with other examiners who were usually members of the cathedral chapter.[21]

As regards the newly created diocese of Huamanga, for which I have found a handful of licenses and examinations dating back to 1615, the examiners were generally members of the cathedral chapter.[22] I have found only one examination from the diocese of Arequipa: in 1654 an applicant for the parish of Camiña in what is now northern Chile (where it is unlikely that Quechua was ever spoken) was examined by two clerics, one of them a canon, who had him "construe" a session from a Latin church council in Spanish and Quechua.[23] Interestingly, there are no references to Quechua chairs as opposed to examiners being appointed in the dioceses of Cuzco, Huamanga, or Arequipa. This is probably because it was presumed that the local criollo clergy in these areas grew up speaking Quechua and/or Aymara.

Even if the Lima university chairs soon gave up their claims to a monopoly of Quechua instruction and examination in the whole audiencia, they continued to be at the center of conflict within the city and archdiocese. In 1591 Juan de Balboa, the first university chair,[24] died and was succeeded by Juan Martínez, an Augustinian. This was still an influential position, as it had the faculty of licensing the parish clergy in the archdiocese, which was separate from its teaching function. In 1592 the cathedral chair was awarded to Alonso de Huerta, a secular cleric from the Spanish town of Huánuco in the central highlands and a favorite of Archbishop Mogrovejo; he also received the cathedral's preachership (Eguiguren 1940–1951: II 1111–1112). In 1613 Juan Martínez accused Huerta of luring his students away to the point where he no longer had anyone to lecture to. As royal chair, Martínez claimed that Huerta was encroaching on a crown monopoly of Quechua instruction, and that this encroachment was part of an attempt by the archdiocese to gain control of language licensing.

Martínez also accused Huerta of teaching with a grammar of his own making, claiming that the anonymous 1586 *Arte y vocabulario* had been made obligatory for Quechua instruction by the same audiencia decree that enforced the use of the Third Council texts.[25] In fact, this decree made no reference at all to a grammar, but in Martínez's mind the *Arte y vocabulario*, of which he had published a reedition under his own name in 1604 (Rivet and Créqui-Montfort 1951: 38–40), was indissociable from the Third Council corpus. Beyond the obvious personal rivalry, the conflict may have been brought on by Huerta's willingness to allow for, and even teach, elements of the Quechua of the Chinchaysuyos, in violation of the dialectal purism of the Third Council tradition (a topic that will be discussed in the next section).

Huerta was strongly supported after the death of Mogrovejo by his successor, Lobo Guerrero. Thanks to his auspices, Huerta was awarded the university chair on Juan Martínez's death around 1614 without having to give up his teaching position at the cathedral (Huerta 1993 [1616]: 10). In 1618 Lobo Guerrero wrote to the king that Martínez had remorsefully confessed on his deathbed to licensing many priests with insufficient knowledge of Quechua. It was a clear effort to discredit the regular clergy and the university chair itself.[26] With archdiocesan support, Huerta dominated Quechua teaching and licensing in Lima for over twenty years, holding both the university and the cathedral chairs until his retirement in the mid- or late 1630s. In 1616 he published a grammar which he claimed was superior as an instrument for teaching Quechua to the existing works because of its brevity, and in which he proclaimed the need for priests in the archdiocese to learn elements of what he called *la lengua chinchaysuyo*. While it is clear that his teaching did not depart significantly from Standard Colonial Quechua, it did expand the boundaries of what was considered dialectally acceptable.

Huerta continued to inspire controversy even after he became the undisputed master of Quechua teaching in Lima. In 1620 he was accused by the archdiocesan prosecutor of neglecting his duties as cathedral chair (he would lecture in the cathedral for only a half hour and then leave for the university) and of illegally charging priests for their language licenses. Huerta was alleged to have made four thousand pesos this way at a rate of four pesos per license over a period of six years.[27] This would mean that between 1614 and 1620 Huerta licensed no less than 1,000 priests who, at least in principle, knew some Quechua and hoped to be assigned Indian parishes. This figure seems greatly inflated, but there can be no doubt that the Quechua teaching and licensing system was functioning on an impressive scale during this period.

The system was undergoing important changes around the time Huerta took over the university chair. His appointment was symptomatic of growing archdiocesan control over language teaching and licensing in Lima—part of a general process by which the secular church consolidated its power and gained greater autonomy from crown officials. Huerta was succeeded as chair by Alonso Corbacho de Zárate, a secular cleric who was priest of the parish of Santa Ana in Lima, and between 1648 and 1652 the chair was held by Juan Rojo Mejía y Ocón, also a parish priest in the city of Lima, who made several attempts to gain a position on the cathedral chapter. It seems likely that Huerta, Corbacho, and Rojo were all beholden either to the archbishop or the cathedral chapter.

Examination and licensing practices were changing, too. When Lobo Guerrero informed the king of Juan Martínez's malpractice as university chair in 1618, he explained that even though he considered Huerta trustworthy, he was now requiring him to carry out the licensing exams in his presence to ensure the fairness of the process.[28] In 1620 a new system was set up whereby the examination was carried out before the archbishop by three examiners—the university chair and two diocesan examiners appointed by the archbishop.[29] By the early 1630s the language examinations had become part of the *concursos*, or competitions between applicants for a specific vacant parish. Instead of presenting a multipurpose license, secular priests were now examined in the presence of their competitors every time they applied for a parish.[30]

The language licensing system had been initially developed by crown officials to ensure that the king was getting his money's worth in terms of pastoral care for Indians. However, the crown soon lost direct control of the system, probably as a result of inertia, and it was taken over by the bishops and cathedral chapters. A comparison of license and exam documents over this period creates the impression that the system was becoming more rigorous: the exams were carried out by committees rather than by a single examiner, and candidates had to demonstrate their knowledge in the presence of their competitors. However, it seems likely that the exams became increasingly elaborate and the certificates more detailed in order to obscure the fact that they were now entirely within the domain of the secular church. As Juan de Balboa, the first royal chair, had argued back in the 1580s, the point of giving licensing powers to crown appointees was that this would prevent the examination process from becoming an instrument for bishops and canons to use the parishes as rewards for their favorites and supporters.

However, the secular church was not successful in imposing its authority in matters of vernacular competence on the mendicant orders. The debate over whether or not the orders should be allowed to keep their parishes had for a while centered on this issue—one of the strongest arguments in favor of the mendicants was their allegedly superior (but largely undocumented) linguistic training. Some said that if they were forced to give up their parishes there would not be enough secular clerics with the necessary language skills to replace them.[31] The conflict came to a head in the late 1610s, when Archbishop Lobo Guerrero demanded that friars who were to be posted in Indian parishes be examined before him for both *suficiencia de lengua* (linguistic competence) and *suficiencia de letras* (knowledge of Latin and canon law), and that those who were already working as parish priests demonstrate their language competence to his visitadores. Even though his demands were backed by royal cédulas, he encountered fierce resistance from the mendicants.[32] The heads of the four mendicant orders responded by arguing that they had a far better record of language competence than the secular clergy, and claiming that their friars had published vernacular grammars, dictionaries, catechisms, rituals, and sermonarios.[33]

The mendicants had until recently been complying with the official examination system, but after the first decade of the seventeenth century it became increasingly unusual for friars to be examined by the university chair, clearly because it was coming under the control of the archdiocese of Lima, which was hostile to their presence in the parishes. The orders were by and large successful in resisting the secular church's effort to monitor their parish priests, and they developed their own language teaching and examining systems. The preface of a 1649 manuscript sermonario by the Franciscan Diego de Molina, which denounced what Molina saw as a lack of language training within the Franciscan order, makes clear that the orders had complete autonomy in examining and selecting candidates for the parishes they held (according to Molina, the Dominicans were more careful about ensuring the competence of their parish priests than his own order) (Romero 1928: 55–59). At the same time, friars were marginalized from the main system of positions and rewards for lenguas—after Juan Martínez, no friar occupied the university chair or was able to publish Quechua texts or linguistic works.

Although there is little information on how language instruction and examination were actually carried out, and to what effects, it is clear that at least initially both were designed to establish the use of the Third Council corpus and the translation standard represented in it among the clergy. It is significant that the first occupants of both the university and Lima cathedral chairs—Juan de Balboa and Alonso Martínez—were members of the council's translation team. Balboa felt that his primary responsibility as university chair was to ensure the use of the Third Council corpus throughout the audiencia, and claimed that the council's efforts for the standardization of catechesis would be to no avail if his full powers as teacher and examiner were not respected. He was not misrepresenting the situation entirely in that his joint teaching and examination powers would have had a major influence on parish priests, and it could be argued that delegating the examination process to the diocesan level led to a diversification in instruction and examination methods. Juan Martínez felt that it was an essential duty of the university chair to teach from the 1586 *Arte y vocabulario*, closely associated with the conciliar corpus. One of the Third Council's decrees ordered that its Quechua catechisms be used for examining would-be parish priests—presumably, the examinee would have to recite the answers to catechism questions recited by the examiner (Vargas Ugarte ed. 1951–1954: I 368). In 1592 Alonso Martínez, while acting as Quechua examiner in Cuzco, approved an applicant who had memorized much of the Third Council's confesionario.[34] Even Huerta approved candidates for parishes on the basis of knowledge of the Third Council books.[35] Huerta's grammar, the only descriptive text that made an apology for Central Quechua, is essentially a Standard Colonial Quechua manual that records isolated Central variants.

However, just as diocesan authorities were taking over the teaching and licensing system, testing procedures were changing, too. In his 1621 extirpation manual the Jesuit José de Arriaga mentioned a decree by Lobo Guerrero ordering that candidates for parishes be examined by having them preach in Quechua (Arriaga 1621: 69), a requirement that would have been born from contemporary concern for idolatry—having a priest recite texts from the Third Council catechisms or confesionario was no guarantee that he would be an effective refuter of idolatries. In the exams of the 1630s and 1640s candidates were required to orally "explicate" or "construe" (*explicar, construir*) in Quechua a Gospel passage chosen from the missal—the Gospel was apparently chosen randomly to force the candidates to improvise.[36] Juan Rojo Mejía y Ocón's grammar, published in 1648 (his first year as the university Quechua chair), was designed specifically to teach students to translate the Gospels from Latin into Quechua. Throughout the book, grammatical rules were exemplified with Gospel passages translated into Spanish and then into Quechua. The emphasis on Gospel translation or paraphrasing reflects the concern that parish priests "preach the gospel"—that is, fulfill the Tridentine requirement that they explain the Gospel reading from the mass in Sunday and feastday sermons.

Notwithstanding these changes, it is clear that Standard Colonial Quechua as codified in the Third Council texts continued to be the gold standard for language teaching and testing. In fact, the language competence system was one of the key institutional contexts for the reproduction and transmission of the standard up to the mid-seventeenth century. Beyond the preparation it required of the parish clergy as a whole, it also generated a significant number of salaried posts (chairs and examiner positions) that encouraged many secular clerics to make a career out of their knowledge of Standard Colonial Quechua. These positions were far superior to an ordinary parish appointment in terms of prestige and financial rewards. Along with the cathedral preacherships, they made it possible for lengua priests to move from rural parishes to a Spanish city and interact with the diocesan elite, and perhaps be admitted to a cathedral chapter, the ultimate career goal of any secular cleric. Nearly all of the secular priests who published in or on Quechua had career paths of this sort, and the latter seems to have been a condition for the former. Royal controls on printing were strict, and publishing required the approval of a whole series of prominent lay and clerical figures, not to mention a significant financial investment, either by the author himself or by a wealthy patron.

But vernacular competence was not just a matter of complying with regulations or of advancing one's career. As a parish priest of the diocese of Huamanga remarked in 1634, it was also a mandate of divine law (*derecho divino*) exemplified in numerous biblical passages.[37] It was a God-given faculty and obligation transmitted to all pastors since the Pentecost. Prominent lenguas frequently cited the New Testament narrative of the foundation of the church (Acts 2), when the Apostles were infused with the Holy Spirit in the form of "split tongues like fire" and were miraculously able to make themselves understood regardless of language barriers. The Pentecostal flames became the most common trope both for the obligation of priests to study Quechua, and for the glory gained by those who already knew it. Juan de Balboa used it in the first sense in 1583,[38] and the Jesuit linguist Diego González Holguín expanded on the subject in the prologue to his 1607 grammar, explaining that the gift of tongues (*don de lenguas*) had been one of the most important powers conferred on the primitive church—"to know many languages . . . is nothing less than to conquer the world for God." In the present day, however, God no longer infused His ministers with the power to effortlessly "speak in tongues," but rather expected them to learn them through the labor of study—"in the sweat of their brows," as it were (González Holguín 1607: n.p.n). The Pentecostal mandate was taken more literally by those who regarded knowledge of the vernacular as a divine gift. In one of the prefatory approvals of Juan Rojo Mejía y Ocón's grammar, the Augustinian Agustín Berrío noted that the "sweet spell" (*dulce hechizo*) of the Pentecostal miracle was repeated in the person of the author, who could preach equally well in Quechua and Spanish, and whose bilingualism was symbolized in the fork in the fiery tongues of the Holy Spirit (Rojo Mejía y Ocón 1648: n.p.n.). A literal interpretation of the Pentecostal mandate can also be found in Archbishop Mogrovejo's claim that he regularly preached to Indians in their own language during his visitas, even though it seems highly unlikely that he ever learned any Quechua.[39]

Non-Quechua Languages, "Chinchaysuyo" Quechua, and Spanish

The overwhelming focus on Standard Colonial Quechua did not preclude limited efforts to formalize the pastoral use of non-Quechua languages. The ability to speak two, three or more different indigenous languages was a paradigmatic quality of the good pastor, and the clearest fulfillment of the Pentecostal mandate. The chronicles of the orders resound with the praise of polyglots like the Jesuit Alonso de Barzana, who on his deathbed was found clutching a paper on which he had written the sentence "God is watching you" in the six Indian languages he had mastered (Quechua, Aymara, Puquina, Chiriguano, Tonocote, and Cacan).[40] A ritual published in 1607 by the Franciscan Luis Jerónimo de Oré contained texts in Quechua, Aymara, Mochica, Puquina, and the lowland languages Guarani and Tupi (although the Guarani and Tupi texts were not the work of Oré himself).[41]

Perhaps the most striking symbol of pastoral multilingualism is a seventeenth-century mural on the baptistery entrance in the church of Andahuaylillas, near Cuzco, in which the baptismal form was written in five languages—Latin, Spanish, Quechua, Aymara, and Puquina. The mural, featured on the front cover of this book, depicts a triumphal arch surmounted by angels holding a medallion which contains the Latin form. Immediately below it, worked into the architectural detail of the frieze, is the Spanish form. The Quechua form appears below the Spanish one, wrapped around the hemicircle of the arch. The internal columns contain the Aymara form, and the external ones the Puquina one, which is barely visible today. The mural has been attributed to the Limeño painter Luis de Riaño, who executed canvases for the Andahuaylillas church in the 1620s, during the tenure as parish priest of Juan Pérez Bocanegra, a preeminent figure of the pastoral Quechua literature (see chapter 5). If the attribution is correct, Pérez Bocanegra himself could be considered the intellectual author of the mural (Mesa and Gisbert 1982: I 79–80, 237–238). There is a similar and apparently contemporary baptistery entrance mural in the church of Checacupe, also in the vicinity of Cuzco, although it lacks the Puquina form (Flores Ochoa, Kuon Arce, and Samanez Argumedo 1993: 142).

The most obvious purpose of such murals was for Indians (parish assistants in particular) to learn the baptismal form in their native language so that they could correctly administer baptism to infants in case of need. The pentalingual inscription in Andahuaylillas can thus been interpreted as evidence that Aymara and Puquina as well as Quechua were spoken in this area in the seventeenth century, but Mannheim argues that the mural served a primarily symbolic function (1991: 47–48). The highly ornate composition served as an expression of the church's Pentecostal multilingualism and as an icon of the translation process itself. The disposition of the forms, both on the vertical (upper-lower) and horizontal (interior-exterior) axes, expressed both hierarchy and a chain of transmission uniting them—the validity of the form in each language is guaranteed by its relation to a hierarchically superior and anterior source. At the same time, the juxtaposition of the five languages, with their increasing degrees of "vernacularness," served to exemplify the impetus and reach of pastoral translation (cf. Rafael 1993 [1988]: 27–28).

In the late sixteenth and early seventeenth centuries the diocese of Cuzco was indeed providing for the pastoral use of Puquina and Aymara as well as Quechua. The 1591 Cuzco synod noted that Aymara and Puquina were spoken in many parts of the diocese (which then included Huamanga and Arequipa) and ordered parish priests in such areas to use these languages in confession and catechesis. The decree noted that dialectal variation within Puquina was considerable, and instructed priests in Puquina-speaking pueblos to put together a brief catechism and a confesionario with the help of *ladino* (i.e., Spanish-speaking) Indians (Lassegue-Moleres 1987: 41–42). The diocese of Cuzco examined priests in both languages, although more frequently in Aymara.[42] After its creation the diocese of Arequipa found the presence of Aymara and Puquina in its territory significant enough to warrant official attention. The 1638 synod, presided over by Pedro de Villagómez, ordered an official translation of the Third Council catechisms and confesionario into Puquina.[43] This synod also produced Quechua and Aymara translations of prayers for adoring the consecrated host and chalice, and the translations were reproduced in one of the decrees.[44]

However, the non-Quechua language that received the most attention in terms of teaching and examination in Peru was not Puquina, nor even

Aymara, but Mochica. The Mochica language, also known in the colonial period as "Yunga," was spoken in a relatively small area in what is now the north coast of Peru and the adjacent highlands. In 1588 the secular cleric Roque de Cejuela, who was priest of the parish of Lambayeque, was named examiner of applicants for Mochica-speaking parishes by the archdiocese of Lima (the appointment was confirmed by the viceroy in 1592). Cejuela also produced Mochica translations of the Third Council catechisms and confesionario, which were approved by Archbishop Mogrovejo in a very cautious decree of 1592 after a lengthy revision process. However, Cejuela was unsuccessful in his attempts to publish his translations.[45] By 1614 the cleric Francisco de Saavedra, priest of the parish of Illimo, was *examinador general de la lengua materna mochica* by authority of Archbishop Lobo Guerrero.[46] In 1626 and 1628 the post was held by García Somorrostro, who had been appointed by the newly created diocese of Trujillo.[47] Following the same pattern we find in Lima, Cuzco, and Huamanga, exams in Trujillo seem to have become more elaborate in the 1630s. A group examination of applicants for the parish of San Martín de Reque held in 1633 was carried out by a lay Spaniard and two Indians who had been named examiners by the bishop.[48] Today it may seem entirely commonsensical to have Indians judging the ability of priests to minister to other Indians who spoke the same language, but given the deeply rooted ethnic hierarchies and the stigma of untruthfulness attached to Indians, it is very surprising to find them in this role. One of the priests examined by this bi-ethnic committee was Fernando de la Carrera, author of a Mochica grammar that was published in Lima in 1644 with the approval of Archbishop Villagómez.

The evidence on the pastoral use of Central Quechua is much more ambiguous. The highland territories of the archdiocese of Lima were dominated by speakers of the Central varieties, with pockets of other languages in some areas (Culli in Conchucos, one of the northernmost provinces of the archdiocese, and varieties of Aymara in the highlands close to Lima and probably in other areas too). The 1613 Lima synod, held under Lobo Guerrero, ordered parish priests to instruct their parishioners only in the "lengua general" and exhorted crown officials such as the corregidores to do what they could so that all Indians spoke it instead of their "lenguas maternas" (Lima Synods 1987: 44). In 1657 Villagómez told the king he was enforcing a "lengua general only" policy.[49] The question is whether the Central Quechua languages were being included in the category "lengua general," which was most often an umbrella term for all varieties of Quechua.

Administrative documents, especially visita records, provide some insight into these questions without entirely resolving them. Ecclesiastical judges and administrators in Conchucos often hired local interpreters in addition to the official "lengua general" interpreters. In the course of a visita in the parish of Cabana y Guandoval in 1612, for instance, the edict announcing the visita was read in both the "lengua general" and the "lengua materna."[50] In all likelihood, however, this does not constitute a recognition of Central Quechua as a language distinct from the "lengua general"—the "lengua materna" referred to here was probably Culli. However, in the same area the priest of Pallasca was found to be fluent in both *la lengua general y la chinchaysuya,* an apparent case of exclusion of Central Quechua from the category "lengua general."[51]

Central Quechua received increasing attention from the archdiocese of Lima throughout the first half of the seventeenth century. For one thing, the term "Chinchaysuyo" or "Chinchaysuyu" was becoming a specific designation for the Quechua of the highlands of the archdiocese (as in *la lengua chinchaysuya*) rather than a very broad ethnogeographical category. Huerta's 1616 grammar provides the clearest definition of Chinchaysuyo Quechua, albeit along geographical rather than linguistic lines:

> While the Quechua language, or lengua general of the Inca, is all one language, it should be noted firstly that it is divided into two ways of speaking. On the one hand, there is the very polished and orderly way known as the language of the Inca, which is spoken in Cuzco, Charcas, and other parts of the upper [southern] province called Incasuyo. The other language is corrupt, and known as Chinchaysuyo, it is not spoken with the civility and order with which the Incas speak . . . the language of the Inca is spoken from Huamanga on up [south], and the Chinchaysuyo language is spoken from there on down [north] until Quito.[52]

"Huamanga" should be understood as the territory of the Spanish town of Huamanga, which at that point was being constituted as a diocese and included the modern provinces of Huancavelica, Ayacucho, and part of Apurímac. The southern border Huerta gives Chinchaysuyo Quechua thus corresponds roughly to the modern boundary between Central and Southern Quechua, but he seems to include the varieties of what is now northern Peru (e.g., the Cajamarca area), which are closer to Southern Quechua, in the "Chinchaysuyo" category. It is not clear if Quito (modern Ecuador) is considered part of the Chinchaysuyo area. Huerta may simply have been unfamiliar with the Quechua spoken north of the archdiocese of Lima, or may have put the central and northern Peruvian varieties in the same bag because, as "corrupt" dialects of the language of the Incas, they were not considered to have their own distinctive grammars. In any case, it is apparent from the contexts in which the term is used, as well as from examples of actual "Chinchaysuyo" forms, that it came to refer specifically to Central Quechua.

The very fact that Huerta, who was from Huánuco and thus a native speaker of the local Central variety, was given such important posts can be seen as a partial recognition of the importance of Central Quechua in the archdiocese of Lima. Huerta declared that his grammar was the first to provide instruction in Chinchaysuyo forms, although it did so only to a very limited degree. He was also in the habit of approving would-be parish priests for their knowledge of Quechua "according to the habit and exercise of speaking with the Chinchaysuyo Indians" (*según el uso y ejercicio de hablar con los indios chinchaysuyos*). It appears that in such cases the examinee had first learned Quechua through interaction with Central Quechua speakers, probably because he had grown up in one of the highland areas of the archdiocese. Huerta's licenses make clear that the Quechua they had acquired was not proper Quechua, but he nevertheless approved them. In one such case, Huerta explains that an ordainee was "perfecting" his knowledge by taking Huerta's course: "Apart from knowing the language according to the habit of speaking with the Chinchaysuyo Indians, he is currently studying it and hears me [lecturing] with great care, and is perfecting himself in it in order to be able to administer the sacraments to the Indians."[53] In other words, a future priest who was a speaker of Central Quechua was taking the university Quechua course, which was a course in Standard Colonial Quechua, to be better able to use the written pastoral literature. Ironically, someone who had already learned Quechua among Indians had to then study it in a different variety in order to minister to those same Indians.

The boom in pastoral Quechua writing and publishing that occurred in the archdiocese of Lima in the late 1640s was accompanied by much debate concerning the viability of Standard Colonial Quechua as a pastoral medium. The Quechua works of this period will be discussed in the next chapter, but some comment should be made here on a phenomenon that could be called "Chinchaysuyoism." There are Central Quechua elements, albeit of a very limited nature, in all of the extant writings of this period.

Two of the authors, the secular cleric Fernando de Avendaño and the Franciscan Diego de Molina, made strident calls for the use of Chinchaysuyo Quechua in pastoral contexts in the archdiocese of Lima. Avendaño stated in the prologue of his sermonario that his translation was intended to be understood by the "people" (*el pueblo*), even if this went against "the opinion of the learned" (*la opinión de los cultos*) (Avendaño 1649: n.p.n.). As Itier notes, Avendaño did not actually state that he was writing in Chinchaysuyo Quechua, and in one of the Quechua sermons he referred to the language he was using as *Ccozcco simi*, "the language of Cuzco" (Itier 2000b: 51). He does say, though, that his sermons were written differently from other pastoral texts and were more suited for a Chinchaysuyo-speaking audience: "In these sermons, which are to be preached primarily in this archdiocese, where the people speak the Chinchaysuyo language, this is the most genuine and current translation, and not the Syriac one, which the learned have introduced so as not to be understood by the people."[54] The expression "Syriac translation" is a reference to an Old Testament episode (Kings 4:18) in which a king of Assyria besieging Jerusalem was asked by the Jewish leadership to speak to them in Syriac rather than Hebrew, so that the Jewish people would not understand the negotiations. Avendaño used this biblical reference to upbraid those pastors who, for motives he does not explain, preferred not to be understood by the masses—in other words, the proponents of Standard Colonial Quechua.

Diego de Molina's position, expressed in the preface to his own sermonario, is very similar to Avendaño's: "If I were an examiner [of applicants for parishes] in the diocese of Chinchaysuyu [i.e., the archdiocese of Lima] I would not examine in the terms of Cuzco, but in its mother tongue, because that is the one its natives speak and understand . . . if I were to go to Cuzco and preach in the Chinchaysuyu language they would laugh and make fun of me."[55] Molina goes on to cite a church canon requiring parish priests to know the local language, with the implication that the requirement was not being fulfilled by those who only knew Standard Colonial Quechua. Most seriously, many Chinchaysuyo Indians had developed basic misconceptions about Christian doctrine because they did not understand the "Cuzqueño terms with which the [Third Council] cartilla was translated" (*términos cusquenses por donde se tradujo la doctrina cristiana*) (Romero 1928: 85).

These attacks on the use of Standard Colonial Quechua in the archdiocese of Lima are somewhat ironic, because the Quechua that Avendaño and Diego de Molina themselves wrote differed little from that of the Third Council. A large part of the reason for this Chinchaysuyoist rhetoric can be found in the occupant of the university chair at their time of writing—Juan Rojo Mejía y Ocón (cf. Torero 1995: 18). He was a native of Cuzco who had come to Lima as a youth, and an unabashed proponent of an exclusively Cuzco-based pastoral medium. In 1648, the year before Molina completed his sermonario and Avendaño's was published, Rojo Mejía y Ocón published a grammar in which he made his case in no uncertain terms:

> . . . I ask the reader not to share the depraved opinion of those who say that the Indians of this archdiocese [of Lima] do not . . . understand [Cuzco Quechua], because they are clearly deceived, as they would be if they said that the *montañés* does not understand the clean and cultured [speech] of Madrid and Toledo, for such is the relation between [the Quechua of Cuzco and that of the archdiocese of Lima] . . . I can say that no Indian who has heard me has not rejoiced and recognized the elegance and efficacy of the language of Cuzco, in which I have spoken to them, as one rejoices at hearing someone who speaks the Spanish or Latin language with eminence and propriety, even though one does not know it and cannot imitate it.[56]

The term *montañés* may simply refer to someone from mountainous, and thus rural parts of Spain. The comparison would then be analogous with the condemnation of Chinchaysuyo Quechua as "rustic" in the linguistic appendix of the Third Council's *Doctrina Christiana*. However, *montañés* is today also a term for the inhabitants of Cantabria in northern Spain and for the form of the Astur-Leonese dialect of Spanish (or Romance language) spoken there (cf. Lapesa 1986: 482–492). The first dictionary of the Real Academia Española suggests that this usage is an old one, defining *montañés* as an inhabitant of the *montes de Burgos* (Real Academia Española 1734: 600). This ethnogeographical sense of the term probably also had connotations of lack of urbanity. In either case, Rojo Mejía y Ocón's claim was that speakers of Central Quechua had no trouble understanding Standard Colonial Quechua, even if they could not speak it, and that there was thus no need to make dialectological adjustments to pastoral speech in the archdiocese of Lima.

There are indications of a personal rivalry between Avendaño and Rojo Mejía y Ocón. The latter wrote to the king in 1648 complaining that his efforts to obtain a position on the cathedral chapter were being blocked, and alleging that since Francisco de Avila's death the previous year there were no canons who knew Quechua—a clear slight on Avendaño, who was not a native speaker (Medina 1904–1907: I 411). Avendaño used the prologue to his sermonario as an opportunity to hit back against these thinly veiled attacks. Molina's comments in the preface to his sermonario also sound like an attack on Rojo Mejía y Ocón, who, as Quechua chair at the university and synodal examiner, was at that time *examinador en el obispado de chinchaysuyu*. Although the university chair did not have much real power over the orders at this point, he was still the official authority in matters of vernacular competence, so his radical Cuzqueñismo must have rocked the boat at a time when it was customary to at least pay lip service to the need to accommodate the speech of the "Chinchaysuyos." Rojo Mejía y Ocón's approach stood in sharp contrast to the policies of Huerta, his predecessor as university chair.

The *lengua del inca* versus *lengua chinchaysuya* debate of the late 1640s should be seen in the light of the personal and institutional rivalries associated with the language competence system. As will be argued in more detail in chapter 6, Chinchaysuyoism seems to have been something of a bluff—the rhetoric was not backed up in actual linguistic practice. It served as a way for ambitious clerics like Huerta and Avendaño to make a mark as Quechuists and to discredit their rivals. There was clearly a real concern that Standard Colonial Quechua was not sufficiently intelligible for a majority of the population of the archdiocese, but this concern is reflected in the Quechua literature produced there only in a very limited way. It was not until the mid-eighteenth century that anything approaching a systematic grammatical description of Central Quechua was published, and the earliest texts that can be considered fully Central Quechua date to the early nineteenth century.

A more serious and widely debated form of the *questione della lingua* concerned whether indigenous languages should be used at all. Hispanization calls had been heard throughout the sixteenth century, but became stronger towards the middle of the seventeenth. In 1634 a cédula ordered the Peruvian clergy to teach Spanish to all Indian children and, most controversially, to have all Indians learn the cartilla in Spanish (Solano ed. 1991: 150–151). The cédula explained that there was a shortage of adequate ministers for the Indians because those who were morally and intellectually apt generally did not know Quechua. In anticipation of complaints that it would be impossible to impose Spanish on the entire Indian population, the cédula noted that such a campaign of language imposition had been carried out by the Incas when they forced their subjects to learn the "lengua general." While it was not unusual for cédulas to be disregarded completely, this one was taken very seriously. It may be that the crown took great interest in this project and made this clear to the bishops, but it appears that the ground had already been prepared in Peru. The cédula was a response to a 1620 letter to the king by Pedro de la Perea, bishop of the newly created diocese of Arequipa, and a 1634 letter from Fernando de Vera, bishop of Cuzco.

Perea based his case on the classic distinction between conversion strategies in civilized and uncivilized societies. The use of the vernacular was justifiable in China and Japan, which were inhabited by rational and civilized people (*naciones de razón y policía*). In such places a native clergy could be formed which would minister to the people in their own tongue. This could not be done among the barbarian peoples of the Indies, because Indians were not suitable for the priesthood. The *iglesia indiana* was thus entirely in the hands of Spaniards, and those Spaniards who were good priests generally did not know Quechua, whereas those who knew Quechua were generally not good priests (a clear condemnation of both criollos and mestizos). Perea also noted the difficulties that diglossia created for the administration of justice, as the ministers could only communicate with the people via mestizo interpreters, who were not to be trusted. Perea clinched his argument by pointing to successful language imposition programs of the past: the Romans with the Spaniards, the Spaniards with the Moriscos (a strange example, given that the Moriscos had recently been expelled from Spain), and the Incas themselves with their subjects.[57] Closer to the date of the cédula, Fernando de Vera, who had only recently arrived in his diocese, presented a similar argument: the bishops could not carry out their duties effectively because they could not hear their flock nor be heard by them. The Greeks had given their language to Asia, but the Spaniards were speaking in the tongue of the conquered even when it came to what mattered most and what was least suited to expression in that language—de Vera repeated the old argument that Quechua was not an apt vehicle for the faith because it lacked terms for "Holy Spirit," "sacrament," and such.[58]

The 1634 cédula met with varied responses. The bishops of Cuzco (de Vera) and Huamanga (Francisco Verdugo) claimed that they were implementing the cédula to the letter. De Vera warned the king not to give credit to those who would claim that the execution of the cédula was impractical, and attacked the Jesuit order for continuing their Quechua training program when they should have been focusing on Hispanization.[59] Verdugo wrote that the Hispanization program was progressing very well in Huamanga—the young were learning the cartilla in Spanish, and both young and old would soon have at least a passive knowledge of Spanish.[60] Although Verdugo claimed that the cédula was well received by the parish clergy in his diocese, he also forwarded to the king a less positive letter from the priest of Pomacocho (a pueblo de indios in the province of Parinacochas), Juan Huidobro de Miranda. Huidobro stated that the cédula had caused considerable dismay among the clergy, and that he and others had argued that it should be resisted because it was contrary to both *derecho divino*, as expressed in the Pentecostal topos from the New Testament, and to canon law in the form of the Third Lima Council (he could also have cited the Council of Trent). The vicar, however, forced them to submit to the cédula by threatening to expel them from their parishes, as a result of which catechesis was being carried out in Spanish.[61] This letter shows that a serious, if short-lived attempt was made to enforce the Hispanization cédula in the diocese of Huamanga, even in the face of considerable opposition from the clergy.

In Lima the cédula was resisted by the archbishop himself. Fernando Arias de Ugarte informed the king that he had forwarded the order to the parish clergy, but stated that there were many obstacles to its execution and even that the alleged precedent of Inca language imposition was a false one, as there were many provinces of the empire where it was not spoken.[62] Arias de Ugarte published the cédula in the edicts of the 1636 synod, but also included among them the Third Council's Quechua cartilla. Pedro de Villagómez, who had replaced de la Perea as bishop of Arequipa, was more subtle than Arias de Ugarte in his response: he stated that he was implementing it *along with the decrees of the Third Council and Francisco de Toledo*, thus pulling the wool over the king's eyes, as these decrees were contradictory with the Hispanization cédula.[63] In the 1638 Arequipa synod, only four years after the cédula, Villagómez maintained the earlier legislation on vernacular instruction and ordered the parish clergy to instruct their parishioners *en su lengua natural*.[64]

What is significant about the 1634 Hispanization cédula is the fact that it was asked for and temporarily implemented by bishops at a time when the status of Standard Colonial Quechua as a pastoral language was fully established. One factor that could help explain the demands for Hispanization was the rivalry between the criollo and the Spanish-born (*peninsular*) clergy, especially within the mendicant orders (Pedro de la Perea and Fernando de Vera were peninsular mendicants).[65] An important portion of the Peruvian-born clergy was Quechua-speaking, and knowledge of Quechua was a key argument for preference over those who arrived from Spain. The Hispanization demands may have come as a reaction against the increasing predominance of criollos in the Peruvian clergy. In 1629, five years before the Hispanization cédula, the archdiocese of Lima had cancelled ordinations *a título de la lengua,* which peaked in the late 1620s, on the grounds that there were not enough Indian parishes to go around.[66] This suggests that in the eyes of the upper clergy, who were mostly peninsulares, the presence of criollos in the Peruvian church had reached a critical level. The demands for Hispanization may thus have been part of a campaign to reduce their presence and give those who arrived from Spain a better chance.

The Limits of Vernacular Competence

Quite apart from the occasional calls for Hispanization, there were clear limits to the colonial regime's dedication to the principle of vernacular competence. Formal instruction and examination seem to have placed little emphasis on practical competence—the courses were essentially lectures in which students "heard" texts and grammatical precepts being read to them. In the 1570s Acosta advised priests who were learning Quechua to memorize grammatical rules and follow the lectures of the chairs, but he also warned them that the real battle would begin when they engaged in actual conversations with Indians (J. Acosta 1984–1987 [1577]: II 75–77). The general assumption seems to have been that priests would pick up true language competence "in the field," and in the meantime would be aided in fulfilling their duties by the pastoral texts, which they would at least be able to read aloud as a result of their classroom training. This was not, of course, what was supposed to happen—in particular, confessors who did not understand each individual sin would be committing sacrilege, according to a Third Lima Council decree (Vargas Ugarte ed. 1951–1954: I 329).

Since the certification system was, in modern terms, "corrupt," clerics who wanted to be ordained or awarded a parish often focused on gaining the support of those in power rather than on learning Quechua. Juan Martínez was accused of falsely approving many priests, and Alonso de Huerta made a small fortune from his position as examiner. Diego de Molina claimed that language competence was generally not taken into consideration in assigning parishes within his order (Romero 1928: 56). In 1620, a Franciscan in Huánuco, the same area where Molina would later work, had informed Archbishop Lobo Guerrero that a local Mercedarian priest who did not know a word of Quechua was able to keep his parish by bribing his superiors with funds obtained by exploiting his parishioners.[67] In all likelihood, the same could be said for much of the secular clergy.

Nor does the system that monitored priests who were already in charge of parishes seem to have been very effective in measuring practical competence. Ecclesiastical judges, whether carrying out a routine visita or investigating accusations by Indian parishioners, do not seem to have had a system for establishing whether or not a priest was competent. The files they produced very frequently contain contradictory statements on the issue. In a 1620 capítulos trial the priest of Chacos (Tarma y Chinchaycocha) was accused of not preaching, catechizing, or confessing because he did not know *la lengua*, but he was able to produce other Indian witnesses who stated that he was a *lenguaraz* (a proficient lengua). Some of his parishioners complained that they found his speech incomprehensible, while others claimed that they had no trouble understanding him.[68] When the priest of one of the urban parishes of Huánuco was similarly accused by his parishioners in 1651, he simply replied that he knew *la lengua* better than his accusers and had his royal language license to prove it.[69] At this everyday level as much as in the higher realms of ecclesiastical politics, whether or not a priest would be considered linguistically competent was largely a function of personal and institutional interests. These contradictions, however, can also be attributed to lack of fit between a homogenizing language certification program and local linguistic reality. Even priests who were proficient in Standard Colonial Quechua would have had difficulty communicating with their parishioners, especially in the archdiocese of Lima, where the local varieties of Quechua were, in effect, different languages.

Finally, it should be noted that the emphasis placed on vernacular competence during this period never resulted in a bilingual clergy. It is likely that in the early seventeenth century a majority of the secular clergy as a whole had some vernacular training, but this was not the case among the *upper* clergy—priests of Spanish parishes, canons, diocesan administrators, and bishops.[70] It is true that most of the clerics who published pastoral texts in Quechua did indeed make it into the upper clergy—in the final stages of his career Francisco de Avila was a canon in the Lima cathedral, as was Fernando de Avendaño, who was named bishop of Santiago, Chile, shortly before his death. The Franciscan Luis Jerónimo de Oré ended an illustrious career as one of the first criollo bishops (of La Imperial in Chile). However, they were able to get their works printed precisely *because* they had made it into the upper ranks, not vice versa. The fact that they persistently identified themselves as lenguas indicates that they were a minority within this elite, which was made up largely of Spaniards and criollos who, thanks to wealth or social standing and achievements in *letras* (which did not include knowledge of Quechua), went straight for the Spanish parishes and the cathedral chapters.

The situation within the Jesuit order, which was especially dedicated to the principle of vernacular competence, is symptomatic. The order's fifth general congregation, held in Rome in 1594, established that *all* Jesuits in the Indies were under the obligation to study the local languages (Castelnau-l'Estoile 2000: 151). That same year the provincial congregation of Peru had proposed that knowledge of the "lengua general" should be required for ordination, and that even those who held positions of authority within the order should study it as a way of setting an example for their subordinates.[71] Claudio Aquaviva, the order's head in Rome, agreed that those who knew Quechua should be preferred for positions of authority.[72]

But this project came up against staunch opposition from the provincial head in Lima, Diego Alvarez de Paz, who believed that the order's elite should be reserved from such requirements. In a letter to Aquaviva in 1601 he wrote that Quechua was a strange language which bore no resemblance to Spanish (*esta lengua es peregrina y . . . no tiene ninguna semejança con la española*), and that mastering it was a question not of months, as some had imprudently claimed, but of years (Alvarez de Paz quoted the famed Jesuit linguist Diego González Holguín on the opinion that at least four years were necessary). He complained that even the theologians and administrators of his order in Peru had been asking leave to study Quechua full-time, and that there was a shortage of men of government and letters because so many were involved in the Indian ministry. To clarify the Andean situation for his superiors in Europe, Alvarez de Paz explained that there was also a *república de españoles* in Peru that required the attention of the Jesuits. He compared pastoral work with Indians to the ministry in hospitals and prisons in a European city, thus equating Indians to the impoverished and criminalized classes of European society, and explained that such work did not require much learning.[73] In Alvarez de Paz's view, dedicating the best intellects of his province to the Indian ministry and to Quechua studies would be like throwing pearls to swine (my simile).

Aquaviva was unswayed by such arguments, and in 1603 he ordered that no Jesuits be ordained in Peru without knowledge of Quechua, that Quechua be preached in the refectories, and that the *superiores* learn the language.[74] Establishing to what extent this policy was actually implemented requires further research. It is likely that most Jesuits in early-seventeenth-century Peru did receive some Quechua training, but this training seems to have been minimal among those destined for *gobierno* as opposed to the Indian ministry. Charlotte de Castelnau-l'Estoile's conclusions regarding vernacular competence in the Jesuit province of Brazil seem applicable to Peru: in spite of repeated instructions from Rome that all members of the order be involved in the study of Tupi and the Indian ministry, a clear differentiation existed between the administrative and intellectual elite and the *línguas* dedicated to missionary activities in the field. The *línguas* were largely excluded from positions of authority and generally did not take their studies very far. Jesuit novices in Brazil were thus faced by a choice *entre le tupi et la théologie* (between Tupi and theology) (Castelnau-l'Estoile 2000: 141–169, 246–252).

The main task of the church in Peru, and the whole justification for the Spanish presence was, at least in theory, the Indian ministry. The 1580 language training cédula made all ordinations in Peru conditional on knowledge of the "lengua general." In 1601, the bishops of Cuzco, Quito, and Popayán informed the king of the obstacles to the conversion of the Indians and suggested, among other remedies, that canonries be reserved for those who had been good priests to the Indians and had preached to them in the vernacular.[75] However, the internal dynamics of colonial society, in particular the explosive growth of the república de españoles, made these projects unrealizable, and the inequalities between Spaniards and Indians were projected onto the relations between priests who worked among Spaniards and those who worked among Indians.

Chapter 5

The Heyday of Pastoral Quechua (1590s–1640s)

The Third Lima Council restricted the subsequent development of pastoral Quechua by establishing a canonical standard for translation practice, by precluding further translations of the cartilla texts and even the composition of basic catechetical texts in general, and by erasing much of the preexisting pastoral literature. At the same time, however, it provided a major stimulus to the composition and publication of texts that did not compete directly with the conciliar corpus. There was now an official and approved model for writing about Christian topics in Quechua, and it became possible, though never easy, to have new works printed in Lima.

The period stretching from the Third Lima Council to the beginning of Pedro de Villagómez's archiepiscopate in 1641, which I will refer to as the "postcouncil period," saw the publication of four books featuring important new Quechua texts: a breviary or hymnal (1598) and a ritual (1607) by the Franciscan Luis Jerónimo de Oré, a second ritual by the secular priest Juan Pérez Bocanegra (1631), and a devotional manual by the Jesuit Pablo de Prado (1641). All four books are primarily liturgical in character, so they represent a significant expansion and diversification of the "genre space" of pastoral Quechua with respect to the Third Council corpus. A variety of new devotional themes were introduced by these authors, in particular the cult of the Virgin Mary, which had been underplayed in the Third Council texts. There were also important stylistic and terminological innovations in these works, mainly the development of Quechua hymns in metered verse and the adaptation of autochthonous religious vocabulary to Christian contexts (Itier 1992d: 397; Mannheim 1998a: 392). The writings of Oré, Pérez Bocanegra, and Prado should be studied jointly with the linguistic works of the Jesuit Diego González Holguín, especially the Quechua dictionary he published in 1608, which reflect many of the same changes vis-à-vis the Third Council standard.

The late 1640s mark the apex of pastoral writing and publishing in Quechua and thus deserve separate treatment. Two sermonarios by Francisco de Avila ([1647, 1649]) and Fernando de Avendaño ([1649]) and a translation of an Italian catechism by Bartolomé Jurado Palomino (1649)—all secular clerics—were published in Lima over a period of three years. Both of the known pastoral Quechua manuscripts from the period of this study—a sermonario by the Franciscan Diego de Molina ([1649]) and a ritual by the secular cleric Juan de Castromonte ([ca. 1650])—were also written during this time. The boom can be attributed in part to the patronage of Archbishop Villagómez, who regarded vernacular instruction, particularly preaching, as an essential part of his anti-idolatry campaigns. Three of the five author-translators—Francisco de Avila, Fernando de Avendaño, and Bartolomé Jurado Palomino—had made their careers largely as extirpators of idolatries. The boom was also clearly a phenomenon of the archdiocese of Lima; while they were not all natives, all five authors made their careers there. However, the connection between the mid-century works and the contemporary extirpation of idolatry campaigns should not be overemphasized, as the refutation of idolatry was a dominant theme only in Avendaño's sermonario.

Postcouncil Pastoral Practices and Discourses

The works of Oré, Pérez Bocanegra, Prado, and González Holguín should be seen in the context of two different developments of the late sixteenth and early seventeenth centuries: growing official stimulus to public worship in the pueblos de indios, and an increased prominence of positive appraisals of Andean religion. The extirpation campaigns that began with the arrival of Archbishop Lobo Guerrero and Avila's *auto de fe* in 1609 are not reflected in the extant pastoral literature until the late 1640s. Pierre Duviols expresses surprise that no sermonario focused on the refutation of idolatries was published previously (Duviols 1977a [1971]: 343), especially considering the detailed program for anti-idolatry preaching and calls for the printing of such a sermonario in Pablo José de Arriaga's extirpation manual (Arriaga 1621: 82–84). The reasons for the delay in the publication of new texts directly concerned with idolatry are unclear, but it seems that the author-translators of the 1590–1640 period had other concerns. It is significant that none of them were based in the archdiocese of Lima, which is where extirpation was most prominent.

Almost immediately after the Third Lima Council, synodal legislation began to call for Indian participation in acts of public worship that were arranged around, or were part of, the traditional liturgy of the canonical hours. In contradistinction to the provincial councils, synods were strictly diocesan affairs involving a different set of agents—in particular, the Jesuits probably did not have much influence in them. A series of synods held by Mogrovejo in the 1580s prescribed three main forms of public prayer: (1) the responsorial Angelus prayer, which commemorates the moment of the conception of Christ and was to be recited every day at noon;[1] (2) the evening prayer for the souls in purgatory; and (3) the singing of the Salve Regina on Saturdays after the evening hour of Compline.[2] The calls for the performance of the Angelus and the Salve Regina in particular reflect the growing importance of the Marian cult in the pueblos de indios. The Saturday evening liturgy for the Virgin was further consolidated thanks to the efforts of Luis Jerónimo de Oré, who in 1605 obtained a decree from Paul V granting indulgences to both Indians and Spaniards in Peru who practiced it. The papal document mentions that the Salve Regina was to be accompanied by a litany to the Virgin in Latin, of which Oré provided a Quechua translation or adaptation (Oré 1607: 335–338).

These liturgical obligations were summed up in a decree of the 1613 Lima synod which specifies that the Angelus was to be recited at both noon and dusk, and that both the Angelus and the Saturday singing of the Salve Regina were to be announced by bell-tolling to congregate the parishioners, or allow them to perform personal acts of devotion such as kneeling wherever they were at the moment the office was taking place (Lima Synods 1987: 64). Early-seventeenth-century instructions for visitas in the archdiocese of Lima called for the visitador to ensure that the three offices were performed in all Indian parishes.[3] The implementation of these offices in the pueblos de indios was no innovation—the synods were approving and systematizing practices that had been instituted by the mendicant orders long before the Third Lima Council. The Mercedarian Diego de Porres, for example, required daily prayer for the souls in purgatory following the evening Angelus in his pastoral instructions from the 1570s, and even suggested that those who failed to chime in be whipped the following morning.[4] It is not clear whether these prayers were to be said in Quechua—the synods themselves did not specify the language. As will be seen below, however, Quechua translations were provided in the pastoral compilations of the period.

The synods of the dioceses of Cuzco and Huamanga sought to ensure the performance of certain daily offices in the pueblos de indios much as the Lima synods did, and in some cases went beyond them. The 1591 Cuzco synod ordered that the hours of first and second Vespers be sung on Sundays and feast days by the parish priest and a choir of Indian cantors, presumably in Latin (Lassegue-Moleres 1987: 48). The first synod of the diocese of Huamanga, held in 1629, required the daily performance of the Angelus and the public prayer for the souls in purgatory, and the Saturday singing of the Salve Regina (Huamanga Synod 1970 [1629]: 38–39). Jesuit reports from the early 1600s also reflect an increased interest in native participation in the liturgy, particularly in the college of Cuzco. Whereas earlier letters stressed catechetical performances, these reports describe traditional liturgical offices, including the Saturday performance of the Salve and the Marian litany. Indians were trained to sing hymns and responsoria for feast day masses and masses for the dead. The Indian *cofradía* or lay brotherhood of the Jesuit college of Cuzco had a key role in the organization of these performances.[5]

Synodal legislation of the late sixteenth and early seventeenth centuries also pointed to another lacuna in the Third Council corpus: eucharistic texts. The 1591 Cuzco synod noted the absence of prayers for adoring the eucharist and ordered that such prayers be translated and taught by parish priests (Lassegue-Moleres 1987: 42). The 1601 Cuzco synod ordered that the Quechua translations of eucharistic prayers and the communion catechism published in Oré's 1598 hymnal be taught throughout the diocese alongside the Third Council texts, even though the prayers translated by Oré were in fact pre- and post-communion prayers, rather than prayers for adoring the eucharist (ibid.: 66). The first synod of the diocese of Arequipa, held in 1638, noted the lack of prayers for adoring the eucharist in terms identical to those of the 1591 Cuzco synod, and ordered that Quechua, Aymara, and Puquina versions of such prayers be taught by parish priests—the Quechua and Aymara prayers were included in the decree itself.[6]

Beyond requiring forms of public prayer, diocesan legislation also implemented the Tridentine requirement that parish priests "preach the Gospel" in the vernacular on Sundays and feast days (in other words, paraphrase and explain the Gospel passage read in the mass). This obligation had been glossed over by the Third Lima Council, which favored thematic sermons of the sort published in the *Tercero cathecismo* as opposed to liturgical sermons. It was established in the 1613 Lima synod, which also instructed parish priests to keep written copies of the sermons they preached, presumably in Quechua, so that visitadores could inspect them (Lima Synods 1987: 37).[7] The 1629 Huamanga synod ordered priests of both Indian and Spanish parishes to begin their sermons by "declaring . . . literally the Gospel of that day" (*declarando . . . literalmente el Evangelio de aquel día*) (Huamanga Synod 1970 [1629]: 15). Translating, or rather paraphrasing Gospel passages from the mass became one of the paradigmatic activities of lengua priests—by the 1630s all candidates for parishes were tested for their ability to "explicate" a Gospel reading in Quechua. Liturgical sermonarios were written to provide parish priests with a sermon for each date in the liturgical calendar, relieving them of the difficult task of preparing their own biblical paraphrases and commentaries.

The church also promoted private acts of devotion which could be performed independently of the temporal and spatial restrictions of the public liturgy, particularly the praying of the rosary. The formal liturgy was thus complemented by a secondary liturgy or "paraliturgy" of personal acts of devotion involving the repetitive recitation of brief prayers dedicated to specific divine persons, events in sacred history, and doctrines. The private devotions complemented the formal liturgy in that they did not require the synchronization of large groups of people and could be carried out on a personal schedule. Although there is no mention of the rosary in the *Doctrina christiana y catecismo*, one of the sermons of the *Tercero cathecismo* instructed Indians to use it on a daily basis (Third Lima Council 1985c [1585]: 709). The importance of the rosary grew considerably during the late sixteenth and early seventeenth centuries. Oré's hymnal included a series of fifteen prayers for dedicating "decades" to the Marian mysteries, which commemorated episodes from the life of Mary (Oré 1992 [1598]: 428–433). The 1611 Dominican chapter ordered parish priests to make a special effort to commend the rosary in their sermons, exemplifying its importance through the narration of exempla and miracles.[8] By the time the Huarochirí Manuscript was written (ca. 1600), the rosary had become emblematic of Indian Christianity—the author noted that *even* Indians who prayed the rosary could be covert idolaters (Taylor ed. 1999 [1987, n.d.]: 138). Guaman Poma's chronicle sets forth a devotional program based on the rosary, in which Indians prayed portions of the rosary followed by prayers to the Trinity, to the Virgin in various avocations, to the saints, and to the souls in purgatory. He also portrayed Indians praying with rosaries in the accompanying drawings (Guaman Poma de Ayala 1980 [1615]: 769–783, 765, 766, 777).

Private devotions came in a variety of other forms and were stimulated by indulgence bulls—individuals who purchased a printed copy of such a bull earned indulgences when they recited specific prayers and performed devotional acts prescribed in the bull. The Third Lima Council texts made no reference to indulgences, probably because of the intense controversy that surrounded them. However, the indulgence bull known as *la bula de la santa cruzada* was already being sold to Indians in the 1570s, and a Quechua plática exhorting Indians to purchase the bull was being preached in 1579.[9] A similar plática written by Juan Martínez was printed in 1600 and has survived (Itier 1992c). The works of Pérez Bocanegra and Prado contain Quechua instructions on how to activate indulgences, as well as Quechua versions of the indulgenced prayers themselves (Pérez Bocanegra 1631: 494–500, 697–701; Prado 1641: f. 161–166). Indulgences rapidly became a central element in Andean Catholicism, with the consequent proliferation of related Quechua texts (only the bulls themselves remained untranslated).

A reaction against the negative appraisals of Andean religion that characterized the reform era is especially visible in the *Relación de las costumbres antiguas de los naturales del Pirú*, a treatise written around 1594 by an unnamed Jesuit (Esteve Barba 1968: li),[10] and in the works of Garcilaso, Guaman Poma, and Pachacuti Yamqui, which date to the first two decades of the seventeenth century. The Anonymous Jesuit opened his text by stating that the Peruvians had believed in a creator God whom they knew as "Illa Tecce" (which he translated as "eternal light"), "Viracocha," or "Illa Tecce Viracocha." His claim that "*Illa* is the same as *El* in Hebrew, *Ela* in Syriac and *Deus* in Latin" (*Illa es lo mismo que El, hebreo; Ela, sir[i]o; Deus, latino*) sounds like a direct refutation of Acosta's statement on the absence of a true equivalent of the word "God" in Quechua (Anonymous Jesuit 1968 [n.d.]: 153).[11] His description of Inca religion drew repeated parallels with Christianity, claiming that the Incas worshipped angels and confessed sins of intent (ibid.: 154, 165, 154–157). His account of the Inca institution of the *aclla*—a class of women who were separated from their communities and dedicated to the service of the state and the Inca sovereign—presented them as nuns *avant la lettre* (ibid.: 169–174). Although he repeated Acosta's claim that the aclla "monasteries" were demonic parodies of the Christian institution (J. Acosta 1987 [1590]: 341–343), he went on to state that at the time of the conquest the acllas converted by the thousands and maintained their virginity as *acllas de Jhesu Cristo* (Anonymous Jesuit 1968 [n.d.]: 172), thus postulating a smooth transition between the pagan and the Christian institution that Acosta would probably not have admitted. Philological proofs had a major role in the Anonymous Jesuit's form of argumentation, and he repeatedly suggested that the reigning misconceptions regarding Inca religion were due to lack of linguistic competence and the misinterpretation of key terms (ibid.: 157). His claims are also supported by references to a variety of texts, most of them unknown and probably apocryphal, including several *quipus,* or knotted-string records.

While the information provided by Garcilaso in his *Comentarios reales de los incas* (1609) is very different from the Anonymous Jesuit's, many of the same themes and arguments recur. Like the Anonymous Jesuit, Garcilaso argued that negative evaluations of Inca religion derived from misunderstandings of Quechua words and utterances (e.g., Garcilaso 1945 [1609]: I 66–67). He emphasized that the Incas had worshipped the one true God under the name "Pachacamac," which he considered to be the correct Quechua term for God, and which he glossed as "he that is to the universe as the soul is to the body" (*el que hace con el universo como el ánima con el cuerpo*) (ibid.: I 68, 66). Pachacamac was in fact the name of an important pan-Andean huaca and oracle located on the coast near Lima, and the site of a major temple. If the place name Pachacamac is read as the Quechua noun phrase /pacha kamaq/ it can be translated roughly as "that which animates/endows/embraces the world/the earth." Garcilaso dismissed the previous identification of Viracocha as the Inca creator God (ibid.: I 67), apparently because he could find no adequate Quechua gloss for the name. Like the Anonymous Jesuit, Garcilaso was influenced by and deferred to Acosta's work, while also contradicting Acosta's claims on key points and presenting a very different overall image of Inca religion (Zamora 1988: 116–119).

These arguments reverberate strongly in the contemporary chronicles of Guaman Poma and Pachacuti Yamqui. Guaman Poma claimed that the first generation of Indians had worshipped a creator God whom they addressed as Pachacamac and Viracocha, and reproduced Quechua prayers which he attributed to them. He also seems to have shared Francisco de la Cruz's belief that recognition of the existence of a creator God was sufficient for salvation (Guaman Poma de Ayala 1980 [1615]: 41–46, 43). Not coincidentally, Guaman Poma's program for Christian life in the pueblos de indios called for the use of native Andean genres in the liturgy, as had been done during the primera evangelización—he mentioned several taqui and haylli genres which were to be performed by curacas and their sons in honor of the eucharist, the Virgin, and the saints on the main feast days, and cited the precedent of David, who danced and played instruments before the "sacrament of the old law" (*sacramento de la ley bieja*) (Guaman Poma de Ayala 1980 [1615]: 731). In Guaman Poma's view, traditional Indian festivities and dances would be as good as Christian if only they were not accompanied by the extrinsic drunkenness, coca chewing, and idolatry (ibid.: 809).

Pachacuti Yamqui presented a more structured account of monotheism in the Andes that focused on the role of the Incas. He claimed that Christianity had been introduced in the Andes by Thomas the Apostle, who left behind a magical staff on which were inscribed the Ten Commandments. This staff went on to become the *tupa yauri*, the royal scepter of the Inca sovereigns. Pachacuti Yamqui presented Inca religion as an attempt to communicate with the Unknown God, and Inca history as a struggle between the monotheistic tendencies transmitted to the Incas by St. Thomas and demonically-inspired idolatry (Pachacuti Yamqui Salcamaygua 1993 [n.d.]). The philological proofs for this account were a series of brief Quechua texts interspersed throughout the chronicle—in particular a prayer attributed to the first Inca, Manco Capac, in which he addressed the creator God as Viracocha—which are very similar in form and content to the prayers recorded in the 1570s by Cristóbal de Molina (ibid.: 200 and passim; cf. Duviols 1993 and Itier 1993).

The claims about the nature of Inca religion made by the Anonymous Jesuit, Garcilaso, Guaman Poma, and Pachacuti Yamqui are far from uniform and coherent, but they reveal a common interpretive trend. There is also a continuity with the earlier writings of Betanzos and Cristóbal de Molina. All these authors shared the same concern for providing philological proof of monotheism or even proto-Christianity prior to the conquest, by citing religious texts and key terms. Attached to the historical argument they were making was the notion that the Quechua language had been an adequate instrument for worshipping God even before the conquest. The implications of making such claims in the early seventeenth century had changed from Cristóbal de Molina's day, primarily in that they had lost much of their political edge. However, these implications continued to be weighty, depending on who was making the claims.

For Indians such as Guaman Poma and Pachacuti Yamqui, or mestizos such as Garcilaso, they were a source of ethnic revindication; Guaman Poma in particular was claiming recognition for Andeans as faithful Christians. From the point of view of the clergy, there were wide-ranging consequences for pastoral practices and translation in particular. If Christian elements, or an inherent Christian potential, could be found in native religious languages, it was then only logical that such elements—especially the terms for native religious institutions and categories that were carefully avoided by the Third Council translators—be assimilated into pastoral Quechua. I will attempt to show that an argument of this sort can be discerned in the writings of Oré, Pérez Bocanegra, González Holguín, and Prado. I am not arguing that they were directly influenced by the Anonymous Jesuit or Garcilaso, let alone Guaman Poma or Pachacuti Yamqui—only that their works reflect certain widespread arguments and perceptions that are expressed in the contemporary chronicle literature.[12]

It can also be argued that the postcouncil author-translators were actively promoting pro-Inca views through their use of native religious terminology, which indicated that the original concepts and institutions were compatible with Christianity. On the other hand, using a Quechua term—any Quechua term—for a Christian concept or institution could serve as a demonstration of sorts that Indians had been familiar with it before the arrival of the Spaniards. When discussing one of the pre-Inca generations of Indians—the *auca pacha runa* (people of the time of warfare), Guaman Poma claimed that they wept while burying their dead because they knew of the existence of hell and recognized that it was their inevitable destination. As evidence for this claim, he adduced that they referred to hell as *ucu pacha* (inner realm) and *supaypa uacin* (house of the devil), even though both of these terms were pastoral neologisms (Guaman Poma de Ayala 1980 [1615]: 56). As Estenssoro Fuchs notes in discussing this passage, "the existence of a native term, however much a Catholic meaning may have been imposed on it, becomes proof of pre-Hispanic knowledge of the new concept" (Estenssoro Fuchs 2003: 135–136). By implication, the same argument could be made for any Christian concept or institution that was referred to with a Quechua term. Because of a widespread perception of religious language as divinely guaranteed, pastoral neologisms were not always recognized as such, nor were the semantic transformations undergone by adapted terms. This form of argumentation throws further light on the strong preference for loan words in the Third Council tradition and also underlines the radical implications of the (re)introduction of Quechua terms into the Christian lexicon in the postcouncil writings.

In examining the development of pro-Andean discourses and their reflections in pastoral translation, it may be useful to take into account analogous developments in other missionary fields. In spite of the obvious contextual differences, the activities of the Italian Jesuit Roberto Nobili in southern India in the early seventeenth century as analyzed by Ines Županov are very reminiscent of the contemporary Peruvian debates. Through extended study of texts in "the Latin of the country" (Sanskrit), Nobili came to the conclusion that Hinduism was a distorted form of Christianity that had key Christian truths, such as the Trinity, at its heart (Županov 1999: 3, 115). These interpretations led him to adopt the persona of a Brahman ascetic and to try to Christianize the elite *through* Hinduism. An equivalent strategy in the Andes would have required missionaries to have reached the Inca empire ahead of the conquistadors. However, Nobili's arguments with more conservative elements in his order have much in common with the polemical strategies of the Anonymous Jesuit and the other authors I have mentioned. In particular, all ground their arguments in exegeses of native texts and key terms, and in a linguistic and cultural expertise which they claim is not shared by their opponents (ibid.: 127–130). Of particular relevance for present purposes is the fact that Nobili's assessment of Hinduism was reflected in unorthodox translation practices whereby he replaced established Portuguese and Latin loan words in "pastoral Tamil" with native terms of Sanskrit origin (ibid.: 48–49, 78–79, 246).

The sort of cultural-linguistic exegesis discussed here may seem characteristically humanist, and indeed one of its prime exponents, Garcilaso, is considered just that (Zamora 1988). However, a concern for interpreting a society, its customs, and religion through its language was par for the course in colonial contexts where significant resources were dedicated to translation and linguistic description and codification. Christianizing readings of the Inca past should not be identified as a "humanist" approach opposed to a "scholastic" orthodoxy characterized by more negative evaluations. Philological tools which may have been humanist in origin had become part of mainstream academic culture, and were used on both sides of the debate. Which side an author-translator positioned himself on is not readily predictable from academic training (of which we generally know very little) or institutional affiliation (different orders, the secular church, and so on), and seems to have been determined on a more contingent basis.

The Postcouncil Works

Luis Jerónimo de Oré (b. Huamanga 1554, d. Concepción [Chile] 1630) was the most renowned of all the author-translators and the first to publish after the Third Lima Council. His main work, the *Symbolo catholico indiano . . .* (Catholic Creed of the Indies . . .) was printed in Lima in 1598 by Antonio Ricardo. The term *símbolo* (*symbolum*), which Oré glossed as "military standard," also meant "creed"—the three creeds (Apostles', Nicene, and Athanasian) were called *symbola* (Stapper 1935 [1931]: 153–154). The title was also a reference to Luis de Granada's *Introducción del símbolo de la fe* (1583), one of the most important pastoral works of sixteenth-century Spain, which Oré cited and borrowed from frequently in his lengthy Spanish prologue. The *Symbolo catholico indiano* can be characterized as a Quechua breviary or hymnal. It contains a cycle of seven hymns (*cánticos*) narrating sacred history from creation up to the foundation of the church at the Pentecost, one for each day of the week, followed by a collection of further hymns, prayers, and catechetical texts, some of them taken or adapted from the Third Council books. The hymns were composed in classical Latin meter, and were intended to be sung in the pueblos de indios as part of the canonical hours.

Oré's *Rituale seu manuale peruanum . . .* (Peruvian Ritual or Manual . . .), a ritual intended for use throughout Spanish and Portuguese South America, was published in Naples in 1607. This book consists mainly of Latin offices and Spanish rubrics, but it also contains short pláticas and other catechetical texts in Quechua, Aymara, Mochica, Puquina, Guarani, and Tupi, as well as some actual sacramental texts in Quechua, Aymara, Puquina, and occasionally Guarani. In contrast to the *Symbolo catholico indiano*, this work is more noteworthy for its multilingual character than for its Quechua texts, which only take up a fraction of the book. The *Rituale seu manuale peruanum* was published with the approval of the papacy, and is the closest thing Peru has had to an official ritual. There are references to other major works by Oré which he never succeeded in publishing and which have been lost, including a Spanish-Quechua-Aymara sermonario and Quechua and Aymara grammars and dictionaries (Oré 1992 [1598]: 67, 208, 458; Oré 1607: 7; Richter ed. n.d. [1600]: 2, 5).

Oré's books became the only post–Third Council pastoral works to achieve a semi-canonical status, in that their use was required by synodal legislation in the dioceses of Cuzco and Huamanga. As mentioned above, the 1601 Cuzco synod ordered parish priests to teach Oré's translations of communion prayers and his communion catechism from the *Symbolo catholico indiano,* and as late as 1669 diocesan legislation required them to have a copy of one Oré's books, probably the *Symbolo.*[13] The first synod of the diocese of Huamanga, held in 1629, required priests to have Oré's *Rituale,* an injunction which was repeated by the 1672 synod (Huamanga Synod 1970 [1629]: 40; Huamanga Synod 1677 [1672]: f. 61).

Oré was born into one of the most prominent conquistador families of Huamanga, where he must have learned the local varieties of Aymara and Quechua during his childhood (Pello 2000: 163). He was ordained in 1582 by Archbishop Mogrovejo (Polo 1907: 77) and may have been present at the Third Lima Council. Franciscan sources state that he was among those nominated by the council to translate the cartilla and catechism,[14] but this claim should not be taken very seriously. Oré's name does not appear in any of the council's documents, and mendicant sources have a tendency to exaggerate the achievements of their members.[15] In 1587 he wrote to the king saying that he had written Quechua and Aymara grammars and dictionaries and a Quechua-Aymara sermonario, but made no reference to the Third Council texts (Armas Medina 1953: 101).

In the late 1580s and early 1590s Oré did an eight-year stint as priest of Coporaque, a pueblo in the Collaguas province, a bilingual Quechua-Aymara area largely in Franciscan hands. The eight-year period during which he composed the Quechua texts in the *Symbolo catholico indiano* (Oré 1992 [1598]: 68–69) probably corresponds to his stay in Coporaque. Oré's hymns were first performed in the Collaguas area by Indians (Richter ed. n.d. [1600]: 33–46; Cook 1992: 41–43). In 1595, shortly after he had completed the *Symbolo,* he moved to the province of Jauja, the other main concentration of Franciscan parishes in the highlands (Cook 1992: 43). In the late 1590s the bishop of Cuzco, Antonio de la Raya, invited him to replace the deceased Alonso Martínez as General Preacher to the Indian population of the town (Richter ed. [1600]: 15). Oré does not seem to have remained for very long in Cuzco—by 1600 he was preaching to the vast Indian population of Potosí (ibid.: 1). Around 1605 he traveled to Spain and Italy and spent the next several years working on official business for his order, including trips to Florida to inspect missions (Cook 1992: 44–55). His career culminated in 1620 when he was named bishop of La Imperial (Concepción) in southern Chile—probably the least desirable diocese in the Spanish empire, but dioceses were hard to come by for criollos. He died there in 1630 (ibid.: 55–60).

The *Symbolo catholico indiano*'s 131-page Spanish prologue is our best source on Oré's perceptions of Andean religion and his connections to other Peruvian writers. More than a prologue, it is a full-fledged theological treatise on the sources of mankind's knowledge of God as well as a description of the New World and its inhabitants. The first chapters of the prologue develop the Neoplatonist *liber mundi* theme, according to which the existence and nature of God is expressed in the visible universe as if in a book or mirror (Oré 1992 [1598]: 82–91). Oré was wary of identifying the natural world too closely with God, but insisted on a very direct analogical or iconic relation between the two, stressing that God was the "exemplar" as well as the "efficient cause" of the universe, since its *idea y forma* proceeded directly from God (ibid.: 97–98). It can be suggested that the purpose of this rather elaborate commentary, which was hardly of a catechetical nature, was to implicitly support the argument that Andeans had derived a knowledge of God from the contemplation of the natural world. As MacCormack notes with reference to Garcilaso, the Neoplatonist belief that "traces of the intelligible universe, the realm of the divine intellect, were imprinted on the visible, material universe that is perceptible to the five senses" provided a basis for reading Christian truths into Inca religion (MacCormack 1991: 346).

Oré repeated a claim by Cristóbal de Molina that the Inca sovereign Inca Yupanqui, also known as Pachacuti, became a monotheist after contemplating the movement of the sun (cf. MacCormack 1991: 258). In Oré's version Inca Yupanqui (or Capac Yupanqui, as he called him), confirmed the existence of a creator God called *pacha camac* or *pacha yachachic* (creator of the world) by sending envoys to Pachacamac, where he then built a great temple dedicated to God. If the Apostle Paul had arrived at that time, says Oré, he would have found the Incas as ripe for conversion as he had the

Athenian worshippers of the Unknown God. As evidence for his claims, Oré quoted a Spanish translation of a prayer with which Capac Yupanqui invoked *el hazedor*, the creator god, and claimed that he had several other similar prayers which were known to be authentic by experts on the matter, but which he was not willing to publish in their original form without official approval (Oré's reticence shows that these prayers were controversial). The Quechua prayer translated by Oré is clearly the first prayer to Viracocha quoted in Cristóbal de Molina's *Relación*, or something very close to it, although his Spanish version differs somewhat from Molina's (Oré 1992 [1598]: 157–159). The connection is made all the more evident by the fact that Oré used some of the unorthodox Quechua epithets for Viracocha that appear in Molina's prayers—notably the terms *usapu*, *tocapu*, and *acnupu*—as epithets for God in his translation of a communion prayer by St. Thomas Aquinas. Interestingly, however, Oré does not mention Viracocha as the object of the prayer and says that the *hazedor* was known as Pachacamac.

The *Symbolo catholico indiano* offered an elaborate liturgical program in which key portions of the canonical hours were performed in Quechua, using either translations of Latin texts or (more frequently) texts originally composed in Quechua that were to substitute for specific portions of the Latin offices. Oré provided direct Quechua translations of the Athanasian Creed, the longest and most complex of the Catholic creeds; the Te Deum, one of the most important texts of the canonical hours; and communion prayers composed by St. Thomas Aquinas and the Venerable Bede. However, his most successful texts were the seven cánticos and a creation hymn which became widely known by its incipit, *Capac eterno*, all composed in Quechua. The *Symbolo* also included the basis for Marian devotions in Quechua: fifteen prayers for dedicating rosary performances to the Mysteries of the Virgin, a Marian hymn, and a Marian litany which differs from the standard Loretan litany and was indulgenced in 1605. Additionally, most of the third (Tuesday) cántico was dedicated to Mary and could be sung as an independent hymn. Oré's work clearly filled a void and had a powerful effect on performers and audiences—a Spanish layman who lived in Collaguas in the 1590s claimed that Quechua-speaking Spaniards who heard the new hymns were "strangely moved" by them (*[les] muebe[n] a devoción extraña*).[16] They were in widespread use even before they were published, particularly in the Franciscan parishes of Collaguas and Jauja where Oré worked, and manuscript copies of his texts were in high demand

(Richter ed. n.d. [1600]: 37). Fragments of some of Oré's hymns are still widely sung today in the Cuzco area and probably elsewhere in Peru.[17]

The success of Oré's hymns derived partly from the fact that he developed a form of Catholic religious poetry in Quechua which combined syllabic verse forms and strophic melodies from the Latin liturgy with native poetic devices such as the semantic couplet, and which merged Christian and Andean religious images and motifs (see chapters 7 and 8). He also presented Christian narratives and doctrines with a new level of detail and employed a much wider range of sources than the Third Council texts: the cánticos reference or echo a variety of patristic and scholastic works as well as liturgical and Old Testament texts. The second and third cánticos, which deal with the creation of the universe, draw extensively on the psalms, as befitted texts that were to be sung as part of the canonical hours.

Oré's work is heavily exegetical and places considerable emphasis on Old Testament types, in contrast to the Third Council texts, which rely on straightforward exemplification and cause-effect arguments, as required by the *estilo llano*. For instance, the fourth cántico discusses the homonymy between the Joseph of the Book of Genesis who saved Egypt from famine and Joseph the husband of Mary as a sign of the fact that Jesus, who was raised and protected by the second Joseph, would become food for a spiritually famished mankind via the eucharist (Oré 1992 [1598]: 275–276). Franciscan devotional motifs and practices are also introduced, especially in the narrative of the passion in the sixth cántico, which goes into extraordinary detail and invites performers and audience to visualize and identify with Christ's sufferings.

Little is known about the precedents of Oré's liturgical "style." It is hard to believe that he created it *ex nihilo*, but this is what the contemporary witnesses say, and there are no traces of earlier hymns of this sort. Margot Beyersdorff states that the main precedents for the cánticos should be sought in a Peninsular tradition of narrative vernacular poems on the life of Christ that developed in the late fifteenth century (Beyersdorff 1993: 223–224). While this is an issue that requires further research, it is clear that Oré's hymns are formally patterned on those of the Latin liturgy, from which they derived their meter and the melodies to which they were to be sung. As for thematic sources that were not biblical or patristic, the first place to look would be the medieval Franciscan tradition, especially the writings of St. Bonaventure, which emphasized the contemplation of the sufferings of Christ. At the same time, it is clear that Oré's theology was deeply influenced by Luis de Granada, from whom he derived the *liber mundi* theme and the general emphasis on the contemplation of nature as a source of knowledge of God.

In spite of its innovative character, Oré's work should not be seen as an open break with the program of the Third Lima Council. His efforts to assimilate elements of pre-Hispanic religious discourse are generally subtle and covert. At orthographic, dialectal, and terminological levels his Quechua texts follow the Third Council norms very closely—only on very few occasions did he use terms that had been excluded from the conciliar vocabulary. Oré also reproduced Third Council texts in both the *Symbolo catholico indiano* and, more extensively, in the *Rituale*. His catechism on communion, published in Spanish, Quechua, and Aymara versions, reads like something out of the conciliar volumes (1992 [1598]: 415–421). Oré's work can be seen as an attempt to reconcile the mendicant emphasis on music and participation in the liturgy with the Third Council's stress on catechesis using a standardized vernacular. The fact that the book was published at all, and that these were the first pastoral Quechua texts to come out of the press in Lima after the Third Council works, indicates that they had strong support from the ecclesiastical hierarchy, and were probably seen in just this light.

Oré's work was part of a broader resurgence in mendicant translation programs. This boom seems to have lasted throughout the first thirty or forty years after the council, a period during which the mendicant orders were locked in conflict with the secular church over their autonomy in the management of their parishes. Augustinian and Dominican sources speak of considerable translation activity, of which we know almost nothing because these works were never printed and no manuscript copies have surfaced.

In 1593 the head of the Augustinian order in Peru informed the king of the achievements of the lenguas in his order, singling out Juan Martínez, who had recently succeeded Balboa as Quechua chair at the university, written sermons and other works, and (allegedly) improved the anonymous 1586 grammar and dictionary.[18] The letter asked the king to make Martínez's appointment permanent and to grant him the same powers Balboa had had as examiner of applicants to Indian parishes. Authorization was also requested to print Martínez's version of the grammar and dictionary, which was done in 1604 (it was essentially a reprint of the 1586 text). A second printed work by Martínez has survived—a pamphlet dated 1600, which contains a Quechua plática exhorting Indians to buy the indulgence bull known as *la bula de la santa cruzada.* The text, which has been published by Itier, does not show any significant deviations from the Third Council standard, as was to be expected from the royal Quechua chair (Itier 1992c). The same letter mentioned another Augustinian, Juan de Cajica (or Caxica), who had written an Aymara grammar, and asked for authorization to print it as no such work was available at that time. Cajica, who was of Basque origin, arrived in Peru in 1573 and worked in the Augustinian parishes of Aymaraes, Pucarani, and Umasuyos (all Aymara-speaking areas in what is now the Bolivian altiplano) during the 1580s and 1590s. He was then moved far to the north, to the pueblo de indios of Cajabamba in the province of Huamachuco, where he died. The Augustinian chronicler Calancha claimed that there were no less than thirty-two volumes of pastoral writings by Cajica in Aymara, Chinchaysuyo Quechua, and Standard Colonial Quechua in the library of the Augustinian convent of Lima. This corpus included liturgical sermonarios, catechisms, confesionarios, commentaries on the sacraments, and exegeses of hymns and psalms (if not actual translations of them) (Calancha 1974–1982 [1638]: 1935–1936, 1940).

The Dominicans did not lag behind, and seem to have been especially active in the 1620s. The Dominican chronicler Juan Meléndez states that Juan de Mercado (d. Cuzco 1625), an outstanding lengua of the Cuzco convent, translated a compendium of the works of Luis de Granada into Quechua "with singular elegance" (Meléndez 1681–1682: III 116). The 1621 Dominican chapter exhorted Mercado to publish this work, specifying that it was a *summa* and translation of Luis de Granada's *Introducción del símbolo de la fe* and his treatise on prayer.[19] Alongside Bartolomé Jurado Palomino's translation of Roberto Bellarmino's Italian catechism, published in 1648, this is the only known case of a Quechua translation of an existing theological work. Meléndez also mentioned a contemporary of Mercado, Juan Arias (d. Huamanga 1645), a native of Pasto (in modern Colombia), as "one of the greatest lenguas of his time in Peru" (Meléndez 1681–1682: III 450). The 1625 Dominican chapter authorized him to publish a "book on the knowledge of God" (*librum . . . de Dei cognitione*), treatises on communion and the rosary, and a liturgical sermonario, all apparently in Quechua. The same decree authorized another Dominican, Miguel Arias, to print his own liturgical sermonario in the vernacular.[20]

The mendicant chroniclers' tendency towards hyperbole aside, it is clear that authors such as Cajica, Mercado, and Juan and Miguel Arias produced an extensive manuscript literature in Quechua which probably surpassed the published literature in size. In spite of the success of Oré's work, there is a clear imbalance in the printed pastoral Quechua literature between the works of the secular and mendicant clergy. Considering their importance as pastoral agents, the mendicants are seriously underrepresented. Oré is the only mendicant who ever succeeded in publishing significant vernacular texts, and even he was not able to publish half of his opus. The rivalry between the mendicant orders and the secular church regarding pastoral administration seems to have resulted in almost insurmountable obstacles for the publication of mendicant works in Quechua.

The first pastoral Quechua work to be published after Oré's *Rituale* was another ritual, Juan Pérez Bocanegra's *Ritual formulario, e institución de curas . . .* (Brief Ritual and Guide for Parish Priests . . .) (Lima, 1631). Pérez Bocanegra was a secular priest who spent most of his career in Cuzco and its environs. His ritual is one of the major works in the pastoral Quechua literature, and also one of the most unorthodox. It is far longer than Oré's (729 pages) and has a much larger proportion of Quechua texts, offering translations of the actual sacramental offices—at least of those parts that had to be said by Indian participants. The ritual proper is followed by an appendix, which contains an extensive general catechism followed by several new prayers and three Marian hymns. The *Ritual formulario* is widely known among Andeanists for the information on Quechua kinship terminology (including a kinship diagram) provided in the section on marriage, and for its references to the use of quipus in the confesionario. Pérez Bocanegra's three Marian hymns have attracted attention for their exuberant poetics—especially the third hymn, which is accompanied by a musical score considered "the first piece of vocal polyphony printed in any New World book" (Stevenson 1968: 280) and which has been the object of the first formal analysis of a colonial Quechua hymn (Mannheim 1998a: 392–401).

There is very little biographical information on Pérez Bocanegra, and several questions arise from what we know of his life and work. I have found no record of his date and place of birth, but he was probably born in Cuzco in the 1560s or early 1570s. Mannheim places his death in 1645 (1991: 146). A secular priest, he is mentioned in the chronicle of the Franciscan province of Charcas because he was a third order Franciscan (Mendoza 1665: 555), but, as will be seen, he seems to have had stronger ties to the Dominican order. He had a brilliant career as Quechua and Aymara examiner, Latinist, musician, and parish priest. After earning his bachelor's degree at the university of Lima, he won a grammar chair there, which he held until 1590 (Eguiguren 1940–1951: II 700).[21] By 1592 he was back in Cuzco and a member of the cathedral choir, where he served as singer and choir book corrector into the 1610s (Itier n.d., Stevenson 1968: 281 n. 30). For much of the first two decades of the seventeenth century he also held the urban parish of Nuestra Señora de Belén and was examiner in Quechua and Aymara for the diocese.[22] In 1617 he became one of the priests in charge of the parish of the Cuzco cathedral (Esquivel y Navia 1980 [1753]: II 31), an obvious promotion, and he seems to have been poised to enter the cathedral chapter.

By 1621, however, he was priest of Andahuaylillas, a pueblo de indios close to Cuzco, where he seems to have remained until his death, preparing his works for publication and working on the pueblo's famous church.[23] Andahuaylillas was certainly a plum parish, and Pérez Bocanegra vigorously defended his possession of it against the Jesuit order, which wanted to found a Quechua training college there.[24] Nonetheless, his assignment to Andahuaylillas seems like a demotion from his previous position at the Cuzco cathedral—however desirable Andahuaylillas may have been, it was still a pueblo de indios. It is possible that Pérez Bocanegra's pastoral vocation may have led him to voluntarily leave Cuzco, but it seems likely that he encountered obstacles to his entry to the upper levels of the ecclesiastical hierarchy. Among other things, a position in the Cuzco cathedral chapter would probably have made it easier for him to complete and publish his works—Pérez Bocanegra never succeeded in publishing his magnum opus, a liturgical sermonario in Quechua.

He encountered considerable difficulties with the *Ritual formulario* itself. Pérez Bocanegra had written a first draft as early as 1610, but had to adapt it on the appearance of the *Rituale romanum* in 1614. The bishop's approval for the final version dates from 1622, but it was not published until nine years later (Pérez Bocanegra 1631: n.p.n.). Thanks to a group of documents recently discovered by Gabriela Ramos, it is now known that Pérez Bocanegra paid for the printing out of his own pocket, and that he was assisted in the process by prominent members of the Dominican order. In 1628 he stated that he had left the *Ritual formulario* in Lima in the hands of the Dominicans Francisco de la Cruz and Luis Cornejo, along with the substantial sum of 2,800 pesos to cover the cost of printing 1,200 copies (Itier n.d.)—evidently, Pérez Bocanegra was not able to take enough time off from his duties in Andahuaylillas to oversee the printing process in

Lima. Luis Cornejo was well known as a lengua within the order, and Francisco de la Cruz, who became provincial in the 1650s, was a harsh critic of the Third Council texts. It is significant, first of all, that Pérez Bocanegra was not able to obtain a patron to finance the publication, and secondly that, being a secular priest, he obtained assistance from the Dominican order, which had not succeeded in printing any Quechua works since 1560. Both facts point to the divergences between his work and the Third Council tradition.

The *Ritual formulario* was unorthodox at several different levels. Pérez Bocanegra's inclusion of a new general catechism of his own creation violated the Third Council's ban on basic catechisms other than those provided in the *Doctrina christiana y catecismo*. In this catechism he went as far as citing the Pater Noster in a significantly modified form (Pérez Bocanegra 1631: 690). Pérez Bocanegra's criteria for selecting which liturgical texts to translate were unusually liberal—he even translated the priest's secret prayers for before and after communion from the canon of the mass (Pérez Bocanegra 1631: 500–502). Additionally, his Quechua diverged significantly from the conciliar norm. First, as Itier has noted, there are dialectal differences: Pérez Bocanegra's Quechua is more specifically Cuzqueño than Standard Colonial Quechua, and thus differs from it lexically and even morphologically (if only in a few minor details) (Itier 2000b: 51–55). But the most important differences are terminological. Many of the loan words consecrated by the Third Council are replaced (though only sporadically) by terms for Inca religious institutions—for instance, "feast day" is sometimes rendered *raymi* or *citua*, which were names of Inca religious festivals, rather than *fiesta* (Pérez Bocanegra 1631: 174, 311). In the prayers and hymns he composed or translated, Pérez Bocanegra also employed a set of distinctly heterodox terms associated with the deified Inca sovereign, the huacas, and celestial objects of adoration as epithets for God, Christ, and the Virgin (Mannheim 1998a: 392–401).

Perhaps because of their unorthodox character, Pérez Bocanegra's texts never enjoyed the success he hoped for. Although Bishop Lorenzo Pérez de Grado, who approved the *Ritual formulario* for publication in 1622, hinted that it would become the official ritual of the diocese, I have found no evidence that it ever achieved that status. Pablo de Prado's 1641 devotional manual, which I discuss below, reproduces several hymns from Oré's *Symbolo catholico indiano*, apparently because they had become part of an established repertoire, but there are no texts by Pérez Bocanegra. However, a

1705 reedition of Prado's manual included several of Pérez Bocanegra's prayers, which suggests that the *Ritual formulario* was still in use more than seventy years after its publication.[25]

The last pastoral Quechua work to appear before the boom of the late 1640s was the *Directorio espiritual en la lengua española, y quichua general del inga . . .* (Spiritual Directory in the Spanish Language and Quechua, the General Language of the Inca . . .) (Lima, 1641) by the Jesuit Pablo de Prado, a collection of texts which can best be described as a devotional manual. Although chronologically Prado's work might be grouped with the mid-century literature, it is much closer in its themes and language to Oré's and Pérez Bocanegra's. Only the bare bones of Prado's biography are available: He was born in La Paz around 1576 and entered the Jesuit order in Lima in 1595. His career as a missionary seems to have been based in the Jesuit college of Huamanga (he was ordained in Huamanga in 1612, and participated in missions and idolatry inspections in the Huamanga area around that time).[26] It is not clear to what extent Prado can be considered the author of the *Directorio espiritual*: it contains several texts taken from the Third Council's *Doctrina christiana y catecismo* and Oré's *Symbolo catholico indiano*, and there are orthographic variations throughout the work. There is at present no way of establishing which, if any, of the texts were actually composed or translated by Prado.

The *Directorio espiritual* has been entirely neglected by Quechua scholars until recently,[27] but it is a rich and important work. It belongs in the same league with Oré's *Symbolo catholico indiano* and Pérez Bocanegra's *Ritual formulario*, as it offers a complete devotional and liturgical program for the pueblos de indios and contains several catechisms and sacramental instructions as well as prayers and hymns. Prado's work is unique in that it was intended to be read by Indians rather than priests—it does not contain any of the liturgical offices that could only be said by priests, and it provides Quechua performance instructions that speak directly to Indians in the second person. Its purpose was to guide Indians in their personal spirituality and prepare them for the reception of the sacraments, especially communion. The *Directorio espiritual* is also worthy of attention because it is the only pastoral Quechua work other than the Third Council texts to have had reeditions: there is a 1651 edition, which is essentially a reprint, and a third edition from 1705, titled *Selectas del directorio espiritual*, which has significant modifications, including the insertion of texts by Pérez Bocanegra (Prado and Manuel 1705). Finally, there is an eighteenth-century manuscript titled

Quaderno de directorio espiritual, which, in spite of significant differences, can still be considered a derivation of Prado's original work of 1641 (Quaderno de directorio espiritual n.d.). This stream of reeditions and adaptations indicates an exceptional popularity, which must have derived from the fact that it was intended for use by Indians.

The *Directorio espiritual* opens with the cartilla and other excerpts from the *Doctrina christiana y catecismo* followed by an *ejercicio cotidiano*—a series of prayers which were to be uttered at different moments in a daily routine—and instructions and prayers for hearing mass, praying the rosary, taking communion, activating indulgences, rendering devotion to the Virgin and Saints, and helping the dying. Prado was especially concerned with stimulating and structuring Indian participation in the mass. He provided a Quechua version of the *Orate fratres* prayer, one of very few texts specific to the mass that were translated into Quechua, and an exegesis of the symbolism of the different stages of the mass whose purpose was to provide a structure for devotional meditation as the mass ran its course (few Indians, of course, could understand what was actually being said) (Prado 1641: f. 49v–56v). There is also a detailed Quechua instruction for Indian acolytes that provided the Latin responses which the acolyte had to say and cued him on what to do at each stage of the mass (ibid.: f. 59v–62v). The latter part of the book contains a series of litanies and hymns, some of them taken from the *Symbolo catholico indiano* (ibid.: f. 211–223v). The language of Prado's texts on the whole stays very close to the Third Council standard in its dialectology, orthography, and Christian terminology. However, a number of unorthodox terms are used as epithets in prayers, hymns, and litanies, and in this respect some of Prado's texts have much in common with those of Pérez Bocanegra.

A discussion of pastoral Quechua during this period would not be complete without some mention of the linguistic works of Prado's correligionary Diego González Holguín. González Holguín's Quechua grammar (Lima, 1607) and dictionary (Lima, 1608) are by far the most detailed descriptions of Quechua from the colonial period and are rivaled by few twentieth-century works. The most obvious innovation in González Holguín's work is the use of an orthography that attempted to distinguish phonemes that had not been represented in the previous literature, but he was also highly innovative in his proposals for Christian terminology and poetics. Clearly, González Holguín did not feel obligated to follow the Third Council standard to the letter (cf. Mannheim 2002).

The prologue of González Holguín's grammar emphasized the need for preachers to use the "natural elegance" (*propia elegancia*) and the "complex, meaningful, and elegant things" (*cosas curiosas, substanciales y elegantes*) of the Quechua language (1607: n.p.n.). There is an implicit criticism here of the *estilo llano* proposed in the prologue of the *Tercero cathecismo*—clearly, if González Holguín felt that preaching style needed revamping, it was because the norms provided by the Third Council were inadequate. His grammar is often critical of the 1586 *Arte y vocabulario* and even points to errors in the Third Council texts themselves.[28] González Holguín's dictionary, like his grammar, was designed as a tool for preachers, and it provided a large number of Quechua terms and expressions for Christian themes that are not present in the Third Council corpus. Juan Vásquez, a fellow Jesuit who approved González Holguín's dictionary for publication, noted this expansion of the pastoral lexicon: "this work [has] an abundance of terms that have been newly adapted to spiritual uses for explaining the mysteries of our holy faith, vices and virtues which this language lacked."[29]

In particular, González Holguín's dictionary proposed Christian meanings for a number of terms for Inca religious institutions and categories. For instance, his gloss for *aclla* contains a suggested Christian adaptation of the term that parallels the Anonymous Jesuit's claims about the acllas: the expression *Diospa acllancuna* (God's acllas) should be used to refer to "the religious or nuns who have been chosen by God for his service" (González Holguín 1989 [1952, 1608]: 15). Although he did not put forward any arguments for Inca monotheism in his prologues, his stand on the issue comes through in his glosses. The word *Pachacamac*, for instance, is glossed as "the temple the Inca [sovereign] dedicated to God the creator next to Lima" (*El templo que el Inca dedicó a Dios criador junto a Lima*) (ibid.: 270). González Holguín also favored the Christianizing adaptation of Andean song genres, against the prevailing policy of the time. His gloss of *haraui* reads: "songs about the deeds of others or the memory of absent loved ones, and about love and endearment, and now they are used as devout and spiritual songs" (ibid.: 152). Similar claims are made in his glosses of the verb *huacayllicu-* and the nouns *huacaylli* or *huacayllicuy*, which referred to a song/dance genre used to ask for rain in pre-Hispanic times. González Holguín, who even provides a verbal sketch of the melody of the *huacaylli*, claims that it addressed God—"it was the invocation they made to God for rain water when it did not rain." He goes on to say that the *huacaylli* was still performed in the present day and that both God and the Virgin were invoked in it (ibid.: 167).

González Holguín was born in Cáceres (Spain) in 1553, joined the order in 1571, and arrived in Peru in 1581. Surprisingly, the order used him primarily as an administrator, giving him charge of several different colleges throughout the Andes. Also surprisingly, he does not seem to have spent much time in Cuzco. He was sent to Cuzco shortly after his arrival in Peru and was ordained there, but by 1586 he was in Quito. Ten years later González Holguín, who was still in Quito as head of the college, reported that he had written part of a *verbal* and asked to be posted to Juli, where he claimed he would complete it in three or four years.[30] His linguistic work was encountering opposition from his superiors, who apparently were concerned that it would distract him from his administrative duties.[31] These difficulties may be related to the unorthodox character of his work and/or to the internal debates over the compatibility of vernacular studies and positions of leadership within the order that were discussed in the previous chapter. After his lengthy stay in Quito, we find González Holguín in Chuquisaca (1600), Arequipa (1601), Juli (where he was head of the college in 1607), and finally in distant Asunción (Paraguay), where he died around 1618—it appears that his wish of completing his linguistic works in Juli was fulfilled before he was sent to Paraguay.[32]

González Holguín's peripatetic career raises certain questions concerning his linguistic research. Both the grammar and the dictionary are extraordinarily detailed, a treasure-trove of specifically Cuzqueño terms and expressions. González Holguín states that his dictionary was essentially the work of the "many Indians from Cuzco" that served as his informants (González Holguín 1989 [1952, 1608]: 8). He could have found such informants in the different places where he resided, although more easily in Arequipa or Juli than in Quito. On the other hand, many of his glosses and the expressions he recorded clearly derive from Christian discourse of a kind that differed significantly from the Third Council tradition, and I would suggest that he was also working from a corpus of Christian texts—perhaps the sort of sermons he wanted priests to be able to preach. A parallel can be suggested here with the work of Ludovico Bertonio, a contemporary and correligionary of González Holguín's who was the main Aymara linguist of the colonial period. González Holguín's dictionary in particular is very similar in its format and descriptive procedures to Bertonio's, especially its abundant use of phrases that sound like excerpts from sermons. Bertonio stated that his Aymara dictionary, published in 1612, was based on a large corpus of pastoral texts in Aymara (sermons, theological treatises, lives of saints, and exempla) translated by Indians of Juli (Bertonio 1984 [1612]: n.p.n). An interesting possibility thus arises. González Holguín had lived in Cuzco around the time of the Third Lima Council, that is, before the council's form of pastoral Quechua was imposed, so that any texts he may have gathered during this period would reflect pre–Third Council translation practices. González Holguín's divergences from the Third Council norm at orthographic and, above all, terminological levels may thus reflect the preconciliar Cuzqueño tradition of pastoral Quechua rather than a personal innovation.

González Holguín's translation program should not be considered representative of that of the Jesuit order as a whole. The single-volume grammar and dictionary by the Jesuit Diego de Torres Rubio (Lima, 1619) follows the Third Council norms very closely, and contains none of the unorthodox terminology we find in González Holguín's dictionary or in the books of Pérez Bocanegra and Prado. Torres Rubio's grammar-dictionary was clearly designed for missionary work because of its concise and accessible character, which contrasts strongly with González Holguín's massive work. Nonetheless, it did share in the liturgical emphasis of the period, as it contains an adaptation of Oré's Marian litany at the beginning of the book, and a sacramental appendix with a confesionario and Quechua versions of parts of the offices of marriage and extreme unction. The standard tasks of a Jesuit missionary included confessing, marrying, and preparing the dying, so Torres Rubio provided a linguistic reference work and a mini-ritual in one volume. The combination was a successful one, and the work went through two reeditions in the eighteenth century (Torres Rubio and Figueredo 1701; Torres Rubio, Figueredo, et al. 1754).

To complete this survey of the postcouncil literature, some mention needs to be made of the pastoral texts in Guaman Poma's chronicle—the only such texts we have any reason to believe were written or translated by an Indian. Because Guaman Poma's work falls outside the central topic of this book, I do not give these texts the in-depth treatment they require but instead ask how they relate to the mainstream pastoral literature. Guaman Poma's chronicle, which was written in Spanish, contains a variety of Quechua texts with Christian content, ranging from prayers that Guaman Poma claimed were addressed to God by the first generation of Indians, to his satires of the sermons of bad priests (Guaman Poma de Ayala 1980 [1615]: 41–46, 576–582). I focus here on Guaman Poma's rosary-based devotional program for Indians (ibid.: 769–783). The inclusion of pastoral texts in Quechua in what was purportedly a chronicle or even a report (*relación*) is unusual, but makes sense in light of the encyclopedic and normative character of Guaman Poma's work—one of his objectives was to provide exhaustive guidelines for the Christian governance of the pueblos de indios.

The section on devotional practices in the pueblos de indios has the highest proportion of Quechua texts in the chronicle: instructions for the performance of an extensive daily regimen of prayer as well as the actual prayers, most of which do not appear elsewhere, are provided in Quechua. The texts instruct Indians to dedicate portions of the rosary to various Christian entities and advocations followed by prayers invoking their aid. In other words, the prayers provided by Guaman Poma were to be said as conclusions to series of Pater Nosters and Ave Marias. Each of them consists of an invocation followed by a list of dangers—which include corregidores and parish priests alongside diseases and snakes—against which the addressee's protection is requested.

These texts are hard to place in relation to the mainstream pastoral literature. It appears that they were composed at least in part by Guaman Poma; it seems unlikely that a priest would have included his fellow clerics on a list of evils against which divine protection was required. The emphasis on the various threats besieging Christian Indians is characteristic of the chronicle as a whole, and does not appear elsewhere in the pastoral literature. The devotional program proposed, in particular the emphasis on Mary and on the rosary, is coherent with the liturgical bent of the post-council literature, but it shows none of the terminological innovations that characterize it—the language of the texts does not deviate from Third Council norms except for a few mainly orthographic variations.

One of the most interesting features of Guaman Poma's brand of pastoral Quechua is his misuse of standard texts and expressions. In the Salve Regina, *caman* 'worthy' becomes *camuan* 'with you,' rendering the final sentence of the prayer nonsensical (Guaman Poma de Ayala 1980 [1615]: 779). Guaman Poma also misinterpreted the phrase *ánimas de purgatorio* 'the souls in purgatory,' using it simply as a designation for purgatory—for instance, he writes *animas de purgatoriopi cac uacchacunapac . . . rrezanqui* (pray for the poor ones who are in the souls of purgatory) and even *animas de purgatoriomanta quispichiuay* (save me from the souls in purgatory) (ibid.: 774, 776). These errors exemplify the difficulties even a highly literate and ladino Indian like Guaman Poma could have in understanding pastoral Quechua texts.

The Mid-Seventeenth-Century Boom

The five extant works that date from the late 1640s and circa 1650 share important features that stand in contrast to the postcouncil literature. First, all participate in the trend of (mostly token) "Chinchaysuyoization" discussed in the previous chapter. Why Central Quechua elements make an appearance at this time is open to debate. It could be suggested that in the interests of anti-idolatry preaching Archbishop Villagómez had encouraged adaptations of Standard Colonial Quechua that would make it more intelligible in his archdiocese, and that consequently author-translators who wished to publish and be rewarded for their efforts were obligated to "Chinchaysuyoize" their writing, if only by inserting a few Central word stems. On the other hand, there is no reason to believe that such adaptations had not been going on for decades, as is suggested by Huerta's 1616 grammar. The fact that they only appear in the pastoral literature in the late 1640s does not argue against this—none of the postcouncil books are the work of priests who were based in the archdiocese of Lima. As suggested in the previous chapter, the evidence for a raging contemporary debate in the prologues to Avendaño's and Diego de Molina's sermonarios can be explained by Juan Rojo Mejía y Ocón's assumption of the university Quechua chair in 1648. Avila and Jurado Palomino make no reference to their use of Chinchaysuyo forms, which suggests that it was nothing new.

The mid-century literature is also characterized by a renewed emphasis on doctrinal instruction by the priest over indigenous participation in the liturgy. The pattern is clearest if one compares what was published in the late 1640s to the printed works of the previous fifty years: two sermonarios and a catechism versus two rituals, a hymnal, and a devotional manual. At the same time, there is a clear shift in discourses on native Andean religion in relation to the postcouncil period—the writers of the mid-century boom tended to harp on the notion that the Indians were *still* not fully Christian. This shift is reflected in the fact that they were fairly conservative in their religious terminology and did not often stray far from the Third Council norms in this respect. All these changes seem to be related to the resurgence in concern over idolatry in the mid-seventeenth-century archdiocese of Lima, although it is not clear that there was a cause-effect relation between extirpation and translation practices. Both may be effects of deeper developments.

The leading figure of the mid-century boom was Francisco de Avila (b. Cuzco ?1573, d. Lima 1647), one of the most studied figures in colonial Andean history because of his role in shaping the seventeenth-century extirpation campaigns and in the genesis of the Huarochirí Manuscript (cf. A. Acosta 1987; Polo 1906). His *Tratado de los evangelios, que nuestra madre la Iglesia propone en todo el año . . .* (Treatise on the Gospels that Our Mother the Church Presents throughout the Year . . .), a seven-hundred-page Spanish-Quechua sermonario published in two folio-size volumes around the time of his death in 1647, has attracted less attention. Avila was, in all likelihood, a mestizo, but was at least partly free of the stigma attached to mestizos because he had been abandoned as a baby and raised by a prominent Spanish couple of Cuzco. Having spent his childhood in Cuzco, Avila must have been a native speaker of Cuzco Quechua. After studying in the local Jesuit college, he moved to Lima for his university studies and became parish priest of San Damián de Huarochirí in 1597. Avila then carried out a series of investigations on clandestine native cults in the Huarochirí area that culminated in an *auto de fe* held in Lima in the presence of Archbishop Lobo Guerrero in 1609. Avila's success led to his promotion to the Spanish parish of Huánuco, the La Plata cathedral chapter, and eventually the Lima cathedral chapter, but his writings continued to draw on his early "fieldwork" in Huarochirí. Avila's reputation as a lengua was certainly a factor in his promotion to the Lima cathedral—in 1640 he was also awarded the cathedral's Quechua chair and preachership.[33]

Avila's sermonario is of the liturgical variety, which means that each sermon is a commentary on the Gospel passage read during mass on a particular Sunday or feast day. Each sermon follows a regular plan and is divided into three parts: (1) an introductory discussion of the significance of that day's feast or moment in the liturgical calendar, (2) a paraphrase of the Gospel passage, and (3) a commentary on the Gospel passage. The first volume contains ninety-one sermons running from the beginning of Advent to Whitsunday (Pentecost or *Pascua del Espíritu Santo*). It was completed by April 1646 and published in 1647. Avila died in September of that year without completing the second volume, which was nonetheless published by the executor of his will, Florián Sarmiento Rendón, probably in 1649.[34] This volume contains only sixteen sermons: it covers the liturgical calendar up to Corpus Christi, and thereafter provides only Sunday sermons (no feast days) up to the fourteenth Sunday after Whitsunday, thus leaving out the middle of the calendar year and the main Marian feasts.

Volume 1 includes anti-idolatry decrees by Viceroy Marqués de Mancera and Archbishop Villagómez, and reproduces a Latin sermon preached by Avila at the 1609 *auto de fe*. Avila's lengthy prologue contains a detailed account of his exploits as an extirpator of idolatries forty years earlier. The sermonario itself, however, is by no means a mere compendium of refutations of idolatry—in fact, the issue of idolatry comes up only occasionally, as permitted by the subject matter of each sermon, which was determined by that day's Gospel reading. The sermons go into great depth and detail in their exposition of Christian doctrines and narrative, and are rich in exempla and comparisons which draw on contemporary events and situations and on Avila's extensive knowledge of native religious practices. Although it made such a strong impression on Georges Dumézil during his stay in Peru that he published an article on it in 1957,[35] the *Tratado de los evangelios* has barely been mentioned by Quechua scholars until recently.[36]

Fernando de Avendaño (1577?–1655) was Avila's contemporary, fellow lengua and idolatry expert, and rival. Like Avila he began his career as a priest and *visitador de idolatrías* in the highland parishes of the archdiocese during the 1600s and 1610s, moved on to occupy a Spanish parish, and became a canon at the Lima cathedral. The parallels between their two careers culminated when they both published Quechua sermonarios in the late 1640s. Unlike Avila, though, Avendaño was of undoubted Spanish parentage and a native of Lima. He was able to climb higher in the ecclesiastical hierarchy, and was named bishop of Santiago shortly before his death. Another key difference for our purposes is that Avendaño was not a native Quechua speaker: he reportedly learned Quechua in eight months in order to obtain the parish of San Pedro de Casta (Huarochirí) (Guibovich 1993: 171–172). In many respects Avendaño seems like a lesser version of Avila: he rode the wave of the extirpation of idolatry campaigns which had been set in motion by Avila, and his sermonario, which appeared the same year as volume 2 of the *Tratado de los evangelios*, comes nowhere near Avila's work in its depth, complexity, or proficiency in the use of the language.[37]

Avendaño's sermonario, titled *Sermones de los misterios de nuestra santa fe catolica. . .* (Sermons on the Mysteries of Our Holy Catholic Faith . . .), was published together with an anti-idolatry instruction by Archbishop Villagómez in a single volume in September 1649, simultaneously with the inauguration of a new extirpation campaign. Villagómez had commissioned Avendaño to write the sermonario as a manual for priests and *visitadores de idolatrías*.[38] The sermonario consists of ten thematic sermons composed by

Avendaño, followed by twenty-two more taken from the *Tercero cathecismo* of 1585, which had long gone out of print. This sermonario was clearly better suited for the purposes of anti-idolatry preaching than Avila's, as its thematic organization made it easier to pick out appropriate texts and arguments, and thus won the formal support of Archbishop Villagómez (cf. Duviols 1977a [1971]: 346–369 for an analysis of the content of Avendaño's sermons).

Diego de Molina's *Sermones de la quaresma* (Sermons for Lent) was completed in 1649 and never published. Like Avila's *Tratado de los evangelios,* it is a liturgical sermonario, although one restricted to the Lenten period (from Ash Wednesday to Good Sunday), which it covers in over six hundred densely-written quarto pages. It is the only surviving pastoral Quechua work written by a mendicant after Oré's 1607 *Rituale,* and a manucript to boot. Molina was born in Huamanga around 1597, and was thus a native speaker of Southern Quechua. In 1609, at age twelve, he was admitted to the Jesuit-run college of San Martín in Lima, but he eventually entered the Franciscan order (his connection to the order probably dated back to his childhood in Huamanga) (Taylor 2001a: 212). Molina was ordained around 1617, and by 1645 was in charge of the parish of Santa María del Valle, one of several Franciscan parishes in the vicinity of the Spanish town of Huánuco, in the central highlands. The sermonario was written over a period of a few years—many of the sermons are signed and dated, the earliest date being 1645.

Molina's lengthy prologue, an important source on contemporary language politics and on the history of Central Quechua, was published in 1928 (Romero 1928). Further study was hampered by a 1940 fire in the Peruvian national library, which badly damaged the manuscript and left parts of it illegible, but Gerald Taylor has published an excerpt from the Good Sunday sermon and is planning further editions (Taylor 2001a). Molina drew freely on Oré's *Symbolo catholico indiano,* particularly for his narrative of the life of Christ and the passion. Some texts appear independently as colophons to sermons—Oré's hymn *Capac eterno* is reproduced in full at the end of the Palm Sunday sermon, as if Molina had intended it to be sung at that point.[39] Other appropriations are less visible: most of the Good Sunday sermon, the last in the sermonario, is taken from Oré's seventh cántico, but the stanzas are presented in prose form, and there are some minimal modifications to the text. The sermonario concludes with a series of prayers commemorating episodes from the life of Christ on the pattern of a rosary which were also adapted from Oré's cánticos (D. Molina [1649]: f. 289–301v, 305–326). Additionally, at least three brief passages were taken from the *Tercero cathecismo*.[40] It should be emphasized, however, that Molina's sermonario is no mere anthology of texts taken from other authors. Most of it is very distinctive in style and content, and there is no reason not attribute these portions to Molina. He drew on the by then classical texts of the *Tercero cathecismo* and Oré's *Symbolo catholico indiano* to cover specific topics.

The sermonarios of Avila, Avendaño, and Molina are important testimonies to mid-seventeenth-century pastoral strategies and discourses, and they present interesting differences and similarities in this respect. Uniquely, we are able to compare three contemporary works of roughly the same nature by different authors. Avila's sermons are characterized by a lively and wide-ranging discussion of a variety of issues that go far beyond the exposition of basic doctrines. The Gospel passages are used as a starting point for moral commentaries on colonial Indian society, and these commentaries are critical both of the Indians for their lack of faith and of the Spanish officials who governed them for their greed—there are numerous attacks on abusive and negligent parish priests and corregidores. Avendaño's sermons, on the other hand, are far more aggressively focused on anti-idolatry argumentation. The arguments, which are not constrained by the need to develop an exegesis of a specific Gospel text, are of an abstract and scholastic nature, whereas Avila tended to rely more on exemplification.

Both Avila and Avendaño, however, used common rhetorical strategies such as the dialogue with an imaginary Indian interlocutor who raises objections to their arguments. Both put the knowledge of Andean religious culture they had gained as extirpators of idolatry on display, discussing cult practices with a wealth of detail that was clearly intended to show the Indians that their priests were well aware of what was going on. Both also place some emphasis on the rational, demystifying explanation of natural phenomena such as the movement of the sun and moon or thunder and lightning, explaining that they were not divine manifestations but had purely mechanical causes. Although comparisons with the works of Oré and Pérez Bocanegra are problematic because we do not know what their sermons were like, a contrast can be suggested with the presentation of nature in their hymns, where natural entities and phenomena appear as manifestations rather than mechanical instruments of God.

Diego de Molina's sermons present numerous contrasts to those of Avila and Avendaño—which is not surprising considering that he was a Franciscan rather than a secular cleric. Anti-idolatry argumentation has a minimal role; as Taylor has noted, Molina draws on the Third Council texts, which at that time were almost seventy years old, on the few occasions when he deals directly with the problem of idolatry (Taylor 2002: 185). Instead, his sermons have a strong devotional emphasis. The gospel passages are read more for their spiritual than doctrinal implications—in the Palm Sunday sermon, Christ's entrance into Jerusalem is given a eucharistic meaning, an interpretation which gives rise to a discussion of the soul as God's house (D. Molina [1649]: f. 251–263). A recurrent theme is the contemplation of Christ's love for man and his suffering in the passion in the *imitatio Christi* tradition, which had been strongly developed by Oré (ibid.: f. 118). The magical powers of Christ's name, which is a characteristic theme in Franciscan spirituality and is featured in one of Oré's hymns, is also present in Molina's sermonario (ibid.: f. 246). Molina's sermons are surprisingly abundant in Latin quotes from biblical and patristic sources, especially St. John Chrysostom. The entire sermonario is a string of anecdotes, exempla, and dicta organized around the gospel readings. In some respects Molina's work appears closer to that of the postcouncil period—it is particularly reminiscent of the exegetical emphasis of Oré's hymns.

There are, however, important commonalities between all three authors with respect to their historical conception of Andean Christianity. The thrust of the numerous historical references in their texts is to emphasize the need for Indians to amend themselves and take advantage of the precious opportunity they had been given to enter the church. The Inca past was no longer something that strengthened the hold of Christianity in the present, but rather a terrible lesson on the urgency of full conversion. Avendaño was thus careful to point out, in response to a question from an imaginary Indian interlocutor, that all of his ancestors prior to the arrival of Christianity had been damned, and to imply that modern-day Indians were wasting their opportunity for salvation (Avendaño [1649]: 115). While many of the Inca references in the sermons of Avila and Avendaño are simple exemplifications in which the Incas are presented in a relatively positive light (Estenssoro Fuchs 2003: 350), and although both writers speak of the monotheistic discoveries of specific Inca sovereigns (Avila [1649]: 4–5; Avendaño [1649]: 13), the balance of the references points to the Indians' idolatrous inclinations.

The new arguments were developed most extensively by Avila, who used the parable of the vine owner from Matthew 21 (in which the rebellious stewards were understood as a reference to the Jews, who had broken their covenant with God) to convey the urgency of a full conversion. The discussion of this parable provided an opportunity to tell a story which he felt concerned the Indians very deeply: Avila had discovered evidence, oral and otherwise, that their ancestors had been evangelized by St. Thomas the Apostle, but that he had been spurned and nearly martyred by them. Thomas was remembered in the Titicaca area, where he had been active, under the guise of the deity Tunupa (Avila [1647]: 230–237). The Indians of Peru were, in a sense, a chosen people who had been given their own apostle, but they had rejected him and returned to idolatry. A second chance was given to them when an Inca instituted the worship of the creator god Pachacamac and dedicated the temple of Coricancha to him (Avila [1649]: 4–5), but the temple was soon defiled by idolatrous sacrifices. Avila explicitly compared the conquest of Peru to the destruction of Jerusalem by the Romans, in that both were divine punishments for idolatry (Avila [1649]: 97–99). The belief that Andeans had had early contacts with Christianity took on an entirely new meaning: while in the early seventeenth century it was a sign that the church had deep roots in the Andes, by the middle of the century it became an indication of the perversity of the Indians and a warning to them not to miss the new opportunity they had been given.

Molina's sermonario presents Indian Christianity in terms remarkably similar to Avila's. The narrative of the destruction of Jerusalem, for instance, is turned into a pointed warning to the Indians against falling out of God's favor (D. Molina [1649]: f. 249v–250v). Molina's exegesis of the parable of the vine owner also has a very similar thrust. He developed the standard interpretation of the parable as a reference to the fate of the Jews, and warned his audience lest they, who had recently been admitted to God's vineyard, suffer a similar fate. Molina went on in the same sermon to describe some recent and successful attempts by his fellow Franciscans to establish missions among the Panataguas, Carapachos, and Payancos, inhabitants of the jungle lowlands east of Huánuco. The reference to the jungle missions is used to exhort his highland audience to be thankful that they had been part of the church for so long, and to upbraid them for carrying on with their old rites, with a warning that those who abandoned the church were far more unfortunate than those who never entered it. There was also an implicit threat here that the jungle Indians, whom the highlanders had historically regarded as a savage "other," could well take their place in God's vineyard (ibid.: f. 120–139v).

There is a marked shift here in relation to the discourses that had justified accommodationist practices before and after the Third Lima Council: while many of the same themes are present, they are used to very different effect. This shift is reflected in the contemporary historiography on the Incas. The Jesuit Bernabé Cobo, the main author of the mid-seventeenth century on the subject, was much closer to Acosta than to his more immediate predecessors in his portrayal of the Inca past. Cobo found no proto-Christian elements in Inca religion, and in general abandoned the practice of interpreting Andean culture through extended comparison with Old World precedents (Cobo 1956 [1653]; MacCormack 1991: 392–405).

The remaining two representatives of the mid-century boom—Bartolomé Jurado Palomino and Juan de Castromonte—were both secular clerics who spent their careers in the northern highlands of the archdiocese of Lima. Jurado Palomino was born in Cuzco in 1591 and moved to Lima in 1614. Around 1618 he began his career as a parish priest, and in 1621 became priest of Cabana y Guandoval in the province of Conchucos, where he was to remain for thirty years. In 1626 he was named *predicador general de los naturales* (official preacher to the Indians of the archdiocese) by Archbishop Campo. By the time he began to put together his información de oficio in 1646 he had completed a Quechua translation of an Italian catechism by the Jesuit Roberto Bellarmino (1542–1621), one of the leading Counter-Reformation theologians, which he mentioned pointedly as a motive for promotion (like most clerics, Jurado Palomino was aiming for a position in the cathedral).[41] Although his translation was approved for publication that same year, it did not appear until 1649—it seems that the publication was made to coincide with the inauguration of the new *visita de idolatrías* and Jurado Palomino's appointment as one of the *visitadores generales*. Jurado Palomino's book is actually a retranslation, as he worked from a Spanish edition by Sebastián de Lirio. The catechism is an extended commentary on the common prayers, articles of the faith, commandments, and sacraments in which the questions are asked by the "disciple" and answered by the "master" (the reverse of the standard arrangement). It is far longer and more detailed than the Third Council catechisms, and each section contains an exemplum taken from a variety of medieval and sixteenth-century sources, especially biographies of saints.

Juan de Castromonte (b. Huánuco 1625, d. Huaraz ?1700), an otherwise obscure figure, wrote a thirty-one-page ritual sometime between 1650 and 1653. The manuscript, titled *Aptaycachana, o manual en que se contiene todo lo que los curas an de deçir y enseñar a los yndios en su lengua quando les administran los santos sacramentos . . .* (*Aptaycachana* or Manual that Contains Everything that Parish Priests Should Teach the Indians in Their Language when They Administer the Holy Sacraments to Them . . .), is held at the Biblioteca Nacional del Peru.[42] Beyond the fact that it is one of three Peruvian rituals and one of two pastoral Quechua manuscripts to have survived from the period of this study, Castromonte's ritual is of interest primarily because it contains more Central Quechua elements than any other colonial text—the title goes on to describe it as being written in *la lengua general Chinchaysuyo del Peru.* It is also the only pastoral Quechua text that does not provide Spanish versions of the Quechua passages and that has a Quechua title—*Aptaycachana* ('something which can be held easily in the hand'), a literal translation of "manual." The manuscript is obviously a clean copy and was probably written to be shown to Archbishop Villagómez or some high-ranking cleric who had control of ecclesiastical appointments.

Castromonte's career followed the standard pattern for lengua clerics. He was born in the Spanish town of Huánuco in 1625 and moved to Lima around 1643, where he was ordained seven years later. His first appointment was the isolated parish of Huancabamba in the province of Tarma y Chinchaycocha, which he held between 1650 and 1653—his ritual dates from this period. He then applied for better parishes, and in 1666 was made priest of San Sebastián de Huaraz, one of the most important of the archdiocese. In 1674 he presented an información de oficio to the crown in the hope of obtaining a promotion to the Lima cathedral, but was unsuccessful.[43] Interestingly, Castromonte barely mentioned his abilities as a lengua in the información and said nothing of his ritual—a clear sign of declining institutional interest in the vernacular during this period. Castromonte, who was fifty years younger than Avila or Avendaño, came too late in the day to have much of a career as a lengua.

Epilogue: Mid- and Late-Colonial Developments

The mid-seventeenth century has long been treated as a watershed by students of colonial Peru, as the beginning of a "mature" or stable phase of colonialism that ended with the Bourbon reforms and the rebellions of the late eighteenth century (Kubler 1946: 347–350; Marzal 1983: 192; Estenssoro Fuchs 2003: 243–244). The development of the pastoral Quechua literature would seem to support this view, which has come under criticism (Mills 1997: 13–15). Including grammars and dictionaries, fourteen original works for aiding priests in their Quechua ministry have survived from the first half of the seventeenth century, and major new works appeared in every decade between the Third Lima Council and 1650, excepting the 1620s. However, not a single pastoral Quechua text can be dated between 1653 (the latest possible date for Castromonte's ritual) and 1690, and the production of pastoral literature in Quechua remained meager for the rest of the colonial period (cf. Mannheim 1991: 71). The three books published in 1649—volume 2 of Avila's sermonario, Avendaño's sermonario, and Jurado Palomino's translation of Bellarmino's catechism—were the last major new pastoral Quechua works to be printed until after independence.

A similar though less abrupt decline in the colonial regime's investment in the vernacular program is apparent in administrative sources. In the series of informaciones de oficio of Peruvian clerics held at the Archivo General de Indias, emphasis on linguistic competence as a reason for promotion declined significantly around the middle of the century, just as emphasis on *limpieza de sangre* and the services of fathers and grandfathers increased. Similarly, the frequency of Quechua exams in the *ordenaciones* and *concursos* series of the Archive of the Archdiocese of Lima drop during this period. By 1685 the visitadores no longer seem to be checking systematically for language competence or the required pastoral books.[44] The cathedral Quechua chair in Lima was closed in 1694, although the preachership continued for another forty years (Castro Pineda 1945: 39). The university chair continued to function until it was abolished in the aftermath of the Tupac Amaru rebellion of 1780–81 (Mannheim 1991: 74), but it appears that the examination system was dormant for most of the eighteenth century.

The causes for the loss of official interest in the vernacular project around the middle of the seventeenth century are unclear. The most obvious explanation would point to demands for Hispanization from the crown, but there is no evidence that they became more insistent at this time. A major Hispanization push did occur throughout the empire in the 1680s, and the principle of Hispanization was enshrined in the *Recopilación de leyes de los reynos de las Indias* of 1681, the first official compilation of royal decrees for the colonies. The usual arguments regarding the difficulty of expressing Christian doctrines in the vernaculars were adduced, and royal officials were ordered to ensure that Spanish teachers were widely available (Solano ed. 1991: 188–197; Mannheim 1991: 70–71). These efforts certainly had an impact and contributed to the overall decline of interest in the vernacular. However, they cannot be seen as the sole or even the main cause for processes that were clearly visible decades earlier.

A fierce debate regarding the level of instruction among Indians that took place in the 1650s bears mentioning, especially with regard to the sudden cessation in the printing of pastoral Quechua texts (cf. Marzal 1983: 119–171). In 1654 an audiencia official, Juan de Padilla, sent a letter to the king claiming that a large portion of the Indian population continued to be ignorant of the basic principles of Christian doctrine, and arguing that the deficiencies in the pastoral regime were due largely to the fact that the bishops did not inspect their dioceses personally.[45] In 1656 and 1657 the Dominican provincial, Francisco de la Cruz—the same man who had assisted Pérez Bocanegra with the publication of his ritual—informed the viceroy that most Indians were "atheists" and did not believe they were descendants of Adam. No instruction at all, said de la Cruz, would be better than the instruction they had been receiving, as the Quechua cartilla and catechisms (of the Third Lima Council) contained numerous errors and heresies, three in the Credo alone, "because the translator of those times must have been a good lengua but not a theologian so as to find the correct terms for the meaning."[46] The Council of the Indies responded by ordering the Lima Inquisition to investigate de la Cruz's accusations by having the Quechua catechism translated into Spanish for examination, while also reprimanding him for remaining silent on the issue for so long.[47] In these same years the new bishop of Huamanga, Francisco de Godoy, joined the fray, complaining of the lack of basic catechetical instruction among Indians, which he attributed to the negligence of the parish clergy, who left catechistic instruction to their assistants and were content with rote memorization.[48]

De la Cruz's criticisms of the Third Council catechism could be interpreted as ammunition in political conflicts and rivalries that had other causes—Archbishop Villagómez had clearly been stepping on people's toes in these years. However, the criticisms of the pastoral system were unusually harsh and came from high places. De la Cruz's attack on the Third Lima Council texts is far more radical than any of the previous criticisms, which never went as far as claiming that they contained doctrinal errors or that the translators were poor theologians. The 1650s were thus a time of intensified debate over the adequacy of vernacular instruction such as had not been seen since the 1570s. One would expect this debate to have led to a new spate of publications of pastoral texts—in fact, de la Cruz was calling for better linguistic training among the clergy. Instead, it appears to have had precisely the opposite effect: if vernacular instruction was considered so inadequate even after the recent boom in pastoral publications, there may have been a crisis of confidence in the utility of such instruction. As seen, the key works of the late 1640s were characterized by an increased pessimism concerning Indian Christianity, as if their providential window of opportunity for salvation as a people was rapidly closing (in any case, this is what Avila, Avendaño, and Molina wanted their flocks to believe). More specifically, the debate over instruction, and especially Francisco de la Cruz's claims that the whole system was flawed, may have made it temporarily difficult to obtain permission to publish Quechua texts.

Clearly, however, one should look for more long-term factors than this crisis. First, it can be suggested that the growing difficulty of maintaining Tridentine standards of catechesis and sacramentation as a result of the gradual breakdown of the reducción and parish system discouraged the clergy from investing much time and effort in developing new vernacular texts. In order to escape tribute and labor drafts, Indians were leaving their formal reducción pueblos to live in smaller, more dispersed settlements known as *estancias* or *anejos*, often returning to their original pre-reducción settlements. This process had been going on since the creation of the reducciones, but seems to have reached a tipping point around the middle of the seventeenth century. The reducción model itself came to be regarded as a chimera: whereas Archbishops Fernando de Arias Ugarte and Gonzalo de Campo had attempted to enforce reducción in the 1620s and 1630s (Campo even carried out resettlements in person during his visitas),[49] in 1663 Villagómez advised the king *against* a proposal for a large scale "re-reducción" on the grounds that it was no longer possible to identify which Indians belonged to which pueblos.[50] Many were abandoning their home parishes entirely, moving into other areas where they lived under the legal category of *forastero* or "outsider" (cf. Wightman 1990, chapter 2). By the middle of the seventeenth century most parishes had large populations of forasteros who formally belonged to other parishes and thus could not be ministered to properly. Migration and the growth of informal settlements were also causing jurisdictional conflicts between parishes, as these settlements were located in the periphery and drew their population from different areas—typically, a large estancia in parish "A" was inhabited largely by forasteros from parish "B."[51]

As the original system of watertight pastoral jurisdictions was breaking down, it was no longer possible for priests to keep a close tab on their parishioners. At the same time, the functions of the priest and his deputies were being taken over by Indian cofradías, which were proliferating as a result of the dispersal process. Although the church sought to limit cofradías to one or two per reducción pueblo, in many areas each ayllu or estancia had its own by the middle of the seventeenth century. The formal purpose of the cofradías was to organize and finance the cult of a specific saint and offer suffrages for deceased members, but they also carried out catechetical and liturgical functions in the absence of the priest. They allowed ayllus and estancias to elude the pastoral regime while maintaining formally Christian lives that required only occasional involvement by a priest. The multiplication of cofradías was aided by the notorious cupidity of the parish priests, since they received payments from each cofradía for saying mass on its feast days. In doing so, they were devolving control over everyday catechesis and liturgy to more or less autonomous Indian agents.[52]

Second, Estenssoro Fuchs suggests that the mid-seventeenth century marked a sea change in colonial attitudes towards the república de indios, in that the Christianization process was increasingly regarded as complete (Estenssoro Fuchs 2003: 243–244). This interpretation seems hard to reconcile with the pessimism of sermon discourse in the 1640s or the calls to arms over lack of instruction in the 1650s. However, it is supported by a variety of other developments of the late seventeenth century. There were growing demands for the ordination of Indians, which would become a reality in the late eighteenth century (Marzal 1983: 324–325), and even for a proposed Indian saint—Nicolás de Ayllon, whose canonization process began in 1683 but was never concluded (Estenssoro Fuchs 2003: 468–492). In 1674 the pueblo of San Sebastián de Huaraz asked the archdiocese for the right to observe the full range of feast days rather than the shortened list for Indians because, they claimed, they were now Christians—*como los españoles*.[53] The petition was not successful, but the mere fact that it was made and heard is indicative of a changed climate. Mills has pointed to the continuation of the extirpation campaigns into the early eighteenth century, contrary to the common perception that they did not extend beyond the 1660s, but by his own account extirpation became increasingly unpopular within the colonial establishment during the 1650s and 1660s (Mills

1997: 157–169). While Indian elites and inhabitants of the Spanish towns and the larger pueblos were gaining recognition of their condition as bona fide Christians, the attitude towards the majority of the Indian population, who were increasingly being left to their own devices in pastoral terms, is best characterized as one of resignation—they were as Christian as they were capable of becoming.

The late seventeenth and eighteenth centuries were not, of course, devoid of new pastoral works in Quechua, and a brief discussion of what has reached us from this period will help bring Part I of this book to a close. There seems to have been a small renaissance during the 1690s and the first decade of the eighteenth century whose circumstances I have not investigated. There is a 1690 grammar by Juan de Aguilar, a canon at the Lima cathedral, which went unpublished, and in 1691 the cathedral chair, Esteban Sancho de Melgar, published his own Quechua grammar. Sancho de Melgar also left a 248-folio manuscript, held at the Colombian national archive, which contains paraphrases of the gospel passages from the missal (Rivet and Créqui-Montfort 1951: 130–131). In 1701 the Jesuit Juan de Figueredo published a reedition of Torres Rubio's 1619 grammar and dictionary, to which he added the cartilla and a brief Chinchaysuyo lexicon (Torres Rubio and Figueredo 1701).

In 1705 another Jesuit, Gaspar Manuel, published a reedition of Pablo de Prado's *Directorio espiritual* under the title *Selectas de el directorio espiritual.* This text could be considered a new work, as it contains only a minority of the texts in the *Directorio espiritual* and adds many more from various sources. On several occasions it replaces prayers that were in the *Directorio espiritual* with equivalent ones from Pérez Bocanegra's ritual. Most of the hymns and litanies of the original edition were omitted, but Manuel's edition contains a long passion hymn titled *Romances de la passion de N. Señor Iesu Christo,* which does not appear in earlier texts. Most interestingly, the book ends with a long list of editorial corrections: the manuscript had been revised by Quechua experts in Cuzco, but their corrections had arrived too late to change the printing so they were simply added as an appendix. Most of the corrections are of an orthographic nature, but others ask for the omission or replacement of unorthodox terms employed in texts originally published by Prado and Pérez Bocanegra (Prado and Manuel 1705).

A second rebirth of interest in pastoral Quechua came in the mid-eighteenth century. In 1754 the archbishop of Lima, Pedro Antonio de Barroeta y Angel, issued a decree ordering priests to study Quechua and warning that both parish priests and ordainees would be examined for their Quechua expertise. Noting that the Hispanization policy of the crown had not had the desired effects, Barroeta y Angel had resurrected the practice of examining candidates for parishes in Quechua (Lima Synods 1987: 398–400). That same year an unnamed Jesuit published a third edition of Torres Rubio's grammar and dictionary. This edition included a greatly expanded Chinchaysuyo section, with a much larger lexicon and a more detailed commentary on Chinchaysuyo grammar that were contributed by the cleric Bernardo de Zubieta y Rojas, Quechua chair at the university, *examinador sinodal,* and a canon of the Lima cathedral (Torres Rubio, Figueredo, et al. 1754).

The issue of vernacular instruction came up again in the Sixth Lima Council of 1772—the first provincial council to be held since 1601 (the Fourth and Fifth Lima Councils were minor affairs). The council ordered the composition and translation into Quechua of a brief catechism which followed closely in the Third Council tradition and was printed in 1773, while also requiring the use of the *Doctrina christiana y catecismo.* A reedition of the Spanish and Quechua texts of the *Tercero cathecismo* was published under the authority of the council that same year (Vargas Ugarte ed. 1951–1954: II 19, 21; Sixth Lima Council 1772; Rivet and Créqui-Montfort 1951: 170–173). The fact that, at a time when calls for uniformity in vernacular catechesis were being heard once again, a provincial council should have fallen back on a corpus of texts that was almost two hundred years old is symptomatic of the lack of official investment in pastoral translation during the second half of the colonial period.

In sharp contrast to the seventeenth century, the eighteenth century is more abundant in Quechua manuscripts than printed texts. These manuscripts are mostly anonymous and undated compilations of catechisms, prayers, and hymns (Rivet and Créqui-Montfort 1951: 200–221). Most of the texts were copied from sixteenth- and seventeenth-century sources, but there are some novelties. The lengthiest such manuscript—an adaptation of Prado's devotional manual titled *Quaderno de directorio espiritual,* which Paul Rivet obtained in Cuzco and dated to the late eighteenth century—contains litanies and versified translations of the psalms *Miserere* and *De profundis* that do not appear in older texts. The *Quaderno de directorio espiritual* also evidences the linguistic changes which occurred in Cuzco Quechua after the mid-seventeenth century, primarily the lenition of syllable-final stops (Quaderno de directorio espiritual n.d.). A contemporary manuscript of very similar content has recently been found in Ayacucho (colonial Huamanga), and it too has versions of psalms, as well as of the hymns of the canonical hours *Sacris solemnis* and *Dies irae* (Untitled Devotionary n.d.).[54] Like the *Quaderno de directorio espiritual,* this manuscript reflects the dialectal peculiarities of its region of origin. The proliferation of manuscripts and the paucity of the printed literature indicate that Quechua liturgy and catechesis had ceased to be a concern of the church and were being carried on at a more informal level. It seems likely that many of these manuscripts were written by and circulated among Indians, as they often do not contain Spanish versions, and what Spanish texts they do contain have errors that could not have been made by a literate Spanish speaker.

The outstanding characteristic of the eighteenth-century literature as a whole is its dialectal diversity (Torero 1995). The 1701 and 1754 reeditions of Torres Rubio's grammar and dictionary are the only known colonial texts that provide anything like a grammatical and lexical description of Central Quechua. It was also during this period that the first pastoral texts in the Quechua varieties of modern Ecuador and Bolivia appeared.[55] The manuscripts from Cuzco and Huamanga differ noticeably from Standard Colonial Quechua and present many of the features of the modern varieties of each area. Something similar can be said of the earliest manuscripts of the colonial plays, which reflect the linguistic changes undergone by Cuzco Quechua (Mannheim 1991: 147–152). The question is to what extent Standard Colonial Quechua continued to be widely studied or used. It is very much alive in the *Selectas de el directorio espiritual* (Prado and Manuel 1705), could be taught with the reeditions of Torres Rubio's work, and the Sixth Lima Council adhered to it strongly. However, it was becoming something of a relic even in Christian discourse, and most Quechua writers tended to fall back on their native spoken varieties. The institutional and ideological contexts that had allowed it to flourish and become a written standard both within and without the church no longer existed.

PART II

Texts

Chapter 6

Pastoral Quechua Linguistics

Issues concerning pastoral Quechua dialectology, terminology, genres, and poetics have been touched on many times in the preceding chapters, but only in passing and in the course of a broad historical narrative. From here on the book takes the reverse approach: the texts themselves are the starting point. Their formal characteristics are examined in detail in order to substantiate and expand on what has been said about the nature and development of pastoral Quechua in Part I. As always, individual texts are approached from a comparative perspective, asking how they express divergent approaches to the practice of Christian translation and the broader issues surrounding it. This chapter deals with the basic linguistic features of the texts—grammar, dialectology and orthography, and Christian terminology—giving way to a discussion of genre and style in chapter 7.

How Quechua Was Pastoral Quechua?

Pastoral Quechua can be considered a new and distinctive "language" at many important levels. It was a written medium whose oral instantiations were closely tied to printed or manuscript books, and it had unique and novel vocabulary, genre models, and stylistic and performance characteristics. Standard Colonial Quechua can be thought of as a new linguistic variety, though only in the limited sense that it was a standardization of an existing one—its "Chinchaysuyoist" or Central Quechua–influenced forms were especially distinctive because of their combinations of Southern and (limited) Central elements. The question dealt with in this section is to what degree pastoral Quechua texts diverged from basic, common Quechua grammatical patterns through misuse or adaptation to European patterns. This is a reasonable question to ask, considering that pastoral Quechua was the creation of individuals who were Spanish speakers first and foremost, and that many modern forms of Quechua show substantial influence from Spanish at grammatical levels—e.g., the use of the Spanish nominal plural *-s* rather than Quechua /-kuna/ in some Bolivian varieties.

Quechua grammatical patterns differ radically from those familiar to speakers of most European languages. First, grammatical relations are expressed primarily by suffixes, so that word order is very flexible. Second, there are a number of grammatical categories in Quechua that seem exotic from a European perspective, such as the distinction between the inclusive and exclusive forms of the first-person plural, and the evidential suffixes that specify the source of the information being conveyed by the speaker.[1] To this day the use of a number of common suffixes is poorly understood, and the explanations provided in modern grammars and teaching manuals are often misleading or erroneous. Colonial linguists such as Domingo de Santo Tomás and Diego González Holguín were especially prone to misinterpreting and misrepresenting grammatical categories because they worked within a Latinate framework. Nonetheless, González Holguín's work in particular surpasses most modern texts in its level of detail and pragmatic richness, and has much to contribute to our understanding of how some of the more obscure suffixes work in present-day varieties.

Although there has been little discussion of the issue, some Quechua scholars have suggested that pastoral texts reflect lack of understanding of Quechua grammar and/or interference from Spanish. Sabine Dedenbach-Salazar Sáenz has gone farthest in developing this line of analysis, arguing that the linguists created a distinctive, grammatically incorrect form of Quechua that was then assimilated by the author-translators (1997a: 314–315). She specifies that there was a tendency to underuse or misuse discourse-level suffixes (also called enclitic or independent suffixes)—a group of suffixes that can be attached to different word classes, operate at the phrasal level, and serve a variety of functions, including conjunction, topic-marking and contrast, and source of information marking (evidentiality) (see Mannheim 1991: 242). Dedenbach-Salazar Sáenz also argues that there was a preference for lexical rather than morphological resources for syntactic conjunction and subordination (1997a: 310).

However, these arguments concerning the ungrammaticality or grammatical distinctiveness of pastoral Quechua are based on a very small sample of texts, and numerous counterexamples could be presented for each alleged case of divergence from normal Quechua patterns.[2] There certainly *are* pastoral texts which were translated in a very literal fashion from a Spanish or Latin original, thus resulting in awkward syntax and a heavier reliance on lexical forms of subordination of the sort that Dedenbach-Salazar Sáenz describes. This is most clearly the case with Avendaño's sermons, and it is no coincidence that he was one of the few author-translators we know to have learned Quechua as an adult. However, these features should not be generalized to pastoral Quechua as a whole. Most of the author-translators were native speakers who would have been unaffected by the errors of the linguists. And while the latter did indeed misrepresent the more unfamiliar categories because they were trying to squeeze them into a Latin framework, this does not mean that they did not know how to use them in communicative practice, which is an entirely different activity.

The use of the evidential suffixes in the pastoral texts, however, requires further discussion both because of the complexity of the topic and because these suffixes will come up again in chapter 9. By most accounts, Southern Quechua (like other varieties of Quechua) has a paradigm of three evidential suffixes, /-mi/, /-si/, and /-cha/, which the speaker uses to specify the source of the information contained in the utterance by selecting the appropriate suffix and tagging it on to a key word. "Direct-witness" /-mi/ indicates direct observation, "reportative" /-si/ implies verbal report, and "conjectural" /-cha/ indicates the absence of either source of information. These suffixes were consistently misrepresented by the colonial linguists, as there was no slot for them in their tradition of grammatical description. Santo Tomás, for instance, approached them as a rhetorical device, claiming that /-mi/ has "no meaning" (which, in terms of semantico-referential meaning, is true) but can be used to "adorn" a sentence—*adorna mucho la tal oración* (Santo Tomás 1995 [1560]: 133).

Itier was perhaps the first to comment on the fact that pastoral Quechua texts "systematically narrate events not witnessed by the authors (for instance, biblical accounts) with the . . . direct suffix."[3] Dedenbach-Salazar Sáenz mentions the prevalence of the direct-witness marker in the Third Lima Council's sermons as an example of the incorrect use of discourse-level suffixes in the pastoral literature (1997a: 310), and Torero notes that in both the Quechua and Aymara versions of the council's *Doctrina christiana y catecismo* there is "no sign of the 'reportative' or 'conjectural' [suffixes], features so characteristic of these languages, and . . . there is an abusive use of the assertive [i.e., direct-witness suffix], which is misunderstood."[4] A study of modern pastoral discourse in Aymara, which has a very similar evidential system, includes the use of direct-witness evidential marking in a list of alleged grammatical errors routinely committed by missionaries (Briggs 1981: 181–182).

While there are, in fact, a number of instances where the reportative suffix /-si/ is used (these instances will be discussed in chapter 9), pastoral texts do tend to employ direct-witness evidential marking (/-mi/) exclusively. Does this reflect a misuse of the evidential system? Would the audience of a priest delivering an Easter sermon be led to believe that he had actually witnessed the death and resurrection of Christ, or was claiming to have done so, by his liberal use of the suffix /-mi/? A first problem with this view concerns participation frames—the relationship between a performer or author and a text. It is not always easy to identify the "speaker" presupposed in the standard definitions of the evidential categories (cf. Mannheim and Van Vleet 1998: 335 on participation frames).

Some pastoral Quechua texts, such as those in the cartilla, came from biblical or other canonical sources and were to be repeated literally, in which case the use of direct-witness marking does not seem to present a problem—it corresponds to the perspective of the original speaker or author. The issue emerges more clearly in pastoral Quechua texts that were composed in Peru by identifiable individuals—in other words, the bulk of the corpus. By a strict interpretation of the evidential categories they should have used the reportative suffix /-si/, since they were transmitting information they had received by verbal report. These texts were also, however, the voice of the church. Francisco de Avila, for instance, has a clear authorial voice in his sermons and sometimes introduces autobiographical references, but his sermons were still an official statement of church dogma which was to be retransmitted by countless parish priests, each of whom would be acting as the ostensible author. How evidentiality works in genres where there is no single identifiable "speaker" is a difficult question—the modern grammatical descriptions have been based solely on the observation of conversational speech and thus presuppose such a speaker—so it is not easy to qualify any particular use as "incorrect."

The question of direct-witness marking in the pastoral literature is further revealed to be a false problem when one notes that the evidential system itself is far more flexible than most linguists have assumed. This is suggested by Martina Faller's analysis of modern Cuzco Quechua evidentiality (2002)—the first in-depth study of Quechua evidentiality, much of which is confirmed by my own informal observations of Ayacucho Quechua. Faller argues that the use of direct-witness /-mi/ indicates that "the speaker possesses the *best possible* source of information for the type of information conveyed by the utterance" (ibid.: 123, my emphasis). In other words, /-mi/ does not necessarily indicate that the speaker has or is implicitly claiming to have direct knowledge of an event or state of affairs—this depends on what Faller calls "evidential licensing conditions" (ibid.: 130). For certain types of information, which Faller calls "personal information," a speaker is expected to use /-mi/ only if she or he directly witnessed an event, but for other types that are not directly observable, which Faller calls "encyclopedic information," it is sufficient for the speaker to have the information on good authority. This includes history, news, and things learned at school or, indeed, in church (ibid.: 133–135, chapter 4). Such licensing conditions are established culturally, and in the cultural context of pastoral Quechua the use of direct-witness evidential marking in discussing Christian dogmas or narratives would have been fully licensed.

Dialectology and Orthography: Preliminary Issues

Questions of dialectology—for example, from what particular spoken varieties the author-translators drew the basic linguistic code they were working with, the degree to which they modified and standardized it, and the degree to which their writings reflected linguistic diversity—are essential for understanding the development of pastoral Quechua. Dialectology is very telling of the role it was intended to have in indigenous society—whether it was meant to be an easily assimilated vernacular or a semi-hieratic language to which its recipients had to be assimilated instead. Dialectological choices reflect general pastoral strategies and broad perceptions of target language(s) and culture(s), and are tied to just about every other level of translation practice. In previous chapters I suggested that the development of Standard Colonial Quechua as an exclusive dialectal standard reflected ideological preconceptions—especially a tendency to hierarchize languages on the basis of concepts of origin and civility—but was primarily inspired by a desire to maintain control over vernacular Christian speech.

Orthography, a seemingly minor topic that has not come up much so far, is discussed in tandem with dialectology. Determining how to use the Roman alphabet to represent Quechua sounds was one of the most basic and also most complex steps in the development of Quechua as a written language. While orthography and dialectology are two separate issues, an understanding of the first is necessary for an understanding of the second. Thus, scholars of Quechua historical linguistics have expended considerable effort in unraveling the orthographic practices of the authors of the pastoral Quechua literature—if these practices are not understood, the texts have little value as witnesses to the varieties they represent, at least at the phonological level. In particular, it is important to be able to distinguish between variations in spelling that are purely orthographic, and those that reflect different phonological systems and hence different language varieties (cf. Cerrón-Palomino 1987; Mannheim 1991). Additionally, orthography is not a neutral, merely technical matter. It is one of the most prominent features of any text or writing practice and carries a variety of cultural, social, and political associations and stigmas—seemingly straightforward orthographic choices are often subjects of considerable debate and even conflict. Orthographies do indeed often have "political" programs behind them that facilitate certain types of readers and reading practices over others (cf. Calvet 1998 [1987], chapter 14; Schieffelin and Doucet 1998).

Some general comments on the intersection between Quechua phonology and Spanish orthography are necessary before discussing individual authors.[5] A first point is that the linguists and author-translators did not simply apply the Roman alphabet to Quechua: they applied it specifically as it was used to write Spanish. In other words, Quechua sounds were usually represented with the letters or combinations of letters used for the Spanish sounds that most resembled them. If Portuguese, Italian, or French missionaries had taken on the task of "reducing" Quechua to writing, they would have employed very different orthographies. For instance, the Quechua palatal nasal sound would have been written {nh} or {gn} rather than {ñ}. A series of digraphs were used in accordance with Spanish conventions: e.g., {ch}, which has the same value as in English, {ll}, the palatal lateral, and {qu}, used for the velar stop (the "hard" *c* sound) before {e} or {i} (as in English, {c} serves as a sibilant in those contexts). In other words, reading colonial Quechua texts is much easier if one already reads Spanish. This is true even of the modern phonological alphabet, which in general has a much closer letter-to-phoneme correspondence (note the continued use of the digraphs {ch} and {ll}).

The real problems arose when it came to representing phonological oppositions which had no equivalents or correspondences in Spanish. Both Central and Southern varieties had an opposition between a velar and a uvular stop—between /k/ and /q/, as they are written in the modern phonological alphabet. There is no such distinction in Spanish (or English), which only has the velar stop ("hard" *c*). Also unprecedented for Spanish ears were the glottalized and aspirate forms of the stops /ch, /k/, /p/, /q/, and /t/—in other words, /ch'/ and /chh/, /k'/ and /kh/, /p'/ and /ph/, /q'/ and /qh/, and /t'/ and /th/—which were restricted to Southern Quechua, and probably to only some forms of it (particularly those of the Cuzco region; see Mannheim 1991: 122–123). Typically, the velar-uvular and plain-glottalized-aspirate stop oppositions were not represented effectively in colonial orthographies, if at all. The main resource employed in this respect was the digraph, that is, a double letter, such as {tt} for /t'/.

The Quechua vowels presented the opposite problem, in that the Spanish used *more* symbols to write them than was necessary. Southern Quechua has three vowels—/a/, /i/, and /u/—but until very recently was always written with five orthographic vowels: {a}, {e}, {i}, {o}, and {u}. Coming from a five-vowel system, the Spanish tended to hear two different vowels each in the allophonic variations of /i/ and /u/, which they recorded as {e} or {i}, and {o} or {u}, respectively. In recent decades attempts have been made to impose a three-vowel orthography for Quechua, but there has been much opposition (Mannheim 1991: 235–236).[6]

One of the most complex issues in Quechua historical linguistics concerns the sibilants, as both the Quechua and the Spanish sibilant systems were undergoing change during the colonial period (the changes in Spanish phonology affected Spanish perceptions and orthographic representations of similar Quechua sounds). Regardless of their phonetic properties, it is clear that sixteenth-century Southern Quechua distinguished between a sibilant written {c, ç, z} and another written {s, ss} in the colonial texts, while in Central Quechua the latter was substituted by a sibilant written {x}, almost certainly a palatal sibilant (like the English sound *sh*). Following Taylor and others, I represent these three sibilants in phonological notation as /s/, /ŝ/, and /sh/, respectively (Taylor 2000d [1985]: 43–44).

The main point to bear in mind is that /ŝ/ {s, ss} and /sh/ {x} were dialectal variants of each other—one of the many shibboleths between Central and Southern varieties. While Central Quechua varieties maintained a sibilant distinction, the Southern Quechua sibilants merged to a single sibilant during the colonial period—indeed, the orthographic distinction breaks down in most of the mid-century texts.[7]

Dialectology and Orthography up to the Third Lima Council

To recapitulate, there is some agreement that Santo Tomás's descriptive works, as well as the brief Quechua texts included in them, correspond to a variety of Quechua spoken on the central coast that disappeared during the colonial period.[8] It has also been suggested that the Incas employed a lingua franca that was of coastal rather than southern highland origin, and that the coastal varieties had long acquired a "vehicular" status (Cerrón-Palomino 1988, 1989, 1995a; Taylor 2000d [1985]; Torero 1974).[9] Mannheim has objected to the first interpretation, pointing out that Santo Tomás's dictionary "culled items indiscriminately from among the Quechua languages" and was criticized by Guaman Poma for this dialectal mix (Mannheim 1991: 260 n. 13). However, Santo Tomás's ecumenicism in recording lexical variants does not mean that his linguistic work as a whole lacked a specific base dialect—it seems far too coherent for that.

The most visible characteristic of Santo Tomás's Quechua is the voicing of the stops in the vicinity of /n/ and /m/. For instance, the second-person subject was written *-ngui* /-ngi/ rather than *-nqui* /-nki/, and the third-person subject future *-nga* /-nga/ rather than *-nca* /-nqa/. It also had a more complex stress system than Southern Quechua—i.e., stress did not fall regularly on the penultimate syllable (several different rules for the placement of stress are laid out in Santo Tomás 1995 [1560]: 157–169). Both features were mentioned in the linguistic appendix to the Third Council's *Doctrina christiana y catecismo* as characteristic of the speech of the Chinchaysuyos and of those who spoke Quechua "corruptly" (Third Lima Council 1985a [1584]: 168). Santo Tomás's Quechua was primarily Southern in lexicon, but may have had significant Central elements. While his dictionary was dialectally inclusive, frequently presenting both Central and Southern forms (Taylor 2001b: 432), the Central term is sometimes preferred over the Southern one.[10]

Santo Tomás's orthography was broadly similar to later ones. In his view, the Spanish alphabet required no modifications to be applied to Quechua—God had providentially made the sounds of the two languages very similar (Santo Tomás 1995 [1560]: 8–9). He did not attempt to distinguish between /k/ and /q/, employing {c} or {qu} (before {e} and {i}) for both, and like every other colonial-period writer he used all five Spanish vowels. The main purely orthographic feature that distinguishes Santo Tomás's writings from the later literature is the use of {gu} for /w/ before /a/, as in *guaca* rather than *huaca* for /waka/ 'divinity.' Additionally, Santo Tomás's use of the {e-i} and {o-u} oppositions is very different from that of later writers, primarily because it seems unsystematic. Whereas later authors used {e} and {o} to represent allophonic variations in /i/ and /u/ produced by the proximity of /q/, this is not the case in Santo Tomas's writings, where {e} and {o} appear far more frequently and in contexts where there could be no /q/ to account for them—for instance, the nominal plural /-kuna/ is consistently written *-cona* rather than *-cuna*. On the other hand, {i} and {u} appear in the vicinity of what should have been /q/s. This has led to suggestions that the /k-q/ opposition had disappeared in the variety of Quechua described by Santo Tomás, but it seems more likely that his use of the {e-i} and {o-u} oppositions was simply unsystematic (cf. Cerrón-Palomino 1989).

The relation between the variety described by Santo Tomás and the Inca lingua franca is open to debate because of the scarcity of testimonies for the latter—primarily, scattered Quechua words and utterances recorded in the early Spanish chronicles, especially Betanzos's (1987 [1551]: 32, 100, 101, 111, 131), and Quechua loan words assimilated into Peruvian Spanish at an early stage, such as *inga* 'Inca,' *hatun luna* 'tribute-payer' or 'commoner,' and *oxota* 'sandal.' This information suggests that the lingua franca shared some important features with the variety described by Santo Tomás, but also differed from it. While stops were voiced in the vicinity of /n/ and /m/, the lingua franca variety also seems to have been characterized by features that are not attested in Santo Tomás's writings: a word-initial /r/>/l/ change, the elision of the agentive suffix /-q/, and the use of {x} (/sh/) in lieu of {s, ss} (/ŝ/) (Cerrón-Palomino 1988: 128–132, 1989; Taylor 2000d [1985]: 37; Torero 1974: 132–133). While Santo Tomás does on occasion use {x}, Taylor has noted that he only does so with very commonly-used words such as *xuti* 'name' and *xamu-* 'come.' He suggests that {x} (/sh/) was the native form of Santo Tomás's base variety but that he preferred to use {s} (/ŝ/) because it derived from a prestige variety (Taylor 2001b: 433). However, it seems more likely that {s} (/ŝ/) was used in the variety described by Santo Tomás, and that palatal {x} (/sh/) was introduced in a few common words because of influence from the lingua franca.[11]

These differences could be attributed to the (unknown) dialectology of the central Peruvian coast. Whereas the Inca lingua franca was said to have come from the Chincha area, to the south of Lima, Santo Tomás's works may reflect Lima usage (cf. Cerrón-Palomino 1995a: xii, xvi). The Inca lingua franca could also have developed through a process of koinéization between coastal and highland varieties, assuming phonological characteristics of some Central varieties such as the /r/>/l/ change and the use of {x} (/sh/). Finally, it is possible that the Quechua described by Santo Tomás lay within an acceptable range of variation for the lingua franca—for instance, the /r/>/l/ change is not represented in Betanzos's texts, which in this respect coincide with Santo Tomás's.

There is scattered evidence that the Inca lingua franca continued to be used as the primary medium of colonial communication into the 1560s. A 1563 lawsuit against a mestizo interpreter mentioned on several occasions that he used the word *landi* ('to sell') to translate the Spanish term *perpetuidad* in an información held among Indian nobles to determine the viability of a plan to make the *encomiendas* perpetual. [12] The interpreter was accused by a judge of the Lima audiencia of mistranslating the proposal, with the result that his indigenous audience believed that the king intended to "sell" them to their *encomenderos* (encomienda recipients). In his defense, the interpreter alleged that the confusion arose from the impossibility of translating the concept of perpetuity, and that the closest he could get was *landi*. While some of the proceedings were carried out in Huamanga, the language the interpreter used was identified as *la lengua general del Cuzco del inga*.[13] The form /landiy/ (Southern Quechua /rantiy/) reflects two of the phonological characteristics of the Inca lingua franca—the word-initial /r/>/l/ change and the voicing of stops after nasals—only one of which appears in the variety recorded by Santo Tomás, who writes *randiy* (Santo Tomás 1951 [1560]: 346). The multiple occurrences of the form *landi* in the court case are open to two interpretations: either the defendant did indeed use it to address Indian nobles in both the Huamanga and Cuzco areas, or this was simply the form to which the Spanish notary who wrote down the proceedings was accustomed. In either case, this document provides another piece of evidence for Torero's proposed Inca lingua franca and its continuity into the early colonial period.

The Quechua prayers recorded by Cristóbal de Molina in Cuzco in the early 1570s are the earliest texts that can be considered Southern Quechua. Although the extant manuscript contains copy errors, it is clear that these texts do not reflect features of the old lingua franca such as the voicing of stops or the presence of {x}. The contrast between Molina's texts and those recorded in the 1540s and 1550s by Betanzos, who was also based in Cuzco, points to a shift from the lingua franca to the local form of Southern Quechua in Spanish understandings of what the "language of the Inca" was. The revisions to the official pastoral texts of the diocese of Cuzco which were carried out around Molina's time of writing seem to have included the use of orthographic signs to represent glottalized and aspirate stops, and could be interpreted as a "Cuzqueñization" of earlier lingua franca texts. It seems likely that such changes reflect the abandonment of the lingua franca by the Inca elite itself, as the older generations died off and the younger ones adopted local Quechua.

The Southern character of Standard Colonial Quechua as codified in the Third Council texts is clear. In order to judge its relation specifically to the Quechua of Cuzco it is necessary to take into account the latter's late colonial transformations as described by Mannheim (1991). During the second half of the colonial period, Cuzco Quechua underwent a process of lenition of syllable-final stops which resulted in the modification of many suffixes, such as the second-person plural /-chik/, which became /-chis/, or the progressive aspect /-chka/, which became /-ska/ and eventually /-sha/.[14] Other phonological and morphological characteristics that can make the language of the Third Council texts seem alien to modern Cuzco Quechua speakers can also be put down to historical change: (1) there were two sibilants—/s/ {c, ç, z} and /ŝ/ {s}—where modern Cuzco Quechua has only /s/; (2) the suffixes /-yku/ and /-rqu/ did not lose their consonants or undergo a /u/>/a/ change before the suffixes /-mu/, /-pu/, and /-chi/; (3) some words and suffixes had /ñ/ where modern Cuzco Quechua has /n/, or (word-finally) /m/ rather than /n/; and (4) there was a variant /-i/ of the "empty" or "euphonic" suffix /-ni/ that appeared after /q/, /ŝ/, and /r/, which no longer exists.[15]

The lexicon of the Third Lima Council texts almost always falls on the Cuzco side of the modern Ayacucho-Cuzco dialectal divide. Even when it comes to semantic differences between terms present in both modern Cuzco and Ayacucho Quechua, the conciliar usage always coincides with the Cuzco usage. For instance, in the conciliar texts the use of the verb /khuya-/ or /kuya-/ seems closer to the modern Cuzqueño sense ('to have compassion for') than to its Ayacuchano sense ('to love'). The verb /yacha-/ means simply 'to know,' without the added meaning of 'to reside' that it has in Ayacucho Quechua (in modern Cuzco Quechua, as in the conciliar texts, 'to reside' is /tiya-/, which also means 'to sit,' while in Ayacucho Quechua /tiya-/ only has this last meaning). One apparent exception is the use of the term /yaku/ 'water,' which is absent from modern Cuzco Quechua, where /unu/ is used. The /unu/-/yaku/ doublet is the most prominent point of lexical differentiation between modern Cuzco and Ayacucho Quechua (as in other cases, the Ayacucho form corresponds to the Central Quechua one). However, the Third Council texts use *yacu* and *unu* interchangeably, as do most colonial texts.

While it is not clear to what extent Southern Quechua had differentiated along modern lines such as the Ayacucho-Cuzco divide at the time of the council, the dialectology of the conciliar texts suggests that we can take seriously the claims that they were based specifically on the Quechua of Cuzco (cf. the mid-seventeenth-century dialectological debate discussed in chapter 4). But if this is the case, why does the linguistic appendix of the *Doctrina christiana y catecismo* state that the translators tailored their Quechua for intelligibility among the inhabitants of the coast and of the highland areas north of Huamanga (Third Lima Council 1985a [1584]: 167)? This suggests that they incorporated forms from the Central and coastal varieties in an effort to develop some kind of koiné, but this was not the case. Not only is there an absence of forms that can be identified as foreign to sixteenth-century Cuzco Quechua in the conciliar corpus, but immediately after making this ecumenical statement the translators went on to proscribe a long list of forms—along with "other details" (*otras menudencias*) which are not mentioned—that seems to exclude anything distinctively coastal or Central Quechua. It includes lexical stems such as *tamya-* rather than *para-* ('to rain'); pronunciations such as *hara* rather than *çara* ('maize') and *chili-* rather than *chiri-* ('to be cold'); suffixes such as first-person subject /-y/ rather than /-ni/ and first-person object /-ma/ rather than /-wa/; and stress patterns that differed from that of Cuzco Quechua (ibid.: 167–168). The translators also proscribed the "corrupt" practice of stop voicing and the word-initial /r/>/l/ change, both of which, ironically, were characteristic of the Inca lingua franca (ibid.: 168). There is a patent contradiction between the ecumenical statements contained in the appendix and the persistent dismissal of anything that diverged from *el uso común del Cuzco*. It appears that there was an effort to hide what was evidently a controversial decision—to use Cuzco Quechua as the exclusive base dialect for Christian discourse in Quechua.

What koinéization was carried out consisted of the exclusion of grammatical forms, terms, and expressions which were used in the Cuzco area but were considered extraneous or irregular by the translators, as well as the codification process itself (i.e., the selection and use of a single form where several different ones were used). One of the forms proscribed in the linguistic appendix involved the use of the passive participle /-sqa/ with an active meaning, as a sort of perfective. The example given is *micusca cani* 'I have eaten' (not 'I am eaten'), which is condemned as ungrammatical even though it was common in areas where Quechua was spoken "with perfection."[16] The "correct" form was *micurcani* 'I ate,' which employed the simple past tense suffix /-rqa/ and was less specific (Third Lima Council 1985a [1584]: 167). Standard Colonial Quechua was thus constructed on the basis of abstract criteria of grammatical regularity and correctness, and was sometimes drastically simplified in relation to its oral model.

An effort was made to avoid "the excessive refinement with which some of the inhabitants of Cuzco and the surrounding area use terms and expressions so rare and obscure that they are beyond the bounds of the language that is properly called Quechua, introducing terms that perhaps were used in ancient times and no longer, or taking them from the Incas and lords, or other peoples with whom they deal."[17] The vehemence with which the translators expressed the need to avoid this *lenguaje exquisito* (complicated or unusual language) suggests that they were reacting against previous translation practices, perhaps the official cartilla and catechism of the diocese of Cuzco that was in use at the time of the council. We know next to nothing about these earlier texts, but it seems likely that they were more specifically Cuzqueño in their lexicon than the Third Council texts, since they were designed for use only in the diocese of Cuzco.

What, then, were these terms and expressions the Third Council translators rejected? It is clear that they did not employ a number of verb and noun stems that can be considered common Cuzco Quechua. Examples include /t'aqa-/ 'to separate' (which is not recorded by the 1586 dictionary, but does appear in González Holguín's), /ch'ikllu-/ 'to select,' and /allpa[ri]-/ 'to suffer.' These terms, which were specifically Cuzqueño, also had close pan-Quechua synonyms in Cuzco Quechua (*raquiri-*, *aclla-*, and *ñacari-* or *muchu-*, respectively) which *were* used by the Third Council translators. Their policy was to favor pan-Quechua terms when a choice was available within the Cuzco Quechua lexicon. The policy is expressed more clearly by the Aymara translation team, who seem to have followed very similar guidelines: "an effort was made to use general terms understood among almost all the Aymara-speaking peoples" (*se procuró usar de vocablos generales entendidos en quasi todos los Aymaraes*) (Third Lima Council 1985a [1584]: 175). The preference for *vocablos generales* did not, however, lead the Quechua translators to introduce terms that were alien to Cuzco Quechua. Additionally, Cuzqueño expressions and turns of phrase whose meaning was not easily inferred from their lexical and grammatical components were excluded (multiple examples can be found in González Holguín's works). Again, the result was a simplified and watered-down form of Cuzco Quechua that would have been easier to understand both for speakers of other varieties of Quechua and for Spaniards who were learning Quechua.

However, the linguistic appendix of the *Doctrina christiana y catecismo* states that the *lenguaje exquisito* the translators sought to avoid was archaic and foreign, perhaps derived from the speech of *los ingas y señores*—that is, of the old Inca elite. This brings to mind Cerrón-Palomino's arguments that this elite was multilingual, speaking Puquina and Aymara before it spoke Quechua, as well as the colonial reports of an Inca "secret language," which he believes to have been a Puquina-ized form of Aymara (1999). As will be seen below, some of the postcouncil pastoral texts used arcane terms derived from Inca religious registers which probably had Aymara and Puquina influences. Some of these terms—for instance, epithets such as *chacllipu, tocapu, acnupu, yalliquiri,* and *huallpayhuana,* for which no transparent Quechua etymologies are available—were first recorded in the pseudo-Inca prayers of Cristóbal de Molina, who was almost certainly involved in the revision of the pastoral corpus of the diocese of Cuzco in the early 1570s. It could thus be proposed that this corpus employed such terms as part of an accommodationist translation strategy, and that the Third Council was reacting against this practice on theological more than dialectal grounds.

The orthography of the Third Council texts was designed for maximum simplicity and ease of use (from the perspective of literate Spaniards, that is). Like Santo Tomás, the translators did not attempt to distinguish the uvular from the velar stop directly, but rather employed {c} or {qu} (before {e} and {i}) for both /k/ and /q/. The most obvious purely orthographic change was the decision to represent /w/ in /wa/

with {hu} rather than {gu}, so that /wawa/ 'woman's child' was now written *huahua* rather than *guagua*. In both cases {g} or {h} was used simply to indicate that the {u} should not be read as a vowel, so the change does not indicate a phonological difference. The motives for the change, which was followed without exception in future pastoral texts, are unclear. It may be that the proscription of the coastal variety as written by Santo Tomás—in which {g} was used to represent voiced /k/s and /q/s, as in *inga*—led to an all-out ban of {g}, even in this entirely unrelated context.[18]

But the most significant orthographic change was the systematization of the {e-i} and {o-u} oppositions. In the Third Council texts {o} and {e} were used exclusively to represent allophonic variants of /u/ and /i/ in the vicinity of /q/. If a vowel adjacent to a {c} or {qu} was {o} or {e}, the reader then knew that the stop was a /q/ rather than a /k/—a hyper-differentiation in the vowels was thus used to compensate for a hypo-differentiation in the stops (if the adjacent vowels were all /a/s, however, the ambiguity remained). However, the translators made an exception to this rule: if the /q/ adjacent to an /i/ or /u/ belonged to another morpheme, the variation was not represented. For instance, /yacha-chi-q/ 'teacher' was written *yachachic* rather than *yachachec*, as later writers would do. Clearly, the translators wished to aid the recognizability of different morphemes for Spaniards who were learning Quechua.

The most difficult issue in understanding the Third Council's orthography is the failure to represent the glottalized and aspirate stops of Cuzco Quechua. While the translators indirectly distinguished /k/ and /q/ in most contexts via the adjacent vowels, there was no attempt at all to distinguish plain, glottalized, and aspirate stops. The rationale on this issue was explained as follows in the linguistic appendix of the *Doctrina christiana y catecismo*:

> . . . the greatest difficulty in pronunciation is in these syllables: *ca, que, qui, co, cu, cha, che, chi, cho, chu, ta, te, ti, to, tu*; the Indians pronounce them more roughly or more softly depending on what they mean . . . just as the word *coya* means 'queen,' 'mine' and a certain kind of grass . . . Some wished to use the following differentiation: *ca, cca, ka, csa, ta, tta, tha, cha, chha, ça, zha*, and others of this sort, but the meanings do not concur and the interpreters do not agree among themselves. And so it seemed better to write these syllables in our way, because no rule covers so much diversity in such a way that one may pronounce in accordance with the letters.[19]

The translators were clearly referring to variants of the plain stops /k/, /q/, /ch/, and /t/ that had phonological value, although they failed to mention /p/ and subsumed the velar-uvular opposition with the simple-glottalized-aspirate oppositions (the notations with sibilants—*csa, ça,* and *zha*—are probably misprints). The word *coya* is cited to exemplify the modified forms of /q/: *coya* 'queen' was /quya/, whereas *coya* 'type of grass' (which González Holguín would later write *koya*) was /q'uya/—it is not clear whether *coya* 'mine' was /q'uya/ or /qhuya/.

There was clearly an ongoing debate over whether and how to distinguish glottalized and aspirate from plain stops, and once again the Third Council team seems to be reacting against a "Cuzco tradition" in pastoral translation. When the Cuzco cathedral chapter "reformed" the diocesan cartilla and catechism in the early 1570s, the cleric Melchor del Aguila was assigned the task of transcribing the texts using a new orthography that probably had special notations for the velar-uvular and plain-aspirate-glottalized oppositions (see chapter 2). The wording of del Aguila's información de oficio suggests that he used diacritics of some sort—*puntos y rasgos*—to represent phonemes that had no Spanish equivalents. However, the diacritic marks probably presented printing difficulties, and the most common way of distinguishing plain and glottalized or aspirate stops, as well as the velar from the uvular stop, was the use of digraphs. The discarded notations mentioned in the linguistic appendix of the *Doctrina christiana y catecismo* involve digraphs, as well as {k}, and are reminiscent of the orthographic practice of González Holguín.

The Third Council team considered these notations inadequate because their proponents did not agree among themselves (*no . . . convienen los intérpretes entre sí*), and because they had not succeeded in creating a system which fully accounted for the semantic differences (*no concuerdan las significaciones*). If González Holguín's work can be considered representative of the earlier notations, they were indeed inconsistent, primarily because they had only one notational resource (the digraph) to represent both glottalization and aspiration, as well as the plain-uvular opposition. As the mid-seventeenth–century authors would argue, however, even an unsystematic representation of the glottalized and aspirate stops, and above all of the velar-uvular opposition, would have greatly enhanced the intelligibility of the Third Council texts. The council's emphasis on uniformity and simplicity outweighed such considerations, and the result was a strongly hypodifferentiating orthography in which {c}, for example, could stand for as many as six different phonemes (/k/, /kh/, /k'/, /q/, /qh/, and /q'/) if the adjacent vowels were /a/s.

In short, the translators were not trying to engineer a phonologically simplified form of Cuzco Quechua; they merely chose not to distinguish certain phonemes orthographically for practical reasons (cf. Mannheim 1991: 136). However, it *does* seem possible that the Third Council orthography served as an indication to both priests and parishioners who were not Cuzco Quechua speakers that the use of Standard Colonial Quechua did not necessarily involve the pronunciation of glottalized and aspirate stops. Significantly, the 1586 *Arte y vocabulario*, the linguistic complement to the Third Council corpus and probably the main teaching instrument of the late sixteenth and early seventeenth centuries, makes no reference at all to the existence of glottalized and aspirate stops. In this limited sense a koinéizing intention could be read into the orthography.

Perhaps the most striking feature of the Third Council orthography is the degree to which it presupposed a knowledge of Spanish, and the complications it created for non-Spanish-speaking writers of Quechua. The indigenous writers of the seventeenth century clearly attempted to use it, but had difficulties on two key points: the digraphs {ch} and {hu}, where they tended to mix up the order of the letters or omit one of them,[20] and the {o-u} and {e-i} oppositions, which they used unsystematically. These oppositions were very useful for Spaniards, since {o} and {e} revealed the presence of the uvular stop /q/, but to Quechua speakers who had not fully assimilated the Spanish five-vowel system the variation provoked by /q/ in /i/ and /u/ was imperceptible (Durston 2003: 216; Mannheim 1991: 134; Taylor 2000d [1985]: 47).

Dialectology and Orthography after the Third Lima Council

Three main tendencies are visible in pastoral Quechua dialectology and orthography from the 1590s to the middle of the seventeenth century: (1) faithful adherence to the conciliar norms; (2) an effort to reflect spoken Cuzco Quechua more exactly, which I will refer to as the *Cuzqueñista* tendency; and (3) Chinchaysuyoism (the effort to adapt Standard Colonial Quechua to Central norms). While the Third Council standard was the dominant model, only two Quechua writers chose (or were able) to reproduce it exactly and unwaveringly. Significantly, they were both Jesuits:

Pablo de Prado and Diego de Torres Rubio. Torres Rubio's 1619 grammar-dictionary and Prado's 1641 devotional manual show no significant divergences from the orthographic and dialectal norms of the Third Council. The texts published by Prado do contain some unorthodox religious terms, but this is not really a dialectological issue. The rest of the author-translators show elements of either tendency 2 or 3, to varying degrees. In some cases both are present.

Oré's work is representative in this sense: by and large he adhered very closely to the conciliar norms, but occasionally one finds examples of tendencies 2 and 3. Quechua scholars have noted that the Central terms *tamia* 'rain' and *marca* 'town' sometimes appear in Oré's hymns in alternation with their Southern equivalents *para* and *llacta* (Cerrón-Palomino 1992: 223–224). This should not, however, be interpreted as an attempt to make the texts more intelligible among Central Quechua speakers. The terms always appear alongside their Southern equivalents *para* and *llacta,* and are used as a kind of "poetic filling" for the construction of semantic couplets (see chapter 7). On one occasion Oré even used the Central Quechua ablative case /-pita/ in the sentence *Infiernopita llocsic allcomanta . . . quespichihuaycu* (save us from the hounds that come out from hell) (Oré 1992 [1598]: 354). The Central form was recruited to avoid the cacophonic repetition of its Southern equivalent /-manta/; Oré even alerts his readers to the presence of an extraneous form in this verse by placing the note *Phrasis de chinchay* in the margin.

However, there are other "Chinchaysuyoisms" in Oré's work that cannot be explained in terms of poetic license. His adaptation of the Third Council confesionario, included both in the *Symbolo catholico indiano* and in the *Rituale seu manuale peruanum,* used the Chinchaysuyo term *uria-* 'to work' next to its Southern equivalent *llamca-* (Oré 1992 [1598]: 448, Oré 1607: 150). The version in the *Rituale* contains a note explaining that the term *uria-* was to be used "on the [coastal] plains of the archdiocese [of Lima]" (*en los llanos del arçobispado*). The *Rituale*'s version of the confesionario also contains the dialectal pair *ranti-/rana-* 'to sell,' Santo Tomás being the only colonial lexicographer to have recorded *rana-* (Santo Tomás 1951 [1560]: 346). In these cases the user of the book was to select the term most appropriate for the audience, rather than use both of them.

A further peculiarity that appears in parts of Oré's work is the use of digraphs to distinguish /q/ from /k/ and the glottalized or aspirate from the plain stops. The representation of glottalized and aspirate stops suggests an effort to reproduce more clearly the speech of Cuzco, which was, as Oré put it, the Athens, the Rome, and the Toledo of the Quechua language (Oré 1992 [1598]: 144). While Oré's writings generally adhere to the Third Council orthography, there are texts in the *Rituale* where /q/ is written {cc}, and where /t'/ and /p'/ are written {tt} and {pp}.[21] Even in the *Symbolo catholico indiano* there are some isolated instances of the use of {k} for /q/, as in *kaka* 'rock,' and *rakay* 'ruin' (Oré 1992 [1598]: 378, 375), and of {pp} for /p'/, as in *mappa* 'filth' (ibid.: 422). This indicates that Oré had been accustomed to these notations, which are very similar to those used by González Holguín, but then abandoned them in favor of the Third Council's orthography—the pressures to do so must have been significant when he published the *Symbolo,* so soon after the council. The variant notations that appear in it seem to be remnants that he failed to correct. Even in the *Rituale* they were not used consistently to represent the corresponding phonemes, but were introduced where they were most necessary to resolve semantic ambiguities. In general, the texts in the *Rituale* diverge more frequently from the Third Council standard on orthographic, dialectal, and terminological points than those of the *Symbolo.*[22] It seems that when Oré published the *Symbolo* he adapted his writing very deliberately and carefully to the Third Council norms as a way of giving what was otherwise a fairly revolutionary translation program a more canonical appearance. He did not feel so constrained when he published the *Rituale,* perhaps because of the time lapse and because it was published in Italy.

The Cuzqueñista tendency is best exemplified in the works of González Holguín and Pérez Bocanegra. In Itier's understanding they represent an earlier, more idiosyncratic form of Cuzco Quechua that was disappearing under the effect of the homogenizing linguistic forces unleashed by the Potosí-Lima commercial circuit, one of whose expressions was Standard Colonial Quechua (Itier 2000b and 2001). I concur with Itier on the point that their writings—Pérez Bocanegra's in particular—show significant if subtle divergences from Standard Colonial Quechua, which result from adherence to localist Cuzqueño norms. In my interpretation, however, Standard Colonial Quechua was simply an abstract, literary standard rather than a new variety that was replacing an older Cuzqueño speech.

The most obvious Cuzqueñista aspect of González Holguín's linguistic work was his all-out use of an orthographic system that represented the velar-uvular and plain-glottalized-aspirate oppositions by using the digraphs {cc}, {chh}, {pp}, {tt}, and {qq[u]}, and the letter {k}. Obviously, these notational resources were insufficient to represent the full range of stops, and the system functioned very inconsistently. Not only were there not enough different notations to distinguish all of the phonemes, but the same phonemes were represented with different notations: /q/, for instance, could be written {cc}, {qq[u]}, or {k} depending on the context. Nonetheless, this orthography must have made the reading and pronunciation of pastoral texts much easier for those who knew Cuzco Quechua, above all because the very productive /k/-/q/ opposition was indicated in a regular way. Although González Holguín stated that his dictionary was "the first to use [true] orthography" (*el primero que ṣaca orthographía*) (González Holguín 1989 [1952, 1608]: 9), the appearance of similar notations in Oré's texts and their mention in the linguistic appendix of the *Doctrina christiana y catecismo* indicate that he was simply resurrecting a pre–Third Council practice.

González Holguín's dictionary and grammar were both conceived primarily as tools for preachers, and his break with the Third Council's orthographic standard is part of a broader program to enable priests to preach in a stylistically more elaborate Quechua. He was clearly at odds with the Third Council's tendency to water down and standardize Cuzco Quechua—in his view, preachers should use a language that reflected how the Indians of Cuzco actually spoke. His dictionary, in particular, records a variety of terms, expressions, and turns of phrase that are generally absent from the pastoral literature (with the exception of Pérez Bocanegra's work) and can be considered specifically Cuzqueño. González Holguín was also the only colonial linguist of Quechua to recognize a debt to Indian informants, who were, of course, natives of Cuzco (González Holguín 1989 [1952, 1608]: 8).

Juan Pérez Bocanegra's orthography in the *Ritual formulario* followed the Third Council model with two minor differences: he represented the variation in /i/ and /u/ provoked by /q/ even across morpheme boundaries, so there are more {e}s and {o}s in his writings, and he tended to write syllable-final /y/ with {i} rather than {y} (this change, which became quite widespread in Quechua writing towards the middle of the century, seems to reflect the development of Spanish orthography). More significant divergences can be found at grammatical levels. Itier notes the presence of Aymara morphological elements in Pérez Bocanegra's Quechua, especially the verbal derivational suffix /-qa/ (Itier 2000b: 52).[23] He also tended to drop third person /-n/ after the past tense suffix /-rqa/, writing *-rca* rather than *-rcan* (as had Santo Tomás) (Itier 2000b: 52–54). These morphological deviations from the standard are fairly minor and occur inconsistently. What makes Pérez Bocanegra's Quechua sound alien if one is familiar with the Third Council texts is, above all, its lexicon, and especially the lexicon of the confesionario. It should be emphasized that this impression does not result exclusively from dialectal differences. Like González Holguín, Pérez Bocanegra was invested in reforming pastoral terminology and introduced a variety of terms that did not appear in the Third Council texts, but for reasons that had little to do with dialectology. Additionally, the extraordinary detail of the confesionario in its interrogation of everyday life led to the use of terms which other authors never had occasion to use.

Nonetheless, it *is* clear that Pérez Bocanegra had recourse to parts of the Cuzqueño lexicon which his predecessors deliberately avoided. In such cases, Pérez Bocanegra tended to pair the specifically Cuzqueño term with a close synonym that was used in Standard Colonial Quechua.[24] Some of these terms do not appear even in González Holguín's dictionary. It can be surmised that Pérez Bocanegra provided both terms to aid the use of his book (which was, after all, published in Lima) among populations that had no familiarity with Cuzco Quechua. In sum, the morphological and lexical forms which set Pérez Bocanegra's writings apart from those of the Third Council tradition reflect his adherence to an actual spoken variety with all its inconsistencies rather than the use of a different base dialect.

Alonso de Huerta is the sole explicit proponent of the use of Chinchaysuyo Quechua in the postcouncil literature, but it is possible that he was not as isolated as he seems. The facts that he published a grammar in which he claimed to record Chinchaysuyo forms and that he held both the university and the cathedral chairs for many years indicate that his "Chinchaysuyoist" position had some backing in the archdiocese of Lima. What exactly this position implied, however, is not clear. He was in the habit of approving candidates for the priesthood or for parishes on the basis of a knowledge of Chinchaysuyo Quechua, but it appears that his courses focused on teaching Standard Colonial Quechua. He certainly believed priests in the archdiocese of Lima should be aware of some of the more characteristic features of Central Quechua, but there is no evidence that he was invested in adapting Standard Colonial Quechua texts for use among Central Quechua speakers to any significant degree.

In his 1616 grammar Huerta simply mixed in a few Central forms with the Southern ones, often without setting them apart. He records /-chaw/ as the Chinchaysuyo locative case and notes that the Chinchaysuyos used

/-ma/ rather than /-wa/ for the first-person object, but mentions the Central first-person subject, marked by the lengthening of the preceding vowel, as an occasional variant of the Southern form /-ni/ (Huerta 1993 [1616]: 22–23, 41, 35–36). Similarly, he mentions the Central progressive aspect /-yka/ indistinctly alongside the Southern form /-chka/, and even combines it with Southern first-person subject /-ni/ (e.g., *ricçicani* /riqsi-yka-ni/ 'I am getting acquainted with' and *ranticani* /ranti-yka-ni/ 'I am buying') (ibid.: 56–57). The grammar also contains one important orthographic innovation: Huerta distinguished /q/ by marking {c} with a *vírgula* {¯} and {q[u]} with a stress mark {´}. The use of a diacritic rather than a digraph for /q/, which could have revolutionized colonial Quechua orthography, was taken up only in the manuscript works of Diego de Molina and Juan de Castromonte.

For all the rhetoric we find in the prologues to Avendaño's and Diego de Molina's sermonarios about the need to use Chinchaysuyo Quechua, Chinchaysuyoist tendencies in the published literature were limited to the insertion of a few Central word stems. Frequently, these word stems were accompanied by their Southern equivalents, thus forming cross-dialectal pairs out of which the reader or performer of the text had to select the locally appropriate term. Avendaño's sermonario contains only a few Central stems, which are sometimes paired with their Southern equivalents, and sometimes appear alone.[25] Avila, who made no statements on the issue of Chinchaysuyo Quechua, used more Central lexicon in his sermonario than Avendaño did.[26] Jurado Palomino's catechism is the most systematic in its use of cross-dialectal pairs—the two terms are usually separated by the notation *l.* (Cerrón-Palomino 1992: 224–225). The manuscript works of Diego de Molina and Castromonte differ in that the Central stems occur independently—Central lexicon is especially prominent in Castromonte's ritual.[27]

Central Quechua morphological elements are very rare in the printed texts. Avila seems to use a verbal plural /-sapa/ in place of /-ku/ on a couple of occasions ([1647]: 4), and Jurado Palomino occasionally used the Central ablative case /-pita/ (Southern /-manta/) (1649: f. 3, 5v, 8, 62v). In both authors the use of these forms appears to be a slip. Diego de Molina discussed Central morphology in the prologue to his sermonario, mentioning the second-person subject past tense /-rqayki/, the locative /-chaw/, and the first-person object marker /-ma/ (Romero 1928: 75), but his sermons contain no Central suffixes. It is only in Castromonte's ritual that we find Central suffixes as well as word stems in significant numbers. Castromonte consistently used /-llapa/ as a second- and third-person verbal plural, sometimes appending it to the Southern second-person plural /-chik/ as if it were a separate word. Apparently, his intention was to convey plurality to Chinchaysuyo audiences who would not recognize the Southern form, but without excessively changing the Southern morphology of his texts. On a few occasions the Central first-person subject marker (the lengthening of the preceding vowel) is recorded, as is /-y/, a first-person subject form not usually associated with Central Quechua, but from which the Central form seems to have derived (Cerrón-Palomino 1987: 140). Other Central suffixes that occur in Castromonte's text include the subordinator /-r/ (one case), the first-person subject/second-person object /-q/ (two cases), the first-person object /-ma/ (two cases), and the second-person subject past tense /-rqayki/ (four cases).[28]

The mid-century literature was quite innovative orthographically. Three of the five authors from this period—precisely the three who published their works—represented glottalized and aspirate stops using notations very similar to González Holguín's. Avila referred admiringly to González Holguín's work in his prologue, but pointed out that his orthography was not used consistently in his works and speculated that this may have been the fault of the printers. Avila also claimed that González Holguín's use of {k} was unnecessary and excluded it from his own orthography (Avila [1647]: n.p.n.). A very similar orthography was used by Avendaño and Jurado Palomino. It is a paradox and something of a mystery that those author-translators who, in the extant pastoral literature at least, first distinguished glottalized and aspirate stops should have been precisely those who were writing for a Chinchaysuyo audience. Avila and Jurado Palomino were both natives of Cuzco and were thus familiar with the distribution of glottalized and aspirate stops in Cuzco Quechua. However, this does not explain why a González Holguín–style orthography became the norm during the 1640s. Unless one is willing to consider the possibility of the existence of glottalized and aspirate stops in the Central Quechua varieties (which goes against everything that is known about the history of Quechua phonology), it has to be assumed that Chinchaysuyoization and the tendency to represent glottalized and aspirate stops were simply two separate processes that coincided in these texts.

Significantly, those authors who were most familiar with Central Quechua—Diego de Molina and Juan de Castromonte—made no attempt to represent glottalized and aspirate stops and focused instead on distinguishing the uvular from the velar stop. Molina's prologue contains a lengthy discussion of Quechua phonology/orthography which harps on the differences between Standard Colonial and Chinchaysuyo Quechua and on the importance of distinguishing the uvular stop, which he refers to as *la gutural.* Molina proposed writing {cc, qq[u]} for syllable-initial /q/, and {ĉ} for syllable-final /q/, and exemplified the system by transcribing the basic prayers first in the Third Council orthography, which he claimed was leading to endless confusion, and then with the orthography he proposed (Romero 1928: 76–87). Oddly, Molina did not use this orthography at all in his sermons, which diverged from what was proposed in his prologue both dialectally and orthographically, and which followed the Third Council norm quite closely except for the occasional lexical "Chinchaysuyoism." Castromonte, on the other hand, made no explicit orthographic proposals but perfected the system proposed by Molina, using /ˆ/ to mark /q/ in all contexts, placing it over both {c} and {q[u]} (Durston 2002).

It cannot be a coincidence that the three authors who singled out /q/ as a sound needing special representation and used diacritics rather than digraphs for this effect—Huerta, Diego de Molina, and Castromonte—were all familiar with Central Quechua. In fact, all three were either natives of or residents in Huánuco, the only Spanish town in a Central Quechua–speaking area (Huerta and Castromonte were born there, and Molina spent much of his career there). I suggest that other writers had not been able to do this because they were steeped in the Cuzco Quechua–based standard and had difficulty distinguishing the velar-uvular from the plain-glottalized-aspirate oppositions. Since the Central Quechua varieties did not have glottalization or aspiration, the only significant hypo-differentiation in the Third Council orthography with respect to their phonology was the absence of a clear distinction between the velar and uvular stops.

The Chinchaysuyoist writers made no attempt to represent specifically Central Quechua phonemes. Diego de Molina made a detailed case for the importance of {x} (/sh/), which is present in most modern Central varieties, but did not use it in his own writings—in fact, {x} does not appear at all in the pastoral literature after Santo Tomás. The only text from this period that throws any light on the phonology of a Central Quechua variety is Castromonte's ritual, but it does so indirectly. On a few occasions Castromonte wrote {g} where he would normally have used {ĉ} (his notation for /q/), and on others he substituted {ĉ} for {g} in Spanish words (e.g., *purĉatorio*). Clearly, /q/ was voiced in Castromonte's native

Quechua, and he had trained himself to replace {g}—his instinctive spelling for /q/—with {ĉ}, to the point where he would sometimes substitute {ĉ} for *Spanish* {g}s, an eloquent testimony to the weight of the Third Council tradition. The voicing of /q/ is a characteristic of the variety of Central Quechua spoken today around Huánuco, Castromonte's birthplace, and his writings show that this change had taken place by the mid-seventeenth century (Durston 2002: 238).

A final aspect of the orthography of the mid-century texts that bears mentioning is the collapse of the sibilant distinction. Avila, Avendaño, and Castromonte used the {c, ç, z}-{s, ss} opposition incorrectly, often writing {ç} where earlier writers consistently wrote {s} (Taylor 2002: 43, 122). Molina, on the other hand, tended to use only {s}. It is known that the two sibilants of Southern Quechua merged during the colonial period (Mannheim 1991: 153–176), so it could be argued that this phonological change is already represented in the orthographies of these writers. However, it would be rash to identify these orthographic changes too directly with phonological changes—it is not at all clear how the Quechua of writers like Avila, for instance, was related to that of ordinary speakers of any given variety. Furthermore, it is clear that some of Avila's contemporaries, such as Pérez Bocanegra, had no trouble maintaining the sibilant system, and the system is more or less intact in Jurado Palomino's catechism. The argument would certainly not apply in Castromonte's case, since Castromonte was a speaker of a variety of Central Quechua which until the present day maintains a sibilant distinction.

In conclusion, the adaptation of Standard Colonial Quechua for Central Quechua–speaking audiences by the mid-century authors was irregular and halfhearted. Central morphemes appear very rarely, and Central lexical stems, if more abundant, are also in the minority, and it is usually not clear why they appear when they do. Apparently, it was not feasible for Spanish authors to actually write in Central Quechua. To do so, they would have had to reinvent pastoral Quechua from the ground up and repeat the same process the Third Lima Council translators had gone through with Southern Quechua—namely, establish a new dialectal standard, orthography, and pastoral terminology—in order to prevent the new Central Quechua literature from diversifying excessively. On the other hand, Spanish writers had difficulty in apprehending Central and Southern Quechua as distinct languages, and saw Central forms as corrupt derivations of their Southern equivalents. This perception seems to have affected even the

Chinchaysuyoists, which would explain why their written Quechua presents such an irregular mix of Central and Southern features. One might ask if using Central forms so sporadically served any real purpose in terms of the intelligibility of the texts, and why these authors bothered to do so. One plausible answer is that they were simply putting on an appearance. As was seen in chapter 4, writing pastoral texts for the Chinchaysuyo Indians became more of a political banner than a linguistic reality.

In some cases, however, it seems that the distribution of Central forms was strategic. This is clearly the case in Castromonte's use of the Southern and Central stems for 'male human being'—*ĉari* /qari/ and *ollĉo* /ullqu/, respectively. In his plática on the sacrament of confirmation, a highly rhetorical text, Castromonte used the Southern form, but in his translation of the baptismal office *ollĉo* is used in the priest's question regarding the baby's gender. Clearly, he preferred not to use the Southern form in a context where an unequivocal answer was needed (Durston 2002: 243). Another systematic variation occurs in the first-person subject: as Torero has noted, the non-Southern forms only appear in the people's responses in the sacramental offices (Torero 1995: 17). Castromonte may have been seeking to represent the linguistic reality of the administration of the sacraments in the parishes of the central highlands, where the priests spoke in Standard Colonial Quechua and their parishioners replied in the local form of Quechua. Alternatively, he may have been instructing fellow priests to have their parishioners respond in their native language to ensure that they understood what they were saying.

Christian Terminology: The Problems of Equivalence

The easiest and least controversial solution to the problem of rendering Christian theological and institutional categories in Quechua was the introduction of the source terms themselves as loan words. Lexical borrowing was greatly facilitated by Quechua's agglutinative morphology: nouns were incorporated unchanged as noun stems, and verbs were introduced by using the Spanish infinitive form minus *-r* as Quechua verb stems. For instance, Spanish *rezar* 'to pray' gave the loan stem *reza-* (thus, "I pray" is *rezani*).[29] Pastoral loan words in Quechua generally used the Spanish rather than the Latin term, even though the Latin terms and expressions always provided the ultimate point of reference and were often invoked for greater clarity on semantic issues. The Spanish terms were probably preferred because they would be more accessible and familiar for all concerned, including the less educated clerics. Loan stems were not adapted to Quechua phonology and morphophonemics, at least in writing. For example, Quechua does not admit consonant clusters, so *cruz* 'cross' should have become *curuz*. The resistance to such adaptation is all the more striking when we consider that nonreligious loan words *were* so adapted—for instance, the word derived from *servir* 'to serve' is often written *sirui-* (/sirwi-/) in pastoral texts.[30]

Of course, the disadvantage of loan words was that they greatly reduced the intelligibility of the pastoral texts, and were probably also an obstacle to their recitation or singing. There were two main alternatives to borrowing: (1) semantically adapting existing Quechua terms, and (2) creating Quechua neologisms that were essentially glosses of the source terms (cf. Itier 1995b: 322–326).[31] Both options were fraught with difficulties: adapted terms could distort the meaning of the entire Christian message because of their baggage of native religious concepts and practices, and neologisms rarely conveyed the sense of the source term accurately. All pastoral Quechua texts use a combination of all three solutions—loan word, adapted term, and neologism—but the proportions varied considerably.

If one can judge from the texts reproduced by Santo Tomás, pre–Third Council translation practices were characterized by a penchant for neologisms, on the model of *Diospa yanan* (God's assistant) for "saint," and for paraphrases that avoided the problem of terminological translation entirely. As Santo Tomás put it, "[t]he things of our faith are explained with the same terms [loan words] . . . or by circumlocutions, or by the names of the causes or effects of the things that one wants to explain or declare."[32] The phrase "full of grace" from the Ave Maria was translated as *hochanac* (sinless), thus conveying the theological concept of grace through its "effect" (Santo Tomás 1995 [1560]: 92). The problem of finding a specific lexical "equivalent" for "grace" does not seem to have troubled Santo Tomás, who was more concerned about the global intelligibility of texts. For the Third Council translators, however, the priorities had changed: a much wider range of doctrines and institutional contexts were involved, and there was a premium on the stability and uniformity of the pastoral terminology. The translators were thus hostile to paraphrases and neologisms, and sought one-to-one correspondences with the source terms.

While the basic pastoral terminology established by the council remained fairly stable in later texts, there was a partial return to the use of neologisms in the works of Pérez Bocanegra, who coined terms such as *chuyanchana* 'place of purification' for "purgatory" (Pérez Bocanegra 1631: 678, 698).

Because of their controversial character, adapted terms were always relatively few in number, especially in the Third Council standard, but they never ceased to have a role in the pastoral terminology. Key adapted terms in the canonical terminology include the noun *hucha*, which originally meant something like 'debt' or 'obligation' and became the pastoral Quechua term for "sin," and the verb *cama-*, which designated the divine activity of infusing a vital force into living things and was used for the Christian concept of creation. The pastoral adaptation of these terms sometimes led to a kind of bifurcation of their meaning; for example, even within the Third Council texts, *hucha* continued to be used in its original sense (Itier 1995b: 323). Itier has suggested that such terms were adapted not so much because their original sense was considered similar to that of the Christian source term, but because there was a *contextual* proximity between their uses (ibid.). Thus *cama-* was applied to God's act of creation because in native religious thought the term designated the essential activity of deities, and *hucha* became 'sin' because it conveyed the sense of a fault which required a form of expiative and restitutive action (more on these terms below). In the postcouncil literature we find a variety of new adapted terms used for church institutions, although these terms never caught on. Pérez Bocanegra, for instance, used *aclla* for "nun," echoing (deliberately or not) the Anonymous Jesuit's claims that the Inca acllas had become true nuns after the conquest (Pérez Bocanegra 1631: 238).

Establishing the correct terms for key Christian categories and institutions did not just involve problems in the interpretation of the target language and culture—very often there was confusion surrounding the exact meaning of the source terms themselves, primarily because there were at least two source languages involved. The problem is exemplified by the variant translations of the verb "to baptize" as used in the baptismal form ("I baptize you in the name of the Father, the Son, and the Holy Spirit"). The Third Council established the standard Quechua translation of the form, expressing the action of baptizing with the loan *baptiza-* (Third Lima Council 1985a [1584]: 112). The use of a loan word in this context was problematic, however, because baptisms were carried out very frequently by Indians, and the sacrament was valid only if the minister uttered the form with full intent. In the early seventeenth century, a variant form had become common in which the Quechua term *sutiya-* or *sutiyachi-* 'to name' was used instead of *baptiza-*, on the misunderstanding that naming was the essential aspect of baptism.[33]

Pérez Bocanegra's ritual contains a lengthy criticism of this practice, which suggests that there was an ongoing debate over the issue (Pérez Bocanegra 1631: 45–47). He explained that the Latin term *baptizare,* which was of Greek origin, actually meant 'to wash' and had nothing to do with naming, and argued that baptisms in which the term *sutiya-* had been used were sacrilegious and void. Pérez Bocanegra was not arguing that the loan word *baptiza-* was obligatory: although this was the established practice, baptisms could validly be administered with Quechua verbs meaning 'to wash,' such as *maylla-, arma-, challa-,* or *chulla-*. In this case, a translation problem arose because the source term, which was a loan word even in Latin, had acquired a vernacular sense in Spanish that was etymologically and theologically incorrect.

The difficulties involved in working from different source languages are also reflected in the pre–Third Council use of the expression *caci quespilla cay* (literally, "be calm and safe") to translate the Latin salutations *ave* and *salve* in the Ave Maria and Salve Regina prayers (Third Lima Council 1985a [1584]: 170). The contemporary Spanish versions of these prayers had *Dios te salve,* "may God save you," for *ave* and *salve,* so *caci quespilla cay* was in fact a translation of these Spanish expressions. The Third Council translators advised against this translation in the linguistic appendix to the *Doctrina christiana y catecismo* and instead used *muchaycuscayqui*—literally, "I will kiss/adore you"[34]—for both *ave* and *salve* (ibid.). This seems a bizarre choice, but as Itier has noted, the expression *muchaycuscayqui* was also a deferential salutation of the sort given to a superior, just as the Latin expressions *ave* and *salve* were (Itier 1995b: 323).

The general nature of religious terminology in pastoral Quechua raises serious issues of intelligibility, especially after the Third Lima Council, when most key concepts were expressed with loan words. Even adapted terms presented problems for intelligibility, since they were familiar terms used with entirely new meanings. Dedenbach-Salazar Sáenz and Itier have attempted the exercise of reading pastoral Quechua texts as they might have sounded to native Andeans. Dedenbach-Salazar Sáenz suggests that the use of adapted terms, especially as epithets for God and the Virgin, would have led native Andeans to simply incorporate Christian entities and concepts into existing cosmologies (Dedenbach-Salazar Sáenz 1997b: 202–203). Itier, on the other hand, suggests that the intention of the author-translators in using adapted terms was to allow for different degrees of "acculturation"—individuals with no Christian training could still make some sense of the texts based on the original meaning of the terms, thus allowing a gradual progression towards a fuller understanding of the terminology (Itier 1995b: 326). While there is little evidence that allows us to speculate on native interpretations of the texts, it seems unlikely that the author-translators would have favored an "unacculturated" reading. I would argue instead that the issue of intelligibility should be approached from the perspective of the textual and performative contexts in which the terms appear. As will be seen, the interpretation of key terms was not meant to occur in a vacuum, and a variety of metasemantic guidelines were provided both by performance practices and by the poetic structure of the texts.

Christian Terminology up to the Third Lima Council

There are some important continuities between Santo Tomás's texts and those of the Third Lima Council. Most obviously, the former used the loan word *Dios* for "God" without any explanation or glossing—clearly, if there was ever a debate as to whether a native term could be used to designate God, it was resolved quickly. It seems very likely that there *was* such a debate. As described in chapter 2, Juan de Betanzos claimed quite vehemently in his 1557 chronicle of the Incas that the name Viracocha was the proper Quechua term for God, which suggests that his catechetical texts in Quechua from the 1540s were written accordingly. By the late sixteenth century Pachacamac was replacing Viracocha as the Inca creator god or "unknown God" in Spanish accounts of Inca religion, but God was never referred to directly as Pachacamac—or with any other native term—in the extant pastoral literature.

To put this issue in perspective, it is useful to look at contemporary Christian literatures in other Amerindian languages. Texts in Guarani and other languages of the Tupi-Guarani family, whether the work of Spanish or Portuguese clergy, consistently used the name of the thunder god, *Tupa*, to refer to God (Meliá 1992: 74). The Dominicans in mid-sixteenth-century Chiapas used another approach with Kakchiquel Maya: the term *qabahuil* or *qabovil* was used both in the generic sense of "god" (with a lowercase *g*) and as the name of the one true God. The original meaning of this term seems to have approximated Quechua "huaca" in that it designated divine things and beings in general. This was, of course, the same time-honored translation practice that resulted in the use of *Deus* in Latin and "God" and its cognates in the Germanic languages. Franciscans working in the same area were in conflict with the Dominicans over this issue and espoused the use of "Dios" on the grounds that *Qabahuil* would blur the distinction between God and the "idols" of the native religion. The Dominicans countered that "Dios" was meaningless for the Mayas, and that it was preferable to show them that the native term had been applied incorrectly to their false gods ("there is no *qabahuil* but *Qabahuil*") (García-Ruiz 1992: 91-92). In Nahuatl, God was designated primarily as "Dios," but the term *teotl* was used for generic "god" and could thus be applied to the one true God (Estenssoro Fuchs 2003: 95; Tavárez 2000: 25). In Christian discourse in Quechua, the candidates for the native term for God were all names of deities. The generic concept of "god" appears rarely if ever— "false gods" are referred to as "huacas" (i.e. idols) and the term "Dios" is applied only to the one true God (cf. Estenssoro Fuchs 2003: 95-96).

Santo Tomás's texts employed some key adapted terms which would remain part of the basic pastoral terminology, especially *hucha* and *huchallicu-* as 'sin' and 'to sin' ('to acquire a *hucha*'), *mucha-* as 'to worship,' and *çupay* as 'devil.' In some cases, the continuities are deceptive. *Hucha* originally designated a duty or debt in a social relationship of reciprocity, especially relationships between a person or social group and a huaca (Taylor ed. 1999 [1987, n.d.]: xxvi–xxvii). *Hucha* in relationships with huacas resulted from negligence in cult duties and from ritual transgressions, and could cause disease, bad weather, and the birth of twins, among other misfortunes. They could be incurred unwittingly and affected entire groups of people. Spanish observers consistently claimed that native Andeans confessed their *hucha* to specialized confessors who prescribed various forms of penance (e.g., Third Lima Council 1985b [1585]: 268–269), but it seems more likely that these "confessions" were in fact divination rituals directed at identifying what particular *hucha* was causing a problem.[35] The Andean concept of *hucha* was thus very far removed from Christian sin—it had none of the sense of a voluntary act which polluted the individual soul and then had to be declared. However, the *hucha* = sin gloss became established at a very early moment, probably because of the analogy in the implications of having acquired one or the other—primarily, the need for a ritual restitution and purification in order to avoid dire consequences.

The primary sense of *mucha-* is 'to kiss,' but at the time of the conquest it was also the term for worshipping a huaca, which involved offering sacrifices as well as oral prayer and gestures (one of the common gestures of worship involved a kiss-like movement of the lips). In all the known pastoral Quechua texts *mucha-* is the main term for the generic worship or veneration of God, Mary, and the saints, while also having the more specific sense of 'to implore, to ask.'[36] *Muchapu-* referred to the intercessive rogations made by the Virgin, the saints, and ordinary people on behalf of a sinner. There must have been theological qualms about equating the worship given to God to the idolatrous worship of the huacas, but the term *mucha-* was one of the underpinnings of the whole pastoral terminology—as in the case of *hucha,* a recognizable term was needed to obtain certain kinds of action. It was also effective in getting across the message that the worship of God excluded the worship of the huacas, expressed in a short prayer from Santo Tomás's *Plática para todos los indios*: *Manañatac guacacta mochacusacchu, Cam çapallata mochascayqui* (I will no longer worship the huacas, I will worship you alone) (Santo Tomás 1995 [1560]: 179).

We find the term *çupay* (/supay/) applied to the Devil and to devils in general in Santo Tomás's texts and in all later works. However, there is an important difference in the way Santo Tomás used the term, as devils are referred to as *mana alli çupay,* 'bad *çupay*.' His dictionary glosses *çupay* as "angel, good or bad" (*ángel, bueno o malo*), indicating that at one point the term was considered an adequate designation for the angels (Santo Tomás 1951 [1560]: 279). The *Plática* does not use *çupay* for 'angel,' preferring instead the more neutral neologism *Diospa yanan* (God's assistant), but nor did it use the term straightforwardly with the meaning 'devil' (Estenssoro Fuchs 2003: 103–106). Taylor suggests that *çupay* originally designated the spirits of the dead, which were objects of worship and were consequently demonized by early Christian observers, who consistently claimed that the Devil was known to Andeans under the name *çupay* (Taylor 2000e [1980]). As Estenssoro Fuchs notes, however, there was an early attempt to adapt the term to the Christian concept of "spirit," such that it could be applied to angels and devils as well as the souls of the dead. This attempt was soon abandoned however, and *çupay* became a specific designation for evil spirits (Estenssoro Fuchs 2003: 103–110, 120–126).

The Quechua terms used in the *Plática* to designate God's creation were also maintained in later texts: *hanan pacha* 'upper realm' for "heaven," *ucu pacha* 'inner realm' for "hell," and *cay pacha* 'this realm' for "world." These terms sound like neologisms, but it may be that they designated specific entities in Andean cosmology, as Itier has suggested for *ucu pacha,* in which case they could be regarded as adapted terms (Itier 1995b: 325). However, there is an important difference in the terms used to express God's act of creating the world: in addition to the more obvious *rura-* 'to make,' the *Plática* used the term *yachachi-*, usually glossed as 'to teach.' Itier argues that *yachachi-* originally had little to do with the act of making and that *pacha yachachic* (in the Christian gloss, 'creator of the world') had been an epithet of Viracocha in his mythical role as facilitator of agricultural production (Itier 1993: 158–161). Consequently, Itier argues, the use of *yachachi-* as a translation of "to create" derived from an accommodationist identification of Viracocha as an "Andean reminiscence of the Christian creator God," which in turn allowed for the pastoral appropriation of his epithets (ibid.: 161). *Yachachi-* was entirely excluded from the pastoral Quechua vocabulary of the Third Lima Council.

Several other discontinuities between the early pastoral terminology and that of the Third Council are apparent throughout the *Plática,* the Confiteor prayer, and Santo Tomás's dictionary and grammar. As has been seen, these discontinuities derive mainly from a greater disposition in the earlier texts to use neologisms and adapted terms as opposed to loan words. In the Confiteor, for example, the act of confession is translated as *huchata uilla-* 'to tell a *hucha*' and the saints are referred to as *Diospa yanan[cona]* 'God's servant[s]'; while in the *Plática* we find *onancha* 'sign' translating "sacrament" and *Diospa yanan* applied to the angels. A variety of terms are used to designate the Christian soul. *Alma* and *ánima* are glossed *songo, camaquen,* and *çamaynin* in the Spanish-Quechua section of the dictionary (Santo Tomás 1951 [1560]: 35, 40). The *Plática* refers to the soul as *songo, camaquen,* and *ucupi cac runa* (Santo Tomás 1995 [1560]: 173). *Ucupi cac runa* 'interior person' is an obvious paraphrase. *Çamaynin*—'breath' followed by the third person possessive marker—probably derived from the European tradition of identifying breath with the spiritual. The ordinary sense of *songo* is 'heart,' and the word may have had connotations similar to its equivalents in European languages. The most interesting of these terms is *camaquen* (/kama-q-i-n/), the agentivized form of the verb *cama-* (which originally referred to the activity of animating or strengthening living beings) followed by the third-person possessive. In native cosmology *camaquen* designated a kind of double that all living things had—the entity that provided them with their vital energy (cf. Taylor 2000a [1974–1976]).

As a rule, the Third Council translators used loan words to designate key Christian entities, institutions, and practices, so many of the neologisms and adapted terms of Santo Tomás's time were set aside, if not proscribed. The search for a Quechua term for "soul" was abandoned, and the Latin form *anima* was incorporated, probably because it was more adaptable to Quechua phonology than Spanish *alma* (the Latinism *ánima* was also used frequently in Spanish).[37] The loan words *santo* and *ángel* replaced the neologism *Diospa yanan* 'God's servant,' and the sacraments were referred to with the loan word *sacramento* rather than Santo Tomás's multivocal *onancha* 'sign.' The act of confession became *confessa-* where Santo Tomás had used the expression *huchata uilla-*, probably because of fears that native forms of dealing with religious *hucha* would be confused with the Christian sacrament. *Ayuno* 'fast' and *ayuna-* 'to fast' were used instead of Quechua *çaciy* and *çaci-*, which designated an Andean ritual fast that required abstinence from specific foods and sexual intercourse and would be used for the Christian fast in later texts. There are no references to Christian fasting in Santo Tomás's texts, but his dictionary glosses *çaci-* as *ayunar por devoción* and *çacii mitta* or *çacii pacha* ('the time of *çaciy*') as *quaresma* 'Lent,' so he seems to have considered it a good equivalent (Santo Tomás 1951 [1560]: 241). While Santo Tomás's version of the Confiteor refers to Mary with the term *tazqui* for "virgin"—*tazqui* or *tazque* being the term for unmarried girls—the Third Council texts used *virgen* both in the title "Virgin Mary" and to refer to her state of virginity. Interestingly, ordinary virgins were designated with another loan word, *donzella,* so that *virgen* was reserved for the miraculous and holy virginity of Mary.[38]

Most of the loan words established by the Third Council correspond to institutions, categories, and entities that do not appear in the brief, bare-bones texts reproduced by Santo Tomás. These include basic terms like *sacerdote* or *padre* 'priest,' *iglesia* 'church,' and *Trinidad* 'Trinity.' The particularly difficult Trinitarian concepts were expressed with a mix of loan words and common, uncontroversial Quechua words. The persons of the Trinity were rendered *yaya* (Quechua for 'father'), *churi* ('son'), and *spiritu sancto*—or *Dios yaya, Dios churi,* and *Dios spiritu sancto* (God the Father, God the Son, and God the Holy Spirit). In Quechua the qualifier precedes the qualified, so one would have expected *churi Dios, yaya Dios,* and *spiritu sancto*

Dios, but perhaps this formulation sounded too much like three different gods. While the Trinity was addressed as *sanctissima Trinidad,* its official title in pastoral Quechua, it was also referred to as *quimça persona* or *quimçantin persona* 'the three persons.' In the latter expression, the suffix /-ntin/ added to the numeral *quimça* 'three' indicated the totality of the three persons (i e., that there are only three persons); it is grammatically identical to the term *tahuantin suyu,* which designated the Inca empire as a unity composed of four *suyu*—parts or provinces.

I have already discussed some of the main adapted terms that were used in the Third Council texts, as these also appear in Santo Tomás's. *Hanac pacha* 'heaven,' *ucu pacha* 'hell,' *hucha* 'sin,' and *mucha-* 'to worship' were used much as they had been in Santo Tomás's Confiteor and in the *Plática para todos los indios.* There appears to have been an important innovation in the adoption of *cama-* (/kama-/) as the main term for divine creation, substituting *yachachi-*. Admittedly, *cama-* was glossed as 'to create' in Santo Tomás's dictionary (Santo Tomás 1951 [1560]: 246), but it does not appear with this meaning in his *Plática,* where *yachachi-* and *rura-* are used and the root *cama-* only appears in the form *camaquen* 'soul' (cf. Taylor 2001b: 435). Taylor has reconstructed the original sense of *cama-* as the action of animating, strengthening, or communicating a life force, typically as exercised by a huaca in relation to crops, animals, and people—a meaning that has been replaced entirely by the gloss imposed by the Third Council (Taylor 2000a [1974–1976]). As occurs with *çupay* 'devil,' it appears that the Christian gloss for *cama-* had not yet been consolidated when Santo Tomás's *Plática* was written.

Some of the more important adapted terms had synonyms that were sometimes used alongside them in a supporting role, apparently as a way of clarifying the meaning of the main term (see chapter 7 on lexical pairing). *Hucha* 'sin' had a synonym in the noun *cama* (/kama/, not to be confused with the verb cama-) which originally had the sense of 'task' or 'responsibility' (e.g., Third Lima Council 1985b [1585]: 239, 240). Similarly, the act of creation was expressed with the words *rura-* 'to make' and *pacarichi-* (/paqari-chi-/) 'to cause to be born' as well as *cama-* (e.g., Third Lima Council 1985a [1584]: 56, 57). They generally appear immediately after *cama-*, the principal term for divine creation, but *rura-* could replace it entirely in contexts where its use was problematic because of its native religious connotations. When it came to translating the phrase "creator of heaven and earth" in the Credo, the term used was *ruraquen* (/rura-q-i-n/—the agentive suffix followed by the third person possessive) because the form *camaquen* was considered ambiguous—it had been lexicalized as the term for the animating doubles or "souls" (in Christian minds) of all living things. As the translators pointed out in the linguistic appendix of the *Doctrina christiana y catecismo,* the phrase *hanac pachap cay pachap camaquen* could thus be interpreted as "soul of heaven and earth" (Third Lima Council 1985a [1584]: 174). They also wanted to avoid bringing together the terms *pacha* 'world' and *camac* 'creator,' as they could be associated with the name Pachacamac.

The Third Council translation program required the semantic transformation of a number of terms that had not had specifically religious meanings. This was the case with *iñi-* 'to believe,' which had probably been a common term for 'to agree.' Mannheim has analyzed *iñi-* as two separate words, interpreting it literally as 'to say "yes",' and argued that it did not convey the sense of belief as "an inner state that can be held by an individual" (Mannheim 1991: 131). However, *iñi-* can be better interpreted as a delocutive verb (among several others in which an interjection followed by the verb stem *ñi-* 'to say' were fused into a single verb stem) whose sense did not imply an actual speech act. (Even the verb *ñi-* itself does not imply speech, as it often refers to thought, intention, or simply the imminence of an action or event.) It can also be assumed that the Quechua terms used to refer to Christian concepts of sign and representation underwent semantic transformations. For instance, the term *imagen* 'image' as used in the doctrine that Man was created "in God's image" was translated with the nouns *ricchay* and *unancha,* which can be very roughly glossed as 'appearance' and 'sign' but were hardly functional equivalents of the Western concept of image (e.g., Third Lima Council 1985a [1584]: 70). The verb stem *unancha-* was used as 'to understand,' but its non-pastoral sense was probably closer to 'to signal.'

Another important area of semantic adaptation was that of divine epithets. The terms *capac* and *collanan* were persistently applied as adjectives to God, Christ, or the Virgin Mary, but their functions are hard to define as they do not consistently translate specific source terms. *Capac,* which could serve as adjective or noun, was glossed by the Third Council translators as "king or thing of royal majesty" (*Rey o cosa de magestad real*) (Third Lima Council 1985a [1584]: 169). It was the primary term for divine power and glory, and God was typically referred to as *capac Dios. Collanan,* which could be roughly glossed as 'excellent,' normally designated the outstanding member of a group of similar things. In the Marian prayers Ave Maria and Salve Regina it was used to translate the term *bendito/a* 'blessed,' applied to Mary and Jesus. *Collanan* seems to have congregated a much broader range of meanings associated with divine glory and holiness, but usually with reference to Christ (*collanan Jesus*) and Mary (*collanan Maria*) rather than God the Father. However, it could also be paired with *capac* as an adjective for God, as if the two terms were synonyms—the phrase *Dios es grande* (God is great) was translated *Diosca . . . ancha capacmi collananpunim* (Third Lima Council 1985c [1585]: 490). In the Salve Regina, Mary is referred to as *çapay coya* 'sole queen,' the formal title of the principal consort of the Inca sovereign (the *çapay inca*), a practice that matches the use of *capac* with reference to God (Third Lima Council 1985a [1584]: 26). As will be seen in chapter 8, a variety of terms associated with Inca royalty were applied to God in later texts, but in the context of the Third Council works *coya* was probably intended as a transparent equivalent of "queen" (*regina, reina*).

In short, the Third Council terminology stands in sharp contrast to the practices exemplified in Santo Tomas's dictionary and grammar and in the short texts reproduced in them. In addition to minimizing the use of Quechua adapted terms and neologisms, there was an effort to establish one-for-one correspondences—be they loan words, adapted terms, or neologisms—for the key source terms. Santo Tomás's suggestion that one could use "circumlocutions" or "the names of the causes or effects" of the referent was no longer acceptable. The changes reflect post-Tridentine standards of doctrinal uniformity and purity as well as growing fears of indigenous misinterpretation and misuse of Christian doctrine, but also the fact that the Third Council implemented a far more detailed and in-depth catechetical program, which required greater terminological precision.

Christian Terminology after the Third Lima Council

The basic religious terminology established by the Third Council translators was never effectively changed. However, the postcouncil writers sought to adapt or expand it in certain areas, and there were attempts to replace specific loan words with Quechua terms, and to substitute new adapted terms and neologisms for the old ones. Although there are important common patterns in the works of Oré, Pérez Bocanegra, Prado, and González

Holguín, their terminological innovations are not identical. One of the few widespread terminological changes in the postcouncil period was the reappearance of *çaciy* and *çaci-* as the terms for 'fast' and 'to fast.' Juan Martínez's 1600 plática on an indulgence bull refers to Lent as *hatun çaçi mita* (the great time of *çaciy*) just as Santo Tomás had done (Itier 1992c: 138), and the confesionario in Torres Rubio's grammar-dictionary, which otherwise adhered very closely to the Third Council norms, used *çaçi punchau* (day of *çaciy*) for the days on which fasting was obligatory for Indians (Torres Rubio 1619: f. 88v).[39] *Çaci-* also appears with the sense of Christian fasting in the works of Pérez Bocanegra (1631: 628, 677), whereas in those of Prado and Castromonte it was used with reference to the kind of fast that only involved abstinence from eating meats and certain animal products, as opposed to the loan stem *ayuna-*, which was applied to the complete fast, required for Indians on only a few dates in the liturgical calendar (Prado 1641: f. 151v–152; Durston 2002: 283 n. 47).

Pérez Bocanegra was by far the most ambitious reformer of the pastoral terminology in the postcouncil period. He substituted Quechua neologisms or adapted terms for many of the loan words of the conciliar terminology, e.g., *Diospa acllan* for 'nun' (Pérez Bocanegra 1631: 238), *Dios pachan* for 'priest' (ibid.: 183, 406, 524, 530) (both neologisms proposed by González Holguín in his dictionary),[40] and *raimi* or *citua* (the names of the main Inca religious festivities) for 'feast day' (ibid.: 174, 311). Santo Tomás's term for Mary's virginity, *tazque*, reappears in Pérez Bocanegra's texts, where Mary is referred to as *purum taçque coya* and *purum tazque sancta Maria* (ibid.: 701, 658).[41] His modifications also extended to the canonical adapted terms. He very visibly replaced *iñi-* with *checanchacu-* 'to resolve a mystery' as "to believe" in his translation of the Nicene Creed, which is the first Quechua text in the *Ritual formulario*.[42] On several occasions Pérez Bocanegra replaced *mucha-* 'to adore' with *hupa-*, always in the form *hupaicu-* /hupa-yku-/ (ibid.: 693, 694, 704). This term appears to be a Puquina loan word—a verb stem *upalli-* was used as 'to worship' in the Puquina texts published by Oré in his *Rituale* (Oré 1607: 400–403).[43] Its use brings to mind Cerrón-Palomino's hypothesis that the Incas had originally been Puquina speakers. The fact that Pérez Bocanegra used it in some fairly strategic contexts (it is the first word in his first Marian hymn) indicates that it carried a certain ritual prestige because of its Puquina origin.

However, it should be emphasized that Pérez Bocanegra did not go as far as actually replacing the orthodox terms entirely. He continued to use *iñi-* and *mucha-* rather than *checanchacu-* and *hupaicu-* in most cases, and many of the terms he introduced usually appear with the conventional forms alongside them. His translation of the Nicene Creed, for instance, renders "prophets" as *Hamauta, unanchac, tococ, prophetas* (Pérez Bocanegra 1631: n.p.n.). The first three terms can be read both as adjectives and as alternate terms for the standard loan word *propheta*.[44] The same happens when "baptism" is rendered *armacui, maillacui, Baptismo* (*arma-* and *mailla-* both being terms for 'to wash,' which is the etymological sense of baptism) (ibid.). Pérez Bocanegra's catechism, which tends to paraphrase and adapt the Third Council catechisms, defines Man as *mana huañoc animayoc, camaqueyoc, huallpacyoc* (possessor of an immortal soul) (ibid.: 646). He provides the old adapted term *camaque[n]*, and a new one, *huallpac*, as alternatives for the loan word *anima* 'soul,' but does not replace it with them.

The majority of the new terms that appeared in the postcouncil literature were epithets for God, Christ, Mary, and the saints drawn from Inca religious and cosmological languages, whose use deliberately provoked identifications between Christian entities and Andean ones. For instance, a series of epithets originally applied to the deified Inca sovereign were used to express God's omnipotence and glory. These terms appear mostly in prayers and hymns and form part of a liturgical tropic register that can be considered separate from the basic pastoral terminology. They are discussed in chapters 7 and 8.

The diversification of the pastoral terminology after the Third Lima Council resulted in part from a concern for intelligibility—hence the tendency to use adapted terms rather than loanwords, and to offer alternatives for key terms which often acted as glosses of the traditional expressions. But the use of terms associated with native practices and institutions in Christian contexts also served as a demonstration that these practices and institutions had approximated Christianity. As suggested in the last chapter, it appears that the author-translators of the postcouncil period were making arguments about the nature of native Andean religion similar to those developed explicitly by Garcilaso de la Vega, the Anonymous Jesuit, and others. This motivation sometimes seems to conflict with the concern for intelligibility—one wonders how widely intelligible Inca religious terminology was in the early seventeenth century, especially outside the Cuzco area.

The mid-century texts did not, on the whole, continue the earlier trend of terminological innovation, but rather tended to adhere to the

Third Council norms in this respect. Some terms that can be considered characteristic of the postcouncil period do crop up—for instance, there are a few examples of the God-Inca sovereign trope in the sermons of Diego de Molina and Avendaño (see chapter 8). In Castromonte's ritual we find the action of belief consistently expressed with the verb phrase *checanmi ñi-* (literally, "to say 'it is true'"), which is reminiscent of Pérez Bocanegra's *checanchacu-*. However, this practice is the result of dialectal considerations: the affirmative /i/ on which the form *iñi-* was based was unknown in Chinchaysuyo Quechua (Durston 2002: 243). The terminological conservativeness of these authors is clearly related to the changing attitudes towards the Inca past that were discussed in the last chapter: there was not much room for proposing continuities and identities when even the positive elements of this past were used to exemplify the inconstancy of Indians in their relationship to Christianity.

Chapter 7

Text, Genre, and Poetics

If dialectology and terminology were essential and highly contested issues in the development of pastoral Quechua, the question of what genres and styles to write in was equally fundamental and problematic. This chapter examines the textual as opposed to strictly linguistic characteristics of the corpus from three main standpoints. I first discuss the range of texts and genres that are represented, with some reference to equivalent literatures in other languages for comparative purposes. I then examine the corpus in terms of the varying relations that existed between pastoral Quechua texts and Latin and Spanish source literatures and how these relations were conceived by the author-translators. A third topic, dealt with in particular detail, is poetics, by which I mean primarily tropes and textual figures. Especially with the development of a Quechua liturgy in the postcouncil period, author-translators confronted the task of developing poetic resources that could produce appropriate levels of devotional engagement. Traditional Christian tropes and images could be "translated" literally, but to very little effect in the absence of the original cultural and textual contexts. Textual figures, such as verse forms, are not translatable in any conventional sense. As a result, some author-translators made systematic use of native Andean religious images and verbal art forms while remaining within a Western genre framework. Poetic language is not, of course, exclusive to liturgical texts—even the Third Council translators, with their declared preference for an expository *estilo llano* and their banishment of tropes, frequently used textual figures, primarily semantic and syntactic parallelism. However, such resources are especially dense and prominent in the Quechua hymns, so special attention is given to them.

Texts and Genres

One of the key points of variation in religious translation programs involves the range of texts and genres that are considered fair game, and the genre space of pastoral Quechua changed considerably during the period of this study. Still, some restrictions applied throughout this period, and it is useful to consider the outlines of the corpus as a whole, especially for purposes of comparison with other religious literatures in translation. A range of texts were excluded from the translation process, most obviously the Bible. The liturgical sermonarios contain paraphrases rather than literal translations of the Gospel passages read in the mass, although they can on occasion be fairly close paraphrases. Admittedly, Juan Rojo Mejía y Ocón's activities as Quechua chair at the university of San Marcos seem to have focused on teaching priests how to translate Gospel passages literally, which suggests that the Inquisition's mid-sixteenth-century ban on Bible translations had been relaxed a century later. However, he never succeeded in publishing his translations, and only isolated sentences appear in his grammar.

Only a handful of texts specific to the mass became available in Quechua. Pérez Bocanegra published translations of the Nicene Creed and the priest's secret prayers for before and after communing with the bread and wine (1631: n.p.n., 500–502), and Prado provided a Quechua version of the *Orate fratres* prayer and the response of the people (1641: f. 53v–54). Several versions of the *Domine non sum dignus* prayer, which was recited prior to receiving communion, became available (see the next section). As for the sacramental liturgies, the rituals of Oré, Pérez Bocanegra, and Castromonte, along with several other works, contain translations of portions of the sacramental offices, usually those that required some form of participation from Indians. Pérez Bocanegra took this process further than anyone else, even providing translations of the forms for extreme unction, which were said only by the priest (1631: 526–527).

While Oré translated key texts from the canonical hours, the psalms remained off limits, probably because they were biblical texts. I have found no Quechua psalms from the period of this study, and (more conclusively) Pérez Bocanegra did not provide Quechua versions of the Seven Penitential Psalms in the extreme unction section of his ritual, although he did translate the Penitential Litanies which were recited alongside them (1631: 528–534). Nor do we find Quechua translations of hymns from the canonical hours such as the Marian hymn *Ave Maris Stella* or the eucharistic hymn *Sacris Solemnis,* even though these were not biblical texts. However, this lacuna does not seem to reflect an actual prohibition, since the Te Deum—which is a hymn in the broader sense of a liturgical song, but not a metrical composition—was translated by Oré (1992 [1598]: 390–394). Rather, it seems that Oré and others refrained from translating hymns proper because of the difficulty of producing Quechua versions which maintained the metrical form of the original so that they could be sung to the same melody.

Fourteen hymns (strophic texts based on a syllabic metrical pattern) originally composed in Quechua survive from the period of this study, and there are a few more from after 1650.[1] This may not seem like a very large corpus, but there is abundant testimony to the success and importance of the genre. Among the dozens of Quechua hymns that have a loyal following in Peru today are some fragments of pre-1650 hymns (specifically, some of Oré's cánticos) and many more that are probably of colonial origin.[2] As will be argued below, the hymn was especially successful in Quechua because the language's morphology and prosody facilitated syllabic meter. Oré's hymns were modeled closely on canonical Latin hymns and were intended for performance as part of a simplified version of the canonical hours (although portions were later excerpted for performance in other contexts). The exact precedents for Pérez Bocanegra's hymns and the brief hymns recorded by Prado and Castromonte are less clear.

The Jesuits developed an extensive repertoire of religious songs referred to as *romances* and *coplas* that were formally modeled on the profane genres of Spanish popular culture (Estenssoro Fuchs 2003: 305–307). Guaman Poma sharply criticized the Jesuits for their use of *coplas,* which he claimed Indians exploited to offend God, presumably through satirical distortions (Guaman Poma de Ayala 1980 [1615]: 771, 778, 782). It is unclear how these *romances* and *coplas* related to the surviving hymns, but it seems that by and large they were simpler in their formal composition and content. An example of the religious *romance* genre has survived in the *Romances de la passion de N. Señor Iesu Christo y su madre santissima,* a lengthy narrative of the passion printed in the 1705 reedition of Prado's *Directorio espiritual* (Prado and Manuel 1705: f. 137v–146v), which was a Jesuit text.

The bulk of the pastoral Quechua literature is made up of catechetical genres, mainly catechisms and sermons which were composed in Spanish for Andean audiences and then translated. The only instructional work of European origin that became widely available in Quechua was Roberto

Bellarmino's Italian catechism for the uneducated, in the translation of Jurado Palomino. There are no theologically complex or "advanced" works in Quechua: the catechisms and sermons provided instruction on basic doctrines, often in elaborate and innovative ways, but did not cater for an audience of educated readers who sought guidance for their personal reflections. It seems to have been assumed that the more learned and sophisticated Indian readers would know Spanish. The vernacular-language devotional literature that was so popular in sixteenth- and seventeenth-century Spain, which included translations of classic works such as Thomas à Kempis's *Imitation of Christ* as well as works originally composed in Spanish, such as those of Luis de Granada, did not carry over into Quechua to any significant degree. The Dominican Juan de Mercado may have translated parts of Granada's book on prayer into Quechua, but this is certainly not representative of what could be considered mainstream pastoral Quechua. The devotional literature, such as the texts in Prado's *Directorio espiritual,* focused on providing instruction for basic private devotional practices and for an elementary participation in the liturgy. Indians were restricted to the mechanical rounds of vocal (as opposed to mental) prayer and were not expected to aspire to a contemplative life.

In comparing the development of a Quechua Christian literature with analogous translation programs into Old High German, MacCormack notes the absence in Quechua of elite or theologically complex texts such as did become available in German, and attributes the difference to the fact that the German translation process was in native hands (MacCormack 1994: 89). Early religious translation into German can thus be classed as endogenous in opposition to the overwhelmingly exogenous Quechua translation tradition. It is important to note, however, that pastoral Quechua is limited in this respect even by comparison to other native languages in Spanish America: there is nothing in Quechua comparable to the 1705 Guarani translation of Juan Eusebio Nieremberg's theological treatise *De la diferencia entre lo temporal y eterno* (On the Difference between the Temporal and the Eternal) (Meliá 1992: 121–123). I have already mentioned the 1723 Nahuatl translation of the Roman Catechism or Catechism of Pius V, which appeared in an edition that also contains the first *Spanish* translation ever printed (Rodríguez 1998: 15).

Another major lacuna is the religious play, whose absence from the pastoral Quechua literature for most of the period between 1550 and 1650 period cannot be attributed solely to the vagaries of manuscript conservation. The religious play had been a key missionary genre for centuries, and the importance of drama in the Christianization of central Mexico is well documented. Several Nahuatl plays dealing with topics such as the Final Judgment, the Annunciation, and the Magi have survived from the seventeenth and eighteenth centuries, and it is known that plays were composed and performed in Nahuatl as early as the 1530s. The performances were elaborate and large-scale productions that became an essential component of Nahua Christian culture (Burkhart 1996; Ricard 1966 [1933]: 194–206). As has been seen, there is an important dramatic tradition in Quechua, including four colonial plays that can be classed as religious dramas, two of them in the *auto sacramental* genre. However, it is unlikely that even the oldest of these plays is earlier than the mid-seventeenth century, and Itier has argued they cannot be considered examples of a *teatro de evangelización* because of their complexity and thematic structure—they were not intended for basic catechetical instruction (Itier 1995c: 98). Garcilaso stated that the Jesuits composed *comedias* on religious topics for Indians to perform, and mentioned one in praise of the Virgin Mary in Aymara that was performed in Juli and a Quechua *diálogo del niño Jesús* (dialogue about or with the Christ Child) performed in Cuzco. He also claimed that the Jesuits found native Andeans to be especially talented in learning and performing such texts (Garcilaso 1945 [1609]: II 127).[3] However, the rarity of such references, even in the extensive Jesuit sources, suggests that these plays were experiments that did not become widespread. The play was a standard component of the Jesuit pedagogical tool kit, so it was only to be expected that they produced *some* Quechua plays. There is no ready explanation for the (initial) lack of success of Christian religious drama in Peru. Notwithstanding Garcilaso's claims, it could be suggested that it did not catch on among the Andean population because of the absence of comparable native performance traditions. It may be worth noting here that the First Lima Council prohibited the performance of any plays representing the birth, passion or resurrection of Christ that had not been expressly licensed by the archbishop, on the grounds that the indigenous population was not responding well to them (Vargas Ugarte ed. 1951–1954: I 51–52).

Finally, the absence of adaptations of native Andean genres in the extant literature requires some discussion. Such adaptations *were* carried out during the primera evangelización. We have seen instances of the haylli (a triumphal song-dance genre performed in military and agricultural contexts) and probably also the haraui (a genre of remembrance and lamentation) adapted to Christian liturgical contexts through the insertion of Christian texts as well as some musical and performative modifications.

Estenssoro Fuchs argues that the use of indigenous genres died out during the reform period of the 1570s and 1580s because they came to be regarded as the musical and textual equivalents of the "idol behind the altar," especially once the church became convinced that Indians were using Christian festivities such as Corpus Christi as a cover for the continued public worship of the huacas (Estenssoro Fuchs 1992, 2003).

In a critique of Estenssoro Fuchs's argument, Itier has pointed out that González Holguín's 1608 dictionary contains very specific references to uses of the haraui genre and of the *huacaylli,* a rain chant, in Christian contexts. Itier also mentions a 1610 description of the celebrations of the beatification of Ignatius of Loyola in Cuzco, during which taquis, presumably of the haylli genre, were dedicated to him (Itier 1992d; cf. Inca Fiestas 1986 [1610]: 43). Nonetheless, I find Estenssoro Fuchs's chronology convincing. Much of the information recorded by González Holguín is more prescriptive than descriptive, and he may have been referring to much earlier practices. The beatification fiesta was not a properly liturgical context, and it is not clear that the taquis were adapted as Christian songs—religious festivities traditionally included the performance of a variety of straightforwardly secular genres. It is also possible that there was a limited rebirth of the adaptation of indigenous genres in the early seventeenth century, a development that would be coherent with contemporary changes in translation practices.

The absence of native genres in the pastoral Quechua literature brings up the question of indigenous participation in the creation of this literature, and here again it is useful to look at equivalent endeavors in other languages. Dominican chroniclers in Mexico speak of Mixtec nobles who translated and composed catechisms, prayers, hymns, and spiritual tracts (Terraciano 2001: 55–56). Many Christian texts in Nahuatl were group enterprises in which the "author," always a Spanish cleric, worked closely with native assistants.[4] Closer to home, Ludovico Bertonio published texts that had been written or translated by Indians from Juli under his direction in the early seventeenth century (see the prologues to Bertonio 1984 [1612] and Bertonio 1612). In the Jesuit missions of Paraguay the Guarani writer Nicolás Yapuguay published two pastoral works in the 1720s (Meliá 1992: 149–152). By contrast, Guaman Poma's are the only extant Christian texts in Quechua that we have any reason to attribute to an Indian author-translator. Even mentions of collaboration between Spaniards and Indians in composing such texts are very rare: In 1583 a representative of Bishop Lartaun of Cuzco told the Third Lima Council that mestizos and Indians had participated in a translation of the cartilla texts carried out under his supervision,[5] and Oré stated that his translation of the Athanasian Creed had been checked by Spanish-speaking Indians (*indios muy ladinos*) (Oré 1992 [1598]: 207). One could speculate that indigenous participation in the production of the pastoral Quechua literature was much more widespread, but there is no direct evidence of this.

Translations and Originals

Pastoral Quechua texts can be divided into three main groups based on their relation to the source literature: (1) direct translations of canonical texts, (2) direct translations of texts composed ad hoc in Spanish for Indian audiences, and (3) texts originally composed in Quechua (i.e., "translations" only in the broader sense discussed in the introduction). Within the first group, there is an important distinction to be made between translations sponsored by the Third Lima Council and those carried out by later writers. The Third Council's translations of the cartilla texts were almost untouchable, and have largely remained so until the present day. No new translations of these texts were undertaken—only Pérez Bocanegra dared to make a modification to the Pater Noster, and he did so in a very discreet way.[6] The postcouncil authors translated a variety of new texts from the canonical hours, sacramental liturgies, and even the mass, but they had no such authority and there was a proliferation of different versions of these texts. For instance, there were at least nine different translations of the *Domine non sum dignus* communion prayer.[7] I have found no evidence that the church attempted to regulate the translation of such texts or establish official versions.

Translations of canonical texts seem to generally have been made from the Latin originals, or at least with the Latin originals in mind, something that is not always evident. The Third Council's cartilla was published in Spanish, Quechua, and Aymara, and the Spanish versions are presented as the originals. However, the linguistic appendix of the *Doctrina christiana y catecismo* often refers to the Latin texts to justify specific translation choices. In discussing the phrase *sancta cruzpa unanchanraycu*, "by the sign of the holy cross," from the *Per signum crucis* prayer, the noun stem *unancha* is glossed in Spanish as *señal* 'sign' but the suffix *-raycu* is equated to Latin *per*, 'by' or 'on account of.' In general, the Latin texts are used as a reference point to explain grammar and doctrinally delicate or important Quechua terms and expressions (Third Lima Council 1985a [1584]: 169–171). Certain comments in the appendix suggest that the Third Council translations of the cartilla texts differed from earlier efforts in their greater adherence to the Latin.[8] Oré emphasized that his translation of the Athanasian Creed "is regulated in all its terms with the Latin language" (Oré 1992 [1598]: 207). Translations of prayers, litanies, and other liturgical texts in the works of Oré, Pérez Bocanegra, and Prado are often accompanied by Latin versions. Clearly, reference to the Latin offered greater guarantees of doctrinal fidelity, especially at the terminological level.

The practice of direct translation of canonical texts was influenced to some extent by contemporary European debates on translation, or in any case, the author-translators tended to explain their practices in the terms of these debates, which revolved around a particular variant of the "literal-free" opposition: *ad verbum* versus *ad sensum* translation. *Ad verbum* translation required both word-for-word and syntactic correspondence with the original text, while *ad sensum* translation focused more on reproducing its general meaning. *Ad sensum* translation corresponds to what today would be considered literal translation, while *ad verbum* translation would be dismissed as absurd or impossible by most. The classical locus for the distinction is a letter written by St. Jerome, the author of the Vulgate, in 395 in which he defended the *ad sensum* principle, but added that *ad verbum* translation was to be preferred for translating Scripture, where "even the order of the words is a mystery [i.e., contains a hidden meaning]" (Lefevre ed. 1992: 47). Theo Hermans argues that while the traditional *ad verbum* principle was under increasing attack in the sixteenth century, especially from humanist circles, it was still regarded by many as the basic norm or "law" of translation. In particular, it was believed that it provided a guarantee of fidelity and transparency that was necessary for the translation of texts of great importance (Hermans 1997).

The Third Council translators were clearly putting themselves in the *ad sensum* camp when they claimed to have followed "the rule of translating meaning for meaning rather than word for word" (*la regla de interpretar sentido por sentido, más que palabra por palabra*) (Third Lima Council 1985a [1584]: 167). The same could be said of direct translation into Quechua in general. The whole notion of *ad verbum* translation may seem absurd, especially when the target language is as different from the source language as Quechua is from Latin or Spanish (the concept had been developed for translation from Greek into Latin). However, the *ad verbum* principle was not completely discarded. Oré claimed to have observed *both* principles in his translation of the Athanasian Creed (Oré 1992 [1598]: 207–209). The result is a very opaque Quechua text that is almost unintelligible without reference to the source text but cannot be dismissed as ungrammatical.[9] The fact that grammatical relations in Quechua are expressed through suffixes rather than word order made it possible to maintain some degree of syntactic correspondence, at least at a phrasal level.

This is an extreme case, but it is symptomatic of a tendency in some of Oré's and, especially, Pérez Bocanegra's translations of liturgical prayers to reproduce the syntax of the original text at the expense of intelligibility (e.g., Pérez Bocanegra 1631: 556–562). These translations are characterized by very long and convoluted sentences because one of the characteristics of liturgical Latin is the use of long relative clauses, and of long series of such clauses (Mohrmann 1957: 75–76). They are difficult to reproduce in Quechua, whose natural resources for relativization are morphological rather than lexical and always appear at the end of a clause, which makes them unsuitable for very long clauses. Oré and Pérez Bocanegra could easily have produced simpler and clearer translations by modifying the structure of the originals, but they chose to maintain it because of the canonical character of the texts, and perhaps because they sought to reproduce something of the cadence of liturgical Latin. In doing so, they were directly contravening the *estilo llano* espoused by the Third Council translators, who specifically advised against the use of long clauses (Third Lima Council 1985c [1585]: 355). The *estilo llano* can to some extent be seen as a corollary of the *ad sensum* principle.

Turning now to texts that were translated from ad hoc Spanish originals or composed in Quechua, a first observation is that it is sometimes difficult to distinguish one from the other. Georges Dumézil argued that Avila's Quechua sermons, which are accompanied by parallel Spanish versions, were the originals: "[it] is obvious that the sermons were thought out and originally written in Quechua . . . the relief and color of the original are lacking [in the Spanish versions]" (Dumézil 1957: 72). Avila himself does not tell us which he wrote first, but my impression is that the sermons were composed in Spanish and translated into Quechua, precisely because the Quechua version often goes into more detail. Adding "relief and color" during translation seems a more natural process than removing it. In Avendaño's case, the author himself explained that the Quechua versions are translations, and his Quechua bears the mark of over-literal translation from the Spanish—his sermons are probably the most Hispanized of all pastoral Quechua texts at semantic and syntactic levels.[10] While Diego de Molina provides few clues as to the process of composition of his sermons, it also seems clear that the Quechua versions are translations, or rather extended paraphrases, of the Spanish texts that accompany them. The fact that the Quechua versions contain a wealth of detail that is absent from the Spanish texts again suggests that the latter are the "originals." The only extant pastoral Quechua texts that one can safely assume were composed in Quechua are the hymns, whose formal requirements excluded direct translation. The Spanish prose versions, titled *declaraciones*, that precede each of Oré's cánticos provide rare examples of Spanish texts that were translated *from* Quechua.[11] No Spanish versions were provided for the hymns that appear in the works of Pérez Bocanegra, Prado, and Castromonte. As descibed in chapter 2, the catechism that was used in the diocese of Cuzco during the 1560s was originally composed in Quechua, and it was only during the revision process in the early 1570s that a Spanish translation was made to accompany it. The dominant pattern, however, was to compose such texts in Spanish and then translate them, however loosely, into Quechua.

This tendency is related to an aspect of the way in which pastoral Quechua texts were presented and transmitted that stands out through comparison with Mexican editions of pastoral literature in Nahuatl. The latter generally present free-standing Nahuatl texts and contain very little Spanish text beyond the prologues (e.g., Gante 1553; Gaona 1582; Bautista 1606; Mijangos 1607).[12] There was an obvious advantage to not including Spanish versions, as they doubled the length and cost of the books. By contrast, pastoral Quechua texts are almost always accompanied by Spanish versions—be they originals, translations, or paraphrases. Only a tiny portion of the overall corpus is free-standing, and the only work that contains no Spanish versions at all is Castromonte's ritual, which, not coincidentally, is a manuscript. Spanish versions served to constrict readings of the Quechua texts while also subjecting them to the scrutiny of the ecclesiastical elite, who generally could not read Quechua. The tendency to first compose sermons and catechisms intended for Indian audiences in Spanish also seems to have served as a guarantee of orthodoxy.

Tropes and Textual Figures

The translation of metaphors and other tropes is a classic problem in translation studies, and three main approaches are usually distinguished: (1) "literal" translation, which runs the risk of lacking intelligibility or resonance in a new linguistic and cultural context; (2) "paraphrase," or the use of a non-tropic gloss, which involves changing the whole tone and style of the text; and (3) "substitution," finding a term in the target language which can stand in a similar relation to the referent—i.e., to use a native trope (cf. van den Broeck 1981). Juan Rojo Mejía y Ocón confronted the issue in an appendix to his 1648 grammar which provides tips for the translation of Gospel passages into Quechua, where he explained that some terms had to be paraphrased rather than translated literally to preserve the meaning of the text. He used the example of the opening phrase of the Gospel of John (*In principio erat verbum,* "In the beginning was the Word"), where *verbum* should be translated *Diospa churin* 'God's son' rather than *simi* 'word, language' (Rojo Mejía y Ocón 1648: f. 85v–86). This could well be a veiled critique of Avila, who in the recently published first volume of his sermonario had opted for *simi* when translating this passage in his Christmas day sermon (Avila [1647]: 56). This "literal" translation is followed by a commentary explaining that the Word is the Son of God, who proceeded from the Father and was made flesh, just as speech is first conceived in the mind and then uttered by the mouth; as Avila explains, *simi* means 'mouth' as well as 'word' and 'language' (ibid.: 59–60).

Such issues arose even in the translation of the cartilla texts and thus had to be confronted by the Third Council translators, who generally sought to avoid the use of tropes. The term *regnum* or *reino* 'kingdom' in the Pater Noster (*venga a nos el tu reyno*—"thy kingdom come") was translated *capac cayniiqui,* "your greatness" or "your kingliness." God's "kingdom" was interpreted as a metaphor and translated through a paraphrase, thus avoiding the use of metaphor in the Quechua text. Years later, in a rare modification of the Third Council's version of a cartilla text, Pérez Bocanegra would use *capac pachaiqui* (roughly, "your kingly time/place"), which seems a more literal translation of Spanish *reyno* or Latin *regnum* (Pérez Bocanegra 1631: 690). Pérez Bocanegra either had a different reading of the expression, perhaps referring to Christ's millennial rule on earth, or sought to maintain the tropic ambiguity of the original in the Quechua version.

The epithet *agnus Dei* (lamb of God), a metaphor for Christ as a blameless and docile sacrifice put in the mouth of John the Baptist in John 1:36, can also serve as an example of the different approaches to Christian tropology. Pérez Bocanegra encountered it when translating the Penitential Litanies for his ritual, and rendered it literally as *Diospa uñan,* "God's lamb," an expression which, prima facie at least, would have meant little to native Andeans (*uña* refers to young mammals in general) (Pérez Bocanegra 1631: 533). Avila had to deal with this same trope in his sermon for the eighth day after the feast of the Epiphany, which paraphrased and commented on John 1:36. As with the Word/Son of God case discussed above, Avila opted for a literal translation followed by an extensive commentary. He rendered *agnus Dei* as *Diospa uña uyçan*—in other words, just as Pérez Bocanegra had, only he specified that *agnus* referred specifically to a young sheep by using the phonologically adapted loan word *uyça* (/wisa/, from Spanish *oveja*) (Avila [1647]: 114). Anticipating confusion among his audience as to how Christ could be compared to a sheep, and knowing that many of them would be familiar with the pictorial version of the metaphor in paintings or statues of John the Baptist that show him pointing to a lamb, Avila explained that just as the Incas had sacrificed llamas to the sun and lightning—sacrifices which (Avila suspects) continue even in the present—so in Christ's time sheep were sacrificed to God in expiation of sins. Thus, when John the Baptist referred to Christ as God's lamb, he was anticipating his death on the cross as an expiatory sacrifice to God (ibid.: 114–116).

The lengthy excursus was necessary because *uña uyça* did not imply the concept of sacrifice. González Holguín's dictionary had proposed a shortcut which is implicit in Avila's comparison of Inca and Jewish sacrifices. González Holguín suggested using *huaccarpaña uña* as an epithet for Christ, *huacarpaña* being the term for a type of llama with pure white wool that was offered in blood sacrifice to the sun deity in the Inca cults (González Holguín 1989 [1952, 1608]: 166; cf. Cobo 1956 [1653]: II 202). This can be considered an example of the third option in tropic translation, that is, substitution: the prototypical sacrificial animal in the Judeo-Christian tradition is substituted by the prototypical sacrificial animal in the Andean tradition, which happens to bear a close resemblance to it. The problem, of course, was that *huacarpañas* had additional meanings and associations, especially the solar connection, which were more than a distant memory. Just five years before González Holguín's dictionary was published, fellow Jesuits extirpating a huaca cult not far from Cuzco discovered an idol of a *huacarpaña,* defined as "a white, spotless llama which they would offer to the sun," that was being kept in a cave.[13]

Dealing with Christian tropology was an especially prominent issue for the postcouncil authors: either they were translating liturgical texts that abounded in tropes, or they were writing new texts that imitated them and thus had to be tropically rich. The Marian images were especially abundant and complex. Making sense of them required a familiarity not only with the culturally specific associations of, say, a star that can be used for maritime navigation (as in the epithet *stella maris*), but also with the canonical textual precedents and contexts that justify their use and account for their full implications. While a sermon could translate a trope literally and then proceed to explain it, as Avila's did, this was not possible in a hymn, litany, or prayer: the trope had to work immediately or not at all. As will be seen in the next chapter, the postcouncil author-translators responded by developing a rich syncretic iconography of Andean substitutes for the conventional tropes along the lines of González Holguín's *huacarpaña uña.*

However, the clearest carryovers from traditional Quechua poetics occurred at the level of textual figures rather than tropes. The single most important formal resource in the pastoral Quechua literature is semantic and syntactic parallelism, whereby a grammatical unit in a text echoes or repeats semantic and syntactic features of the previous unit, which Mannheim has emphasized as the key resource in Andean poetic traditions up to the present day (1986b, 1998b). Prior to the conquest, Quechua verbal art forms did not employ syllabic meter and were non-strophic—poetic units were not composed of precise numbers of syllables as in European verse forms, and were organized instead by semantic and syntactic patterns (Mannheim 1986a; cf. Tedlock 1983: 218). Parallelism predominated both in song and in prayer or ritual address. The most elaborate and complete form of parallelism in modern Quechua poetics is the semantic couplet, in which "two otherwise identical lines are joined together by the alternation of two semantically related word stems" (Mannheim 1986b: 60). In other words, a syntactic unit (sentence or phrase) is followed by a second unit which is identical to it, except for one or more word stems which vary and are consequently opposed to one another, or "matched." These terms tend to form semantic minimal pairs, in that "they differ by a single semantic property, and there is no word stem with a value for that property midway between them" (ibid.). Mannheim assigns great cultural importance to the semantic couplet, seeing it as a "means by which lexical relations are transmitted and reproduced among Quechua speakers" (Mannheim 1998b: 268).

The original forms and functions of parallelism in pre-Hispanic Quechua verbal art are difficult to determine due to the scarcity of representative texts. The following lines from a love song recorded by Guaman Poma, as transcribed and analyzed by Mannheim, can be considered a good example of a pre-Hispanic semantic couplet (Mannheim 1998b: 248, see also 1986a):

> Unuy wiqillam apariwan
> yakuy parallam pusariwan[14]
>
> [Watery tears carry me away
> Watery rain leads me away]

In this couplet there are three pairs of semantically related word stems appearing in identical morphological and syntactic contexts: *unu* and *yaku* 'water' (which today are dialectal variants of each other, but may have been semantically differentiated in the colonial period), *wiqi* 'tear' and *para* 'rain,' and *apa-* 'carry' and *pusa-* 'lead.' In this case there is an identical number of syllables in each line, but this a coincidence rather than an intentional poetic effect.

Non-Christian prayers recorded in the colonial-period literature provide further examples of Quechua parallelism that can be considered representative of pre-Hispanic practice. The following prayer to a newly-built house was recorded by Pérez Bocanegra in his confesionario (1631: 156):

> A
>
> huaman huaci
> cuntur huaci
> ancha, unay huatallatac huacaychanacussun
> mana oncoyhuan
> mana chiquihuan,
> unay huata ñoca
> huacaychayqui
> ricuiqui
> camri cana chay hinallatac huacaychahuanqui.

[O
hawk-house
condor-house
let us take care of each other for many years
without illness
without bad luck
For many years I will
take care of you
look after you
and you will do the same for me]

Stem matching is produced between *huaman* 'hawk' and *cuntur* 'condor,' *oncoy* 'illness' and *chiqui* 'misfortune,' and *huacaycha-* 'care for' and *ricui-* 'look [after].'[15] However, the parallelistic or "doubled" segments are so brief—sometimes consisting of single words—that one might question whether they can be considered semantic couplets.

As Frank Salomon has noted, there are numerous examples of parallelism in the Huarochirí manuscript, mostly in quotations of prayers and other forms of ritual address. He points in particular to a prayer in which the huacas Llacsahuato and Mirahuato are addressed by a sick person who wishes to determine the nature of the transgression (*hucha*) that is causing the disease (Salomon 1994: 232):

A Llacsahuato Mirahuato
cam-mi runa cama-c ca-nque
cam-tac-mi hucha-y-ta chaupiñamuca-cta-pas yalli-spa yacha-nqui
uillallahuay
yma-manta-m huncu-chi-cu-ni
yma hucha-y-manta-m ñacari-spa causa-ni.[16]

[O Llacsahuato and Mirahuato
You are the animators of the people
You know my *hucha* even better than Chaupiñamuca.
Please tell me
How have I made myself sick?
On account of what *hucha* do I live in suffering?]

This constitutes a third form of parallelism that differs both from the semantic couplet recorded by Guaman Poma and from Pérez Bocanegra's house-dedication prayer. The parallelistic units are full sentences, but the parallelism is quite loose: the sentences have similar syntactic structures and a number of stems and suffixes are repeated, but their content differs and no clear stem matching is produced.

Parallelism served a variety of purposes in pastoral Quechua texts. It was particularly frequent in indigenous ritual discourse, and thus gave Christian texts an added gravity. In certain cases it also served to orient the interpretation of key terms in Christian discourse, and even to transform semantic relations within the Quechua lexicon. As Mannheim notes, parallelism is present in the verbal arts of cultures across the world (1998b: 245–248). Perhaps the closest example for present purposes is the Roman Canon of the mass, which is characterized by the use of series of synonyms and synonymous phrases, a feature derived from pre-Christian Latin prayer (Mohrmann 1957: 66–68). However, the persistently binary character of parallelism in the pastoral Quechua texts, and in particular the tendency to form semantic minimal pairs, can be seen as crossovers from native poetic traditions rather than from those of the source languages.

One does not have to search very far to find pastoral Quechua texts that are pervasively parallelistic. The prayer that concludes Santo Tomás's *Plática para todos los indios* is strongly reminiscent in its structure of the prayer quoted from the Huarochirí manuscript (Santo Tomás 1995 [1560]: 177–179):

A athac
appo-y-mi can-gui,
ruraqu-e-y-mi can-gui [ñispa,]
conan-cama guaca-cta mocha-spa, piña-chi-rca-yqui
conan-manta guana-ssac-mi
mana-ña-tac hocha-llicu-ssac-chu
mana-ña-tac guaca-cta mocha-cu-ssac-chu
cam çapa-lla-ta mocha-scayqui
cam-ta tucuy-ta yalli-spa coya-scayqui

[O, alas
You are my lord
You are my maker

Until now I have angered you by worshipping the huacas
From now on I will amend myself
I will no longer sin [commit *hucha*]
I will no longer worship the huacas
I will worship you alone
I will love you above all things]

The author-translator used the same form of loose semantic and syntactic parallelism throughout the prayer, which appears to be modeled on native Andean prayers to huacas. The formal features of Andean prayers are turned against the worship of the huacas, as in the second pair of lines, where the incurrence of *hucha* (*hochallicuy*) is paired with, and equated to, the worship of the huacas (*guacacta mochacuy*), a nonsensical equation if the term *hucha* was understood in the traditional sense.

The Third Council translators sometimes recurred to parallelism of a sort that is more reminiscent of the house-building prayer recorded by Pérez Bocanegra—the parallelistic units are very brief, usually consisting of single words. It is especially prominent in certain texts of the *Confessionario,* such as the following prayer in which the penitent asks forgiveness for his/her sins (the matched stems are underlined) (Third Lima Council 1985b [1585]: 240):[17]

A, capac Dios ñocap çapay yayay,
ñoca huchaçapa
runayquim,
huacchayquim
chica achca
huchayhuan,
camayhuan,
cam Dioniita piñachircayqui:
cunanca canmanmi
cayllaycumuyqui,
çichpaycumuyqui,
tucuy soncoyhuan cutiri[y]cumuyqui,
anchapunim
llaquicuni,
puticuni
huchaymanta,
mana alli cascaymanta.

[O lord God, my only father, I
Your sinful person
Your sinful orphan
Have made you angry
With my abundant sins
With my many transgressions.
Now
I come close to you
I approach you
With all my heart I return to you.
I am very sad
I am very sorrowful
On account of my sins
On account of my evil doing]

This form of parallelism results in abundant stem pairing. The clearest pairs are *runa* 'person' and *huaccha* 'orphan'; *hucha* and *cama,* both terms for 'sin' in the Third Council's terminology; and *llaqui-* and *puti-* 'to be sorrowful.'

Mannheim argues that lexical pairing or stem matching, which carries the implication that the matched terms are inherently related either by synonymy (hyponymy or hyperonymy) or antonymy, plays an important role in the reproduction of Quechua language and culture in that it "brings lexical relationships which are normally tacit to the surface of discourse" (Mannheim 1986b: 64). At the same time, lexical parallelism can be used with rhetorical and ideological purposes to suggest the existence of an intrinsic semantic relationship between terms that are not so related (Mannheim 1998b: 263). By the same token, it can be argued that stem-matching was employed in pastoral texts to inculcate semantic transformations of Quechua terms that were being adapted for Christian use.

These effects are clearly at work in the Third Council texts. Take the following example from the catechism on the Credo, in which the answer to the question "what is man?" (*runaca ymam?*) is translated as follows: *Runaca, padre, Diospa camascanmi rurascanmi, huañuc ucuyoc, uiñay cauçac animayoc, Diospa ricchayninman, unanchanman camascan cascanmanta* (Man, father, is God's creation, possessor of a mortal body and an immortal soul, because he was made in God's image) (Third Lima Council 1985a [1584]: 70). The stem matching can be brought out as follows:

Diospa
camascanmi
rurascanmi,
huañuc ucuyoc,
uiñay causac animayoc,
Diospa
ricchayninman,
unanchanman
camascan cascanmanta.

There are four pairs of word stems in this sentence: *cama-/rura-* (synonyms for 'to create'), *huañu-/uiñay causa-* (antonyms—'to die' and 'to live for ever'), *ucu-/anima-* (antonyms—'body' and 'soul'), and *ricchay/unancha* (synonyms for 'image' or 'likeness').

The pairing implies that the concepts of *cama-* (a function of huacas who cause people and their livestock and crops to flourish) and *rura-* (the mechanical action of 'making,' as in making a pot), were inherently related, thus transforming their meanings. The action of *cama-* in particular is brought more into line with the Christian concept of creation by implying that it also involved "making."[18] Similarly, the noun stems *ricchay* and *unancha*, roughly glossable as 'appearance' and 'sign,' were used jointly to translate the concept of "image," of which neither was a functional equivalent—their original meanings are unclear, but it seems that each contributed something that the other lacked to approximate "image." In *huañuc ucuyoc, uiñay causac animayoc* (possessor of a mortal body and an immortal soul) there is a straightforward relation of antinomy between *huañuc* ('dying' or 'dead') and *uiñay causac* ('forever living'), but the *ucu/anima* ('body'/'soul') pair is composed of an adapted term and a loan word. The pairing of these terms, preceded by more familiar qualifiers, also in a paired relation, served both to cue their correct interpretation and to introduce them into the lexicon. This sort of mutual glossing was a key instrument for the Christian transformation of certain areas of the Quechua lexicon.

The Poetics of the Quechua Hymn

The most densely poetic of all pastoral Quechua texts are the hymns of Oré and Pérez Bocanegra. Like the Latin hymns of the breviary on which they were modeled, they were composed in different forms of classical meter and, at least in Oré's case, they were intended to be sung to the traditional liturgical melodies. Estenssoro Fuchs suggests that once the Christianized hayllis and harauis of the primera evangelización were discarded, the composers of Quechua hymns adopted a more conservative approach and attempted to reproduce the traditional Christian textual forms and melodies as closely as possible (Estenssoro Fuchs 2003: 300). However, echoes of native religious languages do occur in these hymns at the level of individual terms and images and the pervasive use of parallelism. Estenssoro Fuchs thus overstates his case when he claims that the hymns of Oré and Pérez Bocanegra deliberately avoided any dialogue of religious traditions of the sort set off by early texts and performances such as the haylli-*chanzoneta* described by Garcilaso (ibid.: 302). As will be seen in the next chapter, this sort of dialogue is very much alive in Pérez Bocanegra's hymns in particular. However, there is no denying that these hymns were European in their overall metrical and musical composition.

Composing Christian hymns in Quechua thus involved using the traditional meters, which were of classical origin. An anonymous Jesuit who wrote a linguistic survey of several South American languages in the late eighteenth century noted that one of the most unusual features of Quechua was, precisely, its adaptability to Spanish and Latin verse forms:

> The ninth characteristic of Quechua, and it is a very unusual one, is that it admits any type of verse or meter, be it of the sort used in Spanish verse or in Latin verse . . . One only has to note that in [Quechua] verses that are written in imitation of Latin verse, one does not pay attention to the quantity [i.e., length] of the syllables . . . One only pays attention to stress and to the placement of the caesuras. And this is enough for the words to form a complex sound that has that harmonious variety that in Latin is formed through the alternation of long and short [syllables] when they are pronounced by anyone familiar with the language.[19]

What this linguist observed is the fact that Quechua is highly adaptable to syllabic versification due to the flexibility of its syntax, the regularity of its prosody, and the abundance of mono- and bi-syllabic derivational and enclitic suffixes that can be added, omitted, or shifted around relatively freely to vary the number of syllables in a phrase or sentence. Composing Quechua verses in classical meters, such as the ones used in the Latin hymns of the liturgy, was thus relatively easy. The difference was that the rhythm resulted from stress patterns rather than the alternation of long and short vowels, as in Latin verse.

Oré appears to have been the first person to successfully compose Quechua verses on a large scale. The seven cánticos of his *Symbolo catholico indiano* were written in a form of Sapphic meter in which each stanza is composed of five lines: four eleven-syllable lines capped by a five-syllable line. Each of the first four lines is divided into hemistiches by a caesura between the fifth and sixth syllables. In each hemistich the first and the penultimate syllables are stressed. In the final line, the second hemistich is omitted. Vowels were sometimes omitted from word endings when they would have ruined the scansion. The pattern can be exemplified with the following stanza from the second cántico, which describes the heavenly spheres (Oré 1992 [1598]: 230):

> Cay ri | cus | can | chic || ha | tun cie | lo | pu | nim
> huc | pas ha | huam | pi || mas | ta | ra | cun | tac | mi
> huc | pas chay | man | ta || mu | yun | tin | ta pam | pac
> as ha | tun can | mi[20]

> [This sky we see is large indeed, and there is another one spread out on top of it, and yet another even larger one covering and encircling them both.]

Although he quoted a stanza by the classical (and pagan) Latin poet Horace to exemplify the meter, Oré made it clear that his immediate models were several Latin hymns of the Roman breviary that used the Sapphic meter, especially one particular hymn that was sung in the "eighth tone" at Sunday Vespers in Lent (Oré 1992 [1598]: 204). The cánticos were composed in the same meter and were to be sung to the same melody as this hymn. At the same time, Oré's seven cánticos are the only Quechua hymns that maintain a clear rhythm when read as poetry because of their high rate of coincidence of regular prosodic stress and metrical stress, and Oré indicated that they could be recited as well as sung (ibid.: 184).

Oré's *Symbolo catholico indiano* also includes two additional, independent hymns that were composed in different meters and were to be sung to different melodies. The creation hymn *Capac eterno* consists of four-line stanzas—three twelve-syllable lines, with a caesura in the middle of each line, and a final eight-syllable line. It was to be sung to the same melody as the Latin hymn *Sacris solemnis* (Oré 1992 [1598]: 394–399, 184). Oré's Marian hymn *Lira a Nuestra Señora del Rosario* has an entirely different meter—five-line stanzas in which lines 1, 3, and 4 consist of seven syllables, and lines 2 and 5 of ten syllables—and its melody is not specified (ibid.: 434). This hymn presents a further peculiarity in that it uses end rhyme on an ABABB pattern. As Mannheim has noted, rhyme is not an effective poetic resource in Quechua because it is "easily gerrymandered by the addition of identical suffixes to two or more words," and is thus not used in autochthonous verbal arts (Mannheim 1986b: 55). However, rhyme was very common in the Latin liturgical hymns on which Oré's hymns were based, and may have been integral to specific meters.

Of Pérez Bocanegra's three Marian hymns, each has an entirely different metrical pattern, the most complex being that of the third hymn, which has been analyzed by Mannheim (1998a: 393–401). Pérez Bocanegra stated that it was composed in "Sapphic verse" (1631: 707), but its meter differs from that of Oré's cánticos, as the stanzas consist of five eight-syllable lines and one four-syllable line. The hymn also has a pattern of end rhyme on an ABBAAC pattern, in which rhyme C goes on to become rhyme A in the following stanza. Pérez Bocanegra, who worked for several years in the choir of the Cuzco cathedral, provided a polyphonic score for this hymn which has been identified with the villancico tradition—the melody seems to have been derived from a sixteenth-century Spanish villancico which imitated the style of a popular love song (Estenssoro Fuchs 2003: 303). At the musical level Pérez Bocanegra thus diverged quite significantly from Oré, whose hymns were intended to be sung to the more solemn melodies of the canonical hours.

The classical metrical form of these hymns did not exclude the use of indigenous forms of parallelism. Mannheim has noted elements of parallelism in Pérez Bocanegra's third hymn and speaks of a "syncopation of poetic units" between the Andean and European patterns (Mannheim 1998a: 397). This syncopation is most clearly exemplified in Oré's cánticos. Take the following stanza from the fifth cántico, which describes the dispersal of the children of Eve throughout the world (Oré 1992 [1598]: 305):

Achca llactaman, achca marcamanmi
raquinacurcancu, nanac runa caspa,

may quittipipas, mayñec quinraypipas
huntam mirarcan.

[They were dispersed among many towns, as they were very numerous.
In whatever region they lived they multiplied until it was full.]

The first and third lines are each composed of two phrases of almost identical content and morphological and syntactic structure:

Achca llactaman,
achca marcamanmi
raquinacurcancu, nanac runa caspa,
may quittipipas,
mayñec quinraypipas
huntam mirarcan.

[To many towns
To many towns[21]
They dispersed, being very numerous
In whatever region
In whatever area
They multiplied until it was full]

This is the most common form of parallelism in Oré's hymns: two parallelistic lines occur within a syllabic verse line and are separated by the caesura. Due to the constraints of syllabic versification, the parallelism is not always as exact as it would be in freer verse forms.

On occasion the parallelistic lines coincide with the verse lines, as in the following stanza addressed to the Virgin Mary, where the first two lines form a semantic couplet (Oré 1992 [1598]: 257):

Hanacpachapas, canmantam cochucun,
angelcunapas, camraycum cussicun,
çupaycunapas miticaspa, ayquen,
camt[a] uyarispa.

[The heavens delight because of you
The angels rejoice on account of you

The devils, stumbling, flee
When they hear you]

In another variation, the couplet lines overlap across the verse lines (ibid.: 256):

Canmi preciosa margarita canqui,
yupay umiña, quespi rumi hinam,
chipipipinqui, canchac rupay hinam
canananaqui.

[You are a precious daisy
like precious stone, like crystal
you shimmer, like the shining sun
you blaze]

The couplet can be represented as follows:

Quespi rumi hinam, / chipipipinqui
Canchac rupay hinam, / canananaqui.

[You shimmer like crystal
You blaze like the shining sun][22]

Again, however, there is a symmetry between the semantic couplets and the verse lines—in each case the verse line break occurs at the same point in the couplet line.

Stem matching in Oré's hymns can often be seen to work towards the inculcation of the pastoral terminology, much as occurs in the Third Council texts. However, many of the lexical pairs are translinguistic—a Standard Colonial Quechua (i.e., Southern Quechua) term is paired with a Spanish or Central Quechua equivalent. In the first of the three stanzas quoted above, *llacta* and *marca* (Southern and Central terms for 'town') are paired in the first line (see also Oré 1992 [1598]: 258 and 309). Oré also paired *para* and *tamya*, Southern and Central terms for 'rain' (ibid.: 306, 356). Translinguistic pairing was a standard resource in traditional Quechua poetics, as can be seen in the following catchphrase cited in González Holguín's dictionary: *Choquechum corichum tulluyqui? Llamcay camca* (Are your bones made of gold [x2]? Get to work!) (1989 [1952, 1608]: 117). The word "gold" appears twice in identical grammatical contexts: first the Aymara stem (*choque*) and then the Quechua one (*cori*). This pair also occurs in the "idolatrous" prayers cited by Pérez Bocanegra in his confesionario, although in reverse order (*cori/choque*) (1631: 151). In a set of native prayers from Cajatambo that were recorded in an extirpation of idolatry trial and have been studied by Itier, we get Central/Southern Quechua pairs such as *ashua/aca* ('maize beer') (Itier 1992a: 1013). In a majority of cases, the alien stem is the "term b"—in the Cajatambo example, the Southern term *aca* (/aqa/) appears second because Cajatambo is a Central Quechua–speaking area (cf. Mannheim 1998b: 259 on translinguistic pairing in modern song texts). However, in Oré's translinguistic pairs this order is not always maintained. The purpose of such translinguistic stem matching is uncertain. The likeliest and least problematic explanation suggests that stem pairing was an aesthetic end in itself, and that lexical items from other languages were used simply because they provided a limitless supply of synonyms (Itier 1992a: 1014).

Chapter 8

God, Christ, and Mary in the Andes

If a dialogue between Christian and Andean religious thought is ever in evidence in the pastoral Quechua literature, it is in the network of tropes, motifs, and images that the author-translators of the postcouncil period applied to God, Christ, and Mary. Christian divinity was identified with a range of Andean (mostly Inca) divine entities and attributes, either through the use of unassimilated terms directly associated with them or, less explicitly, through certain emphases and details added to traditional Christian narratives and images. Rather than being an unintended side effect of the translation process, the confluence of the Andean and the Christian was deliberately sought out. The purpose of this chapter is to explore this Andean-Christian iconography with an emphasis on the more exotic tropes and their relation to the traditional imagery of divine power and majesty, of the passion of Christ, and of Mary's role in salvation—the themes around which Andean elements seem to have clustered. This involves an effort to decode what are often very opaque terms by identifying their original meanings in Andean contexts and then determining why and how they were used in Christian ones—a task made all the more difficult by our precarious understanding of Inca religion. It should be emphasized that the iconography discussed in this chapter is not representative of pastoral Quechua as a whole. Nonetheless, it merits detailed treatment because it provides relatively clear and precise examples of strategies of accommodation or deliberate syncretism in the colonial Peruvian church, and thus an opportunity to explore the mechanisms and purposes of these strategies. How were Andean religious entities and categories associated with Christian ones, and to what effect? Was the intention simply to ease the assimilation of Christian beliefs, a sort of "coating on the pill" along the lines of conservative understandings of accommodation, or was there more at stake?

Divine Omnipotence

One of the key challenges confronting the author-translators was the development of a vocabulary of epithets that inspired an appropriate sense of awe for divine omnipotence and glory. Some of the standard Latin or Spanish terms could be translated with neologisms: *omnipotens* or *todopoderoso* 'almighty' became *tucuy atipac* or *llapa atipac* 'all overcoming,' and *eterno* 'eternal' became *uiñay cac* 'always being.' However, such expressions were clearly deemed insufficient, and many of the epithets used to convey God's omnipotence were originally associated with the Inca sovereign—to some extent, this is true even in mainstream pastoral Quechua.

The first reference to such adaptations comes from the 1571 Jesuit carta annua, which describes the performance of a taqui by a group of nobles referred to as "Incas" in a Corpus Christi celebration in Huarochirí. The report approvingly notes that the lyrics included epithets originally applied to the sun and to "their king" adapted to Christ.[1] Inca sovereigns were true divine kings—they were objects of direct worship in person, through their effigies, and through their mummies once they were deceased. They were closely identified with the sun god, Inti—the reigning sovereign was referred to as *intip churin,* "son of the Sun," or simply as *inti* (D'Altroy 2002: 91–99; MacCormack 1991: 118–138). As Peter Gose puts it, "[t]he Sun represented the ultimate source and repository of the political authority of each Inka ruler, the deindividuated expression of the permanent influence of the Inkas as a group" (1996: 403). While the Jesuits in Huarochirí distinguished two separate entities—the Sun and the King—as the original referents of the epithets in the Corpus Christi taqui, they were to some extent one and the same thing.

The standard terms that expressed divine power in the Third Council corpus and all subsequent texts were the nouns *capac* and *apu,* normally used in adjectival position (the use of *apu* goes back to Santo Tomás's texts, e.g. 1951 [1960]: 18). *Capac* and *apu* were near synonyms, glossable as 'king' and 'lord,' respectively.[2] A *capac* was an especially exalted *apu,* while the Inca sovereign (the *capac* of Cuzco, or *Cuzco capac*) was given the titles *inca, çapay* ('sole') *inca,* or *çapay capac inca* (cf. González Holguín 1989 [1952, 1608]: 134). It could be said that *inca* was a hyponym of *capac,* which in turn was a hyponym of *apu.* God and Christ were referred to as *capac Dios, capac Iesu Christo, capac yaya* ('father'), *apu yaya,* and *apunchic* or *apuycu* ('our lord').[3] The term *capac* was also applied to the blood of Christ (*capac yahuar*) and to the life of the blessed in heaven (*capac cauçay*),[4] which shows that the term, in pastoral usage at least, had many of the semantic elements of 'holy' and 'glorious.' The use of these terms reflects a long-standing tradition of applying titles of secular power to Christian entities, e.g., Latin terms such as *dominus* or *rex* (for God or Christ) and *regina* (for Mary) and tropes such as "king of kings." A Christian use of the term *capac* was considered viable even by the more conservative author-translators because of a tendency to view the secular as distinct from the sacred (*capac* could thus be considered—wrongly—not to have any religious connotations), added to the fact that the institution of the Inca kingship had been effectively destroyed by the time of the Third Council.

Oré began to push the envelope by using a series of new epithets for God, if in a sporadic and sometimes covert way. At least in Oré's mind, these terms were associated with the Inca creator god rather than the Inca sovereign. His first cántico, a version of the Athanasian Creed, used *usapu* (or *ussapu*) to translate *omnipotens* 'almighty' (1992 [1598]: 219, cf. 252). The stem *usa-* 'to conclude successfully' is followed by the benefactive suffix /-pu/ (indicating that the action is carried out on behalf of someone other than the subject) and the agentive suffix /-q/, whose elision was a characteristic of the Inca lingua franca. González Holguín glossed *usapu* as "he who can achieve anything" (1989 [1952, 1608]: 358), and the term is recorded by Acosta as an epithet of Viracocha (1987 [1590]: 314). In Oré's view, however, the Inca creator god was Pachacamac, not Viracocha—attributes and epithets that earlier authors had associated with Viracocha were transferred by Oré to Pachacamac. He also seems to have associated God with the name Pachacamac in a veiled way—the term appears as the noun phrase *pacha camac* 'creator of the world,' which had been carefully avoided by the Third Council translators (Oré 1992 [1598]: 227, 358).

The most striking examples of Oré's use of unorthodox epithets for God come from his translation of a pre-communion prayer by Thomas Aquinas where, in addition to *usapu,* we find the terms *chacllipu, tocapu,* and *acnupu* (or *acnupo*), all translating *omnipotens* (Oré 1992 [1598]: 421). These terms are morphologically identical to *usapu*—a verb stem followed by the benefactive suffix and the agentive suffix (which is omitted). However, the verb stems do not appear in any other context and are not recorded in the Quechua dictionaries, which suggests that they are not Quechua. The term *tocapu* is familiar to students of Inca culture as the name of the geometrical motifs typically found on military tunics or *uncu,* such as those worn by the Inca sovereign (cf. Cummins 1994; Dean 1999: 123). In colonial usage, it seems to have referred to any elaborate design embroidered on or woven into a textile.[5] References in González Holguín's dictionary and Pérez Bocanegra's confesionario show that *chacllipu* and *acnupu* too were terms for fine and elaborate clothing, and that they tended to be used together with *tocapu*—González Holguín suggests that they referred specifically to the clothes of the Inca sovereign.[6]

Like *usapu,* the terms *tocapu* and *acnupu* appear as epithets for Viracocha in the pseudo-Inca prayers recorded by Cristóbal de Molina (1989 [1575]: 81–95). Insofar as Viracocha and his avatars appear to have been wandering culture heroes who endowed human societies with essential skills and technologies, these epithets may have originally referred to him/them as the originators of the ability to produce elaborate textiles. The Huarochirí Manuscript states that Cuniraya Viracocha was invoked by weavers whenever they attempted a difficult task (Taylor ed. 1999 [1987, n.d.]: 10; cf. Urbano 1991: xxviii). Deities were also pictured wearing such clothing—the Huarochirí Manuscript recounts a myth about a competition between huacas in which two of the challenges involved "dressing up" (Taylor ed. 1999 [1987, n.d.]: 64, 69). Considering the economic, political, and ritual prominence of textiles in the pre-Hispanic Andes (Murra 1962), it is not entirely surprising that rich clothing should have become a symbol of divinity.

It thus appears that part of Oré's intention in using the terms *tocapu, acnupu,* and *chacllipu* was for Andean worshippers to picture God richly dressed in Andean clothing, which would help inspire in them the proper awe and devotion. On the other hand, it seems that he regarded these terms—and, more obviously, *usapu*—as Inca epithets for the creator god. He was familiar with Cristóbal de Molina's prayers to Viracocha, although he believed that they had been addressed to Pachacamac (Oré 1992 [1598]: 157–158). Using such terms was thus a way of proposing a continuity between the cult of Pachacamac (the Inca equivalent of the Unknown God of the Athenians, according to Oré) and Christianity. They served not just as a stimulus to devotion but also as a demonstration that the Incas had been monotheistic—they had understood key aspects of the nature of divinity, and consequently the epithets they had used were appropriate for the true God.

Regardless of whether Oré intended it or not, it appears that some of these epithets also evoked the Inca sovereign. González Holguín associated *tocapu/acnupo* clothing with *el inca,* who in any case seems to have been identified with Viracocha. One of the most important Inca sovereigns in the accounts of the Spanish chroniclers was named Viracocha, and Pedro Sarmiento de Gamboa identified this individual as the inventor of finely woven clothing, which was consequently known as *Viracocha-tocapu* (1988 [1572]: 84). In fact, most of the unorthodox epithets for God one finds in the postcouncil literature as a whole clearly derive from the cult of the Inca sovereign. A good first example is the term *tupa,* which González Holguín glossed as "something royal, pertaining to the king" (*cosa real que toca al rey*) (González Holguín 1989 [1952, 1608]: 347), and whose full form was /tupa-q/ (*tupa* could also be written *tupac*). *Tupa* appears to have been a hyponym of *capac,* and was closely associated with the Inca sovereign.[7] González Holguín suggested that *tupa cocau,* which he claimed was a kind of magical maize given by the sovereign to his emissaries for sustenance on the road, was an appropriate epithet for the consecrated host (ibid.: 347).[8] In fact, the plática on communion in Oré's ritual called the consecrated host *animanchicpa tupa cocauñin* (the *tupa cocau* of our souls) (1607: 96). Diego de Molina described the church as *tupa huaci* (*tupa* house, i.e., palace) in the following passage from a sermon which is also one of the few places where God is referred to as *inca*: "Why do so many angels guard [the church]? The church is *capac* God's *tupa* house, that is why they serve God, their *capac* Inca, crowding around him and humbling themselves. Millions upon millions of angels serve *capac* God in the church."[9] I have seen no pastoral texts in which *tupa* is applied directly to God, although González Holguín did suggest such a practice in his gloss of the term.[10]

The identification is taken farthest by Pérez Bocanegra, particularly in the opening invocation of a pre-confession prayer he translated, which consists of a string of obscure and heterodox epithets used for *omnipotens*—much like Oré's translation of a pre-communion prayer by Thomas Aquinas mentioned above (Pérez Bocanegra 1631: 703). The key terms for present purposes are *titu* and *huanacauri.* González Holguín glossed *titu* (/titu-q/) as 'provider' (ibid.: 344), and Garcilaso discussed the term as a standard epithet for the sovereign that expressed his magnanimous liberality (Garcilaso 1945 [1609]: I 248). The power of the sovereign throughout the Inca empire was expressed and established through gift-giving and largesse on a massive scale (cf. D'Altroy 2002: 263–286). Like *tupa, titu* had been the name of a specific sovereign, and both terms reflect the omission of the agentive suffix /-q/ that was characteristic of the Inca lingua franca. It seems a fairly uncontroversial term to apply to God, but the fact that only Pérez Bocanegra did so suggests that it was not.[11] *Huanacauri* was the tutelary huaca of the Incas, identified both with a mountain in the vicinity of Cuzco and with a stone that was considered to be the lithified remains of one of the founding ancestors of the Incas (ibid.: 163). It was also, however, one of the standard titles of the sovereign, and I would argue that this is the relevant sense here.[12] Calling God *Huanacauri* may seem similar to the conventional practice of calling him *capac,* as was done in the Third Council texts. However, the term established a very direct and explicit identification between God and the Inca sovereign in his role as deity.

Some interesting extensions of the God-Inca sovereign trope can be found in Pérez Bocanegra's texts. The pope is referred to consistently as *apu panaca* or *apu capac panaca* (1631: 497, 534, 535), *panaca* being the term for the royal ayllus of Cuzco, which claimed descent from individual sovereigns. Thus, Paul V is *sanctissimo apu capac panaca yayanchic Paulo* (our father the most holy *apu capac panaca* Paul), and the current pope is referred to as *apu panacaicu* (our *apu panaca*) (ibid.: 497, 535). This use of the term is obscure, but seems to construe the line of successive popes as a *panaca* with the Inca God at its origin. In Pérez Bocanegra's translation of a prayer invoking the Archangel Michael, which stresses his prowess in defeating Satan, Michael is addressed as *Capac Cozco S[an] Miguel* and *Tampu Toco S[an] Miguel* (ibid.: 714–715). *Capac Cozco* can be glossed as "royal Cuzco," while *Tampu Toco* refers to a mountain with caves in the vicinity of the village of Pacaritambo from which the first ancestors of the Incas emerged according to one of the origin myths (cf. Urton 1990). It seems that both terms were metonymic epithets for the Inca sovereign—in early chronicles he was referred to as *el Cuzco* (Pease G. Y. 1995: 127). Like the epithet *Huanacauri, apu panaca, Capac Cozco,* and *Tampu Toco* all refer to the divine origins and descent lines of the sovereigns.

The God-Inca sovereign trope has some intriguing parallels in colonial religious art in Cuzco and the surrounding pueblos, where statues of the Christ Child, and sometimes of the adult Christ, were dressed with Inca regalia such as the *mascapaycha,* a tassel of scarlet wool that hung over the forehead of the wearer and was the main insignia of the Inca sovereign—his "crown" (cf. Cahill 2000: 117–118; Dean 1999: 55–56, 100–110). As David

Cahill observes, the practice of dressing the Christ Child as an Inca sovereign should be seen in the context of the iconographic tradition of the "Little King" with crown and scepter, the Inca sovereign being the local equivalent of a European king (Cahill 2000: 119). But just as occurs with the application of Inca royal epithets to God in prayer, the crowning of Christ with the *mascapaycha* was much more than an attempt to "translate" a trope or motif which could just as well have been omitted.

The earliest known reference to this practice is from a Jesuit source dating to 1610, which speaks of an image of the Christ Child "dressed as an Inca [sovereign]" that was paraded in the celebrations of the beatification of Saint Ignatius Loyola in Cuzco.[13] In 1687 Bishop Manuel de Mollinedo ordered that a *mascapaycha* and a solar pectoral be removed from a Christ Child image in the church of Andahuaylillas, specifying that the more traditional solar rays around the head be allowed to remain (Dean 1999: 230 n. 10; Marzal 1983: 364). It is tempting to relate this Inca Christ of Andahuaylillas to Pérez Bocanegra's presence there earlier that century, but Mollinedo also ordered the removal of the *mascapaycha* in several other pueblos (ibid.: 372). The practice of crowning Christ with the *mascapaycha* was clearly an entrenched one, however: in 1781, almost a century after Mollinedo's efforts, Bishop Juan Moscoso singled it out in a discussion of Inca nostalgia in local society, which he saw as the main cause of the recently defeated Tupac Amaru rebellion. Moscoso had observed Inca regalia both on statues of the Christ Child and in unspecified paintings: "What most pains me is to have seen in the visita I carried out last year how they [the Indians] introduce these vain observances into the church, dressing the image of the Christ Child with the *uncu* and the other insignias I have described [a garment called *yacolla* and the *mascapaycha*], and I have noted the same in some paintings, which convinces me that they adore the true God only when they see him in the garb of their Incas, whom they regarded as deities."[14] The equivalence with the epithets discussed above is not exact, as they were not applied specifically to Christ, but there is clearly a common theme. If, as Bishop Moscoso claimed, the Indians of Cuzco worshipped God "only when they see him in the garb of their Incas," this was because the Inca sovereign was the clearest embodiment of God's key attributes, especially the combination of absolute power and absolute generosity.

Finally, the apparent absence of solar terms in the lexicon of divine power and glory requires comment. As far as I can tell, none of the epithets discussed here referenced the sun directly. Solar symbolism is not very prominent in the pastoral Quechua literature in general, in contrast to contemporary Nahuatl texts, where the traditional Christian image of the solar Christ was merged with indigenous solar categories and associations (Burkhart 1988). Considering the well-known importance of the sun in Inca religion, it seems likely that the author-translators deliberately avoided terms and images that *directly* associated God or Christ with the sun. However, it can be argued that the God-Inca sovereign identification implicitly involved the traditional Christ-sun trope—the sovereign was, after all, a manifestation of the Sun, and vice versa. The connection appears explicitly in the plastic iconography—for instance, the solar pectoral removed from the Christ Child of Andahuaylillas by order of bishop Mollinedo (who nonetheless allowed the solar rays around his head to remain). It is worth noting here that the main representation of the Sun in Inca Cuzco was a gold statue called Punchao ('day') depicting him as a young boy dressed as the sovereign. This statue, which was held in Coricancha, the temple of the Sun, also functioned as a reliquary containing the pulverized hearts of the deceased sovereigns (MacCormack 1991: 113). It is hard not to see a connection between Punchao, which was finally captured by the Spanish in 1572 along with Tupac Amaru, and the popularity of the Inca Christ Childs in Cuzco.

Many of the tropes discussed in this section presume the persistence of an historical memory of the cult of the Inca sovereign well into the seventeenth century, and such a memory would have been strongest in Cuzco, where Pérez Bocanegra was based. In the late seventeenth and eighteenth centuries the indigenous elite of the city claimed descent from the Inca sovereigns and expressed or substantiated these claims by wearing the *mascapaycha* and other Inca regalia in religious festivities, especially Corpus Christi, and in portraits they had painted of themselves (see Dean 1999 for an in-depth discussion of this practice). Self-identification with the glories of the Inca past was also attempted by Cuzco's criollo elite as part of an identity politics—in effect, a form of protonationalism—through which they laid claim to regional leadership in opposition to the Lima criollos and to peninsular Spaniards (cf. Mannheim 1991: 71–72). In particular, it played into the historical rivalry between Lima and Cuzco—while Lima was the political, religious, and economic center of Peru, Cuzco had been the capital of the Inca empire and bore the symbolic title *cabeza de los reinos del Perú,* "head of the kingdoms of Peru." Incaism may seem like a paradoxical move for a Spanish/mestizo elite that also sought to distance itself from "the Indians," but it was made far less problematic by the conviction that prior to the conquest the Incas had been Christian in all but name. While Incaism is generally considered a phenomenon of the late seventeenth and eighteenth centuries, it probably began to develop at an earlier date; high-ranking Spaniards in Cuzco were wearing Inca costumes in public festivities as early as 1607 (Estenssoro Fuchs 2003: 308).

In this context, the *mascapaycha*-wearing Christ Childs can be interpreted as, in part, jingoistic expressions of the belief that God held the Indians of Cuzco, and Cuzqueños more generally, in special favor. An identity politics dimension can also be seen in the unorthodox epithets used by Pérez Bocanegra, which both verbally crowned God with the *mascapaycha*, and allowed the Christian worshipper to pray as an Inca would have—an act not unlike that of donning Inca garb on special occasions. Viewed in the broader context of his work, with its persistent emphasis on Cuzqueño linguistic and cultural forms, these epithets suggest the existence of a specifically Inca, and thus Cuzqueño Christianity, a suggestion that carried implications not just for the Inca past but also for the present and future of the city.

The Sacrifice of Christ

The terrible but redeeming nature of Christ's death on the cross was one of the most crucial and difficult themes the author-translators had to express in Quechua, and its importance was all the greater in liturgical contexts. Christ's sacrifice had to be presented in a way that conveyed a complex and paradoxical theology, while also provoking deeply emotional responses. The topic of the passion was developed most extensively by Oré, in accordance with a Franciscan emphasis on the contemplation of the sufferings of Christ which dated back to the thirteenth century and became widespread in the fourteenth and fifteenth centuries.

Oré's sixth cántico, intended to be sung every Friday as part of the morning office in Indian parishes, is the longest and most powerful of the Quechua passion hymns. The effectiveness of this hymn derives largely from its systematic adaptation for Andean audiences of the traditional passion iconography. The main trope, an identification of Christ's blood with irrigation waters, first appears during the whipping at the column (Oré 1992 [1598]: 346):

Chaupi huaçantam, yahuar puca mayu,
yahuar llocllaspa, pachaman suturcan:
capac yahuarhuan macchircayariscam
allpapas carcan.

[A river of red blood cascaded down the middle of his back and dripped down to the ground, the soil was thoroughly sprinkled with *capac* blood.]

The ground around the column is drenched, "irrigated," with blood—the terms employed are *macchi-* and (in the following stanza) *challa-*, which mean 'to sprinkle' or 'to irrigate by hand.' The same motif appears in a passion hymn printed in 1705, only it is used once Christ is on the cross (Prado and Manuel 1705: f. 146):

Huchanac capac yahuarin
Ucullanmanta paraspa
Sayascan pachatam co[ñ]i
Llocllan, surun, chacchun, carpan.

[His blameless *capac* blood warmly [irrigated x4] the ground where the cross stood, raining down from His body.]

The last line of the stanza consists of four terms for the flowing or dripping of liquids, of which the last two refer specifically to irrigation—*chacchu-* is a synonym of *macchi-* and *challa-*, and *carpa-* is 'to irrigate by canal.' The blood-irrigation water trope also appears in Diego de Molina's account of Christ's sweating blood in the garden of Gethsemane at the beginning of the passion, which states that his blood irrigated the trees and flowers in the garden and made them more beautiful.[15]

Oré's sixth cántico further develops the trope in the account of the crucifixion. The spear wound in Christ's side is referred to as a *gloria puncu* (door of/to glory) from which flows a *yahuar mayu* (river of blood), which becomes the addressee of two stanzas (Oré 1992 [1598]: 360):

A yahuar mayu, yacuhuan chacrusca,
canmi llocsinqui Paraysomanta:
animaycupac Christop sonconmantam
llocllarimunqui.

A llumpac yacu, viñay cauçac pucyu,
animaycucta mayllaripullahuay:
chaquiscallpacta[16] yacunan soncoyta
carparipuay.

[O river of blood mixed with water
You come out of Paradise
For our souls from Christ's heart
Your surge forth

O pure water, eternally living spring
Cleanse our souls
The parched soil of our hearts
Irrigate for us]

These stanzas are followed by an invitation for Man to build a city in the concavity in Christ's chest. In addition to the figuring of Christ's blood as flowing water, Christ's body is identified with the earth itself.

Margot Beyersdorff has suggested that the vocabulary and imagery used by Oré in his description of the shedding of Christ's blood established an implicit parallel with a form of ritual offering known in the present as /ch'alla-/, in which an alcoholic beverage is sprinkled as an offering to the earth and mountain deities (Beyersdorff 1993: 231). However, the dominant image is clearly irrigation, and it derives from late medieval exegeses of the passion, specifically a tradition of interpreting the great flood in Genesis as a "type" for the shedding of Christ's blood and its power to redeem humanity (to "wash away" sin), which in turn led to identifications of Christ's blood with rain and rivers (Marrow 1979: 138–139). The figuring of Christ's body as the earth also had late medieval origins (Areford 1998). However, Oré added a new dimension or "spin" to these images through the emphasis on irrigation, which is not necessarily implied in the flood trope.

This emphasis would have had special resonance in the Andes, where irrigation waters were a precious commodity whose flow was controlled by the huacas—the water of springs in particular was identified as the "urine" of huacas (cf. Polia Meconi ed. 1999: 170). The *yahuar mayu* is today a standard motif in folk songs and peasant cosmology. *Yahuar mayu* refers to the swollen and reddish rivers of the rainy season, when the water-blood similarity is most evident and the rivers are charged with power and danger (Montoya, Montoya, and Montoya 1987: 43–44). The verb used for the gushing forth of the *yahuar mayu* is *lloclla-*, which refers to rivers that overflow their banks, causing mudslides and transforming the landscape. All this is formally coherent with the Old Testament flood type, but it is equally clear that the selection of specific images and terms was intended to set off Andean resonances—in particular, a vision of the cosmos as sustained by a circulation of precious liquids that required sacrifice to the source of these liquids.

Another sequence of stanzas in Oré's sixth cántico focuses on the paradox that Christ, who is pictured as embracing and stabilizing the world with his hands and arms, was himself fixed to the cross and could not move without further destroying his body (Oré 1992 [1598]: 358–359). The audience is invited to contemplate his arms "which embrace the entire earth" brutally stretched out on the cross (*hinantin muyu macallic ricranta / ricullay cruzpi chutarayascacta*). The motif of the world-embracer immobilized by the cross continues in several stanzas, e.g.:

> Tecci muyucta hinantin pachacta,
> clauospi tacyac, canmi tacyachinqui
> yallinmi aychayqui lliquircaricurcan
> cuyuriptiyqui
>
> [You who are fixed [to the cross] by nails are the one who stabilizes the earth and the entire world. Your flesh was ripped even more when you moved.]

The image of Christ as embracing and stabilizing the earth comes from the late medieval passion devotion, as does the emphasis on the crucified Christ's inability to move (Areford 1998: 228, 233; Marrow 1979: 167–169). However, I would suggest that these two motifs were chosen and combined specifically in order to promote an identification between the crucified Christ and Pachacamac with regard to the huaca's main attribute, which was control over earthquakes, rather than his alleged role as the Inca creator god.

As presented in the Huarochirí Manuscript, Pachacamac, a huaca of the coastal plains near Lima, was so large that he would cause earthquakes just by moving his head—were he to move his entire body, the world would be destroyed. Pachacamac's title was *pacha cuyochic Pachacamac* (earth-mover Pachacamac) (Taylor ed. 1999 [1987, n.d.]: 286, 248). In the sequence of stanzas in question Christ's nailed hands are referred to as *pacha camac* (creators of the world) (Oré 1992 [1598]: 358, cf. also 227). Further evidence for the Christ-Pachacamac identification can be found in the fact that the two most important Christ images in Peru, Señor de los Milagros in Lima and Señor de los Temblores in Cuzco (both crucifixes), are attributed control over earthquakes. In a study of the colonial origins of the Señor de los Milagros cult, María Rostworowski has suggested that it developed when devotion to Pachacamac shifted to a miraculous crucifix painted on the wall of a local church which was invoked for protection against earthquakes (Rostworowski 1998). Señor de los Temblores, a colonial crucifix held in the cathedral of Cuzco and unofficial patron of the city, has been attributed a similar role, as his title indicates, since the mid-seventeenth century (Sallnow 1987: 75–78).

Oré may have been the first to associate the world-shaking and world-stabilizing power of Pachacamac with the crucified Christ, thus providing a conceptual basis for the Señor de los Milagros and Señor de los Temblores cults, or he may have drawn on an existing tradition. In either case, I would suggest that the purpose of the identification was to remind native Andeans that the agonizing and impotent crucified Christ was at the same time the all-powerful creator, who even as he hung from the cross was holding the world together with his outstretched arms. Giving the crucified Christ the powers of Pachacamac was a way of making the crucifix, and the passion as a whole, easier to assimilate as an object of adoration as well as pity.

A different, more condensed set of syncretic associations revolving around the passion is apparent in the texts of Pérez Bocanegra and Prado, and in González Holguín's dictionary. These associations centered on an identification of Christ's sacrifice with the blood sacrifices of the Inca state religion, and are set off by the use of the verbs *arpa-* and *pira-*. *Arpa-* was the term for blood sacrifice, while *pira-* referred to a part of the sacrificial ceremony in which the officiants drew lines on their faces and bodies with the blood of the victim (González Holguín 1989 [1952, 1608]: 34, 287). Juan Polo de Ondegardo mentioned a particular form of blood sacrifice in which lines were drawn on the faces of the mummies of past Inca sovereigns with the blood of children—although he did not use the term, this clearly corresponds to the action of *pira-* (Third Lima Council 1985b

[1585]: 267). One of Avila's sermons used both terms to describe idolatrous sacrifices in the Coricancha temple in Cuzco prior to the conquest: *caipim arpaicocc carccan llamacta, ccoicta yahuarñinhuan runacta piraspa* (here they sacrificed [*arpa-*] llamas and guinea pigs, and marked [*pira-*] the people with their blood) (Avila [1649]: 97). The two terms are emblematic of idolatrous worship.

The use of *arpa-* as a term for Christ's sacrifice developed gradually. Oré employs it in a cautious, qualified fashion. It is applied in his narrative of the passion to Abraham's attempted sacrifice of his son, i.e., to the kind of sacrifice that was displeasing to God (Oré 1992 [1598]: 347), and at the end of the narrative Oré refers to Christ's death as *Diosman checan arpay* (the true sacrifice [*arpa-*] to God) (ibid.: 361). In other words, for Oré the term implies the idolatrous sacrifice of the "old law." In the texts of Pérez Bocanegra and Prado, however, we find *arpa-* applied directly to the sacrifice of Christ (e.g., Pérez Bocanegra 1631: 684, 696; Prado 1641: f. 32, 56).

The Christian adaptation of *pira-* was proposed in González Holguín's dictionary entries on the term (González Holguín 1989 [1952, 1608]: 34, 287):

> Pirani. Era una ceremonia que del carnero o cordero que avían de sacrificar con la sangre nueva y fresca se embijavan con rayas en la cara, o cuerpo para tener parte en aquel sacrificio.
> Pirascca. Los embijados, o sulcados con sangre, y se puede aplicar a nuestro cordero Christo.
> Pirasca. [sic., Pirascca] Con su sangre unjidos los que participan del.
>
> [*Pirani.* It was a ceremony in which they painted lines on their faces or bodies with the fresh blood of the alpacas or llamas that were sacrificed in order to partake of the sacrifice.
> *Pirascca.* Those who are painted with lines of blood, and it can be applied to our lamb Christ.
> *Pirascca.* Those who are annointed with his blood and partake of Him.][17]

González Holguín suggested two different metaphoric uses of the passive participle *pirasca,* which normally would refer to the sacrificer or participant who is marked with the blood of the victim. It can be applied to Christ himself, paradoxically because Christ is the sacrificial victim; and to those who take communion and thus participate in the sacrifice of Christ. As discussed in the previous chapter, González Holguín also suggested that the term *huacarpaña,* name of the white sacrificial llama of the Inca solar cult, would be a good epithet for Christ in the form *huaccarpaña uña* (*huacarpaña* lamb) on the model of the *agnus Dei* epithet (ibid.: 166). The *huacarpaña* llama is mentioned as a typical victim of *arpay* sacrifices by Pachacuti Yamqui (Pachacuti Yamqui Salcamaygua 1993 [n.d.]: 210), which indicates that the *arpa-/pira-* and *huacarpaña* tropes were related.

González Holguín's suggested uses of *pira-* occur exactly as he indicated in hymns by Pérez Bocanegra and Prado. Pérez Bocanegra's second Marian hymn describes Christ as a shepherd who descended to earth to care for his llamas, and revived them with his blood (Pérez Bocanegra 1631: 706):

> Yaca huañunayactam
> Yahuarinhuan <u>pira</u>spa,
> Cauçachirca,
>
> [He brought them back to life when they were almost dying by marking [*pira-*] them with his blood.]

Pérez Bocanegra employs González Holguín's second suggested metaphor: the followers of Christ, and by implication those who take communion, are presented as the recipients of the action of *pira-*. The first of González Holguín's suggested metaphors appeared in Prado's passion hymn, which pictures Christ's body on the cross as follows (Prado 1641: f. 230):

> Riti yallic ucunri,
> Yahuarinhuan <u>pira</u>sca
> ñauray rurac maquinri
> Ancha yallin chutasca.
> Alau alau
>
> [And his body whiter than snow
> Streaked [*pira-*] with his blood
> And his hands that made everything
> Terribly stretched
> Alas, alas]

Here it is Christ, the sacrificial victim, who is paradoxically described as *pirasca.* The metaphor conveys in a highly condensed fashion the idea that Christ, who is both man and god, is both sacrificial victim and recipient (i.e., sacrifices himself to himself).

In these instances, the "Andeanization" of Christ's sacrifice was carried out in a very different fashion from that seen in Oré's work. The images here focused on Christ's condition as a docile sacrifice rather than on his world-transforming powers. Instead of a force that irrigates, nourishes, and transforms landscapes, Christ's blood is equated to that of llamas sacrificed to the huacas. These identifications reflect an effort to clarify the properly sacrificial nature of Christ's death and its relation to the eucharist. The word *arpa-* conveyed the concept of sacrifice with more clarity and force than any other Quechua term, while *pira-* had an even greater specificity, expressing the relation between victim and officiants/beneficiaries. In particular, *pira-* allowed for the creation of a trope which expressed the paradoxical nature of Christ's sacrifice more effectively than any amount of explanation.

The Marian Cosmos

Mary's crucial role in Counter-Reformation Catholicism stemmed from her function as an intermediary between Man and God, and from the belief that although she was one of the children of Eve she had a unique proximity to God through the Incarnation and her physical assumption into heaven. While the doctrine of the Immaculate Conception (Mary's conception free of original sin) was not officially proclaimed until the mid-nineteenth century, and was a subject of intense debate during the sixteenth and seventeenth centuries, the Spanish monarchy was fully invested in it, and it was affirmed explicitly in the pastoral Quechua literature. Extensive portions of the daily liturgy in the pueblos de indios were dedicated to Mary: the Angelus was performed every evening (sometimes also at noon), and the Salve Regina and a Marian litany on Saturday afternoons. There were also a host of private devotional practices dedicated to Mary, the most important of which was the rosary. In terms of the variety of textual and performative expressions and the time devoted to it both in the formal liturgy and in private devotions, the Marian cult surpassed that of the crucified Christ. Beginning in the late sixteenth century a series of

Marian shrines and pilgrimage centers sprang up in pueblos de indios and acquired regional importance, most notably that of the Virgin of Copacabana on Lake Titicaca (cf. MacCormack 1984).

Oré's *Symbolo catholico indiano* laid the foundations for the Marian cult in Quechua. It provided two Marian hymns in different metrical forms: in addition to the *Lira a Nuestra Señora del Rosario,* which appears at the end of the book, thirty-eight stanzas from the third (Tuesday) cántico could be performed as an independent Marian hymn, an abbreviated version of which was reproduced by Prado (Oré 1992 [1598]: 434, 248–259; Prado 1641: f. 230v–234v). The *Symbolo* also provided fifteen prayers narrating the fifteen mysteries of the Virgin, which were to be used for praying the rosary (Oré 1992 [1598]: 428–433). Finally, the *Symbolo* contains a Marian litany in Latin and Quechua versions which was to be performed on Saturday afternoons while the choir processed into the church, prior to the singing of the Salve Regina (ibid.: 435–438, 191). The Quechua text is actually an abbreviated version which omits several of the epithets in the Latin text. This litany was indulgenced in 1605 by Paul V on Oré's request, and shortly afterwards Oré published the indulgence document and the Latin version of the litany in his ritual (Oré 1607: 335–338). It became the official Marian litany of the Peruvian church and should be considered one of the most important sources for colonial Marian iconography in Peru. I have not been able to identify its sources, but it differs substantially from the Litany of Loreto, the standard Marian litany of the Church—it is longer, its iconography is different, and it contain references to the Marian Mysteries.[18]

Pérez Bocanegra's *Ritual formulario* contains the most important collection of Marian texts in Quechua after Oré's *Symbolo.* Pérez Bocanegra was clearly invested in spreading Marian doctrines and devotions, and he published Spanish and Quechua versions of an Immaculist adaptation of the Ave Maria that had been indulgenced by Alexander VI (1631: 700–701). The *Ritual formulario* concludes with Pérez Bocanegra's three Marian hymns, of which the first and third provide the most radical and complex examples of the Andeanization of the Marian iconography (the second hymn speaks more of Christ) (ibid.: 704–712). The first hymn is simply a series of epithets in sixty-nine eight-syllable lines with no apparent division into stanzas and no indications as to its musical performance (ibid.: 704–706).[19] The third hymn, whose formal properties were described in the previous chapter, has become widely known under the incipit *Hanac pachap cussicuinin* ("Joy of Heaven") after several commercial recordings based on Pérez Bocanegra's score (ibid.: 707–712).

Traditional Marian iconography symbolized Mary's virtues and her role in the history of salvation with flowers, stars, and architectural forms. Flower and plant names were signs of her beauty and virginal purity, and celestial epithets (stars, moon, dawn) pointed to her role as guide and intercessor between heaven and earth. Mary's function as a vessel and mediator was indicated with architectural epithets such as "tower," "temple," "cistern," "enclosed garden," "door," "ladder," etc. This iconography derived from a long tradition of exegetical commentary on biblical texts, in particular the Song of Songs. As discussed in chapter 7, there were obvious difficulties in reproducing these tropes in Quechua. One could call Mary "rose" by using the loan word *rosa,* but even Indians who had actually seen one would probably be unaware of the rose's extensive cultural associations and of the textual sources of the Christian rose iconography (see Winston-Allen 1997: 82–89). Thus, Oré and (in particular) Pérez Bocanegra substituted Andean botanical and constellation names for European roses and sea-stars. However, it seems unlikely that there was a true correspondence of attributes and associations between the original images and their Andean substitutes. On what basis the latter were selected is thus an important but difficult question.

Ethnohistorical and archeological research has shown that astronomical observation was of crucial importance in pre-conquest Andean society at both imperial and local levels (Bauer and Dearborn 1998). Stars and constellations that were carefully observed to regulate the agricultural and ritual calendars were also objects of worship, and were thought to control the reproduction of specific animal and plant species (Cobo 1956 [1653]: II 159; Taylor ed. 1999 [1987, n.d.]: 372–379). The Pleiades, known as Collca ('granary') or Oncoy ('sickness'), were at the top of the list, and are still observed in the present day to predict the quality of the maize harvest and determine when planting should begin (Taylor ed. 1999 [1987, n.d.]: 378; Urton 1981: 118–122). The constellations Orcochillay and Catachillay, imagined as a male and female llama respectively, were objects of special adoration by shepherds because they controlled the reproduction of llamas. Catachillay was identified by most Spanish observers as a cross-shaped constellation they knew as *el cruzero,* perhaps the Southern Cross (Third Lima Council 1985b [1584]: 265; Urton 1981: 131).[20] Chacana, the Belt of Orion (popularly known in Spanish as *las Tres Marías*), appears at the center of a sketch of the Andean cosmos by Pachacuti Yamqui—Gary Urton explains that "it marks the point at which the sky is divided into two parts; also, its rising and setting points coincide with those of the equinox sun"

(Pachacuti Yamqui Salcamaygua 1993 [n.d.]: 208; Urton 1981: 139). Other stars or constellations that are mentioned in colonial sources as having religious importance include the unidentified Tupatarca, Mamanmirco, and Queantupa (Third Lima Council 1985b [1584]: 265; Cobo 1956 [1653]: II 160; Urton 1981: 131, 138).

The celestial objects associated with Mary in the traditional iconography were rather generic. They derived primarily from John's vision in Revelation 12:1 of a woman "clothed with the sun, and the moon under her feet, and upon her head a crown of twelve stars." Apart from comparisons to the sun and moon, Mary was referred to as *stella maris* (star of the sea) and *stella matutina* (morning star) in the original Latin version of Oré's Marian litany. The *stella matutina* was Venus, but *stella maris* seems to be a generic term for any star that could be used for navigation. Oré's conservative Quechua version of this litany was equally generic, using the epithets *chasca coyllur* (shaggy or hairy star) and *cori coyllur* (golden star). *Chasca* is today a generic term for the brightest stars and planets (Urton 1981: 107), although in colonial usage it seems to have referred to the "morning star" Venus (Pachacuti Yamqui Salcamaygua 1993 [n.d.]: 208), and was thus the equivalent of *stella matutina*. *Cori coyllur* does not seem to have referred to any specific star.

Pérez Bocanegra greatly expanded the range of stellar epithets for Mary, incorporating precisely those stars and constellations mentioned in colonial sources as having religious significance for native Andeans. His hymn *Hanac pachap cussicuinin* contains the consecutive epithets *chipchiicachac catachillay* (sparkling Catachillay) and *punchau pussac queantupa* (Queantupa that leads the day)—Catachillay is also mentioned once more further in the hymn. As Mannheim suggests, Catachillay, the female llama constellation in opposition to the male Orcochillay, may have been an appropriate epithet for the Virgin because of its generic femaleness (Mannheim 1998a: 397). Queantupa is mentioned only by Cobo (1956 [1653]: II 160) and cannot be identified with any specific star or constellation, but from the way it is described in the hymn it seems to have been especially visible before dawn. Mannheim identifies *Hanac pachap cussicuinin* as a "Pleiades song," pointing to R. T. Zuidema's argument that the term *Catachillay* designated the Pleiades (Zuidema 1982: 211).[21] This identification is unclear: although Ludovico Bertonio's Aymara dictionary associated the Pleiades with the name *Catachillay*,[22] several other colonial sources distinguished clearly between the two.[23] However, Mannheim's identification is also supported by the appearance of the term *collca* with its more common meaning 'granary,' which can be interpreted as a veiled reference to the Pleiades. The hymn contains several epithets alluding to harvesting and food storage, both activities closely associated with the Pleiades. Pérez Bocanegra's first Marian hymn mentions a different set of stars/constellations: Chacana, Mamanmirco, and Tupatarca. As in the case of the Pleiades in *Hanac pachap cussicuinin*, the reference to Chacana, which literally means 'ladder,' is ambiguous, occurring in an epithet that compares Mary to a celestial ladder in accordance with the traditional *scala coeli*. Tupatarca is described as *Mama cochacta huampocpa / ñan catinan* (which shows the way to those who sail the sea). This sounds like a paraphrase of *stella maris*, which if translated literally (*cocha coyllur*), as it is in some modern Quechua hymns, would probably have meant little to native Andeans. Why Tupatarca in particular was chosen for this role is unclear.

Before discussing the botanical epithets, some mention should be made of references to the earth and agricultural fertility in Marian contexts. In the Marian section of Oré's third cántico Mary is referred to as *camac allpa* (fertile soil) and *çumac orco* (beautiful mountain) (1992 [1598]: 258). *Camac allpa* is a particularly striking expression in that it seems to echo *camac pacha*, "fertile earth," an entity identified as an object of pagan worship in one of the Third Council catechisms (Third Lima Council 1985a [1584]: 81). As Mannheim has noted, *Hanac pachap cussicuinin* contains several references to fruitful trees, bountiful harvests, and food storage, which again seems to relate Mary to agricultural fertility (Mannheim 1998a: 397–398). Images of Mary as a harvest or storehouse were also eucharistic references to Christ as food for mankind, as in the epithet *Capac micui aimuranca* (harvest of *capac* food).

The profusion of botanical epithets in the texts of Oré and Pérez Bocanegra grew out of the traditional Marian iconography, which in turn was based on exegeses of the Song of Songs, a love dialogue between bride and groom. The bride is compared to the rose and the lily, for her beauty, and to an enclosed garden and a sealed fountain, for her virginity (cf. Winston-Allen 1997, chapter 4). Oré's Marian litany contains the standard symbols: the rose, the lily, the palm, the cedar, and the enclosed garden (*hortus conclusus*). However, his Quechua version of the litany uses the autochthonous cantut, hamancay, and chihuanhuay flowers as epithets in addition to the standard European trees and flowers listed in the Latin version. Flower metaphors have special prominence in his *Lira a Nuestra Señora del Rosario,* as this hymn focuses on the rosary iconography. Interestingly, flower epithets are also applied to Jesus—Mary is presented as having produced the hamancay flower Jesus in the *Lira* and in the Marian section of the third cántico (Oré 1992 [1598]: 434), and Pérez Bocanegra's *Hanac pachap cussicuinin* refers to Christ as a hamancay bud. These images have European precedents, as Christ was sometimes figured as a rose produced by Mary (Winston-Allen 1997: 89)—the question is why the hamancay was chosen for this specific role.

At least twenty flower and plant names are used as Marian epithets in Pérez Bocanegra's first hymn (in some cases the identification of an epithet as a plant name is contextual, because the term does not appear in any of the Quechua dictionaries). Five different autochthonous vines are described as woven into the fence of the *hortus conclusus.* One flower image is particularly complex: Mary is presented as "Jesse's esteemed and royal descendant / golden younger child of his flowering" (*Iesep yupai capac pitan / çiçascampa cori sullcan*). The image draws on patristic exegeses of Isaiah 11:1, which speaks of a stem that would spring from the root of the tree of Jesse and bear flower, as a prophetic reference to Jesus and Mary, who were figured as flowers on the tree of Jesse in medieval iconography (Winston-Allen 1997: 89).

Itier has noted that flower metaphors are very common in Quechua folklore, especially love songs, where loved ones are referred to with the names of specific flowers selected on the basis of conventional attributes inspired by the growth cycle and habitat of a plant as well as its appearance (Itier 1995a: 72–76). It seems clear that this "flower language" is of pre-Hispanic origin and that it was merged with the floral components of the Marian iconography. The following stanza from Oré's *Lira a Nuestra Señora del Rosario* provides one of the best examples of the specificity of the attributes (1992 [1598]: 434):

Hamancaytam yuyayqui
Christo Iesusta huachascayquimanta
Pantictam unanchayqui
Cruzpi huañuscanmanta.

[I consider you a hamancay
Because you gave birth to Jesus Christ
I consider you a panti
Because he died on the cross.]

The meanings associated with plants like the hamancay and the panti might still be recoverable through research on present-day botanical folklore.

The Construction of the Andean-Christian Iconography

As occurred with the increasingly specific associations between God and the Inca sovereign that grew out of attempts to translate traditional epithets such as *dominus,* the conventional Marian imagery provided the "stem" for a "flowering" of ever more complex and syncretic iconography. Even the most exotic-sounding Marian epithets can be traced back to traditional motifs. Most of the epithets in Pérez Bocanegra's first Marian hymn can be matched with those of the Latin litany published by Oré (cf. Durston 2004: 494–498), and this is also the case with *Hanac pachap cussicuinin,* if to a lesser extent. However, the relation between the source images and the Andean variants or substitutes was often a superficial or very generic one, and it is clear that the latter were partly selected on the basis of specifically Andean contexts and associations.

A comparison of Pérez Bocanegra's first Marian hymn and *Hanac pachap cussicuinin* reveals one very specific selection criterion. There is a pattern in the differences between the epithets used in the two hymns which has a clear seasonal basis (the seasonality of a hymn would not in itself be unusual, since much of the Catholic liturgy has a seasonal character). *Hanac pachap cussicuinin* contains prominent references to harvests and granaries, the harvest occurring early in the dry season (*chirau,* during the southern hemisphere winter), while the first hymn, with its references to falling water, rainbows, and dew, and its profusion of flower and vine names, can be identified with the wet season (*pocoy,* during the southern hemisphere summer). Catachillay, which is featured prominently in *Hanac pachap cussicuinin* but does not appear in the first hymn, was placed by Pachacuti Yamqui in the left-hand side of his cosmological drawing, which is labeled *verano* 'summer' (by which he meant the dry season) in opposition to the right-hand side, labeled *imbierno* and *pocoy* (Pachacuti Yamqui Salcamaygua 1993 [n.d.]: 208). Moreover, in the first hymn the moon is termed *pacsa,* while *Hanac pachap cussicuinin* uses the more common *quilla, pacsa* being a term that referred specifically to the veiled moon visible on cloudy nights.[24] This seasonal bias may be related to the fact that *Hanac pachap cussicuinin* presents the Virgin as powerful as well as compassionate (she is even compared to lightning at one point), whereas in the first hymn she appears in a more passive role (either distant or accessible), the dry season/harvest time being the decisive and most active time of the agricultural cycle. Pérez Bocanegra seems to have intended for Andean parishioners to praise Mary by affirming her control over, and presence in, the natural entities and processes that were foremost in their minds at a given time of the year.

Any given image in these hymns, in other words, could be read either in terms of the European symbol that it substituted for or "translated," or for its specifically Andean seasonal and cosmological associations. Mannheim, who argues that *Hanac pachap cussicuinin* doubled as a hymn to the Pleiades, states that it was intended "to be understood within two quite different interpretive horizons by distinct interpretive communities, who could thereby maintain the comfortable fiction that they were engaged in the same ritual endeavor" (Mannheim 1998a: 401). Reading the imagery in relation to its canonical Christian sources required a familiarity with these sources that would only have been common among Spaniards and the Indian elite; for the rest, the imagery still made sense in Andean terms.

Several examples of this duality or open-endedness can be found in Pérez Bocanegra's first Marian hymn. As already mentioned, Mary is termed *Mamanmircoman cecarcoc / Iacobpa çuni chacanan,* "Jacob's tall ladder that reaches up to Mamanmirco." The expression derives from the epithet *Scala coeli* (ladder of heaven), which occurs in the Latin litany but was omitted from Oré's Quechua version. It is a reference to a passage in Genesis in which the Patriarch Jacob dreamed of a ladder connecting heaven and earth. Mary could be seen as a bridge between heaven and earth in that the Incarnation brought God down to earth and opened the gates of heaven for Mankind. Another association is provided in Oré's cántico on the passion, which equated Jacob's ladder to the ladder used to bring Christ's body down from the cross—this ladder is metonymically connected to Mary because she was pictured weeping at its foot (Oré 1992 [1598]: 365). At the same time, it is significant that Jacob's ladder reaches up specifically to the star or constellation Mamanmirco: the term for 'ladder,' *chacana,* was also the Quechua name for Orion's Belt, a constellation known to the Spanish as *las Tres Marías,* "the three Marys" (Urton 1981: 131–132).[25] In the first reading, Mary is figured as a ladder reaching up to the heavens, for which Mamanmirco simply served as a synecdoche. In the second reading, Mary is identified with the constellation Chacana, which already had Marian connotations for the Spanish but whose significance in Andean cultural contexts is unknown.

To Mannheim's analysis of a double register in Pérez Bocanegra's Marian iconography I would add Estenssoro Fuch's concept of disjunction, discussed in chapter 2. In the "highbrow" reading of those familiar with the canonical symbolism, the Andean "substitutes" were not intended to merge seamlessly with this symbolism. They were selected and positioned in such a way that they would stand out and attract attention to themselves, and were meant to be interpreted in a dialogical and oppositional relation to the traditional iconography expressed in the Latin litany published by Oré. Such a relation is suggested by the fact that Pérez Bocanegra's hymns and the official litany were intended for similar performance contexts—like the litany, *Hanac pachap cussicuinin* was to be sung by the choir while processing into the church on Marian feast days (Pérez Bocanegra 1631: 707). The litany would thus have been evoked as a co-text.[26] Another interpretive clue is provided by Pérez Bocanegra's score for *Hanac pachap cussicuinin,* which was composed in the villancico tradition (Estenssoro Fuchs 2003: 303–304). An important part of the intended audience would have been familiar with the different registers of ecclesiastical music, and would have recognized it as a semiformal, "vernacular," and self-consciously "indigenizing" variant or play on the official Marian texts. This genre context served to justify the heterodox elements in the hymn's iconography, while also producing a "disjunctive" effect that stimulated the audience to reflect on what the star or constellation named Tupatarca, say, had in common with the Mary and her conventional attributes—that is, to find a Christian meaning for it.

The overall picture that emerges from the syncretic Andean-Christian iconography is a fairly coherent one. In a seemingly innocent movement, basic Christian tropes were "translated" with Andean categories that appeared comparable at some level—kings for kings, stars for stars, flowers for flowers, and so forth. But these substitutes proliferated and took on a life of their own. While more conservative author-translators kept the substitute tropes very general—God as the generic *capac,* Mary as the generic *coyllur*—others set the ball rolling by introducing more specific images selected on the basis of their Andean religious and cosmological meanings—the divine Inca sovereign who is also the Sun, or a star that governs plant and animal reproduction. The result is a much more daring iconography in which we find Andean divinities serving as tropes for Christian ones.

While there can be no doubt that one of the functions of this imagery was to make Christian devotional themes more familiar and emotionally engaging, I would argue that what was really at stake was the presentation of the Andean as Christian, rather than vice versa. The way Andean tropes were selected suggests an effort to Christianize the native religious functions, categories, and symbols that were most deeply entrenched in Andean culture and language. It is as if the key areas of Andean cosmology were divided up among the primary manifestations of Christian divinity: The Inca sovereign and the top Inca deities (the Sun and Viracocha/ Pachacamac)—in other words, the state religion—were associated with God the Father and with the young Christ. The huacas, the more localized, earth-bound deities with their control over telluric movements and over rivers and irrigation waters were apportioned to the crucified Christ. Mary held sway over the fertility of the earth, the growing cycles of plants, over the seasons, and over the stars and moon. It is also apparent that author-translators like Oré and Pérez Bocanegra privileged Christian iconographic themes that could be related at some level to prominent Andean religious functions, categories, and symbols—for instance, the stellar epithets in the Marian cult, or the identification between Christ's body on the cross and the earth.

This strategy of promoting a Christianization of Andean religion through a syncretic iconography could also have the effect of presenting it as being already essentially Christian, much as occurred with the terms for Inca institutions used in reference to Christian ones. This is most apparent in epithets, as opposed to more diffuse images and motifs that did not rely on single terms. Especially in disjunctive contexts such as Pérez Bocanegra's Marian hymns, the indigenous elements were highlighted as such, inviting an exegesis of their relation to their Christian referents and, more generally, of the relation between Andean religion and Christianity. In other words, these deliberately and explicitly syncretic tropes generated a "metasyncretic discourse" (Stewart 1999: 58), one that explained and justified mixture in terms of preexisting, providential similarities.

Chapter 9

Performance and Contextualization

Pastoral Quechua reaches us as a written literature, and it is easy to forget that this literature consists of scripts for oral performances, most of them public and carefully orchestrated ones. In the broad sense of the term employed here, translation does not stop with a "finished" textual product, but goes on to ensure that it is properly consumed and contextualized, especially when the consumers tend to be unfamiliar with the interpretive conventions of the source culture. This chapter begins by locating pastoral Quechua texts in the daily rounds of catechetical, liturgical, and devotional performance in the pueblos de indios, with an emphasis on those genres that were performed by Indians (which were the vast majority). I then examine the problematic role of native assistants and of indigenous media—specifically, the quipu—in the production of these performances. My account of both topics refers to a status quo that developed in the late sixteenth and early seventeenth centuries.

The remaining half of the chapter examines how pastoral agents and the author-translators themselves sought to orient participation stances and understandings of the nature and purpose of pastoral texts and performances among the indigenous population.[1] In other words, it deals with the metalanguages that enabled and required the correct identification and contextualization of these texts and performances. My understanding of the issue of contextualization is influenced by linguistic anthropological approaches in which the concept of "context" includes the codes and conventions by which a text is to be interpreted and its relation to other texts and semiotic phenomena, as well as the social and spatiotemporal sites where it is created or enacted. Rather than being a set stage that preexists the text or performance, context has to be actively established and constructed. This is achieved in large measure by a stratum of metapragmatic signs, or contextualization cues, embedded in textual, linguistic, and performance forms that tacitly and reflexively "tell" participants what is going on in an interaction, what their expected roles are, and how the text in question concerns them and relates to other texts (see especially Bauman and Briggs 1990; Hanks 1989; Silverstein 1998; Silverstein and Urban 1996; Duranti and Goodwin eds. 1992; and Silverstein and Urban eds. 1996). Thus, for instance, the presence of meter and rhyme in a text informs the reader or listener that it is a poem, and is to be interpreted and experienced in accordance with a specific set of expectations.

This sort of metapragmatic guidance was of crucial importance to the pastoral regime. The baptismal form, for instance, was only effective if the minister—who in the absence of the priest, could be anyone—uttered it with the appropriate intentionality and with an adequate understanding of its effect and of his or her own role as minister. It was necessary for indigenous audiences and performers to understand the difference between, say, a purely catechetical exercise and a liturgical performance in which one addressed God or the saints directly. Beyond such recognition of the functions and requirements of texts and genres, performers and audiences also needed to understand and accept the multilingual character of the liturgy and the place of Quechua in a hierarchy of other languages used by the church. Just as texts and genres had different functions and efficacies, so did languages.

To some extent, such understandings could be transmitted through explicit metalinguistic discourse, but given the referential problems always involved in making language double back on itself and the fact that such understandings need to be instantaneous and highly situated, a key role was played by the sort of tacit metapragmatic cues or indices studied by linguistic anthropologists. Such cues are present in virtually all levels of a communicative event—in nonlinguistic performance features such as music and spatiotemporal distribution, in formal aspects of the composition of a text, and in grammatical categories that index or stipulate aspects of participation and context. Quechua texts are particularly interesting in this last respect because of the existence of metapragmatic categories that have no equivalent in European languages, such as the evidential suffixes (discussed in chapter 6).

The Catechetico-Liturgical System

With the exception of the sermon and the confesionario, all of the major pastoral Quechua genres were intended to be recited or sung aloud by Indians in highly regimented performances. This was the case even with the private devotions, which however personal were still directed at an audience and had to follow set scripts. An audiencia decree published in the Third Council sermonario instructed corregidores to encourage curacas "and other ladino Indians" to read the conciliar volumes as a practice in literacy (*para que se exerciten en la letura*) and for the good it would do to their souls (Third Lima Council 1985c [1584]: 348), but it is clear that this was not the main use for which the council's works were intended. Prado's *Directorio espiritual* was meant to be read by Indians, and Pérez Bocanegra's ritual contains instructions and headings in Quechua which suggest that it too could be used directly by Indians as well as priests. However, both books were intended primarily to provide texts for liturgical and devotional performance. The only pastoral Quechua book that may not have been intended for public recitation/singing or private prayer is Jurado Palomino's translation of Roberto Bellarmino's catechism—the questions and answers are far too long, detailed, and chatty. The degree to which pastoral Quechua texts were read privately should not be underestimated, but this was not their primary purpose.

In the Indian parishes of Peru catechetical instruction did not take the form of an individual dialogue between priest and catechumen, as would appear from the printed catechisms, but rather of carefully choreographed group performances. Catechesis acquired many of the characteristics of liturgical performance and tended to blend into it. The mass recitation or singing of the cartilla texts and the catechisms, a performance known as *doctrina* (the same term was applied to the Indian parish itself), took place every Sunday, Wednesday, and Friday morning in the atrium, a walled courtyard between the church and the plaza which also served as the cemetery. Children had doctrina on a daily basis. First, the priest or (more commonly) one of his Indian assistants (a cantor or fiscal) recited or sang the sentences of the basic prayers for the people to repeat or continue. The performance of the cartilla texts was followed by that of the catechisms, which also had a responsorial or antiphonal structure—one of the documents of the Third Lima Council explained that the question-answer structure of the catechisms was intended to facilitate memorization and public performances in which different individuals or groups were assigned the role of reciting the questions or answers (Third Lima Council 1985a [1584]: 14). Catechesis was given an even more liturgical quality by the practice of having parishioners sing the cartilla prayers in processions. In Oré's catechetical program, doctrina began with the people singing the common prayers while walking in procession into the church from the atrium. After adoring the eucharist, the procession returned to the atrium to recite the catechisms (Oré 1992 [1598]: 185–187). Jesuit missions in particular orchestrated elaborate performances in which the ayllus of a parish marched through the streets in carefully ordered groups while singing the basic prayers.[2]

Catechetical performance was part of a broader liturgical program which often included the canonical hours. By the mid-seventeenth century some of the texts of the canonical hours were available in Quechua translations, and prayers and hymns originally composed in Quechua had become part of the hours, substituting for Latin texts that had a similar content. In Oré's program for the performance of the canonical hours, each day began at the hour of Prime with the choir singing the Marian office (for which no Quechua versions were provided), followed by that day's cántico, which Oré refers to as *el himno del símbolo*. The first of the seven cánticos, which was an adaptation of the Athanasian Creed, was to be sung on Sundays—since the Athanasian Creed itself was traditionally sung on Sundays at Prime (Stapper 1935 [1931]: 172), it seems that this cántico was intended to replace it in the Sunday morning office in the Indian parishes. The day's cántico was followed by a Quechua translation of the Te Deum and the responsorium of Prime, thus concluding the morning office. The evening office (hour of Compline) began with the *símbolo menor quotidiano*, in other words, Oré's creation hymn *Capac eterno*, which was sung to the melody of the hymn *Sacris Solemnis*, followed by a Quechua translation of the responsorium of that hour. The evening office concluded with the Angelus (referred to as the *antíphona del tiempo de Nuestra Señora*), partially translated into Quechua, and a responsorium for the souls in purgatory, also in Quechua. Saturday afternoons after the office of Compline were dedicated to the Virgin Mary, with the recitation of Oré's Marian litany while the choir processed into the church, followed by the singing of the Salve Regina (Oré 1992 [1598]: 182–193).

Oré was thus calling for the performance of a simplified version of the canonical hours in the Indian parishes. Instead of a constant round of prayer such as would be found in a convent or cathedral, where groups of liturgical specialists were available to maintain continuity, Oré proposed the performance of offices at two times of the day, the early morning and the evening. This allowed the members of the choir to spend most of the day taking care of agricultural and other tasks. Nonetheless, even this program may have been excessively burdensome for many parishes, and there is very little concrete information on the performance of the canonical hours in Indian parishes. It seems likely that programs of this type were more often adhered to in the mendicant parishes, given the mendicants' historical emphasis on training Indians for the liturgy. Diocesan legislation enforced the performance of only a part of this program—specifically the evening Angelus, the prayer for the souls in purgatory, and the Saturday singing of the Salve Regina. The 1591 Cuzco synod ordered that the office of Vespers be sung on Sundays and feast days by the parish priest and the choir, a practice of which there is no mention in Oré's works (Lassegue-Moleres 1987: 48).

It is not easy to establish what portions of the mass were said in Quechua. The existence of a Quechua translation of a text specific to the mass does not mean that it was actually performed in Quechua. For instance, it seems unlikely that Pérez Bocanegra's translations of the priest's secret prayers for before and after communing with the bread and wine, which were said in a low voice, were intended for actual use in the mass (Pérez Bocanegra 1631: 500–502). Basic prayers such as the Credo and Pater Noster were probably said in Quechua, as were other short prayers that were said by the people or required a response from the people, such as the *Domine non sum dignus* and *Orate fratres*. Prado, who published a translation of the *Orate fratres* prayer (1641: f. 53v–54), was especially interested in stimulating Indian participation in the mass. He provided instructions in Quechua for Indians who assisted in the mass in the role of acolytes, a task usually carried out by the sacristan (ibid.: f. 59v–62v), and a lengthy exegesis explaining the symbolic significance of each part of the mass intended to aid silent meditation while it was taking place (ibid.: f. 49v–56).

The liturgy acquired special characteristics on feast days. Indians were exempted by a papal bull from most of the feast days of the liturgical calendar, and were only required to observe a total of thirteen, the most important being Christmas, Easter, Pentecost, Corpus Christi, and three Marian feasts (of the Purification, Annunciation, and Assumption) (Third Lima Council 1985b [1585]: 310). Pérez Bocanegra's Marian hymns were intended for performance on the Marian feasts, and sections of Oré's cánticos were sung as independent hymns on feast days, in particular the Marian *carmen* in the third cántico, which was reprinted separately by Prado. This tendency to dismember Oré's program for the canonical hours suggests that it was too ambitious for conditions in the pueblos de indios, and that liturgical performances were organized more by yearly than daily or weekly cycles.

This raises the issue of Holy Week and the reenactment of the passion. There is only one independent passion hymn from the period of this study—Prado's hymn contemplating Christ on the cross. Again, it seems likely that priests drew on Oré's cánticos for Easter performances. The sixth cántico was probably sung as an independent passion hymn—it too was published separately in Prado's devotionary (1641: f. 218v–229v). In present-day Quechua-speaking communities the main event of the Easter liturgy is the performance of the Via Crucis, in which a procession follows a prescribed route commemorating the stations of the cross with prayers and hymns. Margot Beyersdorff has suggested that Oré's sixth cántico was a Via Crucis hymn (Beyersdorff 1993: 229–230), but Oré omitted the stations of the cross from his narrative of the passion. It may be that the practice of the Via Crucis developed later on in the pueblos de indios. Alternatively, Oré may have skipped over this part of the passion precisely because it was narrated by Via Crucis hymns which have not survived.

The liturgy of public worship was complemented by a "paraliturgy" of private devotional acts. The most important of these was the praying of the rosary. The rosary provided a structure for individual prayer in which a "decade" (ten Ave Marias and one Pater Noster marked off by fingering the beads) was dedicated successively to each of the fifteen "mysteries" or key episodes of the life of Mary. The "mysteries" were divided thematically into groups of five, each of which corresponded to one "turn" of the rosary, or fifty-five prayers. Both Oré and Prado provided Quechua prayers narrating the mysteries for dedicating decades of the rosary (Oré 1992 [1598]: 428–433; Prado 1641: f. 90v–96). The rosary allowed individuals to perform lengthy rounds of prayer, and had originally developed to replace participation in the canonical hours, which was too cumbersome for most laypeople (Winston-Allen 1997: 4). The indulgence bull known as the *bula de la santa cruzada,* which was being sold to Indians since the 1570s, provided an important stimulus to private devotions. Indians who purchased printed copies of the bull earned indulgences when they performed devotional acts such as accompanying the eucharist in procession when it was taken to dying persons in their homes, reciting new prayers to specific devotions such as the Holy Shroud or the Immaculate Conception, and performing prayer "marathons" (e.g., praying at five different churches in one day) (Pérez Bocanegra 1631: 494–500, 697–701; Prado 1641: f. 161–166; cf. Itier 1992c).

The liturgy of the sacraments was distinct from that of public worship, as it was not bound to schedules and temporal cycles (with the exception of regular communion, which was part of the mass). The sacraments can be divided into two main classes: those which could be administered on a regular basis, and required preparation (confession and communion), and those which, at least in principle, were administered only once in a person's lifetime (baptism, marriage, and extreme unction and the accompanying Last Rites). The administration of the sacraments required the use of rituals or manuals which advised priests on the necessary circumstances for each sacrament and guided them through the complex sacramental liturgies. The canonical ritual was the *Rituale romanum,* but the Seville and Toledo rituals were widely used before and even after its appearance.[3] Peru never had an official ritual—the closest thing was Oré's 1607 *Rituale seu manuale peruanum,* which contained the full Latin offices, only small portions of which were translated into Quechua and other languages. It was followed by Pérez Bocanegra's 1631 *Ritual formulario* and Castromonte's manuscript *Aptaycachana* (ca. 1650). Unlike Oré's work, these last two rituals had to be used jointly with a Latin ritual, as they only provided those portions of the offices that could be said in Quechua, although Pérez Bocanegra included Spanish translations of the rubrics, or preliminary instructions for each sacrament from the *Rituale romanum.*

Confession was a private act, involving only the priest and the penitent, and had a very simple sacramental liturgy. The penitent recited the Confiteor or General Confession prayer, which was included in the Third Council cartilla, and was then examined by the priest for his or her knowledge of the cartilla, which often involved reciting further prayers. The priest would then question the penitent using a confesionario. The process was concluded by the priest imposing penances on and admonishing the penitent, and reciting the Latin text of the Absolution. Confession often required a lengthy preparation—the penitent had to take stock of his or her sins and achieve the necessary state of contrition—for which Prado's devotionary provided guidelines. The Act of Contrition, a prayer which served both to prepare for confession and to postpone it when a priest was not available, became one of the most widely translated pastoral texts of the seventeenth century—the proliferation of Quechua versions by different authors was permitted by the fact that this prayer was not among the texts translated by the Third Lima Council.[4] During the late sixteenth and early seventeenth centuries it was common for Indians to record their sins on quipus, which they would then "read" to the priest during confession (see the next section).

Of all the sacraments to which Indians had access, communion inspired the greatest controversy and produced the greatest variety of texts: communion catechisms, prayers for before and after communion, and at least eight different translations of the *Domine non sum dignus* prayer. Instructing Indians on the eucharist, thereby preparing them spiritually for the reception of the host, was seen as one of the most important and difficult tasks of the pastoral regime. This preparatory process was as much liturgical as catechetical: more than an abstract understanding of the doctrine of Transubstantiation, it required the performance of concrete, indexical acts of faith in the Real Presence before the consecrated host. There are two surviving eucharistic hymns that served this purpose: Castromonte's *Cantarçillo,* which appears at the end of his ritual, and a fifteen-stanza sequence at the end of Oré's fifth cántico (Oré 1992 [1598]: 324–326), parts of which are still performed as an independent hymn known by the incipit *Canmi Dios canqui,* which is a common part of the mass in the Cuzco region today. In Castromonte's hymn performers addressed a Christ hidden *inside* the host (Durston 2002: 288):

Tanta vino ricçhaĉ
Ucullampim ĉam
Ĉapaĉ Dios tianqui
Manam sucçhu chay

[You, great God, are inside what seems bread and wine, and nothing else.]

In Oré's eucharistic sequence Christ is portrayed as looking out at the speaker from the host (Oré 1992 [1598]: 325):

Muchaycuscayqui apu Iesu Christo,
chay hostiamanta cahuarimullahuay:

rurahuascayqui huaccha runayquicta
quespichihuaytac.

[Hail lord Jesus Christ
From that host please look upon me
Your orphan whom you created
And save me]

The portrayal of a Christ "inside" the host is a metaphor, but it would seem that this metaphor involved a serious risk that the doctrine of Transubstantiation would be misunderstood. However, the stress on belief in the Real Presence superseded such considerations.

While confession and regular communion could be repeated indefinitely in an individual's lifetime and required an intensive preparation, baptism and the Last Rites were administered only once and irrespective of the individual's state of preparation, and were thus less controversial.[5] The baptismal and Last Rites liturgies were said mainly in Latin using the *Rituale romanum* or the Seville or Toledo rituals. However, certain portions were said in Quechua, especially those that required some response from the participants. Quechua versions of parts of the baptismal liturgy were provided in the manuals of Oré, Pérez Bocanegra, and Castromonte. Under ideal circumstances, newborns were brought to the church to be baptized with the full liturgy, in which the godparents spoke on behalf of the child who was baptized. Very often, however, children were born far from the church and had to be baptized immediately if there was any danger they might die before reaching the church. In such cases baptism could be administered by anyone who knew the form and uttered it under the right conditions and with the correct intention. The baptismal form was thus the first sacramental form to be translated into Quechua—the canonical translation first appeared in the Third Lima Council catechism on the sacraments (Third Lima Council 1985a [1584]: 112).[6]

The Last Rites liturgy was a complex ceremonial in several stages that was performed in the dying person's house rather than the church. The sacraments of viaticum and extreme unction were followed by a liturgy of psalms, litanies, and prayers on behalf of the person's soul which was to continue until the moment of death. While the only essential participants were the priest and the dying person, it was customary for others to help perform this liturgy, and cofradías were set up specifically for this purpose.

Quechua versions of parts of the Last Rites were available in different compilations, particularly those of Pérez Bocanegra, Prado, and Castromonte, and the Third Council's *Confessionario* provided a series of texts which served similar purposes, even though they were composed ad hoc rather than taken from a ritual (see chapter 3). Pérez Bocanegra's extensive Last Rites section contains Quechua translations of the Penitential Litanies, of a series of prayers to be said by and on behalf of the dying person, and even of the extreme unction forms, which could be said only by the priest. However, he also stated that while sacramental forms could, in principle, be said in any language as long as the translation was faithful and they were uttered with the necessary intent, it was preferable that the Latin forms be used in this case. The Quechua translation of the forms was intended to allow Indians to understand what the priest was saying and thus observe or receive the sacrament with greater devotion (Pérez Bocanegra 1631: 525–527). The Last Rites liturgy extended into the funerary ceremonies. The key stage of the funerary process was not so much the burial as the procession which carried the deceased from his or her home to the parish church. This procession would make stops (*posas*) on street corners and the corners of the plaza and atrium—where small chapels were often set up—for a litany to be recited in responsorial fashion for the dead person's soul by the priest and the accompanying crowd. The priest charged a fee for each *posa* that had to be paid from the dead person's goods, and the number of posas to be performed was often stipulated in the will.[7]

In short, native Andeans prayed in what must have been a bewildering variety of different ways. The lengthiest explanation in Quechua of the nature and powers of prayer was provided in sermons 28 and 29 of the Third Lima Council's sermonario (1985c [1585]: 700–731). Following the council's policy of explaining such issues with a maximum of simplicity and orthodoxy, the sermons say that prayer is just a way of talking to God and asking for what one needs, just as a child does with its parents. The sermons anticipate a fear on the part of the Indians that they would not know how to address God, just as they were wary of petitioning the viceroy or the bishop because of their ignorance. The solution recommended is to memorize the cartilla prayers and recite them constantly, as these were formulas which had been approved by God himself—more or less (by implication) like the approved legal genres and formulas that an Indian petitioning a colonial authority had at his disposal (ibid.: 708–709, 715–717). The vast repertoire of texts in the mass, canonical hours, and sacramental liturgies are alluded to only briefly, and Indians are advised not worry about these other, more complex forms of prayer (ibid.: 730–731).

Clearly, the Third Council's explanation of the nature of prayer did not come close to covering the variety of actual practice. Prayer could be an offering or sacrifice as much as a form of communication. Oré's Marian hymn *Lira a Nuestra Señora del Rosario* reflexively equated the act of praying or singing to Mary to that of offering her a floral wreath or a crown made of flowers (Oré 1992 [1598]: 434). The figure derives from the iconography of the rosary: the cycles of Ave Marias and Pater Nosters were pictured as floral crowns placed on the head of the Virgin. In Prado's manual, a prayer for dedicating decades of the rosary refers to the act as a sacrifice: *Collanam Virgen santa Maria Diospa maman. Cay chunca Aue Mariacta, uc Padre nuestroctahuan ullpuycuspa ofreçimuyqui, arpamuyqui* (Holy Virgin Mary Mother of God, I humbly offer you [x2] these ten Ave Marias and one Pater Noster) (1641: f. 90v). The term employed for 'to offer' alongside the loan stem *ofreçi-* is *arpa-*, which refers specifically to blood sacrifice. A very definite, quantitative value was attributed to the performance of prayers, especially as a result of the indulgence system. Prayer was tied to a logic of exchange and sacrifice—it was a way of activating or "charging" on one's behalf the accumulated "credit" created by Christ's sacrifice (Prado 1641: f. 159–159v). Diego de Molina's sermonario contains an extensive parable about the power of prayer, in which angels are compared to bees who collect the "honey" of people's prayers and exchange it for God's forgiveness for their sins and other blessings ([1649]: f. 130v).

While the *Tercero cathecismo* advised Indians that God understands all languages and that what mattered was *what* one said (Third Lima Council 1985c [1585]: 706), the liturgy was structured by a marked linguistic hierarchy. Certain key texts could be said only in Latin, but even those texts that were regularly performed in Quechua acquired an added valence in Latin. This point is exemplified in an episode in the Huarochirí Manuscript in which the Indian noble Cristóbal Choquecasa is accosted by a demonized huaca. He first attempted to exorcise the huaca by reciting the cartilla "from beginning to end." When this failed, he invoked the Virgin Mary and recited the Salve Regina, which he would already have recited as part of the cartilla, only now in Latin. When Don Cristóbal was halfway through the prayer, the huaca suddenly disappeared.[8] The powers of Latin were also expressed in an exemplum translated by Prado in which two lads were struck by lightning and one of them was spared because he had heard mass that day. The exemplum ends with the following moral: "you too should say the words *et verbum caro factum est* ["and the Word is made flesh"] when it rains and you see lightning falling. God makes us hear this [in the mass] in order to save us from lightning."[9] To some extent, the magical character of the powers attributed to Latin eased the pressures created by linguistic hierarchy, in that these powers were available to all who could utter the texts, regardless of whether or not they understood them. What Indians needed to know about the phrase *et verbum caro factum est* was not so much its content as the fact that it was said during the mass.

Native Agency and Media

The production of catechetico-liturgical performance was largely the work of an official cadre of native assistants. In every pueblo de indios there were one or two fiscales whose main duty was to enforce attendance in the catechesis sessions and the mass. They also had a variety of supervisory duties—they were to inform the priest of births, illnesses and deaths, and of any "public sins" such as adultery, drunkenness, and idolatry. In short, the fiscal was the main intermediary between the priest and his parishioners. Another group of Indian assistants worked within the church itself, beginning with the sacristan, whose duties included bell ringing and serving as acolyte. In the larger pueblos de indios there were choirs whose responsibility was to sing in the mass and the canonical hours. Frequently, these performances were accompanied by organ or flute music. Like the fiscales, cantors and choir masters (*maestros de capilla*) carried official titles and were exempt from tribute and the labor drafts.[10]

The Indian cofradías too had a key role in organizing catechetico-liturgical performance and in mediating between the priest and the general population, with the difference that the clergy had little effective control over these largely self-regulating institutions. Their role was especially prominent in estancias or anejos as opposed to formal pueblos. In 1626 a cofradía founded in the pueblo of Huacaña (diocese of Huamanga), but which was to function in the estancia of Uyupacha, far from the priest, included among its tasks the performance of the Angelus and the prayer for the souls in purgatory every evening, along with vigilance against idolatry and superstition.[11] One of the reasons why Indians were so eager to establish cofradías was that they provided a sort of alibi for groups who abandoned the pueblos: the cofradía took on the responsibility of ensuring that they remained good Christians. This was precisely what the clergy feared, and efforts were made to curb the proliferation of the cofradías.[12]

Ecclesiastical suspicion was directed even at the official pastoral assistants. Guaman Poma claimed that choir members who showed zeal and independence in performing their duties when there was no priest around—which was often the case even in the larger pueblos—met only with contempt:

> In absence of the priests, the cantors bury the dead with litanies, prayers, and responsoria; they sing Vespers with instrumental music and pray the Salve Regina to the mother of God; and on Sundays and feast days they sing the prayers [of the canonical hours]; all this they pray like Christians, and they do it in the absence of the priest . . . And on the established days, Friday and Wednesday, they say the Angelus at dawn . . . and the stations and responsoria for the dead, and the whole town prays, and they announce the feast days of each week and their vigils . . . and the priests are opposed to all this and punish them for it, calling them "saintly little ladinos."[13]

Guaman Poma, who had himself worked as an assistant for several priests, remembered the highly charged insult *santico ladinejo*,[14] applied to Christian Indians who were biting off more than they could chew. Two different fears are reflected here: that the assistants were usurping the powers of the clergy, and that they were carrying out their duties incorrectly and distorting Christianity.

There are few sources that explain exactly what distortions were seen to result from the reliance on native assistants. Indians were not under the jurisdiction of the Inquisition, and ecclesiastical investigations into their religious lives generally resulted from accusations of idolatry or witchcraft. There are scattered references to the parody and manipulation of Christian texts by pastoral assistants. Guaman Poma, a sharp critic of priests who preached with insufficient knowledge of Quechua or to intimidate their parishioners, notes that their sermons were satirized by their own assistants. He cites the sermon of a certain Father Varica [Barriga?] as follows (italics indicate Quechua text in the original): "Father Varica's sermon: *My beloved children, don't make me mad. When I'm mad I'm a puma, when I'm not mad I can be led around like a horse by the bridle*. His own boys [parish assistants] made fun of this sermon, saying: *My children, don't make me mad. When I'm mad I'm a pussycat, when I'm not mad I'm a mouse.* His assistants had a good laugh at this, and nothing more was understood."[15] José de Arriaga, the Jesuit extirpator of idolatries, mentioned that the fiscales had to be examined by extirpating judges because they often distorted the cartilla texts and transmitted doctrinal errors to the entire town: "it has been necessary when arriving at a town to see if the fiscal or the boys who teach the catechism know it well, because in some places they teach it with many errors, changing or switching some words or letters, as a result of which they change the meaning; for example, in the Credo instead of saying *hucllachacuyninta,* which is 'the communion of the saints,' they might say *pucllachacuyninta,* which is 'the horseplay or merriment of the saints.'"[16] Arriaga does not explain whether saying *pucllachacuyninta* rather than *hucllachacuyninta* was innocent error or satire. However, it seems likely that such an unfortunate slip was a deliberate one. Further references in Guaman Poma's chronicle suggest that certain Christian song genres were especially subject to satire and misuse. In particular, he criticized the Jesuits for their catechetical use of the *copla,* a popular Spanish song genre, and suggested replacing such songs with prose prayers because the Indians used the *coplas* to "offend" God (Guaman Poma de Ayala 1980 [1615]: 778, 782). We do not know exactly what sort of offenses were being committed with the Jesuit *coplas,* but the fact that the *copla* was originally a profane, popular genre may have made it especially subject to satire and distortion.

Our most detailed account of the misappropriation of Christian practices by indigenous assistants comes from the prologue to Pérez Bocanegra's confesionario (1631: 111–115). Pérez Bocanegra warned his fellow priests of the existence in the city of Cuzco and surrounding areas of a sort of clandestine native clergy who called themselves *hermanos mayores* or *hermanas mayores* ('older brothers' and 'older sisters'). The main activity of the *hermanos mayores* was to help Indians prepare confession quipus, but they were also in the habit of discussing points of doctrine among themselves. Pérez Bocanegra condemned them as *alumbrados* (ibid.: 111), thus comparing them to a heretical sect that had developed about a century earlier in Spanish cities and sought direct illumination from God, avoiding the hierarchical mediation of the church (Andrés 1976: I 423). Judging from the way Pérez Bocanegra described them, it is unlikely that the *hermanos mayores* were official pastoral assistants of the sort I have been discussing so far. However, it is fairly certain that they were a Jesuit creation: the Jesuits were strongly invested in the training of Indian intermediaries who taught other Indians how to confess using quipus, and they encouraged their more advanced pupils to discuss points of doctrine among themselves.[17] The Jesuits also had a predilection for using the blind in intermediary roles, and Pérez Bocanegra mentioned that the *hermanos mayores* were often blind. Within the Jesuit order, the title *hermano* was given to a class of lay members who performed a variety of auxiliary functions. These intermediaries were necessarily unofficial because the Jesuits did not have any parishes in the area, so they could not appoint their own fiscales.

Pérez Bocanegra stated that the *hermanos mayores* were in the habit of holding meetings (*juntas*) on feast days, especially the patronal feasts of pueblos and cofradías, to discuss Christian doctrine and to comment on sermons they had heard. These discussions were filled with serious doctrinal errors, which they claimed had been taught to them by the priests they grew up with (Pérez Bocanegra 1631: 114–115). In order to put an end to this practice, Pérez Bocanegra suggested banning the discussion of points of doctrine by Indians entirely: "The most convenient thing is to preach to them often and reprimand them, without allowing these gatherings to be held, nor that they speak among themselves anything other than the prayers they are obligated to know, and the catechisms, with their holy songs, which it seems very well that they sing and pray, preventing them from talking about anything else."[18] The verbalization of church doctrine was to be restricted to the recitation of fixed texts: the cartilla prayers, the catechisms, and the *cantares divinos*, i.e., hymns of the sort that he himself composed.

Most of Pérez Bocanegra's discussion of the activities of the *hermanos mayores* deals with the use of quipus in confession, which is why he brings up the issue in his confesionario. Quipus had long since acquired a variety of functions in missionary and pastoral contexts that are as yet poorly understood, notwithstanding the recent advances in the study of quipu codes (Salomon 2004; Urton 2003). As early as 1555 Archbishop Loayza stipulated that the *alguaciles de doctrina* (i.e., the fiscales) were to record births and illnesses on quipus so that they could report them to the priests, and parish assistants continued to use quipus for information-gathering purposes into the mid-seventeenth century at least.[19] The Mercedarian Diego de Porres's pastoral guidelines, which probably date from the 1570s, suggested that quipus be used to record conciliar legislation and the liturgical calendar.[20] Porres's correligionary Martín de Murúa, author of an important chronicle, was priest of a parish where an old curaca had the entire liturgical calendar recorded on a quipu—the curaca had made the quipu with information supplied by another Mercedarian (Murúa 1987 [1590]: 376). This suggests a Mercedarian tradition of stimulating Indians to use quipus to keep track of feasts, an important task, as the failure to observe calendrical obligations such as fasts and rest days was a mortal sin.

Quipus also had a role in catechetical instruction. Diego de Porres suggested that quipus be used to record the basic prayers and the Ten Commandments, and that all Indians be required to carry these quipus with them.[21] A Jesuit mission report from Soras in 1600 speaks of an Indian woman who saved her soul by using a quipu for recording prayers—the Jesuits rewarded her with a rosary and a penitential scourge.[22] A kind of exchange is implied here—the Indian presented a quipu and in return received quipu-like Christian artifacts. It seems likely that the rosary and its associated textual practices had special success among native Andeans because of its generic similarity to the quipu—both systems involved a tactile "reading" of markers on a string, although the quipu code was infinitely more complex. A sermon from the Third Council's *Tercero cathecismo* instructed Indians to use quipus in lieu of rosaries if none were available: "You must pray by the rosary every day. You must all have a rosary, and if you do not, then pray on a quipu" (*uiñay punchaucuna rossarioyquipi rezacunqui, ama pillapas mana Rosarioyocca caychicchu mana captinri, quipullapipas Rezacuychic*) (Third Lima Council 1985c [1585]: 709).

The most common pastoral use of quipus was as an aid for confession, a use which was prescribed in one of the Third Council texts. Although quipus are not mentioned in the *Confessionario* itself, the sermon on confession encouraged Indians to prepare quipus of their sins in order to "read" them during confession (Third Lima Council 1985c [1585]: 482–483). Most references to confession quipus come from Jesuit sources, and it is clear that the Jesuits were one of the main promoters of the practice—previous to their arrival, little attention had been given to Indian confession at all. In the mission reports collected in the cartas annuas there are frequent references to Indians who spontaneously made confession quipus and through this device were able to save themselves—a 1603 report mentions a blind man who made a confession quipu of such dimensions that his confession lasted four whole days.[23] The same carta annua speaks of blind Indians in La Paz who were trained by the Jesuits to teach other Indians how to confess with quipus, which suggests that the use of confessional quipus was not as spontaneous as other reports would have one think.[24]

By the 1630s and 1640s a reaction against this practice seems to have developed in clerical circles. Quipu confession had created the need for unofficial Indian specialists whose task was to help other Indians prepare their quipus. According to Pérez Bocanegra, the crux of the matter was that Indians who followed the instructions of the *hermanos mayores* confessed sins that they never committed, confessed actions that were not sins, and omitted the sins they *had* committed. Worse still, the same quipus were employed on different occasions and by different people. Indians who confessed with quipus were even under the impression that their use somehow sanctified their confessions and left them better prepared to receive communion (Pérez Bocanegra 1631: 112–113). The activities of the *hermanos mayores* seem to reflect an attempt to reconcile Andean and Christian concepts of *hucha* and to practice Christian confession in a way that made sense to Andeans. Pérez Bocanegra's account does not explain exactly what their interpretation of Christian confession was, but it seems that they had people confessing Andean *hucha* that did not qualify as Christian sins. The use of the same confessional quipu by different people is reminiscent of the fact that Andean *hucha* affected social groups rather than individuals.

Pérez Bocanegra went on to say that when a priest attempted to correct Indians who had confessed according to the instructions of the *hermanos mayores,* he would become himself the object of criticism: "they go and discuss what the priest told them and the penance he gave them with these Indians [the *hermanos mayores*], and they make fun of him, saying that he does not know how to ask the questions for confession, or that he does not understand their language, and they ridicule his way of absolving, along with other very scandalous things that I have learned about them."[25] Here again the accusation of *alumbradismo* comes to the fore: the penitents would actually report back to the *hermanos mayores,* who would use the priest's often incomplete knowledge of Quechua as a weapon against him and criticize his procedures as if they had greater authority. Pérez Bocanegra's recommended solution was that quipus be banned entirely from confession and that Indians be punished for consulting the *hermanos mayores* (1631: 113–114).

The sense that quipu confession was producing dynamics that were out of the church's control was probably widespread at Pérez Bocanegra's time of writing. Prado's 1641 devotionary, which provides detailed instructions on preparing for confession, omits the use of quipus—instead, Prado recommends *reading* a confesionario and then making an effort to remember the resulting list of sins until they were confessed: "you will examine yourself by reading a confesionario, and retaining [the sins] in your memory you will confess them to the priest, the representative of God."[26] The omission is especially significant because Prado was a Jesuit. The admonition that the penitent was to keep the sins *in his memory* and go straight to the priest (whose status as God's representative is pointedly mentioned) directly excludes the use of quipus and recourse to native intermediaries.

Performance as Metalanguage

The complexity of the catechetico-liturgical system, added to the problems that were seen to emerge from the reliance on native assistants, only heightened the need to orient understandings of the nature, purpose, and context of a particular text or performance, and of individual performance roles. Explicit metapragmatic discourse, of which we have seen some examples, only produced more texts that were susceptible to misinterpretation, and it can be argued that the development of the necessary metalanguages was especially difficult in Quechua. Mannheim argues that "unlike their Mesoamerican and Central Mexican counterparts, neither modern Southern Peruvian Quechua speakers nor (I suspect) their Inka ancestors have had well-developed traditions of linguistic and cultural exegesis" (Mannheim 1998a: 387). In comparison to European languages (and, apparently, Mesoamerican languages as well), Quechua has very few terms that refer unequivocally to forms of speech or textual genes, or to textual activities and media. The term for "word," *simi,* also means 'mouth' and 'language.' Most of the pastoral metalinguistic lexicon consisted of loan stems such as *reza-* and *oracion.* Terms for the interpretation and exegesis of texts were also scarce. The verb typically used for "to understand" or "to interpret" (*unancha-*) also meant 'to represent,' 'to mark,' or 'to symbolize,' and its present-day uses range from 'to create' (in Christian discourse) to 'to slaughter.'

The development of a pastoral Quechua metalanguage also confronted grammatical obstacles, especially the fact that Quechua has no regular mechanisms for indirect quotation and the objectification of speech, a problem that is related to the lack of lexical resources for relativization. Discussing an utterance in Quechua usually involves a full direct quotation. As can be seen in Avila's sermonario—the most ambitious attempt to develop a language of textual commentary in Quechua—detailed and involved metalinguistic discourse is both cumbersome and ambiguous. As noted at the beginning of this chapter, the necessary understandings of text in context were more effectively stipulated by implicit cues embedded in textual form and performance practice which worked simultaneously (requiring no interruptions of the performance) and subliminally. This section discusses music and the spatiotemporal organization of performance as tacit metapragmatic "metalanguages." They were themselves, of course, important aspects of the context of pastoral Quechua texts and performances, but they are examined here as aids to their identification.

Catechetico-liturgical performance relied on a profound reorganization of lived space and time whose key component was the pueblo de indios itself, invariably built on a square grid plan with a central plaza. Imposed during the reducción process of the 1570s, the pueblo provided a standard, homogenized, and geometrically regular space with a monumental center consisting of the church, plaza, and the walled courtyard of the atrium-cemetery, which mediated between the closed, sacred space of the church and the open, multifunctional space of the plaza. Small chapels (the *capillas posas* where processions paused) were placed strategically throughout the central area and the grid of streets—especially at the corners of the atrium and of the plaza, and often at the corners or main entry points of the pueblo itself (cf. Durston 1994).

This architectural matrix provided the stage for a very consistent spatialization of catechetico-liturgical performance whereby both texts and performers were assigned to set locations or routes. The church interior was the basic stage for the liturgy, while catechesis generally took place in the atrium. The church imposed a very clear distribution of texts and performance roles dictated by architectural features such as the altar, presbytery, pulpit, pews, choir loft, and baptistery. The open space of the atrium was also subdivided, though here there was more room for variation. Diego de Porres's pastoral guidelines from the 1570s suggested that the floor of the atrium-cemetery be marked with a grid of lines in which each individual could be assigned a specific box to stand during catechetical performance, so that absentees could be noted immediately.[27] The Jesuits, on the other hand, were in the habit of organizing participants according to native systems of rank and segmentary division, and assigned to different groups specific performance roles, such as the recitation of questions or answers from the catechisms. Such roles could also be attached to specific areas of the performance space, as when Jesuit priests recited the questions and answers from opposite corners of the atrium.[28]

Catechetico-liturgical performance could also be highly mobile. In Oré's program it was distributed through the entire church-atrium-plaza complex via processional recitation. He indicated that his adaptation of the Marian litany was to be sung by the choir while processing from the atrium into the church, and Pérez Bocanegra suggested something similar for one of his Marian hymns (Oré 1992 [1598]: 191; Pérez Bocanegra 1631: 707). For the daily evening prayer for the souls in purgatory, which was a universal practice, the choir was to process around the plaza while singing the common prayers as suffrages, and pause at the corners to recite a text that summoned the parishioners to join in (Oré 1992 [1598]: 400).[29] Almost as frequent were the funerary processions going from the homes of the deceased to the church, which recited litanies and responsoria at the *capillas posas.* As occurred with the stationary performances in the atrium or church, processional groups were clearly regimented, with the choir or pastoral assistants leading both the procession and the recitation or singing, and internal divisions along gender, social, or segmentary lines in the body of the procession.[30] The importance of movement and the completion of circuits is exemplified in a reference to (literal) foot-dragging from a 1617 Jesuit mission report. Missionaries in the province of Huaylas reached a town where the members of one of the local ayllus would persistently fall out of catechetical processions around the borders of the atrium on the belief that they would contract leprosy it they completed the circuit. The Jesuits made a point of arranging a procession and forcing the recalcitrant ayllu to complete it.[31]

Several different purposes can be attributed to this spatialization of performance. First, it had disciplinary and surveillance functions of an almost Foucauldian sort, allowing the priest and his Indian assistants to enforce and monitor individual and group participation (this is especially evident in Porres's suggested grid of cells for individual participants in atrial catechesis). Spatialization also had inculcatory and mnemonic functions, perhaps along the lines of the classical and medieval arts of memory, whereby information or segments of text were attached in the "eye of the imagination" to places (*loci*) in a building, imagined or real (Yates 1966). Participants could identify the character of a performance based on the area where it was taking place, and probably also determine what stage they had reached in an ongoing performance and what texts or text segments were coming up next based on their location on a processional route. Spatialization was also the clearest possible stipulation of performance roles, as participants could infer their expected contribution from their location relative to architectural markers and to other participants.

Temporal organization fulfilled analogous functions, in that the nature of a performance could also be inferred from the time of day, day of the week, and time of the liturgical year. Morning and evening prayers were different in nature, with the more catechetically oriented performances in the morning, and the evening marked by the Angelus and the prayer for the souls in purgatory. Wednesdays, Fridays, and Sundays were doctrina days for the entire pueblo, and Saturday evenings were dedicated to the Virgin Mary. Oré's seven cánticos followed a weekly cycle. There was also a calendrical rhythm to the performances that was structured by the liturgical seasons (Advent, Lent, Easter, and Pentecost) and by the main feast days.

The bell tower was a key instrument for keeping liturgical time and recruiting participation in catechetico-liturgical performance. Oré described the regime of bell-tolling as follows:

> What should be observed [in the parishes] is first of all that the bell be tolled very early in the morning, and this is the sign for the cantors to congregate in the choir, and for the fiscales and alguaciles to go through the houses and streets searching out the children to bring them to the catechesis sessions. And if it is Wednesday or Friday or a feast day, they congregate the whole town, for this effort is very necessary for them to come to mass, sermon, and catechesis. The bell must also be tolled for high mass, for Vespers and for the Angelus, and at nocturnal Prime the bell must be tolled for the prayer for the souls in purgatory.[32]

One of the tasks of ecclesiastical visitadores was to ensure the observance of this regime, in which the ringing of the church bells summoned the town's inhabitants either to congregate in the church or to acknowledge the key liturgical moments with a private prayer. These moments were the elevation of the host during mass, the performance of the Angelus at noon and in the evening, and the evening prayer for the souls in purgatory.[33]

Music provided a range of contexts that guided the "interpretation" (both in the sense of exegesis and in the sense of performance) of pastoral texts. Musical training had been an essential element in the schooling of the native elite since the mendicant establishments of the mid-sixteenth century, and continued to be so throughout the seventeenth century. This training was intended primarily, if not exclusively, for liturgical purposes. Oré explained the importance of having schools in the pueblos de indios in the following terms: "it is very necessary that there be a school and a schoolmaster, and named cantors paid with a sufficient salary to teach the Indians to recite the cartilla, to read and write, sing and play instruments . . . the school is like the soul of the whole town . . . if there were none, all I have said about catechesis, music, adornment, and service of the church, altar and choir will be lacking."[34] Singing and playing instruments (*cantar y tañer*) are mentioned in the same breath with reading and writing. It appears that the posts of schoolmaster and choirmaster were often held by the same person—Guaman Poma's drawing of a school scene from a pueblo de indios features a musical score on a lectern, and the teachers are referred to as "choir and school masters," *maistros de coro y de escuela* (Guaman Poma de Ayala 1980 [1615]: 634). The importance of music for the pastoral regime is further underlined by the fact that two of the main author-translators were also accomplished musicians. It was said of Oré that he could have sung in the cathedral choir of Toledo,[35] while Pérez Bocanegra spent part of his career as a singer and choirbook corrector in the Cuzco cathedral choir, and composed the first piece of polyphonic music to be published in the Americas. Singing was not restricted to the hymns proper. Ecclesiastical music had traditionally focused on the singing of prose texts such as prayers and psalms to continuous melodies that worked in any verbal context. Oré developed a melody of this sort for the cartilla texts and had intended to publish it in his *Symbolo catholico indiano*, but did not do so, probably because of typographic constraints (1992 [1598]: 187).[36] His Quechua version of the Te Deum, which was not a strophic composition, was probably sung to the same melody as the Latin original. By contrast, hymns proper were sung to strophic melodies which were more distinctive because they required a specific verse scheme.

The fact that most catechetical and liturgical texts were sung contributed greatly to group synchronization and to the spatial and temporal regularity of performance. Singing regulated the duration of a performance, facilitating its spatialization—the performance of specific texts could be assigned to specific parts of a processional route, such as a side of the plaza or atrium. Music also provided a metalanguage that clarified the nature of texts and performances. One can assume that participants and performers often had a basic familiarity with a range of melodies and musical genres and styles that carried specific implications. For instance, Oré's cánticos were sung to the melody of an important hymn of the canonical hours, and his evening hymn *Capac eterno* used the melody of *Sacris solemnis,* a hymn that Pérez Bocanegra suggested be sung in the processions that carried the eucharist to the homes of dying people (1631: 488). Oré's decision to give his hymns these melodies reflects his aspiration that they be considered part of the liturgy of the hours. As discussed in chapter 8, the fact that Pérez Bocanegra's score for *Hanac pachap cussicuinin* was composed in the villancico tradition marked the hymn as a "paraliturgical" piece that was not subject to the same standards of conventionality and orthodoxy as Oré's more solemn compositions. These musical genre frames have important consequences for our understanding of how the texts were meant to be interpreted—for instance, the paraliturgical status of Pérez Bocanegra's hymn throws light on its very unorthodox terminology and imagery.

Textual Figures

Specifically textual contextualization cues came in a variety of forms, beginning with the visual indices provided by the layout and composition of the printed and manuscript books. Admittedly, not many Indians owned printed books, but it seems likely that pastoral assistants did have regular access to them. The most general level of metacommentary provided by the form of a "text artifact" was the printed book–manuscript opposition. The fact that a given text was taken from a printed book provided some guarantee of its legitimacy, since printing required a series of official inspections and approvals. Variations in font style and size and in formatting had an important role in distinguishing the function and importance of texts. For instance, the Third Council catechisms used a smaller font for quotations from the basic prayers in order to distinguish them from the main commentary. Similarly, important loan words such as *Dios* and *Iesu Christo* are often written in uppercase letters, perhaps to indicate a special emphasis in oral performance. Prayers, hymns, and litanies were usually printed or written with a distinctive layout to indicate genre frames and performance styles that set them apart from catechisms or sermons.

The format of pastoral Quechua works also conveyed important messages regarding the status of Quechua as a Christian language. Quechua texts are surrounded by a web of Spanish and Latin originals, citations, commentaries, and titles, and rarely appear as freestanding texts. The kinds of relations that existed between originals and translations, and between source languages and target languages, were expressed visually in the organization and graphic design of the printed or manuscript pages. Pastoral books were arranged to allow for as close a juxtaposition as possible of Spanish or Latin and Quechua texts.[37] At the same time, different font types and sizes distinguished and separated them while also emphasizing their equivalence. As Ines Županov has observed in relation to early Christian texts in Tamil, "choice of lettering . . . and graphic design succeeded in both underscoring and containing the difference [between source and target languages], as well as reassuring the audience with a perfectly analogical translation/transcription" (2003: 116). Such elements contributed to the presentation of pastoral Quechua as part of a broader array of languages in which it occupied a derivative and subordinate position, just as occurred with the arrangement of the different versions of the baptismal form in the Andahuaylillas baptistery mural.

The most elaborate and pervasive forms of metacommentary were provided by the formal or poetic structures of the texts. Independently of layout and composition, formal textual features such as syllabic versification and parallelism cued understandings of the generic nature and performative function of a text. For instance, the prose exhortations of the Third Council *Confessionario,* which were intended to be recited by the priest, contain prayers that were to be said by Indians after confession or on their deathbeds but are not distinguished visually from the larger texts (e.g. Third Lima Council 1985b [1585]: 241, 288–289). The fact that they were, or could be, independent devotional texts seems to have been deliberately hidden from the casual observer and from readers who did not know Quechua. However, they are distinguished from the surrounding texts by higher rates of parallelism and stem matching. Parallelism is a common mark of ritual speech and produces a formal "tightening" in texts that allows them to be used in multiple contexts (Keane 1997). In these prayers it served both as an invitation to the audience to extract them from the texts in which they were contained, and as an indication that, as poetically enhanced texts, they were suitable for addressing God.

One of the most interesting and metapragmatically significant textual figures in Oré's work is the insertion or retention of terms, and sometimes of entire phrases, from the source languages—a phenomenon referred to by linguists as "code switching" or "code mixing" that is distinct from lexical borrowing. These inserts are most often Spanish, but Oré's hymns also contain scattered Latin, Greek, and even Hebrew and Aramaic terms. There is one full sentence in Aramaic in the sixth cántico, which reproduces Christ's final cry from the cross as it appears in the Gospels of Matthew and Mark (Oré 1992 [1598]: 354). But the most striking example comes from Oré's translation of Christ's prayer in the Garden of Gethsemane from Mark 14:36, also in the sixth cántico (ibid.: 340):

> Cay huañuy caliz Abba Pater Yaya,
> yachacuptinca, ñocamanta richun:
> huañuy upiayta ama upiassacchu,
> munaptiiquica.

> [Father [x 3], if it is possible, let this chalice of death go away from me. If you so wished, I would not drink the drink of death.]

In Oré's Quechua version of the prayer, Christ says the word "father" three times: first in Aramaic (*abba*), then in Latin or Greek (*pater* in both languages), and finally in Quechua (*yaya*).[38] The Vulgate Bible, which was Oré's source and is cited in the margin, has *abba pater,* and the original Greek text does something similar. Both versions seem to add a Greek or Latin gloss parenthetically to the word *abba,* which is retained from Christ's original utterance. However, if Oré had followed this practice, he would have written *abba yaya,* just as the King James Bible has "Abba, Father."

Oré's triple designation calls to mind Augustine of Hippo's suggestion that Christ had used *both* the Aramaic and the Greek word in his original utterance in order to symbolize the fact that Christ's church was to be constituted by Gentiles as well as Jews (Augustine 1980 [1888]: 184). Put differently, each term functioned as a "token" of its language and of the peoples who spoke it. Following Augustine's rationale, adding the Quechua term had the effect of explicitly including Quechua speakers in the fold. Oré's triple designation can also be seen as an "indexical icon" of the translation process itself as it moved from the more distant and original languages to the more proximal ones (Aramaic > Greek/Latin > Quechua).[39] The translation process is thus presented as a hierarchical chain or relay, whose earlier stages cannot be erased from the translation. This unerasability of the previous stages of the translation process is a prevalent figure in pastoral Quechua in general, and in Oré's hymns in particular.

The following stanza from the third cántico is also worth discussing as an example of the insertion of terms from the sacred languages (Oré 1992 [1598]: 248):

> A capac Diosya, quespichic Iesusya
> yschiros Diosya, Dios Athanathosya,
> sancto Messias, sanctissimo Christo
> Dios Heloynya.
>
> [O great God, O savior Jesus
> O *yschiros* God, O *athanathos* God
> Holy Mesias, holiest Christ
> O *elohim* God.]

The stanza consists of seven epithets in a row in which only two words have Quechua stems: *capac* 'royal' and *quespichic* 'savior'. Excluding the common loan words or names *Dios, Iesus, Christo, messias,* and *sancto/sanctissimo,* we have the Greek terms *yschiros* 'strong' and *athanathos* 'eternal,' and the Hebrew *elohim* 'God' (rendered as *heloyn*). In two cases—*Dios Athanathos* and *Dios Heloyn*—the internal order of the noun phrase is inverted, with the term that has the adjectival role appearing at the end of the phrase (this kind of inversion is not unusual in pastoral Quechua poetics).

The first point to be made about the stanza is that it echoes a prayer known as the *Tersanctus,* which is part of the Good Friday office. In the *Tersanctus,* the Greek invocations *Agios o Theos* ("holy God"), *Agios ischyros* ("holy strong one"), and *Agios athanatos* ("holy immortal one") are sung by one choir, while a second choir repeats the same invocations in Latin (*Catholic Encyclopedia,* "Agios o Theos"). Oré's stanza not only "retains" Greek terms from the prayer but also imitates its multilingual character and produces a similar juxtaposition of sacred languages. Second, there is some degree of parallelism between the first and second lines, each of which consists of two epithets. Quechua *capac* is paired with Greek *yschiros* 'strong,' although the matching of the second epithets in each line is obscured by the inversion in the order of the terms in the second line (which may have been intended to prevent the pairing of *quespichic* 'savior' and *athanathos* 'eternal,' which would have been unjustified semantically).

The retention of words and phrases from the source texts is, most obviously, a reflection of a common practice in the New Testament which was imitated in the early Christian liturgy (Mohrmann 1957: 19–24). Christine Mohrmann explains that it was intended as a form of "respect for the word in the form in which it was originally pronounced"—especially where Christ's Aramaic utterances were involved—which became an important element in the development of a distinctive Christian liturgical style (ibid.: 22–25). The inserts or retentions also tied a text to its ultimate source, and served as a reminder that this source was in another language. Oré seems to combine this practice with the Quechua tradition of translinguistic stem pairing, in which synonymous terms from different languages were juxtaposed in identical grammatical contexts. The Quechua poetic ear thus admitted and was accustomed to interpreting such intrusions. Pairing also created an iconic effect, in which the terms functioned as tokens of their languages and the text operated as a diagram of the way in which these languages have been brought into relation with each other via the transmission of the gospel. In this context, it could even be suggested that Oré's use of Standard Colonial Quechua–Central Quechua pairs was intended to express the continuation of the translation relay on towards a further vernacular—Central Quechua.

Grammatical Categories

Quechua grammar is characterized by the use of suffixes that stipulate aspects of the context of an utterance that are left unspecified in most other languages. In addition to the evidential suffixes /-mi/, /-si/, and /-cha/, which index the speaker's source of information for an assertion, two verbal suffixes deserve special mention: "cislocative" /-mu/, which indicates the spatial relation between the event referred to and the site of the speech event (/-mu/ generally meaning "not here"), and /-sqa/, which has been identified as a "narrative tense" that implies lack of direct knowledge of the narrated events. Analyses of the use of these suffixes in pastoral Quechua texts, and in colonial Quechua texts more generally, have argued that they were misunderstood by Spanish writers, or that the medium of writing itself was an obstacle to their proper use. These categories have been seen as characteristic of the "oral" culture in which Quechua developed, as it is presumed that their pragmatic relevance is dependent on the immediacy of oral discourse. Consequently, it is argued, their use in written communication, which involves a separation between the text and the context in which it was originally created, leads to anomalies and irregularities (cf. Adelaar 1997, Itier 1992b). I suggest that these categories were not as rigid and narrow as would seem—a point that has already been made with regard to evidential suffixes in chapter 6—and that instead of being an obstacle to translation, Quechua's metapragmatic suffixes were exploited by the author-translators to establish features of context and to elicit specific responses from performers and audiences, just as occurs in any other form of Quechua discourse, particularly the more rhetorical ones.

"Cislocative" /-mu/ is a verbal derivational suffix added to verb stems before person markers and after other verbal derivational suffixes. With most verbs it indicates that the event referred to takes place somewhere other than "here," which may be the "here" of the speech event or a "here" in the realm of reference, such as the location of a character in a story. There are two derivative uses of /-mu/ in which the category functions somewhat differently. The first occurs when speaker and addressee are considered to be at distinct locations, in which case the point of orientation can also be the location of the addressee (thus, the speaker will apply /-mu/ to verbs designating actions that take place at his/her own location, as they are "not here" from the perspective of the addressee, and vice versa). A second derivative use occurs with verbs which denote movement in a definite direction, such as *chaya-* 'arrive,' *llocsi-* 'exit,' or *yaycu-* 'enter.' In such cases /-mu/ indicates that the terminus of the movement is "here." The main thing to keep in mind about all of these functions is that /-mu/ is employed when there is a definite, specifiable spatial relation between "here" and the event referred to, and can otherwise be omitted. The use of /-mu/ thus implies that such a relation exists.

Occurrences of /-mu/ in the pastoral texts only rarely take the location of the speech event (as opposed to a point in the realm of reference) as the point of orientation, as is to be expected in standardized, transposable texts. When the category *is* used in this way, the "here" of the speech event is usually framed as the world as a whole in opposition to heaven. This occurs primarily in prayers or hymns to Mary, who was believed to be physically in heaven. Take the following sentence from the Salve Regina: *camtam huacyamuycu Euap carcosca huahuancuna, camtam yuyamuycu, huacaspa, anchispa, cay hueque pachapi* (we the expelled children of Eve call [/-mu/] to you, we think [/-mu/] of you, weeping and sighing in this world of tears) (Third Lima Council 1985a [1584]: 26). By assigning /-mu/ to the verbs which, reflexively, refer to the act of praying which is being carried out at that moment from "this vale of tears," the speaker recognizes that he/she is definitely "not here" from the perspective of the Virgin. This does not usually occur in prayers to God, perhaps because of the attribute of Omnipresence. Exceptions can be found in eucharistic prayers and hymns. In the stanza by Oré quoted earlier in this chapter, in which Christ in the host is asked to look out on the speakers, /-mu/ is applied to the requested action—*chay hostiamanta cahuarimullahuay* (look upon on me from that host). A first effect of /-mu/ assignment here is to distinguish the location of the worshipper from that of the host on the altar, thus emphasizing a hierarchical separation. At the same time, it helps to concretize the physical presence of Christ in the host, eliciting awe and reverence.

The verbal suffix /-sqa/ (not to be confused with passive participle /-sqa/) is usually identified as a "narrative tense" opposed to the "simple" or "direct" past tense /-rqa/ with the same implications as the /-si/ (reportative) versus /-mi/ (direct-witness) opposition (e.g., Mannheim and Van Vleet 1998: 338). It is used abundantly in oral tellings of myths and other narratives of temporally and epistemically remote events. However, there is evidence that /-sqa/ is not a tense suffix at all and carries no evidential implication. If /-sqa/ implied indirect knowledge of an event, then the "simple" past tense /-rqa/ would imply *direct* knowledge, which is clearly not the case, as it is frequently combined with reportative evidential marking (similarly, /-sqa/ can be combined with the direct-witness suffix /-mi/). In conversational speech /-sqa/ functions as a sudden-disclosure marker that does not specify tense and has no evidential implications, indicating instead that the information conveyed is new and surprising for the speaker.

González Holguín, who analyzed verb forms in great detail, mentions /-sqa/ only as a sudden-disclosure category (which he terms *de desengaño*), and states that it has no tense implications. He goes on to say that its use can also indicate that the speaker anticipates that the information transmitted is "new and surprising" *for the audience* (González Holguín 1607: f. 27). Along these lines, González Holguín suggested that /-sqa/ be used for telling exempla: "And so *casca* can be used to tell news, or an exemplum, or to teach things about heaven, virtues, hidden things, sudden events, or things unheard of that the audience tends not to know."[40] In just this way, Pérez Bocanegra used /-sqa/ when explaining that confirmation, which was only rarely administered to Indians, was a sacrament too (Pérez Bocanegra 1631: 82). The presence of /-sqa/ here indexes an assumption on the part of the speaker that the information is new and surprising for the audience, and at the same time solicits an appropriate response. However, exempla and other narrative pastoral texts use /-sqa/ only very rarely, and this is also the case in colonial Quechua texts authored by Indians, such as the Huarochirí Manuscript. It appears that the modern function of /-sqa/ as a staple in storytelling developed more recently as a genre-specific offshoot of the "sudden disclosure" category.

I have already argued in chapter 6 that the persistent use of the "direct-witness" evidential suffix /-mi/ in the pastoral literature does not constitute a misuse of the category, which has been more correctly glossed by Martina Faller as "best possible grounds." What requires analysis is not so much the prevalence of direct-witness marking in pastoral texts as the cases where reportative marking (/-si/) is employed. There are several instances of switching from direct-witness to reportative marking in sermons and exempla. Sermon 30 of the Third Council sermonario, for example, paraphrases Christ's parables of Lazarus and of the miser from Luke 16 with reportative marking (Third Lima Council 1985c [1585]: 749–751). The sermon explaining the sacrament of confession (sermon 12) contains exempla with reportative marking which tell of the punishments incurred by those who omitted sins from their confessions (no source is cited for these exempla) (ibid.: 484–485). There are also instances of reportative marking in Avila's sermonario. One of the lengthiest is an account of Thomas the Apostle's evangelization of the Andes, ending with his near martyrdom at the hands of the Colla Indians on the shores of Lake Titicaca, a story attributed by Avila to elderly Indians he had encountered "from Lima to Potosí." Avila shifts back to direct-witness marking to describe how a miraculous cross Thomas left behind had been discovered by a bishop some seventy years before his time of writing (Avila [1647]: 234–235). The exemplum, an especially propitious context for the use of reportative evidential marking, appears as a freestanding genre in the works of Prado (1641: f. 62v–75, 78v–81) and Jurado Palomino (1649: passim). Prado's exempla are unusual in that, while each one opens with reportative marking, the body of the text carries no evidential marking at all, and the conclusion (usually a moral) has direct-witness marking. The exempla in Jurado Palomino's translation of Bellarmino's catechism, which are appended as conclusions to the catechism sections, use reportative marking consistently. Both Prado's and Jurado Palomino's exempla begin with references to the works from which they were taken.

Instances of reportative marking can also be found in hymns, especially Oré's cánticos. It is used briefly early in the sixth cántico, which narrates the passion, to tell John's vision of the heavenly hosts singing the praise of the Lamb in Revelation 5 (Oré 1992 [1598]: 339):

> Euangelista Apostol San Iuanmi
> Apocalipsis sutioc quellcampi,
> hanacpachapi uyaricuscanta
> uillacuanchic.
>
> Apu yayaycu, yahuarniiquihuanmi,
> rantihuarcanqui Diosman quespincaypac
> ñispas taquircan, ñispas tinyacurcan,
> Diospa cayllampi.
>
> [The Apostle and Evangelist St. John [/-mi/] in his writing called "Revelation" tells us what he heard in heaven.]
>
> ["Our Lord, you redeemed us with your blood [/-mi/] so that we might be saved and reach God" thus saying [-si] they sang and played drums in the presence of God.][41]

Towards the end of the narrative of the passion, reportative marking is used once again to tell Jacob's dream of a heavenly ladder, which is compared to the ladder used to bring Christ down from the cross (ibid.: 365). A further example comes from the Marian *carmen* in the third cántico, where reportative marking appears in John's vision of a woman clothed with sun and with the moon at her feet from Revelation 12:1 (ibid.: 258). In all three cases, it is used to tell things seen in divinely inspired visions or dreams granted to holy men that were recorded in the Bible.

In general, the use of reportative marking was a choice that served specific rhetorical purposes rather than a grammatical necessity.[42] These purposes varied depending on the context. In the exempla, reportative marking seems to serve as an interpretive cue indicating that the narrative was to be read for its moral implications—in other words, as a story. In the other cases, there appears to be a desire to set apart or "frame" a specific narrative within a broader text—to individualize it with respect to a particularly important source, often reinforcing an attribution that was also being made explicitly. The heavenly visions of John and Jacob were unique events, and reportative marking helped them stand out from Oré's overall narrative. Choosing reportative rather than direct-witness marking does not rob a statement of certitude—depending on whose speech is being reported, it can enhance it. In the case of Avila's story about St. Thomas in the Andes, there could be no more convincing source from the perspective of his audience than the elderly Indians he had met "from Lima to Potosí." Somewhat like the "retentions" from the source languages discussed above, reportative marking underlines the intertextuality of pastoral discourse, tying it to previous and more prestigious utterances.

Conclusion

Much of this book has been dedicated to charting variation in translation practice, and in what follows I sum up the broad patterns that have emerged, before discussing how pastoral Quechua writing in general both reflected and contributed to the construction of its colonial context. First, however, I would like to suggest that when viewed in a comparative perspective, Christian translation into Quechua stands out for its *lack* of overt variation, especially if one takes into account the linguistic diversity and unrivaled demographic importance and geographic spread of Quechua. I have occasionally referred to contemporary Christian literatures in Mesoamerican languages to highlight specific characteristics of pastoral Quechua whose significance might otherwise go unnoticed. Broader comparisons are a risky undertaking because of the uneven nature of the research on both sides and, above all, the absence of studies that undertake such comparisons directly. However, it seems safe to say that as well as being more prolific, pastoral translation in Mexico accommodated greater terminological and linguistic diversity.

Terminological diversity is difficult to gauge—it is a question of registering not only the occurrence of variant terms but also their frequency and distribution through time and different genre contexts. However, it is apparent from what research has been done on the subject, as well as from a glance at the prologues of Mexican pastoral works, that there was more flexibility and overt variation in terminological practice in Mesoamerica than in Peru.[1] And while Nahuatl was in widespread use as a pastoral medium, its use did not preclude extensive writing and publishing in several other languages. A greater openness to linguistic diversity is expressed in the use not only of more languages but also of closely related linguistic varieties. In the relatively tiny Mixtec area of Oaxaca, for instance, an early pastoral book went through two editions to accommodate different varieties of Mixtec.[2] It is highly significant that a canonical body of vernacular texts comparable to the Third Lima Council corpus was never produced in any Mesoamerican language. Efforts to limit experimentation and diversity in line with the global requirements of the Counter-Reformation did take place in Mexico around the same time as in Peru—the Third Mexican Council of 1585 required on pain of excommunication that all vernacular texts be approved by the local bishop (Tavárez 2000: 28). However, the council did not produce its own body of texts and thus could not truly regulate translation practice.

There was, of course, much significant change and variation in Christian writing in Quechua even after the Third Lima Council, but such variation tended to be covert and inconsistently aligned with institutional divisions within the church. Sources from Mexico and Paraguay record terminological debates that sometimes developed into full-fledged institutional conflicts pitting order against order, or the secular church against an order. In mid-sixteenth-century Mexico, the archdiocese prosecuted a Franciscan over a catechism he wrote in Tarascan, while a debate raged between the Franciscan and Dominican orders in Chiapas over the correct term for God in Kakchiquel Maya (Fernández del Castillo ed. 1982 [1914]: 4–37, 81–85; García-Ruiz 1992: 91–92). There continued to be open debate over key terminological problems in Nahuatl well into the seventeenth century (León 1611: n.p.n.; Alva 1634: f. 48–50; cf. Tavárez 2000: 32). Looking further afield, there was a serious conflict between Franciscans and Jesuits in mid-seventeenth-century Paraguay over the terms used in the main Guarani catechism (Salas 2000: 126–131).[3]

Explicit criticisms of specific texts and translation practices were very rare in Peru: it was not until the end of the period of this study that we find the Chinchaysuyoists in the archdiocese of Lima critiquing the Third Council standard, and then only on dialectal grounds. The first real attack on Third Council practice came from Francisco de la Cruz in the mid-1650s, after the printing of new pastoral texts had practically ended for the rest of the colonial period. Nor does one find corporate groups such as orders openly espousing specific translation strategies in Peru. This is not to say that there were no correspondences between corporate membership and translation practices—the Third Council's translation program was very much the work of the secular church and of the Society of Jesus to the exclusion of the mendicants, who had been the main agents of translation until that moment. The extant works by Franciscans (those of Oré and Diego de Molina) are distinctive in their use of certain devotional themes centered on the passion, but neither author felt free to diverge significantly from the Third Council norms on key issues such as dialectology and basic terminology. When we look at the far more abundant writings of secular clerics and Jesuits, we find the full range of variability within each group. Admittedly, our understanding of this issue is severely limited by the loss of the extensive manuscript literature—in particular, we have no Dominican works later than the very early writings of Santo Tomás. However, there is no reason to assume that Dominican writings diverged more significantly from the Third Council standard than did Franciscan ones.

The lack of open splits and debates over terminological issues in pastoral Quechua is coherent with other points of contrast with Mexican practice that have been noted, such as the apparent absence of native authors or contributors and the fact that Quechua texts rarely appear unaccompanied by a Spanish version: in short, translation was subjected to far greater controls and restrictions in Peru. Different reasons can be proposed for this contrast. Peru was from the beginning a more problematic colony than Mexico: it presented greater geographical challenges, its indigenous population put up a more effective long-term resistance, and its settler population was more fractious and rebellious. These obstacles to crown control, added to Peru's greater importance as a source of revenue, led to a much more heavy-handed royal reorganization. Since political and economic reform was inseparable from religious reform, Peru also experienced a more profound and radical Counter-Reformation. Further, Peru's Counter-Reformation came at an earlier stage in the development of the colony: not only was Peru conquered at a later date, but the period of military and political stabilization that followed on the conquest was longer than in Mexico. This made it possible for the reformers to impose an orthodox standard before the diverse and experimental translation practices of the primera evangelización had had time to fully develop and become institutionally entrenched.

Patterns of Variation

The existence of a dominant standard makes it easier to identify and interpret historically significant variation in pastoral writing in the Andes than in Mesoamerica. After the council, any given author-translator can be characterized as working either for or against the standard in one respect or another. Summing up the overall patterns apparent in the variation, though, is not a straightforward task. One cannot predict translation practices on the basis of institutional affiliation, and the variations are rarely reflected in contemporary debates. Co-variation at different levels of translation practice is also limited: works that diverged significantly from the Third Council standard dialectally did not do so in their Christian terminology. The most straightforward classification that can be proposed for the entire corpus is of a chronological nature. Four main groups have been distinguished: (1) the literature of the primera evangelización (1550s through 1570s); (2) the literature of the reform period of the 1570s and 1580s (represented by the Third Lima Council corpus); (3) the postcouncil literature (ca. 1590–1640); and (4) the mid-century literature (late 1640s).

The first group cannot be described in any detail because only a few fragments of pastoral Quechua discourse have survived from the period. Those provided by Santo Tomás were probably among a corpus approved by the First Lima Council and by the archdiocese of Lima under a Dominican prelate. In dialectal terms, they reflect the continued importance of the Quechua-speaking population of the central coast and of the Inca lingua franca. Terminologically, there is a penchant for periphrastic neologisms and a willingness to use key Andean religious categories. We also have tantalizing bits of information about an independent translation program developed by the diocese of Cuzco in the 1560s and 1570s, if not earlier. This program may bear some relation to the efforts by Juan de Betanzos (in the 1540s and 1550s) and Cristóbal de Molina (in the 1560s and 1570s) to depict Inca religion as centered on the cult of the creator god Viracocha. Betanzos, a resident of Cuzco, was responsible for some of the earliest Christian writings in Quechua and probably used the term "Viracocha" to refer to God in them; Cristóbal de Molina, who was part of the circle of clerics that revised the diocesan pastoral corpus in the 1570s, recorded a series of prayers to Viracocha in which Inca religious language was adapted to monotheistic themes. Hypothetical as these connections may be, it is clear that the translation practices of this period were characterized by an experimental diversity, by a relative openness to the use of adapted terms and neologisms as opposed to loan words, and by the use of Andean ritual genres in Christian liturgical contexts. The accommodationist practices of the time were related to, and justified by, a tendency in the chronicle literature to construe Inca religion as having strong monotheistic and even proto-Christian elements.

The reaction against this primera evangelización is expressed in the Third Council corpus, which was the keystone of the development and imposition of a standard pastoral language. The corpus should be seen as part of a broader process that developed throughout the 1570s and 1580s, including the early translation efforts of the Jesuits (which have not survived, but probably provided the most immediate models for the Third Council translators) and Viceroy Toledo's program for the standardization of vernacular instruction. The Third Council works were characterized by an effort to minimize associations with native religious categories through the use of loan words, by an emphasis on the unicity of key terms and expressions, and by a similar standardization effort at dialectal and orthographic levels. The internal uniformity of the standard served to facilitate its reproduction in further texts and utterances, and its exclusivity as the only legitimate form of pastoral Quechua was to act as a powerful control mechanism over the assimilation of Christian discourse by Indians. The development of Standard Colonial Quechua on the basis of the Cuzco variety resulted both from a conception of language as having fixed centers and origins, and from regional economic dynamics derived from the mining circuit. It is not clear, however, that the Spanish ever attempted to impose it as a spoken language. While viceroys and archbishops did command the Quechuization of populations that spoke non-Quechua languages, Standard Colonial Quechua seems to have remained tied to written communication and to formal pastoral speech, which was based on written texts.

The postcouncil period was above all a time of expansion and diversification of the pastoral literature in genre and stylistic range, terminology, and (to a much lesser degree) dialectology. All but one of the Quechua hymns and the majority of the prayers and sacramental texts come from this period. There was a general move away from the Third Council's emphasis on plain, expository prose—the *estilo llano*—and an effort to produce a more complex, poetically rich Christian discourse. While the basic pastoral terminology established by the Third Council remained in use, Pérez Bocanegra and González Holguín developed "nativizing" alternatives for many of the key terms. The postcouncil literature was also characterized by the development of syncretic poetic registers employing terms and images derived from native cult languages—God, Christ, and Mary were partially identified with Andean deities, or at least acquired some of their attributes. While the mainstream translation program sought to erase the indigenous cultural contexts of adapted terms, the postcouncil author-translators developed a more culturally sensitive, but also more insidious strategy: they used unassimilated terms and motifs precisely on account of their indigenous religious meanings, seeking to generate an *interpretatio christiana* of the referents themselves. These tendencies were related to a cumulus of institutional and ideological developments of the late sixteenth and early seventeenth centuries. One such change was the increasing, or rather, renewed emphasis on Indian participation in the liturgy, which required the development of new poetic registers. At the same time, there was a return to the pro-Inca discourses of the primera evangelización, which had fallen out of favor during the reforms of the 1570s and 1580s. This shift was interdependent with the terminological experimentation, through which implicit parallels between native Andean and Christian religious institutions and practices were proposed. At the same time, it should be stressed that by and large the postcouncil author-translators worked around the conciliar translation program instead of trying to supplant it—they stopped well short of discarding its basic terminological and dialectal norms, and their most striking innovations were restricted to poetic registers.

The mid-century literature was not a continuation of what I have called the postcouncil literature—it was not the next "phase" in an evolution. The trend towards terminological experimentation did not continue in these texts. Instead we find a clear adherence to Third Council practice. Partly as a result of intensified concern over idolatry, there was also a renewed emphasis on catechesis. While the image of the Incas continued to be invoked, it served now as a warning to present-day Indians rather than a bridge between the native past and the Christian present. Dialectally, this literature is characterized by the use of Central word stems with varying frequency and prominence, and even, in some cases, the use of Central suffixes. There was a public debate regarding the utility of "Chinchaysuyo" Quechua as opposed to Standard Colonial Quechua as a pastoral medium. However, it should be emphasized that with the exception of Castromonte's ritual, the dialectal divergences between the mid-century works and the Third Council standard were very limited. Even the relatively few Central Quechua terms employed were usually accompanied by their Southern equivalents, as if the writers were wary of violating the integrity of Standard Colonial Quechua.

When examined in this chronological perspective, translation seems to follow a pendular movement between more accommodationist and liturgically oriented tendencies, and more conservative and catechetically oriented ones. This pendular movement reflects a dialectic between two contradictory requirements that all author-translators experienced, if to different degrees: on the one hand, that of developing a stable doctrinal language that minimized "slippage" and maximized control of Christian discourse in Quechua; and on the other, that of engaging indigenous audiences at devotional levels, a task that required the manipulation of native poetics and religious and cosmological categories. The pendulum image does indeed capture an important part of the history of pastoral Quechua, but when the variations in the corpus are seen through a regional rather than a chronological lens, a different pattern emerges.

Beginning with the Third Lima Council's attempt to impose a standard, two continuous traditions can be discerned: an orthodox one associated with Lima and its archdiocese, and a more accommodationist tradition that had Cuzco and the southern highlands in general as its base. This is a highly conjectural model because neither area is continuously represented in the extant literature: there was no printing in Cuzco and no manuscripts from the area have survived, and the Lima presses published works by the local clergy only towards the end of the period of this study. Additionally, many of the author-translators were regionally mobile. Nonetheless, it is significant that the postcouncil author-translators were all linked, if not to Cuzco itself, to the southern highlands. Pérez Bocanegra was probably a Cuzqueño *tout court*, and González Holguín's formative years, especially in terms of data-gathering, were spent in Cuzco. Oré was from Huamanga and spent most of his career in what was then the diocese of Cuzco. Prado was a native of La Paz, but his career seems to have developed primarily in Huamanga. On the other hand, the author-translators of the mid-century literature are all associated with the archdiocese, if not with the city of Lima. Admittedly, Avila and Jurado Palomino were natives of Cuzco, but they spent their entire careers in the archdiocese. It can be suggested that author-translators in the archdiocese of Lima tended to be conservative terminologically but innovative at dialectal levels, whereas their colleagues in the southern highlands tended to fret against the bounds of terminological orthodoxy imposed by the Third Council.

On the whole, the "Lima tradition" was characterized by loyalty to the Third Council standard. The archdiocese of Lima was the center of the Peruvian church, and the standard had been developed under its auspices. At least in the initial designs of the crown, the guarantor of its proper use throughout Peru was the Quechua chair of the University of San Marcos, also located in Lima. While pastoral writing and vernacular instruction in the archdiocese soon incorporated Central Quechua elements, the modifications to the standard were minimal even at dialectal levels. The diocesan clergy of Cuzco, on the other hand, had been very active during the years prior to the Third Council in the development of their own corpus of pastoral texts, which may have been influenced by the Incaist discourses and translation practices of Betanzos and Cristóbal de Molina. Unlike their counterparts in Lima, Cuzqueño criollos and mestizos were constantly reminded of the glories of the Incas, and soon began to identify with them. Although the Third Council translators adopted Cuzco Quechua as the base dialect for the standard, they also systematically ironed out dialectal idiosyncrasies and perhaps also Inca religious terminology that had been appropriated by the Cuzqueño translators. I would suggest that the postcouncil authors drew on this Cuzqueño tradition. It is clear that the register of syncretic epithets for God which many of them employed was most resonant in the Cuzco area itself, as it derived largely from the state cults. More generally, the Andean-Christian iconography discussed in chapter 8 tended to draw on specifically Inca traditions, although it is not always possible to distinguish them from more broadly Andean ones. I have proposed that González Holguín's appropriations of native religious terminology, which match the usage of the postcouncil authors (Pérez Bocanegra in particular) very closely, derived from pastoral texts written in Cuzco before the Third Lima Council. It does not seem likely that González Holguín on his own could have had such an influence on the postcouncil terminology. Instead, he, Pérez Bocanegra, Prado, and Oré all appear to have drawn on an existing translation tradition.[4]

The two patterns—chronological and geographic—are not mutually exclusive, but in order to balance and flesh them out new research is needed on related historical processes. The institutional, social, and political development of the colonial church in Peru is still poorly understood. Discourses on Andean Christianity as expressed in the chronicle literature have received far more attention, but the scholarship has tended to focus on key works and ideas in abstraction from local circumstances. Above all, connections need to be established between the two areas of research. The patterns apparent in the pastoral Quechua literature can contribute to the unraveling of institutional cultures and politics, especially by suggesting new topics and questions, both general and specific: In what sorts of contexts did Incaist discourses and associated translation practices flourish? To what extent did the clergy of the highland dioceses (i.e., the diocese of Cuzco up to the early seventeenth century) develop different social and ideological characteristics from that of the archdiocese of Lima? What was the background to the mid-century boom in pastoral Quechua writing and publishing in the archdiocese of Lima and the dialectological debate that accompanied it?

Translation and Colonialism

Pastoral Quechua was no missionary pidgin. It was the product of a concerted, institutionalized effort that developed over several decades, and of individuals who were both native speakers and career specialists in translation and linguistic description/codification. The texts they produced made full use of Quechua's unique poetic and grammatical resources, and in some cases employed images and tropes that were intended to work simultaneously in different interpretive registers, and to imply daring commentaries on the links and similarities between Christianity and Andean religion. Pastoral Quechua was disseminated through an elaborate performance system that involved the bulk of the Peruvian clergy and countless native assistants, and its spread went hand-in-hand with a profound reorganization of native society. It had lasting (if largely unstudied) effects on multiple aspects of Andean cultural history—most obviously on literacy and religious thought. However, pastoral translation into Quechua was also marked by hierarchy and restriction, and some of the features I have listed as examples of its virtuosity were also control mechanisms that limited its development.

Literary theory and experimentation aside, translation tends to be viewed as a process that erases its own tracks, producing texts and literatures that can function freely and independently from their source languages. Good translations should not appear as such, and in some cases can even acquire canonical status as "new originals," as happened with the Vulgate (cf. Barnstone 1993: 141). However, religious translation in colonial contexts may be better understood as a process of creating a target language that is capable of supplementing the source language rather than substituting for it. Just as the república de indios was subordinate to, and dependent on, Spanish priests and officials, pastoral Quechua was never intended to develop into a full-fledged Christian language. It was restricted to a limited range of functions, constantly referenced and required the use of the source languages, and remained the domain of a cadre of specialists within a Spanish-speaking clergy.

A variety of mechanisms were deployed to ensure that pastoral Quechua remained "pastoral"—that is, never passed into the hands of its target audience—and that it did not become emancipated from the source literature. Terminological and dialectal standardization was a key instrument in this respect, facilitating clerical supervision and control. Christian speech in Quechua was restricted to a single, highly codified linguistic variety and to a set terminology which the clergy studied and used with only limited attention to the language of their parishioners. Standardization also made deviations from the norm immediately apparent. For similar reasons, pastoral Quechua performances were of a very public and routinized nature, and when they were not, they attracted the suspicion and censure of the church. The abundance of "untranslations" of key terms, texts, and genres was also a control mechanism. The reliance on loan words especially served as an obstacle to the full assimilation of pastoral Quechua by its intended audience: any Spaniard could claim a better grasp of its key terms simply on the grounds of knowing Spanish. Similarly, the Spanish-based orthography—in particular the use of five written vowels—was very difficult for Indians to reproduce, making their writings easy to discern from those of Spaniards.

Pastoral Quechua texts were pervasively marked as secondary and dependent instances of a universal translation process. Loan words were not only difficult to assimilate, they were also a constant reminder of the derivative character of pastoral Quechua. As Vicente Rafael puts it in his discussion of the use of loan words in Christian texts in Tagalog, "[t]he coupling of translation with the notion of untranslatability was intended to position Tagalog as a derivative of Latin and Castilian and therefore an instance in the divine production of signs" (1993 [1988]: 29, cf. 213). In the spatial distribution of a printed page, in the organization of performance in real time/space, and in its own linguistic and textual features and poetic forms, pastoral Quechua was always placed on the edge of, and referred to, Spanish, Latin, and even more remote source languages. Far from being erased, the process of translation was constantly retraced.

The hierarchies established between Quechua and the source languages were projected onto relations among the Andean languages, in particular different varieties of Quechua—a characteristically colonial move. Just as linguistic diversity in nineteenth-century Senegal was interpreted in terms of "a history of conquest and conversion that paralleled the European conquest and the hierarchical relationships thought to obtain between Europeans and Africans" (Irvine and Gal 2000: 55), Cuzco Quechua, or rather the standard based upon it, was identified as the only authentic form of Quechua, a civil and imperial language that was uniquely and providentially suited as a vehicle for Christianity. Even proponents of Chinchaysuyo Quechua in the archdiocese of Lima recognized the superiority of the Cuzco standard in much the same terms as it was expressed by the Third Council translators. The exaltation of one native linguistic and cultural tradition over others served, in effect, as a form of colonial control, contributing to the essentialization and manipulation of the indigenous. It was the central justification for standardization and for the failure to develop non-Southern forms of pastoral Quechua after the Third Lima Council. This failure in turn has served to perpetuate the myth of the primacy of "Inca" Quechua up to the present day. While the development and promotion of Standard Colonial Quechua led to the period of greatest florescence of Quechua literacy, establishing a true written tradition, it also seems likely that its standardized and exclusive character prevented this tradition from taking root and perpetuating itself.

Of course, it is not just the monolithic and hierarchical dimensions of pastoral Quechua that make it characteristically colonial. Colonial societies are defined by radical cultural divides that are reflected in tensions and fractures within both the colonizing and colonized sectors. Christian translation in Peru acted as a forum where conflicting understandings of the indigenous were expressed and worked out. Because of the extent to which they were naturalized, terminological practices in particular carried major implications, providing evidence for (and also guiding) views on pre-Christian religion. Using a native religious expression in a Christian context implied that its original meaning had approximated its Christian one, and applying a Quechua term to a specifically Christian institution or category was proof positive that it had been practiced or understood before the conquest (cf. Estenssoro Fuchs 2003: 135–136). Translation thus functioned as an instrument of intercultural exegesis and of colonial cultural politics.

Pérez Bocanegra's practices in particular often seem to have been directed at exemplifying and performing a Christianizing reading of the Inca past and at suggesting the existence or possibility of an Inca Christianity, as much as at communicating points of doctrine to, or inspiring devotion among, his Indian contemporaries. His use of the phrase *Diospa acllan* (God's aclla) as "nun," for instance, resurrects a specifically Inca politico-religious institution that had disappeared a century before the *Ritual formulario* was published, and one might ask to what extent the term still had resonance among Indian audiences. However, Inca institutions *were* remembered and debated among the Spanish clergy: while Acosta had seen the institution of the aclla as a demonic imitation of the convent, for the Anonymous Jesuit it was only a step away from the real thing, and González Holguín's dictionary suggested that the similarity justified applying the term for the pagan institution to the Christian one. Such a reading should not be identified too lightly with a sympathetic perception of present-day Indians. As has been seen, Pérez Bocanegra was very repressive of indigenous agency in pastoral contexts, and his Incaist translation practices may instead reflect an incipient criollo Cuzqueño identity politics—the exaltation of the Incas resulted in the exaltation of Cuzco vis-à-vis other centers of colonial power in ways that did not necessarily include Indians.[5] This may have been one of the dominant concerns of the hypothetical Cuzco translation tradition: if Christianity was best expressed in Quechua using the religious language of the Incas, then Cuzco and its ecclesiastical institutions could claim to be the true arbiters of Quechua translation and ultimately of Andean Christianity.

Garcilaso de la Vega's narrative of the fateful encounter at Cajamarca between Atahuallpa and Pizarro in 1532 can serve as a coda for this book, exemplifying the pregnancy of translation for colonial politics and cultural/historical interpretation (Garcilaso 1944 [1617]: I 59–68; cf. MacCormack 1989 and Seed 1991). In Garcilaso's account of the events, the speech delivered by Friar Valverde to Atahuallpa prior to his capture was a version of the *requerimiento,* a legal-religious text used by conquistadors to request recognition of the sovereignty of Spain from native lords by outlining the basic principles of Christianity, the history of the world, and the basis of the king's claims. Characteristically, Garcilaso stated that Atahuallpa already regarded the conquistadors as emissaries of Pachacamac (i.e., of God) and was prepared to surrender his sovereignty to them—in other words, he had already understood and accepted the message of the requerimiento. However, the act of communicating it was bungled by the Spaniards and their incompetent and malicious Indian interpreter, Felipillo. The implication of this account was that Atahuallpa would have converted eagerly to Christianity, and the Inca empire would have continued to exist as a Christian kingdom subject to Spain, if only the conquistadors had handled the act of translation properly (MacCormack 1989: 160).

However, the political onus of such an interpretation was excessive, and Garcilaso sought to relieve it by arguing that, even under the best of circumstances, it would have been *impossible* to adequately translate the religious contents of the requerimiento because of the absence of appropriate Quechua terminology. It would have been more in character for Garcilaso to claim that the translation was feasible because Atahuallpa already knew God under the name Pachacamac and was expecting his emissaries, but it was necessary to provide Pizarro, Valverde, and even poor Felipillo with an alibi. Garcilaso found it in the Third Lima Council's *Confessionario para los curas de indios,* of which he owned a copy. The impossibility of adequate translation at the time of the conquest was demonstrated by the fact that the *Confessionario*'s Quechua texts, written by the most capable translators after fifty years of experience with Quechua, relied on Spanish loan words for most key concepts. The Spaniards at Cajamarca could only be "exempted of the blame that could be attributed to them for that bad translation" (*descargados de la culpa que se les podía imponer por aquella mala interpretación*) (Garcilaso 1944 [1617]: I 68). Garcilaso thus chose to justify the conquest as the event that would make translation possible.

Glossary

aclla (Q.): Class of women under the Inca empire who were detached from their communities and dedicated to the service of the state.

audiencia (Sp.): Spanish high court with wide-ranging administrative as well as judicial powers. Also applied to the jurisdictional territory of such a court.

ayllu (Q.): Ostensibly kin-based Andean segmentary unit of social organization.

breviary: Book containing the psalms, hymns, and biblical readings recited during the canonical hours or divine office.

cántico (Sp.): Hymn or religious song.

capítulo (Sp.): One of a series of formal complaints against an official, especially in a lawsuit initiated by parishioners against their priest ("capítulos trial").

carta annua (Lat.): Annual report to Rome from a Jesuit province.

cartilla (Sp.): Compilation of basic Christian texts, usually containing the basic prayers, commandments, articles of the faith, and lists of sins, virtues, and other theological categories. Also referred to as *la doctrina cristiana.*

cédula (Sp.): Royal decree.

Chinchaysuyo (Q): Name of the northwestern quarter of the Inca empire, applied during the colonial period primarily to the central Peruvian highlands and coast and to the varieties of Quechua spoken there.

cofradía (Sp.): Lay religious association, confraternity.

confesionario (Sp.): Questionnaire to be used by priests in hearing confession.

corregidor (Sp.): Spanish provincial governor.

criollo (Sp.): American-born Spaniard.

curaca (Q.): Native Andean noble.

Cuzqueño (>Cuzqueñismo, Cuzqueñista) (Sp.): Something from, and characteristic of, Cuzco and its region.

fiscal (Sp.): An assistant of the parish priest responsible for enforcing observance of sacramental and catechetical requirements.

haraui (Q.): Mournful song/dance genre.

haylli (Q.): Celebratory song/dance genre originally used in military and agricultural contexts.

huaca (Q.): Native Andean divinity, usually identified with a mountain or other feature of the landscape.

información (Sp.): Notarial transcript of depositions from several witnesses made in support of a claim before a court. *Informaciones de méritos* or *de oficio* supported requests to the Council of the Indies for merit-based promotion.

ladino (Sp): non-native Spanish speaker, used especially with reference to Spanish-speaking Indians (*indios ladinos*).

lengua (Sp.): Translator/interpreter, bi- or multilingual person; applied mainly to Spanish clergymen who knew Quechua well.

lengua general (Sp.): Lingua franca, linguistic variety used as a means of communication between speakers of different languages. Mostly used with reference to Quechua in colonial Peru.

mestizo (Sp.): Person of mixed Indian-Spanish parentage.

missal: Book containing the texts to be read in the mass in accordance with the liturgical calendar.

mita (Q.): Labor draft imposed on the indigenous population, used especially with reference to the drafts that supplied the mines of Potosí and Huancavelica (based on an Inca institution of rotating labor service to the state).

pastoral Quechua: Used here with reference to Christian discourse in Quechua in general.

patronato real (Sp.): "Royal patronage," authority granted to the Spanish crown to run the affairs of the secular church in Spanish America.

plática (Sp.): 'Talk,' a brief pedagogical sermon-like text.

primera evangelización (Sp.): Term used for missionary and pastoral practices prior to the reforms of the 1570s and 1580s (cf. Estenssoro Fuchs 2003).

pueblo de indios (Sp.): Indian village of colonial origin of the sort formed in the resettlement campaigns of the 1570s. Characterized by Spanish-style architecture/layout and municipal institutions.

quipu [khipu] (Q.): Native Andean device for recording information using strings in which knotting, coloring, and a variety of other elements had semiotic functions.

reducción (Sp.): Process of forced congregation into large nucleated settlements—cf. *pueblo de indios.*

ritual: Book containing instructions and texts for the administration of the sacraments of baptism, matrimony, communion, confession, and extreme unction.

sermonario (Sp.): Book of sermons.

Standard Colonial Quechua: Used here with reference to the standardized form of Southern Quechua codified in the works of the Third Lima Council (1582–83) and employed by most sixteenth- and seventeenth-century writers.

taqui (Q.): Native Andean song-dance (see haraui and haylli).

villancico (Sp.): Religious song genre with vernacular lyrics formally inspired by popular/profane musical traditions.

visita (>visitador) (Sp.): Administrative inspection of a specific area carried out by a judge on behalf of a bishop or viceroy. Ecclesiastical visitas were directed mainly at evaluating parish priests.

Notes

Introduction

1. The Quechua-speaking population exceeds that of the next largest Amerindian language families, Maya and Tupi, by a considerable margin (see the latest Summer Institute of Linguistics statistics at http://www.ethnologue.com/ethno_docs/distribution.asp?by=family). Quechua has been compared to the Romance and Slavic families in terms of the degree of internal differentiation, but such comparisons are subjective and may create an exaggerated impression of how different the Quechua varieties really are. See Adelaar and Muysken 2004 for an excellent survey of the modern and historical linguistic landscape of the Andes.

2. This is not to deny that a number of studies have made key contributions to the study of missionary uses of native languages. See Burkhart 1989, Sell 1993, and Tavárez 2000 on Nahuatl (central Mexico); Meliá 1992 on Guarani (Paraguay); and Rafael 1993 [1988] on Tagalog (Philippines). For the contemporary activities of Portuguese and Italian Jesuits in southern India and Japan, see Županov (1999, 2005) and López Gay (1966, 1970), respectively.

3. Johannes Fabian's *Language and Colonial Power* (1986) is exceptional for its focus on language policies in the Belgian Congo. See also Cohn 1996, chapter 2, and Comaroff and Comaroff 1991: 213–243. Brigit Meyer's more contemporary research on Ghana has a chapter on translation (Meyer 1999).

4. I still speak of "missionary" activities with regard to earlier periods, before the establishment of a parish system.

5. The term translation will also be used in the ordinary sense, to distinguish texts that had specific models ("direct translations") from those that followed more generic ones.

6. The terms "source" and "target" are applied to languages and cultures as well as specific texts.

7. This tends to be the case even in the most recent studies of translation by anthropologists, including many of the essays in Rosman and Rosman eds. 2003.

8. The letter can be found in Shorter 1988: 141–142. Shorter specifies that Gregory's instructions are not true inculturation, but includes them in a genealogy leading up to it.

9. Congregation for Divine Worship and the Discipline of the Sacraments 2001.

10. The only extant pastoral Quechua texts that can be attributed to an Indian are a series of short prayers contained in Felipe Guaman Poma de Ayala's 1615 chronicle (Guaman Poma de Ayala 1980 [1615]: 769–783).

11. An *audiencia* was a royal court with important administrative powers whose jurisdiction extended over a large territory, often equivalent to one of the modern nation-states.

12. The earliest known Quechua texts from what is now Bolivia and Ecuador date to the eighteenth century, when three books with pastoral texts written in the local varieties were published in Lima (Rivet and Crequi-Montfort 1951: 141–147, 156–158; Dávila Morales 1739). There is an eighteenth-century manuscript copy of a Quechua grammar that appears to be from Ecuador and which may date to the seventeenth century. It contains a few brief texts, but these were adapted from the Third Lima Council's catechism, which was published in Lima in 1584 (Dedenbach-Salazar Sáenz ed. 1993).

13. Barry David Sell has elaborated a pie diagram showing the number of works printed in or about indigenous languages in the Spanish empire between 1539 and 1821. Nahuatl takes an easy first place, with 34 percent and 112 works. A category of "other Mesoamerican languages" takes second place, with 26 percent. Surprisingly, Tagalog and "other Asian languages" take third and fourth place, with 16 percent and 14 percent, respectively. Quechua appears in fifth place, with 19 imprints (including linguistic works) and 6 percent of the total (Sell 1993: 4). There is thus a clear imbalance between Quechua's importance as a vehicular language for the Spanish empire and the amount of printing that was done in or about it.

14. *Ollantay,* the most famous of the Quechua plays, is not exempt from Christian undertones even though it is set in pre-conquest times.

15. *El hijo pródigo* and *El robo de Proserpina y sueño de Endimión* are both attributed to Juan Espinosa Medrano (ca. 1630–ca. 1689), in which case they cannot be much earlier than 1650 (Itier 1999). The plays *Ollantay, Usca Paucar,* and *El pobre más rico* have been dated on the basis of phonological evidence to a period stretching from the late seventeenth to the late eighteenth century (Mannheim 1991: 147–152).

16. Something similar can be said of *El hijo pródigo* and *El robo de Proserpina y sueño de Endimión,* which are elaborate spiritual allegories. The main characters of

El robo de Proserpina y sueño de Endimión are Proserpine, Endymion, and Pluto, representing the Soul, Christ, and the Devil, respectively (Itier 1999), and those of *El hijo pródigo* include the Christian [Soul], the Body, the World, the Flesh, and God's Word (Middendorf ed. 1891).

17. This being said, there is an urgent need for more systematic research on the colonial plays, especially their relation to the pastoral literature. Their study is hampered by the fact that they are mostly anonymous and undated, by a lack of critical editions of the extant manuscripts (none of the colonial plays were printed before the nineteenth century), and by the absence of information on their contexts of production and performance.

18. The list of important missing works includes a group of texts composed/translated by Juan de Betanzos in the 1540s; a cartilla approved by the First Lima Council of 1551–52; a confesionario commissioned by the Second Lima Council in 1567; a groups of texts produced by the diocese of Cuzco which dated back to the 1560s or 1550s; and the sermonarios of Luis Jerónimo de Oré and Juan Pérez Bocanegra, which date from the late sixteenth and early seventeenth centuries, respectively.

19. When I began my research I had hoped to locate missing or unknown pastoral Quechua manuscripts, but I was unsuccessful in this respect. It is likely that new works will appear if and when the libraries of the mendicant orders in Lima and Cuzco become fully accessible (I have had partial access to the libraries of the Franciscan convents of Lima, Arequipa, and Ayacucho, where there appear to be no important Quechua manuscripts from the period of this study).

20. The diocesan archive of Cuzco, the oldest in South America, has lost most of its early documentation, while access to the archive of the cathedral chapter, which may still contain important records, is restricted. The diocesan archive of Ayacucho (Huamanga) was also off-limits at the time of my research, and the equivalent archive in Arequipa, while accessible, contains few documents from the period of this study.

21. The archive of the Franciscan convent in Lima (ASFL) is open to researchers and contains important documentation. I also had access to the Dominican archive in Lima (ASDL), but this collection has been badly depleted. Several other mendicant archives in Lima and Cuzco remain uncharted territory.

22. Of the collections that I have not had the opportunity to work in, the central archive of the Jesuit order (Archivum Romanum Societatis Iesu) is certainly one of the most promising. The *Monumenta Peruana* series only reaches up to 1604, and it appears that the editors sometimes excluded controversial documents.

23. Cf. Clifford 1982 on Martin Leenhardt in Melanesia and Fabian 1986 on the Belgians in the Congo for two cases involving Catholic missionaries; and Meyer 1999 (chapter 3) on Protestants in Ghana.

Chapter 1 Background

1. The power exercised by the archbishops of Lima over the suffragan bishops was limited to the fact that the Lima ecclesiastical court acted as a court of appeals for the diocesan courts.

2. The mendicant provinces were ruled by locally elected prelates, while the Jesuits had a far more centralized structure and reported to their superiors in Rome.

3. For two classic studies of the impact of colonial rule on indigenous society in the Andes, see Stern 1993 [1982] and Spalding 1984.

4. See Bossy 1970 and Hsia 1998 on the Council of Trent and the Counter-Reformation or Catholic Reformation. Studies dealing with Spain include Nalle 1992 on the diocese of Cuenca and Kamen 1993 on Catalonia.

5. The authority of the Vulgate, however, was not directly challenged. Serious discrepancies were avoided by correcting the original rather than the translation (Bataillon 1950 [1937]: I 49).

6. The *villancico* was a type of vernacular religious song that drew on profane and popular musical traditions. It was defined by a "perpetual dialogue and interaction with other genres" rather than by a set of formal characteristics (Illari 2001: 140).

7. February 8, 1574 cédula, Lissón Chaves ed. 1943–1946: II 674–675.

8. See Pagden 1986: 181–185 for an overview of the arguments in favor of and against the imposition of Spanish.

9. For an overview of Quechua phonology, grammar, and dialectology, see Adelaar and Muysken 2004: 194–233 and 183–191.

10. For Bruce Mannheim, however, Santo Tomás's works represent a mix of dialects drawn from different informants, and the Inca lingua franca was a form of Southern Quechua (1991: 113, 178, 260 n. 13). There has never been an in-depth discussion on the issue, at least in print. Cerrón-Palomino, Itier, Taylor, and Torero all adhere to the coastal lingua franca hypothesis, which I also follow. As will be discussed in more detail in chapter 6, the narrative of a coastal variety that became the Inca lingua franca but rapidly disappeared under Spanish rule is supported by many scattered pieces of information and is coherent with the broader picture of developments during the second half of the sixteenth century. However, the evidence is far from overwhelming, and there is ample room for dissenting views.

11. For instance, areas that are now Quechua-speaking are often full of Aymara placenames—this is the case in Cuzco itself (see Cerrón-Palomino 1999, 2005).

12. Cerrón-Palomino's claims are based partly on the analysis of an Inca victory song recorded by the chronicler Juan de Betanzos, which appears to be in a

form of Aymara with Puquina influence (1999: 151–152). I have found at least one term of Puquina origin in a Christian Quechua hymn from the Cuzco area, which might support the identification of Puquina as the ancestral language of the Incas (see p. 218).

13. See Woolard 2002 on the early-seventeenth-century debate concerning whether Spanish was one of the original root languages or was derived from Latin, and its political implications.

14. . . . aunque no puedo afirmar de cierto que la lengua del Inca y la Aymara fueron de las setenta y dos lenguas matrizes que Dios enseñó, con todo esso me parece que el inca no pudo inventar de nuevo una lengua tan hermosa y de tanto artificio como la lengua latina, y por esto digo que la lengua del inca y la aymara no fueron del todo inventadas en esta tierra, sino que Dios las enseñó a los nietos de Noé, y alguna familia de Noé habló en la lengua del inca, y otra en la lengua aymara, o que salieron de la lengua latina, porque se parecen mucho en el artificio, y otras lenguas que ay en esta tierra son hijas destas setenta y dos lenguas matrizes . . . (Avendaño [1649]: f. 112v). I quote the Spanish rather than the Quechua version of this passage of the sermon, as the former is clearly the original.

15. Much of Itier's argument is based on observations in contemporary Spanish sources concerning the spread of *la lengua general* or *la lengua del inga,* but these terms are notoriously unstable—they could just as well refer to Quechua in general. Most Spanish observers were not very careful about distinguishing varieties of Quechua. As evidence for the claim that much of the current Ayacucho Quechua area was originally Central-speaking, Itier points to colonial references to "Huamanga" as a point to the north of which there was a significant change in the way Quechua was spoken (Itier 2000b: 49; cf. Third Lima Council 1985a [1584]: 167; and Huerta 1993 [1616]: 83). Itier interprets "Huamanga" as meaning the city of Huamanga (modern Ayacucho), well to the south of the modern Central-Southern frontier. However, "Huamanga" could also mean the district or territory of the city, which became a diocese in the early seventeenth century. This territory corresponds quite closely to the area of Ayacucho Quechua today, immediately to the north of which Central Quechua is spoken. Linguistic evidence pointed to by Itier, such as Central influence in Ayacucho Quechua, can be explained in other ways (in this case, geographical proximity to Central areas).

Chapter 2 Diversity and Experimentation

1. See Bossy 1970. Sara T. Nalle notes that around 1530 "no clear division between parishes existed" in the Spanish diocese of Cuenca (1992: 25).

2. Foundation documents of the Lima cathedral's Quechua chair, ACML Papeles Varios volume 6, f. 8v–10.

3. The term *huaca* referred to divine beings and things in general, but was applied particularly to the local, tutelary deities that controlled the destinies of specific groups of people and were associated with specific places and geographical features, especially mountaintops (see Salomon 1991 on the concept of huaca).

4. Lope García de Castro, April 31, 1565 letter to the king, Lissón Chaves ed. 1943–1946: II 295.

5. *Relación de la visita del Doctor Cuenca* 1566–1567, Lissón Chaves ed. 1943–1946: II 329–331; *Relación de los capítulos que el doctor Cuenca envió al concilio provincial de Los Reyes* 1567, ibid.: II 351–352.

6. Jerónimo de Loayza, April 20, 1567 letter to the king, Lissón Chaves ed. 1943–1946: II 363.

7. The original Latin decrees of the Second Lima Council are published in Vargas Ugarte ed. 1951–1954: I 97–223. Vargas Ugarte also published a Spanish summary of the decrees made by order of the Third Lima Council in 1583 (ibid.: I 240–257). There are important discrepancies in content between the two versions (Estenssoro Fuchs 1992: 367).

8. Petition of the Franciscan order in Peru to the king, 1563, Lissón Chaves ed. 1943–1946: II 551. On Franciscans training local boys to perform liturgical music in Jauja, see a 1563 viceregal decree in ASFL, Registro 14, f. 255–257.

9. Testimony to the services of Luis de Olvera in Parinacochas, 1562, AGI Lima 316.

10. . . . mudó aquel llanto en canto de la letanía en esta manera: que iban los muchachos de la escuela cantores en procesión, apartados unos de otros de dos en dos, y diciendo en lengua de indios y cantando "Santa María" o "San Pedro," etc. Y respondían todos, llorando en su lengua: "ruega por él y por nosotros" (Abril Castelló and Abril Stoffels eds. 1996–1997: I 638–639).

11. The language used in these songs was probably Aymara rather than Quechua, as the events took place in Pomata. However, it is clear that there were many commonalities in genre forms across the two languages.

12. La más singular de estas danzas fue la de los nobles que se llaman ingas, y el más noble dellos decía la letra, de quatro sílabas cada verso, muy sentida. Y de repente dio a los españoles y padres que allí estaban, porque en la letra dezían epítetos muy buenos a Nuestro Señor. Y preguntando de dónde los sacaban, dezían que los mesmos que antiguamente daban al sol y a su rey, éstos conbertían en loor de Jesuchristo, tomando materia de lo que oían predicar (1571 carta annua, Egaña et al. eds. 1954–1986: I 423–424).

13. Salieron ocho muchachos mestizos de mis condiscípulos, vestidos como indios, con sendos arados en las manos, con que representaron en la procesión el cantar y hailli de los indios, ayudándoles toda la capilla el retruécano de las coplas, con gran contento de los españoles y suma alegría de los indios de que con sus cantos y bailes solemnizasen los españoles la fiesta del señor Dios nuestro (al

cual ellos llaman Pachacámac, que quiere decir "el que da vida al universo") (Garcilaso 1945 [1609]: I 229). See Estenssoro Fuch's interpretation of the expression *el retruécano de las coplas* as *un breve estribillo* (a brief refrain) (2003: 150–151).

14. Esta puesta en diálogo de los ritos no busca facilitar la conversión por medio del sincretismo. Todo lo contrario, nos encontramos frente a un fenómeno que quiere ser la inversa del sincretismo, que se funda en la disyunción: las formas son preservadas, o levemente modificadas, para alterar su significado. Si el antiguo haylli debía subsistir, no era para conservar su antiguo sentido, sino para revelar su 'verdadero significado' oculto, para hacerse anuncio del catolicismo. El contrafactum actúa entonces como una clave de lectura, exigiendo un esfuerzo de exégesis, obligando a la resemantización (Estenssoro Fuchs 2003: 152–153).

15. An anti-idolatry *instrucción* published in one of the Third Lima Council volumes explained that Corpus Christi came at the same time of the year as Inti Raymi, one of the main Inca festivals, and added that there was also an unfortunate resemblance in the songs and dances—*algún género de semejanza . . . en las danças, representaciones o cantares*—of the Christian and the pagan festival (Third Lima Council 1985a [1585]: 272).

16. Cf. Taylor's study of the term *cama-* and its colonial appropriation as the Quechua word for divine creation (Taylor 2000a [1974–1976]).

17. . . . las oraciones comunes de Pater noster, Ave María, Credo, mandamientos e obras de misericordia, artículos de la fée, etc., sean en nuestra lengua castellana, conforme a la cartilla que esta Santa Sínodo tiene ordenada. Y porque en estos reinos del Perú hay una lengua más general y de que más contínuamente usan los naturales della, en la cual está compuesta una cartilla y ciertos coloquios en declaración della, permitimos que desta se pueda usar, y no de otra ninguna (Vargas Ugarte ed. 1951–1954: I 7).

18. This last claim was made by Francisco de Toledo in a March 25, 1571 letter to the king, Levillier ed. 1921–1926: III 496–497.

19. Meléndez 1681–1682: I 327–328; Cerrón-Palomino 1995a: vii–ix; AGI Indiferente 425/23, f. 464 and 467.

20. Estenssoro Fuchs argues that the contents of the *Plática para todos los indios* are closer to those of the 1545 *Instrucción* than to those of the outline of basic doctrines provided by the First Lima Council, which would reflect a more dogmatic and punitive pastoral project, especially as it includes a discussion of hell. He thus suggests that the *Plática* was one of the texts approved by Loayza in 1545, but not by the First Council (2003: 59–60). However, this may be reading too much into the omissions of the *Plática*, which was a very condensed introductory text.

21. By "neologism" I mean a new term that employs Quechua word stems, usually a noun phrase glossing the original term—e.g. *hanac pacha* 'upper place' for 'heaven.' I refer to preexisting terms that were used with Christian meanings as "adapted terms" (see chapter 6 on pastoral Quechua terminology).

22. E.g., *cartilla y sermón y cathecismo fecho en la lengua general deste obispado,* in a 1567 title, and *cartilla y catheçismo deste obispado fecho en la lengua general* in a 1571 title (1597 información de oficio for Blas de Leiva, AGI Lima 320). Cf. 1567 title to Francisco Churrón de Aguilar, AGI Lima 316.

23. Priests were now ordered to instruct their parishioners with a *cartilla y catheçismo deste obispado nuevamente heçho y enmendado en la lengua general de los naturales y romançado en la nuestra castellana* (cartilla and catechism of this diocese newly made and corrected in the lengua general of the natives and translated into Spanish) (1574 parish title in 1597 información de oficio for Blas de Leiva, AGI Lima 320; 1577 parish title in 1592 información de oficio for Pedro Samaniego, AGI Lima 209/16/1; 1577 title to Alonso León, AGI Lima 315; 1579 title to Francisco Muñoz, AGI Lima 315).

24. . . . [uno] de los clérigos de mayor erudiçión y partes, muy enseñado y diestro en la lengua general del inga, y en ella a escripto la cartilla y cateçismo para doctrinar los naturales con idiomas y términos propios y legítimos, de que a resultado y resultará mucho y notable fruto (1574 información de oficio for Melchor del Aguila, AGI Lima 316, n.f.n).

25. . . . uno de los diputados para enmendar la cartilla christiana y catheçismo por donde se enseñan los naturales y para lo poner en perfiçión y más congruidad de términos y vocablos (1574 información de oficio for Melchor del Aguila, AGI Lima 316, f. 2).

26. [le cometieron] el muy illustre señor deán y cabildo desta sancta iglesia el limarlo todo y el escrevirlo por sus caractheres proprios naturales y con la orthografía de la lengua general y el apuntarlo con sus puntos y rasgos, y últimamente la traduzión de todo ello en nuestro romançe castellano para que en su lengua general de los indios y en la nuestra anduviesen junto cartilla y catheçismo así como de presenta anda encorporado, y por ello en esta horden, como dicho es, se muestra la dotrina cristiana (1574 información de oficio for Melchor del Aguila, AGI Lima 316, f. 2).

27. 1574 información de oficio for Melchor del Aguila, AGI Lima 316, f. 2v, 14, 16 and 18v.

28. 1574 información de oficio for Melchor del Aguila, AGI Lima 316, f. 2v.

29. 1583 accusations against Sebastián de Lartaun before the Third Lima Council, Lissón Chaves ed. 1943–1946: III 61.

30. 1583 reply by Sebastián de Lartaun to the charges made before the Third Lima Council, Lissón Chaves ed. 1943–1946: III 73.

31. 1575 decree by Francisco de Toledo, Urteaga and Romero eds. 1916: 193–194.

32. 1574 información de oficio for Melchor del Aguila, AGI Lima 316, f. 11v.

33. Lindsey Crickmay and Sabine Dedenbach-Salazar Sáenz have argued that Molina's prayers should be considered authentic because Molina had no reason to modify them and they were recorded at too early a date for his native informants to have assimilated Christianity. They also point to native poetic and semantic elements in the prayers as evidence of their authenticity (Crickmay 1999: 153; Dedenbach-Salazar Sáenz 1997b: 206). It should be kept in mind, though, that a central objective of Molina's chronicle was to present Inca religion as having strong monotheistic and proto-Christian elements, and even if we assume that he obtained the prayers from Indian informants, it is certainly not far fetched to think that, more than a generation after the conquest, specific native individuals had come to understand something of Christianity and retrospectively apply it to Inca religion. The presence of native religious terms and poetic forms in the prayers does not exclude the possibility that they were fabricated: this is precisely what would have given them plausibility as Inca prayers.

Chapter 3 Reform and Standardization

1. *Despacho que se dio a Don Francisco de Toledo Virrey del Perú sobre la doctrina y gobierno eclesiástico,* 1568, Lissón Chaves ed. 1943–1946: II 451–452.

2. Cf. *Instrucción general para los visitadores,* 1569–70, Lohmann Villena and Sarabia Viejo eds. 1986–1987: I 1–39; *Ordenanza para la reducción de los indios de Huamanga,* 1570, ibid.: I 65–68; and *Provisión con las normas para los reducidores de indios,* 1573, ibid.: I 245–249.

3. Francisco de Toledo, 1582 *memoria* to the king, Jiménez de la Espada ed. 1881–1897: I cliv.

4. *Instrucción general para los visitadores,* 1569–70, Lohmann Villena and Sarabia Viejo eds. 1986–1987: I 15.

5. Francisco de Toledo, February 8, 1570 letter to the king, Lissón Chaves ed. 1943–1946: II 504.

6. Francisco de Toledo, February 8, 1570 letter to the king, Levillier ed. 1921–1926: III 385.

7. Foundation documents of the Lima cathedral's Quechua chair, 1571, ACML Papeles Varios, volume 6, f. 2–2v.

8. December 2, 1578 cédula, AAL Cedulario, volume 1, f. 378.

9. Francisco de Toledo, November 27, 1579 letter to the king, Levillier ed. 1921–1926: VI 188.

10. September 19, 1580 cédula, ASFL Registro 13, f. 288.

11. December 2, 1578 cédula, AAL Cedulario, volume 1, f. 96.

12. Francisco de Toledo, November 22, 1579 letter to the king, Levillier ed. 1921–1926: VI 186.

13. Juan de Balboa, March 13, 1583 letter to the king, AGI Lima 126.

14. Francisco de Toledo, March 25, 1571 letter to the king, Levillier ed. 1921–1926: III 496–497.

15. Francisco de Toledo, September 24, 1572 letter to the king, Levillier ed. 1921–1926: IV 407.

16. Francisco de Toledo, March 20, 1574 letter to the king, Levillier ed. 1921–1926: V 409.

17. Cf. 1569 carta annua, Egaña et al. eds. 1954–1986: I 258; 1575 carta annua, ibid.: I 708; 1577 carta annua, ibid.: II 252, 273, and 280.

18. Cf. 1577 carta annua, Egaña et al. eds. 1954–1986: II 280; 1579 carta annua, ibid.: II 631; 1601 carta annua, ibid.: VII 389; Mateos ed. 1954 [ca. 1600]: II 36, 421.

19. While there are some references to Indian participation in the liturgy in the Jesuit reports, these tend to come from the exceptional places where the Jesuits had taken permanent charge as parish priests, especially Juli—e.g., 1579 carta annua, Egaña et al. eds. 1954–1986: II 624.

20. Jerónimo Ruíz de Portillo, May 8, 1567 letter to Francisco Borgia, Egaña et al. eds. 1954–1986: I 130.

21. 1569 carta annua, Egaña et al. eds. 1954–1986: I 258.

22. Acts of the first provincial congregation of Peru, Cuzco 1576, Egaña et al. eds. 1954–1986: II 67.

23. Acts of the second provincial congregation of Peru, Cuzco 1576, Egaña et al. eds. 1954–1986: II 96–97.

24. Annals of the Lima cathedral chapter, ACML Acuerdos Capitulares, volume 2, f. 27v.

25. . . . si queremos en lengua de indios hallar vocablo que responde a éste, 'Dios', como en latín responde Deus y en griego Theos, y en hebreo El y en arabigo Alá, no se halla en lengua del Cuzco, ni en lengua de México . . . De donde se ve cuán flaca y corta noticia tenían de Dios, pues aun nombrarle no saben sino por nuestro vocablo (J. Acosta 1987 [1590]: 315).

26. The Spanish translation of this passage is as follows: . . . no hay que preocuparse demasiado de si los vocablos fe, cruz, ángel, virginidad, matrimonio y otros muchos no se pueden traducir bien y con propiedad al idioma de los indios. Podrían tomarse del castellano y apropiárselas, cosas que cualquier simiyachac prudente, como se llama al profesor de lengua india, suele ya poner en práctica (J. Acosta 1984–1987 [1577]: II 75).

27. The original Latin version of the council is published in Vargas Ugarte ed. 1951–1954: I 261–312. The Spanish translation, which was produced by the council itself on the grounds that there were not enough scribes who knew Latin to make the necessary copies, is published in ibid.: I 313–375.

28. 1583 información on behalf of mestizo ordainees, Barriga ed. 1933–1954: IV 254–286 (cf. the complete original document in AGI Lima 126); Third Lima Council 1583: f. 33v.

29. See also the audiencia's 1584 decree and the two "epistles" from the council printed at the beginning of the catechism (Third Lima Council 1985a [1584]: 8–18).

30. Aunque oviese cosas que por ventura se pudieran decir mejor de otra suerte (que forçoso es que aya siempre en esto de traductión diversas opiniones) . . . hase juzgado, y lo es, menos inconveniente que se passe por alguna menos perfectión que tenga por ventura la traductión que no dar lugar a que aya variedad y discordias, como en las traductiones de la sancta scriptura saludablemente lo ha proveydo la iglesia cathólica (Third Lima Council 1985a [1584]: 17). The statement concerning Bible translations seems to refer to the Council of Trent's proclamation of the Vulgate as the only correct and legitimate version.

31. The contents of this cartilla are: the basic prayers (Per Signum Crucis, Pater Noster, Credo, Ave Maria, and Salve Regina), the fourteen articles of the faith, the ten commandments of God, the five commandments of the church, the seven sacraments, the fourteen works of mercy (*obras de misericordia*), the three theological virtues (*virtudes teologales*), the four cardinal virtues, the seven deadly sins, the three enemies of the soul, the four last things (*quatro novíssimos*), and finally the Confiteor, or General Confession prayer.

32. Pius V's catechism was in fact designed for the instruction of parish priests, who were to consult it to ensure that their explanations of Christian doctrine were correct, and was thus not a text directly adaptable as a catechism for Indians.

33. The identification is not a firm one. The author of the anonymous *Arte y vocabulario* stated in his preface that he had the intention of writing an Aymara grammar too, and it is known that Barzana was familiar with both Quechua and Aymara (Anonymous 1603 [1586]: n.p.n.). More generally, the fact that Barzana was the leading Jesuit linguist of the time points to him as the author—it is also likely that he had a hand in writing the linguistic appendix to the *Doctrina christiana y catecismo.*

34. There are few surviving copies of the original edition, so I have worked from the 1603 Seville reprint.

35. The council's translation of the Credo, for instance, is cited to exemplify the use of *caymi* as a relative pronoun (Anonymous 1603 [1586]: f. 31).

36. Above all, the Spanish of the council decrees published in the volumes seems more Latinate than that of the actual pastoral texts (the former were translations of the original Latin decrees). For instance, on some of the first pages of the *Doctrina christiana* we find the word "translation" written *traduction* (the Latinate form) in a text produced by the council and *traduccion* in the titles at the top of the page (Third Lima Council 1985a [1584]: 16, 17).

37. . . . se ponen a predicar a indios cosas exquisitas o en estilo levantado, como si predicassen en alguna corte o universidad, y en lugar de hazer provecho

hazen gran daño, porque offuscan y confunden los cortos y tiernos entendimientos de los indios (Third Lima Council 1985c [1585]: 353).

38. Otras muchas cosas muy lindas y maravillosas tiene la sancta iglesia enseñada por el Espíritu Sancto de cantares y psalmos y officios y oraciones y bendiciones, y tiene bestiduras sagradas y ceremonias con gran concierto y horden, y todas son cosas llenas de misterio para que con el alma y el cuerpo honrremos y sirvamos a nuestro gran Dios. Mas a vosotros hijos mios, basta os por agora saber bien esto que os he dicho . . . (Third Lima Council 1985c [1585]: 730–731).

39. The Quechua version of the litany has *yayaycu hanac pachacunapi cac* (our father who is in heaven), an expression taken from the Pater Noster.

40. It is not clear how Haroldus reconstructed the rationale for the modifications. He may have been speculating, but it seems likely that he was working from an unknown document sent by the council to the Roman curia.

41. Enrique Bartra's richly documented note on the subject contains most of the relevant information (Bartra 1967). See also Durán 1982, chapter 4.

42. The claim made by Juan de Balboa in a 1583 letter to the king that he had been assigned the task of writing the Quechua *and* Spanish versions of the catechism, sermonario, and confesionario, which seems to indicate that he worked together with Acosta on the Spanish originals (Bartra 1967: 362), is clearly hyperbolic.

43. The translators' signatures are in Third Lima Council 1583: f. 63v–64v and 68–68v. This volume also contains the manuscript versions of the Spanish originals of these texts, which were signed only by the bishops, thus further concealing the identity of the author[s].

44. 1583 información on behalf of mestizo ordainees, Barriga ed. 1933–1954: IV 255; 1584–85 información de oficio for Francisco Carrasco, AGI Lima 316, f. 3v.

45. 1584–85 información de oficio for Francisco Carrasco, AGI Lima 316, f. 4–6.

46. . . . con no pequeño trabajo, por la mucha difficultad que ay en declarar cosas tan difficíles y desusadas a los indios, y después de aver mucho conferido, viendo diversos papeles, y todo lo que podía ayudar a la buena traductión . . . (Third Lima Council 1985a [1584]: 17).

47. 1584–85 información de oficio for Francisco Carrasco, AGI Lima 316, f. 8v.

48. 1596 información de oficio for Alonso Martínez, AGI Lima 211/12/1, passim; foundation documents of the Lima cathedral's Quechua chair, 1571, ACML Papeles Varios, volume 6, f. 4.

49. 1583 información on behalf of mestizo ordainees, Barriga ed. 1933–1954: IV 261.

50. 1584–85 información de oficio for Francisco Carrasco, AGI Lima 316, f. 8v.

51. 1584–85 información de oficio for Francisco Carrasco, AGI Lima 316, f. 13.

52. 1589 carta annua, Egaña et al. eds. 1954–1986: IV 573.

53. 1583 información on behalf of mestizo ordainees, Barriga ed. 1933–1954: IV 255.

54. Bishops at the Third Lima Council, September 30, 1583 letter to the king, Lissón Chaves 1943–1946: III 81.

55. Mogrovejo's 1585 synod, dated July 17, speaks of the catechism and confesionario as already available in print, and says that the printing of the sermonario was imminent (Torres ed. 1970: 46–47).

56. There is no trace of the manuscript originals of the confesionario or sermonario.

57. The most significant and frequent of these orthographic changes is the replacement of {z} by {s} in some words—e.g. *canchiz* 'seven' becomes *canchis*, and *chazqui-* 'to receive' becomes *chasqui-*. {s} and {z} represented different phonemes, but there was some vacilation among colonial authors as to how the opposition applied to certain words (see chapter 6 on pastoral Quechua orthography). The question-answer exchange that was modified is as follows: *P. Cay animanchiccunari yma cauçaytam cauçanca? R. Animanchiccunaca quiquin ucuncunahuanmi Diospa cayllampi uiñaypac capac cauçayta cauçanca . . .* (Q. What life will our souls have? A. Our souls with their own bodies will forever live gloriously at God's side . . .). It was changed to: *P. Alli christianocunap animancunari yma cauçaytam cauçanca? R. Quiquin ucuncunahuanmi, Diospa cayllanpi uiñaypac capac cauçayta cauçanca . . .* (Q. What life will the souls of good Christians live? A. With their own bodies they will forever live gloriously at God's side . . . ") (Third Lima Council 1583: f. 58v; Third Lima Council 1985a [1584]: 108–109). The Spanish original reads: *P. Y las almas que vida ternán? R. Juntamente con los cuerpos, vivirán vida eterna reynando con Dios. . . .*

58. . . . no usen de los dichos cathecismos comfisionario ni permitan otras personas lo usen de mano por los yerros que puede aver en escrevir, y lo mesmo se haga y cumpla cerca de los dichos sermones después que estuvieren impressos (Torres ed. 1970: 46–47).

59. . . . que la doctrina de los naturales . . . fuesse uniforme, sin hacer diferencia ni aun en solo una sílava por el gran daño que ha resultado de no averse hecho assi en lo passado (Third Lima Council 1985c [1585]: 347).

60. . . . no se use dellos de mano sino de molde, sin hacer inovación, enmienda ni interpretación más de como alli está . . . os aveys de informar en particular si en todo vuestro distrito se haze la doctrina por la dicha traducción, sin mudar sola una sílava (Third Lima Council 1985c [1585]: 348).

61. Toribio Alfonso Mogrovejo, October 5, 1592 letter to the king, AGI Patronato 248 R. 28/1/80.

62. Toribio Alfonso Mogrovejo, 1598 relación to the pope, ACML, Liber Erectionis, f. 35.

Chapter 4 The *Questione della Lingua* and Vernacular Competence

1. Cf. the documents edited by Taylor (2000b [1995] and 2000d [1985]), and references to a further document from the central highlands in Durston 2003: 210–211.

2. . . . es menester saber la lengua general de los indios y la particular de cada repartimiento para poderlos confesar, porque con las mugeres ni los hombres baxos no se pueden tratar sino en cosas generales, pero para descender a lo particular no se puede entender si no es con su lengua particular de cada repartimiento (Luis López, January 21, 1570 letter to Francisco Borgia, Egaña et al. eds. 1954–1986: I 366).

3. 1576 carta annua, Egaña et al. eds. 1954–1986: II 230–232.

4. *Ordenanzas generales para la vida común en los pueblos de indios*, 1575, Lohmann Villena and Sarabia Viejo eds. 1986–1987: II 251.

5. Martín Enrríquez, March 25, 1582 letter to the king, Lissón Chaves ed. 1943–1946: III 17.

6. Conde del Villar, April 25, 1588 letter to the king, Lissón Chaves ed. 1943–1946: III 496.

7. Attempts to describe, or translate into, other Andean languages were mostly the work of the mendicant and secular clergy. Mochica was studied by Fernando de la Carrera and other secular clerics of the Spanish town of Trujillo throughout the first half of the seventeenth century. The Augustinians seem to have produced catechisms and other pastoral texts in Culli (Castro de Trelles ed. 1992 [ca. 1560]: 45) and Uruquilla, a low-prestige language of the altiplano (Calancha 1974–1982 [1638]: 1469). The only Jesuit known to have written in an Andean language other that Southern Quechua and Aymara was the polyglot Alonso de Barzana, who translated the cartilla into Puquina, but his work was continued by the Franciscan Luis Jerónimo de Oré, who adapted, expanded, and published it (Oré 1607: 385).

8. Mercury was used in the silver refining proces. There was thus a direct link between the mines of Potosí and Huancavelica, and both were served by regional mitas.

9. These regional developments also explain why Aymara was the only other Andean language that the Third Council chose to employ as a lengua general.

10. When Barzana died in Cuzco in 1599, the head of the Jesuit college wrote that he had begun his Quechua studies in Spain (using Santo Tomas's linguistics works) but "perfected" his Quechua when he arrived in Cuzco alongside

Viceroy Toledo in 1571 and was chosen to catechize Tupac Amaru and Carlos Inca (1599 report by Gregorio de Cisneros, Egaña et al. eds. 1954–1986: VI 631).

11. . . . de la lengua quichua . . . la ciudad del Cuzco es el Athenas, que en ella se habla con todo el rigor y elegancia que se puede imaginar, como la Ionica en Athenas, la latina en Roma, el romance castellano en Toledo (Oré 1992 [1598]: 144).

12. Bishops at the Third Lima Council, March 19, 1583 letter to the king, Lissón Chaves ed. 1943–1946: III 101.

13. 1584 decree of the audiencia of Lima in Alonso Gutiérrez's 1595 información de oficio, AGI Lima 319.

14. Juan de Balboa, March 13, 1583 letter to the king, AGI Lima 126.

15. Viceroy Conde del Villar, 1586 decree BNP A49.

16. Conde del Villar, April 25, 1588 letter to the king, Lissón Chaves ed. 1943–1946: III 489.

17. 1580 license in Juan de Mendoza's 1583 file, AGI Lima 315; 1582 license in Juan de Vargas's 1583 información de oficio, AGI Lima 315.

18. 1591 license in 1597 información de oficio for Baltazar de Aguilar, AGI Lima 318; 1591 license in 1599 información de oficio for Juan Gutiérrez de Benavides, AGI Lima 322; 1591 license in 1615 información de oficio for Francisco de Lorido, AGI Lima 326; 1593 license in 1600 información de oficio for Francisco García de Medrano, AGI Lima 213/6/1, f. 14; see also 1596 información de oficio for Alonso Martínez, AGI Lima 211/12/1, f. 3 and 8.

19. The nominations were confirmed by Luis de Velasco in a 1599 decree (Egaña et al. eds. 1954–1986: VI 737–739).

20. 1602 and 1607 licenses in 1609 información de oficio for Gonzalo de Ana, AGI Lima 324; 1606 license in 1607 información de oficio for Juan Rodríguez de Rivera, AGI Lima 323; 1609 license in 1610 información de oficio for Juan de Miranda, AGI Lima 325; cf. Esquivel y Navia 1980 [1753]: II 31.

21. 1627 license in 1629 información de oficio for Fernando Ladrón de Guevara, AGI Lima 330; 1628 and 1630 licenses in 1636 información de oficio for Juan de Esquivel, AGI Lima 331.

22. Language licenses and examinations from the diocese of Huamanga can be found in: AAL Concursos I/20 (1615); AGI Lima 226/1, f. 49v–50 (1622); AAL Concursos I/48 (1623); BNP B416, f. 52–52v (1633); AGI Lima 235/5, f. 5v (1639); AGI Lima 252/7, f. 29v (1646); AGI Lima 241/8, f. 86 (1647).

23. 1654 exam, AAA Concursos, Legajo 1. Even though I have had access to the archive of the archdiocese of Arequipa and not to that of Huamanga (Ayacucho), I have had better luck finding language licenses and examinations from Huamanga.

24. The foundation date of the university chair is unclear, but the first reference to it dates from 1579, and Juan de Balboa held it from 1582 at least (Eguiguren 1940–1951: I 185).

25. Juan Martínez Ormachea, 1613 petition against Alonso de Huerta, Eguiguren 1940–1951: III 367.

26. Bartolomé Lobo Guerrero, April 10, 1618 letter to the king, AGI Lima 301. Lobo Guerrero's accusation must be taken with a pinch of salt, because he was strongly anti-mendicant and was fighting them precisely over issues of language certification.

27. 1620 suit against Alonso de Huerta, AAL Causas Criminales XVIII/5.

28. Bartolomé Lobo Guerrero, April 10, 1618 letter to the king, AGI Lima 301.

29. Fernando Arias de Ugarte, May 20, 1631 letter to the king, AGI Lima 302.

30. Cf. the exams in AAL Concursos II/12 (1631); AGI Lima 238/4/1, f. 9v (1635); AGI Lima 241/4/1, f. 36v (1639); AGI Lima 238/9/1, f. 11 (1639); AGI Lima 248/6/1, f. 31–32 (1643); AGI Lima 303 (1646); and AAL Curatos II/1 (1648). Many of the exams of the 1630s and 1640s were carried out by the canons Fernando de Avendaño and Francisco de Avila, both extirpators of idolatries who published Quechua sermonarios in the late 1640s, alongside the university chairs Alonso de Huerta, Alonso Corbacho de Zárate, and Juan Rojo Mejía y Ocón.

31. Fernando de Mendoza, March 3, 1613 letter to the king, AGI Lima 305. Fernando de Mendoza, the bishop of Cuzco, was also a Jesuit.

32. The main source on this conflict is a 312-folio suit between the mendicant orders and Archbishop Lobo Guerrero held before the audiencia between 1617 and 1620 (AGN Tribunal Eclesiástico 43/4). Cf. also a series of 1620 *pareceres* or juridical opinions in ASDL "Libro 2 de cédulas y cartas reales," f. 1, 104, 408, 450v–452v.

33. Suit between the mendicant orders and Archbishop Lobo Guerrero, 1617–1620, AGN Tribunal Eclesiástico 43/4, f. 235–235v.

34. 1592 license issued by Alonso Martínez, Barriga ed. 1933–1954: III 302.

35. 1616 license issued by Alonso de Huerta, AAL Curatos I/26a.

36. E.g., the following examinations from the archdiocese of Lima: 1635 examination of candidates for the parish of Ciguas in 1646 información de oficio for Gaspar Roman, AGI Lima 238/4/1, f. 9v; 1639 examination of candidates for the parish of Mangas in 1646 información de oficio for Pedro Ruiz de Garfias, AGI Lima 238/9/1, f. 11; 1643 examination of candidates for the parish of Santo Domingo de Ocros in 1655 informacion de oficio for Rodrigo Durán Martel, AGI Lima 248/6/1, f. 31–32; 1646 examination of candidates for San Marcelo de Lima, AGI Lima 303; and 1648 examination of candidates for the parish of Piscobamba (Conchucos), AAL Curatos II/1, f. 11.

37. Juan Huidobro de Miranda, December 21, 1634 letter to Francisco Verdugo, Bishop of Huamanga, AGI Lima 308.

38. Juan de Balboa, March 13, 1583 letter to the king, AGI Lima 126.

39. Undated relación to the pope by Archbishop Mogrovejo, ACML Liber erectionis, f. 34. A myth which persists up to the present day attributes the Que-

chua texts of the Third Lima Council, or even a Quechua translation of the Bible, to Mogrovejo.

40. Gregorio de Cisneros, January 2, 1599 letter to Claudio Aquaviva, Egaña et al. eds. 1954–1986: VI 635. Chiriguano, Tonocote, and Cacan were spoken in what is now southern Bolivian and northwestern Argentina (see Adelaar and Muysken 2004: 430–432, 385–386, and 407–409).

41. Oré seems to have been the author of most of the Quechua and Aymara texts, while the Puquina texts were written partly by Barzana and were revised by Oré (Oré 1607: 385). The Mochica, Guarani, and Tupi texts came from other sources.

42. Pérez Bocanegra acted as diocesan examiner in Aymara as well as Quechua under three different bishops during the first two decades of the sixteenth century (Oré 1607: 7; Pérez Bocanegra 1631: n.p.n.). In 1596 Pedro Alonso Bajo was appointed to the parishes of Yauri and Coporaque (Collaguas) after being examined in Quechua, Aymara, and Puquina by Alonso de Robleda. Bajo was found able to preach and confess in Quechua, but only to confess in Aymara and Puquina. Alonso de Robleda, a Dominican based in Arequipa, was commissioned as examiner by the diocese of Cuzco, to which the Arequipa area then belonged (1596 parish title for Pedro Alonso Bajo, AGI Lima 326). In 1627 Fernando Ladrón de Guevara was appointed to the parish of Taraco (Omasuyos) with an Aymara certificate issued in Cuzco by the Mercedarian Baltazar Gutiérrez (1629 información de oficio for Fernando Ladrón de Guevara, AGI Lima 330).

43. Arequipa synod of 1638, BNP B1742, f. 72 and 128–128v. The translations were committed to Alvaro Mogrovejo, priest of Carumas, and Miguel de Arana, priest of Ilabaya, who were known as the best Puquina lenguas in the diocese.

44. Arequipa synod of 1638, BNP B1742, f. 72–73.

45. Several documents related to Roque de Cejuela's career and translation activities can be found in his 1592 información de oficio (AGI Lima 318).

46. 1614 license in 1634 información de oficio for Rodrigo de Paz Vivero, AGI Lima 330.

47. 1626 exam in 1643 información de oficio for Fernando de la Carrera Daza, AGI 235/12, f. 26v–27; 1626 parish title for Juan de Mori, AGI Lima 332; 1628 parish title for Rodrigo de Paz Berrero, AGI Lima 330.

48. 1633 exam in 1643 información de oficio for Fernando de la Carrera Daza, AGI Lima 235/12, f. 35v.

49. Pedro de Villagómez, July 21, 1657 letter to the king, AGI Lima 59.

50. 1612 visita to Cabana y Guandoval (Conchucos), AAL Vistas I/7.

51. 1620 visita to Pallasca (Conchucos), AAL Visitas I/7.

52. Aunque la lengua quichua y general de el inga es una, se ha de advertir primero que está dividida en dos modos de usar de ella, que son, el uno muy pulido y congruo, y éste llaman de el inga, que es la lengua que se habla en el Cuzco, Charcas, y demas partes de la provincia de arriva, que se dize Incasuyo. La otra

lengua es corrupta, que llaman Chinchaysuyo, que no se habla con la pulicía y congruidad que los Ingas la hablan . . . [y] empieçan, la del Inga desde Guamanga arriva, y la de Chinchaysuyo desde alli abajo hasta Quito (Huerta, 1993 [1616]: 18).

53. Demás de saber la lengua según el uso de ablar con los indios chinchaysuyos, al presente la cursa y me oye con mucho cuydado, y se va perfiçionando en ella para poder administrarles los santos sacramentos a los indios (1616 license, AAL Ordenaciones II/31). See also the 1628 licenses in ASFL Registro 13 f. 501v and AAL Ordenaciones IV/17.

54. En estos sermones, que principalmente se han de predicar en este arçobispado, en que el vulgo habla la lengua chinchaysuyu, es ésta la más genuina y corriente traducción, y no la syriaca, que los cultos han introducido para que no los entienda el pueblo (Avendaño [1649]: n.p.n.).

55. Si fuese yo examinador en el obispado de chinchaysuyu, no examinara en los términos del Cuzco, sino en su [lengua] materna, pues ésta es la que hablan y entienden sus naturales dél . . . si yo fuese al Cuzco y predicase en la lengua chinchaysuyu se reirían de mi, y harían burla (Romero 1928: 75).

56. . . . pido al lector no sea de los de la depravada opinión que dizen que los indios deste arçobispado no . . . entienden [la lengua del Cuzco], porque es conocido engaño, como lo fuera el dezir que el montañés no entiende la asseada y culta [lengua] de Madrid y Toledo, pues asi se han unos indios con otros . . . Puedo decir que ningún indio me ha oido que no se aya holgado y reconocido la elegancia y eficacia de la lengua del Cuzco, en que les e hablado, como qualquiera se huelga de oir a quien con eminencia y propiedad habla la española o latina, aunque no la sepa ni pueda imitar al oyente (Rojo Mejía y Ocón 1648: n.p.n.).

57. Pedro de la Perea, March 7, 1620 letter to the king, AGI Lima 309.

58. Fernando de Vera, April 15, 1631 letter to the king, AGI Lima 302.

59. Fernando de Vera, March 1 and February 24, 1635 letters to the king, AGI Lima 305.

60. Francisco Verdugo, May 5, 1635 and May 5, 1636 letters to the king, AGI Lima 308.

61. Juan Huidobro de Miranda, December 21, 1634 letter to Francisco Verdugo, AGI Lima 308.

62. Fernando Arias de Ugarte, April 24, 1635 letter to the king, AGI Lima 302.

63. Pedro de Villagómez, April 27, 1635 letter to the king, AGI Lima 309.

64. Arequipa synod of 1638, BNP B1742, f. 71.

65. Bernard Lavallé argues that the criollo versus peninsular rivalry within the mendicant orders reached a critical stage in the early seventeenth century (Lavallé 1993: 159, 163).

66. The prohibition is mentioned in a 1629 ordination petition (AAL Ordenaciones IV/31).

67. Juan de Santa María, March 8, 1620 letter to Bartolomé Lobo Guerrero, AGI Lima 301 (Lobo Guerrero wasted no time in forwarding the letter to the king).

68. 1620 suit against Alonso Pérez, AAL Capítulos III/8.

69. 1651 suit against Agustín de Aller, AAL Capítulos XV/5.

70. These estimates are based on impressions rather than actual figures.

71. 1594 provincial congregation, Egaña et al. eds. 1954–1986: V 604.

72. Claudio Aquaviva, October 1596 letter to the province of Peru, Egaña et al. eds. 1954–1986: VI 191.

73. Diego Alvarez de Paz, December 12, 1601 letter to Claudio Aquaviva, Egaña et al. eds. 1954–1986: VII 605–617.

74. Claudio Aquaviva, April 2, 1603 letter to the province of Peru, Egaña et al. eds. 1954–1986: VIII 137–140.

75. Bishops of Cuzco, Quito, and Popayán, 1601 letter to the king, AGI Lima 332.

Chapter 5 The Heyday of Pastoral Quechua

1. 1584 Lima synod, Torres ed. 1970: 20. Franciscus Haroldus, the annotator of the 1673 Roman edition of Mogrovejo's councils and synods, had some trouble identifying exactly what prayer this decree refers to, but concluded that it is the Angelus (Haroldus 1673: 213).

2. 1588 Lima synod, Torres ed. 1970: 119; 1585 Lima synod, Torres ed. 1970: 27.

3. E.g., 1609 visita of Piscobamba (Conchucos), AAL Visitas I/2.

4. *Instrucción que escribió el P. Fr. Diego de Porres . . .* , Barriga ed. 1933–1954: IV 182.

5. 1601 carta annua, Egaña et al. eds. 1954–1986: VII 389; 1602 carta annua, ibid.: VIII 717; Mateos ed. 1954 [ca. 1600]: II 36.

6. Arequipa synod of 1638, BNP B1742, f. 72–73.

7. Duviols associates this decree with the contemporary extirpation campaigns (Duviols 1977a [1971]: 339), but it makes no reference to idolatry, and the type of sermon referred to was not the most appropriate for use in an extirpation campaign.

8. 1611 Dominican provincial chapter, in typescript volume of Dominican provincial chapters 1611–1784, ASDL, f. 11.

9. 1579 comission in Gaspar de Zamora's 1586 información de oficio, AGI Lima 317.

10. I disagree with Sabine Hyland's identification of the *Relación de las costumbres antiguas de los naturales del Pirú* as the work of Blas Valera (Hyland 2003:

82–87). The identification is based on the fact that some rare pieces of informaton provided in the *Relación* are also present in excerpts from a lost work by Valera in Garcilaso's *Comentarios reales de los incas*. However, there are also key differrences between the two works—the portrayal of Inca culture in the *Relación* is very unorthodox, not to say unique, in its content and sources (particularly its references to quipus), and the same cannot be said of Valera's writings as preserved by Garcilaso.

11. *Illa* had a very complex range of meanings: González Holguín defined it as a stone amulet thought to bring wealth to its owners (González Holguín 1989 [1952, 1608]: 366–367), but according to the author of the anonymous 1586 grammar-dictionary it meant *ditado de los incas señores* (decree of the Inca lords) (Anonymous 1603 [1586]: f. 79v.). Clearly, the Anonymous Jesuit claimed it as the Quechua word for God because of its similarity to the Semitic terms (he may have subscribed to the Jewish origin theory).

12. Oré met Garcilaso in Spain, where he received a copy of the *Comentarios reales de los incas* (Pease G. Y. 1998: 39). However, this encounter took place years after the publication of the *Symbolo catholico indiano*, Oré's main work.

13. Capítulos suit against the priest of Taraco, AAL Apelaciones del Cuzco XIX/1, f. 23, 172.

14. 1621 testimony of Buenaventura de Fuentes, Franciscan informaciones, BNP C341, f. 28.

15. Oré was fairly young at the time and had only just become a priest. He probably lacked the rank and the institutional backing necessary to have played much of a role in the translation, especially given the marginalization of the mendicant orders in the council.

16. 1594 testimony by Gonzalo Gómez de Butrón, Franciscan informaciones, BNP C341, f. 46.

17. The last fifteen stanzas of the fifth cántico, which invoke Christ in the eucharist, are a standard part of the mass in Cuzco today.

18. Juan de San Pedro, May 13, 1593 letter to the king, AGI Lima 318.

19. 1621 Dominican provincial chapter, in typescript volume of Dominican provincial chapters 1611–1784, ASDL, f. 5. Cf. Meléndez 1681–1682: II 494. In 1601 Mercado had been one of the Quechua experts who examined applicants for Indian parishes in the diocese of Cuzco (1601 license in 1608 información de oficio for Fernando de Salazar, AGI Lima 324, f. 15v).

20. 1625 Dominican provincial chapter, in typescript volume of Dominican provincial chapters 1611–1784, ASDL, f. 5v.

21. It was not unusual for outstanding students to occupy university chairs at an early age before moving on to a parish (cf. Fernando de Avendaño's case in Guibovich 1993: 171).

22. See Oré 1607: 7 and Pérez Bocanegra 1631: n.p.n. Pérez Bocanegra was acting as examiner by 1602 and was priest of Belén by 1604. Baptismal records

from the parish of Belén signed by Pérez Bocanegra survive for the years 1614–1617; starting in 1618 another priest was in charge (Libro de Bautizos de la parroquia de Belén 1614–1652, AAC).

23. The earliest reference to Pérez Bocanegra as priest of Andahuaylillas is in an April 10, 1621 letter to the king from the Cuzco cathedral chapter (AGI Lima 312). A canvas of the baptism of Christ by the painter Luis de Riaño that is still held in the church refers to Pérez Bocanegra as parish priest and bears the date 1626. The church's famous murals, which have earned it the title "Sistine chapel of the Andes" and made it part of the Cuzco tourist circuit—including the pentalingual baptistry mural discussed in chapter 4 and featured on the front cover—may also be Riaño's work. It has been suggested that Riaño and Pérez Bocanegra established a close working relationship in designing these very elaborate murals (Mesa and Gisbert 1982: I 79–80, 237–238).

24. While it is often stated that the Jesuits were in control of the parish between 1628 and 1636, an examination of the original file on the dispute shows that this was not the case. Pérez Bocanegra was *cura propietario* (he was "tenured"), and the December 31, 1628 cédula that apparently granted the parish to the Jesuits was conditional on Pérez Bocanegra's acceptance (AGI Lima 312). The cédula was revoked entirely in 1636 after Pérez Bocanegra stated that it was not in his interest to give up Andahuaylillas, and argued that the Jesuits wanted the parish to use local labor in a nearby hacienda and take over its "sumptuous" church (March 15, 1634 *poder*, AGI Lima 312).

25. Many of the prayers in the *exercicio quotidiano* section (Prado and Manuel 1705: f. 47v–56v) are taken from the equivalent section of Pérez Bocanegra's ritual (1631: 692–697), even though the 1641 edition provided different Quechua versions of some of the same prayers.

26. 1595 catalogue of the province of Peru, Egaña et al. eds. 1954–1986: V 766; Medina 1904–1907: I 331; 1613 carta annua, Polia Meconi ed. 1999: 327.

27. Taylor's anthology of Quechua sermons and exempla contains exempla taken from the *Directorio espiritual* (Taylor 2002).

28. E.g., González Holguín 1607: f. 73, where he points to an omission in the *Arte y vocabulario* and mentions a printing error in the *Tercero cathecismo*.

29. . . . [tiene] esta obra grandíssima copia de términos y vocablos nuevamente acomodados a lo espiritual para la declaración de los mysterios de nuestra sancta fee, vicios y virtudes de que tenía falta la lengua (González Holguín 1989 [1952, 1608]: 4).

30. Claudio Aquaviva, April 8, 1596 letter to Juan Sebastián, Egaña et al. eds. 1954–1986: VI 83. The term *verbal* is unusual—it is not clear whether it refers to the grammar, the dictionary, or to both.

31. Claudio Aquaviva, April 8, 1596 letter to Juan Sebastián, Egaña et al. eds. 1954–1986: VI 83; May 6, 1596 letter to Diego González Holguín, ibid.: VI 123; and October 21, 1596 letter to Onofre Esteban, ibid.: VI 173.

32. Torres Saldamando 1882: 69; Mateos ed. 1954 [ca. 1600]: I 87, 292; Egaña et al. eds. 1954–1986: IV 75 (note 1); 1601 catalogue of the province of Peru, ibid.: VII 255. Juli, a model parish run by the Jesuits, was in an Aymara-speaking area. However, around 1600 the order was using it as a *seminario de lenguas* (language training center) for Quechua as well as Aymara (cf. 1600 report by José Tiruel, ibid.: VII 42). There must thus have been a permanent staff of Quechua speakers, perhaps Indians from Cuzco, which may explain González Holguín's desire to work there.

33. A. Acosta 1987; Polo 1906: 37; cf. *Autos de oposición a la cátedra de la lengua* . . . , 1647, ACML Papeles Varios volume 6, f. 3.

34. Neither volume of Avila's work is dated, but the archive of the Lima cathedral chapter contains a March 27, 1647 petition in which Avila explained to the rest of the chapter that he had completed the first volume of a bilingual sermonario and that a lengthy and laborious printing process would begin in April. He asked to be exempted from choir duties so that he could work full time on supervising the printing and on preparing the second volume, which was to run from the feast of the Trinity to the end of the liturgical year—the two volumes were to cover a total of twelve hundred folio-size pages. It appears that this petition was blocked by Fernando de Avendaño, his superior in the chapter, who at that time was preparing his own Quechua sermonario (ACML Acuerdos Capitulares, Libro 5, f. 245–246). Volume 2 was probably printed in 1649, as the dedication of Sarmiento Rendón's prologue is dated December 8, 1648.

35. Dumézil tells us that he was loaned a copy in 1952 by a canon of the Cuzco cathedral, who "with Sibylline insistence" persuaded him to remain in Cuzco to read it. "Within an hour," Dumézil wrote, " I had forgotten space and time, Indians and landscape—when the ten days had elapsed, my lender graciously granted me a few hours more. The sermons of Francisco Davila are a great book" (Dumézil 1957: 72).

36. Taylor's 2002 anthology of pastoral Quechua texts has a section on Avila.

37. Taylor has a higher opinion of Avendaño's abilities as a Quechua prose stylist, and considers his sermons to be the most outstanding in terms of their literary qualities (Taylor 2002: 42, 123). Although Taylor's opinion on these matters has some weight, I find that Avendaño's texts reflect an over-literal translation of the Spanish originals that often renders his Quechua convoluted and stiff, as could be expected from one of the few author-translators who was not a native speaker.

38. Pedro de Villagómez, November 21, 1648 letter to the king, AGI Lima 302; March 9, 1650 letter to the king, AGI Lima 303.

39. D. Molina [1649]: f. 263–264. A stanza from one of the cánticos appears at the end of the sermon for the sixth Friday of Lent (f. 250v), and Oré's fourteenth rosary prayer appears at the end of the Good Wednesday sermon (f. 433).

40. F. 106v–109v, 195v–199, and 300–301v correspond to Third Lima Council 1985c [1585]: 473–474, 546–547, and 769–777.

41. AAC Libro de Bautizos de la parroquia del Sagrario 1577–1609, f. 85; Eguiguren 1940–1951: II 155; AAL Concursos I/24, I/29; 1646 información de oficio for Bartolomé Jurado Palomino, AGI Lima 239/15, f. 1, 6, 9v.

42. I refer the reader to my edition of the *Aptaycachana* (Durston 2002) for more details on Castromonte and his work, and for full references. The *Aptaycachana* was first published in 1965 by Raul Rivera Serna, but this edition provides little historical context and contains numerous errors in the transcription of the Quechua texts.

43. 1674 información de oficio for Juan de Castromonte, AGI Lima 260/21.

44. I have not carried out systematic research with administrative sources beyond the middle of the seventeenth century; these impressions need further research.

45. Juan de Padilla, October 15, 1654 letter to the king, AAL Cedulario vol. 2, f. 260–260v.

46. La doctrina christiana y catheçismo en su lengua tiene erejías, y no pocas. En el credo ay tres, y en lo demas innumerables barvaridades, porque el que lo tradujo en aquellos tiempos devió de ser lenguarás pero no theólogo para poder aplicar en propiedad de términos el sentido (Francisco de la Cruz, July 20, 1657 letter to the viceroy, AGI Lima 59, f. 3; cf. his August 14, 1656 letter to the viceroy, AGI Lima 304). It is interesting to note that de la Cruz was unaware of the fact that the translation had been done by a team.

47. Concejo de Indias, July 17, 1660 parecer, AGI Lima 59. I have found no information on the results of the investigation—it may never have been carried out.

48. Francisco de Godoy, July 28, 1653, July 10, 1656, and June 18, 1657 letters to the king, AGI Lima 308.

49. 1626 información before Gonzalo de Campo, AGI Lima 302; Fernando Arias de Ugarte, May 13, 1633 letter to the king, AGI Lima 302.

50. Pedro de Villagómez, July 26, 1663 letter to the king, AGI Lima 303.

51. Cf. 1679 lawsuit between the parishes of Cabana and Huacaña, AAL Apelaciones de Huamanga XIV/5; and 1661–1662 lawsuit between the parishes of Yucay and Urubamba, AAL Apelaciones del Cuzco XVI/13.

52. Cf. 1626 foundation document of the cofradía of Santiago in 1679 lawsuit between the parishes of Cabana and Huacaña, AAL Apelaciones de Huamanga XIV/5, f. 14–14v, 16–16v; see also the documents on cofradías in Huarochirí during the 1660s in AAL Cofradías LVIII, especially documents 17 and 24.

53. 1675 ecclesiastical suit, AAL Capitulos XXI/12.

54. I thank Xavier Pello, who discovered this manuscript, for providing me with a photocopy of it.

55. In 1725 Bishop Luis Francisco Romero of Quito published a pastoral letter and a catechism in the Quechua of Quito, and a grammar appeared in 1753 (Rivet and Créqui-Montfort 1951: 141–147, 156–158). In 1739, Juan Antonio Dávila Morales, priest of Yotala in the archdiocese of La Plata, published a Spanish catechism which includes texts in a form of Quechua similar to that spoken today in the Sucre area (Dávila Morales 1739). All three works were printed in Lima. An eighteenth-century manuscript copy of a grammar which appears to be from Ecuador contains dialectally modified versions of some of the Third Council cartilla texts (Dedenbach-Salazar Sáenz ed. 1993).

Chapter 6 Pastoral Quechua Linguistics

1. In the inclusive form of the first-person plural the addressee is explicitly included in the "we," whereas the exclusive form excludes the addressee, resolving what is a common ambiguity in other languages such as English or Spanish where one has to infer this information from context. This amounts to a different person system of a sort encountered for the first time by the European grammatical tradition in missionary descriptions of Quechua and Aymara (see Adelaar and Muysken 2004: 211–213; Mannheim 1982). The evidential suffixes are discussed later in this chapter.

2. For example, in spite of Dedenbach-Salazar Sáenz's claim that the authors-translators barely made use of morphological resources for subordination, an abundant recourse to the subordinating suffixes /-spa/ and /-pti/ can be seen in most pastoral texts. Lexical resources, such as the *may pacha* construction for the subordinator "when," are relatively infrequent (nor is there any evidence that this construction is of colonial origin).

3. [En el material catequístico] sistematicamente se refieren acontecimientos no presenciados por los autores (por ejemplo los relatos bíblicos) por medio del . . . sufijo directo (Itier 1992b: 13).

4. [N]o hay asomo del 'reportativo' ni del 'conjetural', rasgos tan característicos de estas lenguas [Quechua and Aymara], y, en cambio, se hace uso abusivo del 'asertivo', mal entendido (Torero 2002: 15).

5. What follows is based primarily on Mannheim 1991, especially chapters 6 and 7.

6. See also many of the essays in Goddenzi ed. 1992.

7. See Mannheim 1991, chapter 7, for an in-depth discussion of the colonial Quechua sibilants.

8. See Cerrón-Palomino 1991 for an independent example of coastal Quechua that is contemporaneous with Santo Tomás's texts

9. See Cerrón-Palomino 1995a in particular for a thorough study of Santo Tomás's linguistic works and texts.

10. For instance, in the Spanish-Quechua section *llamar* ('to call') is glossed *cayani.gui, o guacyani.gui,* thus giving both what is today the Cuzco form (/waqya-/) and the Ayacucho and Central Quechua form (/qaya-/). However, the Spanish participle *llamado* ('called') gives simply *cayasca* (/qaya-sqa/). More convincingly, *llover* ('to rain') is glossed *parani.gui, o tamyani.gui, para-* being the Southern Quechua (both Ayacucho and Cuzco) form, and *tamya-* the Central Quechua form, but the Central form alone is used to gloss *lluvia* ('rain'—*tamyaynin*) and *lluvioso* ('rainy'—*tamyaçapa*) (Santo Tomás 1951 [1560]: 161, 162).

11. The existence of /sh/ in the Inca lingua franca is suggested by, among other texts, the Spanish prologue of Oré's *Symbolo catholico indiano.* While Oré's Quechua texts were written in Standard Colonial Quechua, so {x} never appears, he used it in the terms *maxcapaycha* (a wool tassel that was the insignia of the Inca sovereign) and *Xairi,* the name of one of the Inca sovereigns (1992 [1598]: 159, 160).

12. An encomienda was a grant of tribute (and, initially, labor services) from a specific group of Indians to a prominent Spaniard, typically a conquistador. The encomienda was the key institution of early Spanish colonial society, but was phased out by the crown in the central areas of the empire during the sixteenth century. The información in question concerned a proposal to make the encomiendas of Peru inheritable.

13. This important document (AGI Justicia 434/2/1) was discovered by Thomas Abercrombie (Abercrombie 2002: 106).

14. The fact that Standard Colonial Quechua does not present these changes makes it sound more like modern Ayacucho Quechua, which was not affected by the consonant lenition process, but this is a chronological illusion. There are a large number of lexical differences between Standard Colonial and modern Ayacucho Quechua, and even some morphological ones, such as the absence of the subordinator of simultaneity /-stin/ in the former.

15. As in *yachachiquey* 'my teacher,' *yahuarii* 'my blood,' or *sipasioc* 'man who has a concubine.'

16. This form no longer exists in Cuzco Quechua, but is common in other varieties—cf. Adelaar and Muysken 2004: 229.

17. . . . la demasiada curiosidad con que algunos del Cuzco y su comarca usan de vocablos y modos de dezir tan exquisitos y obscuros que salen del lenguaje que propriamente se llama quichua, introduziendo vocablos que por ventura se usavan antiguamente y agora no, o aprovechándose de los que usavan los ingas y señores, o tomándolos de otras naciones con quien tratan (Third Lima Council 1985a [1584]: 167).

18. I owe this suggestion to José Cárdenas.

19. . . . la mayor difficultad en la pronunciación está en estas síllabas: ca, que, qui, co, cu, cha, che, chi, cho, chu, ta, te, ti, to, tu; pronunciándolas los indios más ásperamente, o más blandamente conforme a lo que quieren significar . . .

como este vocablo coya significa reina, mina, y cierto género de heno . . . Algunos quisieron se usase de esta differencia: ca, cca, ka, csa, ta, tta, tha, cha, chha, ça, zha, y otras a este modo, mas no concuerdan las significaciones ni convienen los intérpretes entre sí. Y assí pareció mejor escrivir estas síllabas a nuestro modo, porque no se puede dar regla general que comprehenda tanta diversidad para que conforme a los caracteres se pronuncie (Third Lima Council 1985a [1584]: 169).

20. The {h} in the digraph {hu}, which represents /w/ before /a/, was used to indicate that the {u/v} was neither a vowel nor the consonant [v]. This practice was unnecessary in Quechua, where there are no diphthongs and no [v], so the digraph's only purpose was to ease pronunciation for Spaniards who were learning Quechua.

21. E.g.: *huacca-* 'to weep, to cry out' (Oré 1607: 133, 136, 152), *huaccaycha-* 'to protect' (ibid.: 97, 136), *macca-* 'to beat' (ibid.: 150), *hattali-* 'to hold' (ibid.: 58, 133, 134), *mitta* 'occasion' (ibid.: 56, 134), *sutti* 'clear' (ibid.: 87), *humintta* 'maize dumpling' (ibid.: 97), *tantta* 'bread' (ibid.: 98, 103), and *mappa* 'filth' (ibid.: 58, 134).

22. On the dialectal side, we have words like *huallcayachi-* 'to lessen' (Oré 1607: 97), *simi poccha* 'bearer of rumors' (ibid.: 152), *uria-* 'to work' (ibid.: 150), and *rana-* 'to buy' (ibid.: 151); as well as the odd morphological elements in *canillayaspa* (ibid.: 97), *amullayaspa* (ibid.: 133), *cutarcaacuyta* (ibid.: 133–134), and *atitmascanta* (ibid.: 155). On the terminological side, one can point to *yachachi-* 'to make' (ibid.: 56) and *tupa* 'royal' (ibid.: 96).

23. This suffix is also found in Third Council texts, but here it is fused to a few word stems like *cipcica-* /sipsi-qa-/ 'to spread rumors.' In Pérez Bocanegra's texts it appears to be productive, as in the phrase *raicucacchu canqui* /rayku-qa-q-chu ka-nki/ ("do you induce people to . . . ?") (Pérez Bocanegra 1631: 278). Antonio Cusihuamán's grammar notes the existence of this suffix in modern Cuzco Quechua, but it appears to have a very minor role, such that its meaning could not be determined (Cusihuamán 2001 [1976]: 197–198). Also indicative of Aymara influence is the occasional use of the anomalous form *-ssuncu* /-sun-ku/ for the first-person plural inclusive future rather than /-sun-chik/ or simply /-sun/ (ibid.: 334, 534, 655, 682), which can be attributed to interference from Aymara morphology.

24. Such pairs include: *huateca-/caumi-* 'to tempt' (Pérez Bocanegra 1631: 202), *unanchai/cuscui* 'sign, mark' (ibid.: 82), *yacha-/hacaicha-* 'to know' (ibid.: 83), *puchuca-/pallua-* 'to finish, to complete' (ibid.: 88), *paca-/huanlla-* 'to hide, to reserve' (ibid.: 140), and *huanana/timina* 'incorrigible' (ibid.: 200).

25. E.g., the verbs *para-* and *ttamya-* ('to rain') are paired (Avendaño [1649]: f. 9v).

26. E.g., *ichoca* 'left' and *allauca* 'right' (Avila [1647]: 29), *marca* 'town' (ibid.: 42, 178, 458), *huallca* 'little' (ibid.: 5, 183), *pucuta* 'cloud' (ibid.: 4), and *tamia* 'rain' (Avila [1649]: 43, 72).

27. Although Taylor states that Molina's sermons show no Chinchaysuyo elements (Taylor 2001a: 213), common Central terms like *marca* 'town' and *caya-* 'to

call' appear throughout the sermonario (e.g. D. Molina [1649] f. 257v). See Durston 2002 on Castromonte's lexicon.

28. For a more detailed analysis of Castromonte's Quechua, see Durston 2002: 236–243.

29. There are a few exceptions to this principle: the loan words based on *casar* 'to marry' and *pagar* 'to pay' were *casara-* and *pagara-* rather than *casa-* and *paga-*; probably because the latter would have sounded too similar to the Quechua verbs /qasa-/ 'to frost' and /paqa-/ 'to hide.'

30. E.g., Third Lima Council 1985b [1585]: 286.

31. E.g., Santo Tomás's *Diospa yanan* 'assistant of God' for "saint."

32. Las cosas de nuestra fe explícanse o por los propios términos . . . o por circunloquios, o por los nombres de las causas o effectos de las cosas que se quieren explicar o declarar (Santo Tomás 1995 [1560]: 92).

33. Guaman Poma recorded and proposed this form in a drawing which shows an Indian baptizing a child (Guaman Poma de Ayala 1980 [1615]: 784). González Holguín has the following entries for 'to baptize' in the Spanish-Quechua section of his dictionary: *Bautizarse. Baptizacuni, sutiyacuni. Baptizarle. Baptizani sutiyachini* (1989 [1952, 1608]: 430). However, the fact that González Holguín recorded the term *sutiya-* does not mean he thought it could be used in the sacramental form.

34. /mucha-yku-sqayki/—the stem /mucha-/ 'to kiss, to worship, to implore' is followed by the derivational suffix /-yku/, which in this case indicates deference, and the future form of the first-person subject/second-person object suffix.

35. Cf. the episodes of *hucha* resolution in the Huarochirí Manuscript, especially Taylor ed. 1999 [1987, n.d.]: 42–56, 184, 448.

36. There does not seem to have been an attempt to establish a lexical distinction in pastoral Quechua between the "adoration" of God and the "veneration" of the saints.

37. The council's translators considered that *camaquen* had a sense that approximated "soul"—the linguistic appendix of the *Doctrina christiana y catecismo* explained that in the Credo the phrase "creator of heaven and earth" was translated *hanacpachap, cay pachap ruraquen* rather than *hanacpachap, cay pachap camaquen* because the latter could be understood as "soul of heaven and earth" (Third Lima Council 1985a [1584]: 174). However, the verb stem *cama-*, from which it derived, was now being used consistently to express the act of divine creation. The council's policy of making theological terms as distinct and univocal as possible excluded the use of *camaquen* in such an important role. It was probably also considered that the concept of soul was too important to be translated with an adapted term.

38. When male penitents were asked whether they have deflowered any virgins in the Third Council confesionario, the term used was *donzella* (Third Lima Council 1985b [1585]: 218).

39. Avila used *çaçii pacha* for Lent (Avila [1647]: 427).

40. *Dios pacha* or *Dios pachan* seems to derive from *Diospa pachacan,* "God's majordomo." González Holguín records the following sentence: *Diospa pachacancuna. sacerdotecaman, o çapam. Los mayordomos o despenseros de la gracia que es hazienda de Dios acá son todos los sacerdotes* (the Spanish translation reads: "the majordomos or dispensers of grace, which is God's trade here on earth, are the priests") (1989 [1952, 1608]: 270).

41. *Purum* can be glossed as 'wild' or 'uncultivated' and apparently served to narrow the semantic range of *tazque.*

42. Cf. González Holguín 1989 [1952, 1608]: 270 on *checanchacu-*. The translation of the Nicene Creed was showcased at the beginning of the book to exemplify Pérez Bocanegra's critiques of and improvements on the Third Council texts. Apart from the use of *checanchacu-*, it expresses the event of the Incarnation of Christ as *runa ruracurca* 'he made himself a person' rather than the standard *runa tucurcan* 'he became a person'—probably because this last expression could also be read as "he pretended to be a person" (Pérez Bocanegra 1631: n.p.n.; cf. the catechism, ibid.: 646).

43. *Hupa-* is a fairly predictable Quechua adaptation of Puquina *upalli-*. The final syllable of what appears to be the Puquina stem was dropped because Quechua verb stems never have more than two syllables (additionally, there is a Quechua verbal derivational suffix /-lliku/, in which /-lli/ was probably an independent suffix at one point). Word-initial /h/ is variable, and in this case could be associated with glottalization or aspiration in /p/ (although it is not known whether Puquina had glottalized or aspirate stops).

44. The verb *toco-* /tuqu-/, whose meaning is obscure, is used with reference to the predictions of Old Testament prophets regarding Christ and the Virgin Mary in Prado's devotional manual (Prado 1641: 53).

Chapter 7 Text, Genre, and Poetics

1. The fourteen are Oré's seven cánticos, *Capac eterno,* and *Lira a Nuestra Señora del Rosario;* Pérez Bocanegra's three Marian hymns; a short passion hymn published by Prado; and a eucharistic hymn included in Castromonte's ritual.

2. On the modern hymns, see Arguedas 1955.

3. The 1579 Jesuit carta annua mentioned the performance of Aymara *comedias* in Juli (Egaña et al. eds. 1954–1986: II 624).

4. The authors of two major printed works (Bautista 1606 and Mijangos 1607) named individual Nahuas who assisted them in the writing process, and in 1576 the renowned Franciscan lengua Bernardino de Sahagún "stated unequivocally that the only ecclesiastical texts [in Nahuatl] free of heresies were those that had been written with the help of, and examined and corrected by, the kind of church-educated Nahuas he worked with" (Sell 1993: 47).

5. 1583 reply by Sebastián de Lartaun to the charges made before the Third Lima Council, Lissón Chaves ed. 1943–1946: III/11 73.

6. Pérez Bocanegra's adaptation of the prayer appears inconspicuously in his catechism, where the sentence "thy kingdom come" is rendered *capac pachaiqui ñocaicuman hamuchun* (may your kingly place/time come to us) rather than *capac cayniyqui ñocaycuman hamuchun* (may your kingliness come to us) (1631: 690).

7. Oré 1607: 123; Torres Rubio 1619: f. 97v; Pérez Bocanegra 1631: 457 and 484; Prado 1641: f. 59 and 121; Castromonte [ca. 1650] (see Durston 2002: 264); Prado y Manuel 1705: f. 91. Pérez Bocanegra, Prado, and Castromonte each provided two different translations. Prado's and Pérez Bocanegra's versions were distinguished by the fact that one was a briefer and more concise translation, and the other a longer and more explicit one. Castromonte provided a standard version and a version for ladinos and mestizos whose Quechua had become Hispanized (Durston 2002: 228–229).

8. See the comments on the translation of the phrase "who was conceived of the Holy Spirit" in the Credo (Third Lima Council 1985 [1584]: 170).

9. Take, for instance, the following sentence: *Checan iñiimi ari, iñisunsi, rimasuntacsi, apunchic Iesu Christo Diospa churin, Diostac runatac cascanta* (Oré 1992 [1598]: 215). The construction is obscure, especially because of the odd use of the reportative evidential /-si/. It only becomes intelligible when compared to the Latin original: *Est ergo fides recta, ut credamus et confiteamur, quia dominus noster Iesus Christus Dei filius, Deus et homo est* (Thus the correct faith is that we believe and confess that Our Lord Jesus Christ, the son of God, is both God and Man). A closer correspondence in the word order would not be possible. The suffix /-si/, which usually indicates that a statement is based on verbal report, seems to "translate" the Latin relativizer *ut*. This sentence could be translated far more simply and intelligibly using a construction along the lines of: *Checan iñiica, apunchic Iesu Christo Diospa churinpa Diostac runatac cascanta iñiimi, rimaymi.*

10. For instance, *y el demonio ha quedado desterrado y vencido* (and the Devil has been exiled and defeated) reads in Quechua *çupairi atiscca, ccarccosccatacc qqueparirccan* (and the Devil stayed behind defeated and exiled) (Avendaño [1649]: f. 10v). The verb *qquepari-* was used, incorrectly, because it translated one of the senses of Spanish *quedar*, as if the translator were relying on a dictionary.

11. Taylor suggests that the Quechua verses are translations of the Spanish *declaraciones*; he points to the occasional breakdown of the correspondence between the Spanish prose text and the Quechua verses, and the fact that the cánticos contain details that are absent from the *declaraciones* (Taylor 2003: 120). However, the formal complexity and fluidity of the cánticos indicate that *they* are the originals. There is also a distinct awkwardness to the Spanish texts. Other motives have to be sought for the occasional omission of details from the *declaraciones*. In at least one case, Oré seems to have been concerned that such details would have sounded shocking or unfamiliar to Spanish readers: at the end of the

third cántico Christ is equated to a hamancay flower, and the trope is absent from the corresponding *declaración* (Oré 1992 [1598]: 258, 242).

12. Bautista 1606, an extensive Nahuatl sermonary, provides brief Spanish summaries or subject headings in the margins.

13. 1603 carta annua, Egaña et al. eds. 1954–1986: VIII 223–224.

14. I underline the matched word stems.

15. The *huaman/cuntur* pair also occurs in modern house-building songs from the town of Antabamba, in the Apurimac region (Montoya, Montoya, and Montoya 1987: 206, 210).

16. My transcription marks the morpheme (stem and suffix) boundaries in the parallelistic portions, and the repeated morphemes are underlined to bring out the parallelism.

17. The parallelistic elements are absent from the Spanish original, which reads *O señor mio y Dios mio, yo te offendí y he sido gran pecador, agora me buelvo a ti, y me pesa mucho del mal que hize* (O, my lord and God, I offended you and have been a great sinner, now I turn to you and am very sorry for the evil I did).

18. The *cama-/rura-* pair is especially frequent, e.g., Third Lima Council 1985a [1584]: 47, 57, 70.

19. La 9ª particularidad de la [lengua] quichua, y muy particular y rara, es que admite qualquier especie de verso o metro, ya sea a semejanza de los versos castellanos, ya a semejanza de los latinos . . . Solo hay que advertir que para semejantes versos que se hacen a imitación de los latinos, no se atiende ni observa alguna quantitad escrupulosa de sílabas . . . Atiéndese solo a los accentos y a que las cesuras sean oportunas. Y esto basta para que pronunciadas las palabras por qualquiera intelligente de la lengua formen un sonido complexo que tenga esa armoniosa variedad que en latín se forma mediante la alternación de largas y breves (Anonymous Jesuit^2 n.d.: 16).

20. I use a vertical bar to indicate a syllable boundary, and a double bar to represent a caesura. The stressed syllables are underlined.

21. The second of the two terms for "town," *marca,* is the Central Quechua equivalent of the first, *llacta.*

22. Quechua has several different verbs for direct and refracted luminosity which are hard to translate accurately. The reduplication of the last syllable of the word stem in these two cases has an iconic effect.

Chapter 8 God, Christ, and Mary in the Andes

1. 1571 carta annua, Egaña et al. eds. 1954–1986: I 423–424.

2. *Capac* is also glossed in colonial dictionaries as 'rich,' which is the meaning /qhapaq/ has today in Cuzco Quechua. In the pre-Hispanic Andes there was no money or private property, so a "rich" person was one with extensive social

relations and influence—similarly, the term for "poor," *huaccha* /wakcha/, originally meant and still means 'orphan.' Interestingly, in Ayacucho Quechua /apu/ means rich, while /qapaq/ is used only in Christian contexts.

3. For the use of these terms in the Third Council corpus, see especially the exhortations and litany for the dying in the *Confessionario* (Third Lima Council 1985b [1585]: 285–309).

4. E.g., Arequipa synod of 1638, BNP B1742, f. 72v, and Pérez Bocanegra 1631: 696 (*capac yahuar*); Third Lima Council 1985b [1585]: 302 (*capac cauçay* and *capac yahuar*).

5. Cf. the following reference from one of Avendaño's sermons: *ccompiscca chhuspacta, huayaccacta ruraspa, chai chhuspap chaupimpi, manachu huc tticacta, huc ttoccapucta ccompinqui?* (when you weave a coca pouch or a bag, do you not weave a flower, a *tocapu*, in its center?) (Avendaño [1649]: f. 37v). See Cummins 1994 on *tocapu* in pre-Hispanic textiles.

6. González Holguín defines *acnupoy ttocapuy* as *cosa muy galana, o qualquier gala, o buen vestido, que éstos lo eran del Inca* (something very handsome, or any finery or good costume, for these were worn by the Inca sovereign), and goes on to cite the noun phrases *Acnopucta tocapucta ppachallicuk. El que se engalana y viste galanamente* (he who attires himself very finely), *Acnopuy ttocapuy ppachayok. El que tiene muy galanos vestidos, o los trae* (he who has fine costumes, and wears them), and *Acnopullicuni ttocapullicuni. Vestirse galanamente* (to dress finely (1989 [1952, 1608]: 16). Pérez Bocanegra's confesionario contains the following question for confessing women: *Llipec pachahuan, tocapu, acnupo, chacllipo, cumpi, ima çumac pachahuampas, pachallicocchu, caçacocchu canqui?* (do you dress up with lustrous clothes, with *tocapu, acnupo, chacllipo, cumpi* [a finely woven textile] or with any other beautiful clothes?) (1631: 254).

7. A native prayer used for kindling hearths invokes the flames as *thupa nina, Inca nina* (translated *noble fuego, Inca fuego* by Pérez Bocanegra), thus pairing *tupa* and *Inca* (Pérez Bocanegra 1631: 156).

8. *Cocau* is the food carried on a journey, equivalent to Latin *viaticum*, a term applied to communion when it is received during the Last Rites, as a preparation for the "last journey."

9. Ymapactac chica nanac Angelcuna Diospa huaçinta huacaychan? Capac Diospa Tupa huaçinmi ari iglesia, chaytacmi Dios capac yncanta yntuycuspa, ullpuycuspa siruicun. Hunu hunum Angelcuna iglesiapi, hunu hunum capac Diosta yglesiapi siruicun (D. Molina [1649]: f. 130).

10. *Tupa. Es nombre de honor para honrrarse, o llamarse honrrosamente, como nosotros dezimos señor: A tupay, O señor, A tupay Dios, O señor Dios, A tupay San Pedro, O señor san Pedro* (*Tupa*. It is an honorable name to honor oneself, just as we say 'lord': *A tupay*, O lord, *A tupay Dios*, O lord God, *A tupay San Pedro*, O lord Saint Peter) (González Holguín 1989 [1952, 1608]: 347).

11. Avendaño ([1649]: f. 2v) and Diego de Molina ([1649]: f. 144) used *titu* to translate "providence."

12. Guaman Poma's drawing of the execution of Tupac Amaru puts a lamentation in the mouths of Indian spectators in which he is addressed as *inca huanacauri* (Guaman Poma de Ayala 1980 [1615]: 418). The term also appears in an early (1562) prayer quoted in a literary text in which the absent Inca and the Sun are invoked by an Indian. The prayer ends with the request "lead me away, O Sun, lead me away, O Huanacauri" (*pusaguai indiya pusaguai huanacaureya*) (Cerrón-Palomino 1991: 398). Sabine MacCormack notes that "a statue of Manco Capac [the first Inca sovereign] that the Incas took with them into battle was . . . known as Guanacauri" (MacCormack 1988: 968).

13. An Indian cofradía carried its *niño Jesús*—a statue of the Christ Child—*en hábito de Inga, vivamente aderezado, y con muchas luces* (dressed as an Inca [sovereign] and with much finery) in a procession (Inca Fiestas 1986 [1610]: 43).

14. Lo que más lastima a mi corazón [es] el haber observado en la visita que hize el año pasado como introducen al santuario estas vanas observancias, bistiendo la imagen del Niño Dios con el uncu y demas insignias referidas [yacolla y mascapaycha], notando lo mismo en algunas pinturas, que nos persuaden adoran únicamente al verdadero Dios quando le ven en el trage de sus incas, que tenían por deidades . . . (Bishop Juan Moscoso, April 13, 1781 letter to the viceroy, Tupac Amaru 1983: 273).

15. . . . *huertoman yaucuspa, capac yahuarta humpispam, mallquicunata, huaytacunatapas carpaspa sumachircan* (. . . entering the garden and sweating *capac* blood, he made the trees and flowers beautiful by irrigating them) (D. Molina [1649]: f. 262v). The Spanish original says simply *entró en el guerto y labolo y lo rregó con su preciosa sangre* (he entered the garden and washed and watered it with his precious blood) (ibid.: f. 260).

16. *Chaquisca allpacta*—the last segment of *chaquisca* and the first segment of *allpacta* are merged to obtain the required number of syllables.

17. *Pirani* is the first-person subject form and *pirascca* is the passive participle form.

18. Rubén Vargas Ugarte reproduced this litany in his *Historia del culto a María en Iberoamérica,* considering it "the first garland of choice flowers that Christian America deposited before the altar of Mary" (*el primer ramillete de escojidas flores que la América cristiana depositó ante el altar de María*) (1956: II 64–68). He notes that it was incorrectly attributed to Archbishop Mogrovejo, an identification that has persisted until the present day. A short adaptation of the Quechua version was published by Torres Rubio (1619: n.p.n.). Oddly, Prado's ritual contains the Loreto Litany in Latin alongside Oré's Quechua version, as if the latter were a translation of the former (1641: f. 206–209v). Regardless of the meaning of this discrepancy, it is clear that Oré's litany was used widely and was a centerpiece of the liturgy in the pueblos de indios.

19. See Durston 2004: 494–498 for an annotated translation of this hymn.

20. Avendaño mentions Catachillay in his sermonario, pointing to its cross shape as a sign that God had made the heavens. He adds that Catachillay was used for navigation by sailors ([1649]: f. 20v). While Urton identifies it as the Southern Cross, Bauer and Dearborn point to the constellation of the Swan, also known as the Northern Cross (1998: 136). R. T. Zuidema argues that *Catachillay* was a term for both the Pleiades *and* for Alpha and Beta Centauri—the "eyes" of a dark cloud constellation identified as a llama (1982: 210).

21. Zuidema identifies *Catachillay* as a name for the Pleiades in the context of an argument regarding the astronomical dimensions of the ceque system of Cuzco (a radial system of sight lines that emanated from Inca Cuzco). Zuidema believes that the term *Catachillay* was applied to both the Pleiades and Alpha and Beta Centauri because the two constellations had "complementary roles in Inca astronomy and calendrics" (1982: 210).

22. Bertonio glossed *Cabrillas,* the Spanish name for the Pleiades, as *Catachilla huara huara* (Catachilla stars) but his gloss of *Catachilla* reads *una estrella o nebulosa en la via lactea, o las estrellas sobre la nebulosa* (a star or dark cloud constellation in the Milky Way, or the stars in that dark cloud constellation) (1984 [1612]: 107, 38).

23. Pachacuti Yamqui represents the difference graphically in his cosmological drawing, where a group of several stars labelled *huchu* (an Aymara name for the Pleiades) appears close to, but is clearly distinct from, Catachillay (Pachacuti Yamqui Salcamaygua 1993 [n.d.]: 208).

24. *Pacsa,* which probably derived from Aymara *pacsi* 'moon,' is glossed by González Holguín as *claridad de la luna nublada* (the light of the cloudy moon) (1989 [1952, 1608]: 271, 308).

25. González Holguín states that Mamanmirco was a constellation close to *el cruzero,* in other words, to Catachillay (1989 [1952, 1608]: 225).

26. Few Indians would have been able to understand the original Latin litany, but Oré had provided a partial Quechua version, and there may also have been full translations in circulation. Moreover, many were probably familiar with the iconography of the litany via its pictorial expressions.

Chapter 9 Performance and Contextualization

1. While "text" and "performance" are increasingly viewed as dimensions of a single process (Silverstein and Urban 1996), I speak of "performance" with reference to the purposeful enactment of the preexisting texts we find in the pastoral Quechua books. There was not always a one-to-one correspondence between one and the other, as the same text could be used in entirely different performances—for instance, the baptismal form was recited during the performance of the Third Council's catechism on the sacraments, but this was very different from using it in the act of administering the sacrament.

2. Cf. 1569 carta annua, Egaña et al. eds. 1954–1986: I 258; 1575 carta annua, ibid.: I 708; 1577 carta annua, ibid.: II 252, 273, and 280.

3. The *Rituale romanum* was the product of the Tridentine attempt to standardize the sacramental liturgies, but it was not published until 1614, and even after its use was ordered by the Lima synod of 1636, parish priests were allowed to use other rituals (Lima Synods 1987: 279, 280). The 1671 Huamanga synod ordered the use of the Toledo ritual and made no reference to the *Rituale romanum* (Huamanga Synod 1677 [1672]: f. 61).

4. Cf. Torres Rubio 1619: f. 98v; Pérez Bocanegra 1631: 703–704; Prado 1641: f. 116v–117; Huamanga Synod 1677 [1672]: f. 13v–14.

5. When it was administered to adults, baptism required extensive preliminary catechesis, but baptisms of adult Indians were rare during the period of this study.

6. Cf. Prado's instructions to Indians on how to perform a baptism (1641: f. 237–238v).

7. E.g., AAL Testamentos XXI/5a (Cajatambo 1634–1635) and AAL Visitas II/22 (Matahuasi, Ancash, 1649).

8. When first confronted by the huaca at night in an abandoned house, Don Cristóbal said the Pater Noster and Ave Maria while fleeing. When further accosted, he said all the prayers he knew, reciting the *doctrina* (i.e., the cartilla) "from beginnning to end several times." It is not specified whether Don Cristóbal said these prayers in Quechua, Latin, or Spanish, but it can be presumed that they were in Quechua (or possibly in Spanish). This round of prayers was followed by a personal, improvised call to the Virgin for aid, which is quoted in Quechua, and finally by the Salve Regina, which the narrator specifies he said "in Latin"—*cayta ña pochucaspas latinpi salue regina mater misericordia ñispa rresarcan* (having finished this he prayed in Latin, saying *salve regina mater misericordia* [*sic*]) (Taylor ed. 1999 [1987, n.d.]: 258, 260, 262).

9. Chayraycu campas paraptim rayocunacta cacya illapacunacta urmacta ricuspa cay simitatac. Et verbum caro factum est ñiscanta hocarinqui. Caytam Diosninchic rayomanta quespichinanchicpac uyarichihuanchic (Prado 1641: 71v–72).

10. Cf. Francisco de Toledo's *Instrucción general para los visitadores*, 1569–70, Lohmann Villena and Sarabia Viejo eds. 1986–1987: I 15; and a 1581 *ordenanza* by Martín Enrríquez, ASFL Registro 13, f. 226–227v. See also a 1644 *fiscal mayor* title, AAL Papeles Importantes XXIII/9, and a contemporary *cantor* title in the same location. Guaman Poma discussed the fiscales, sacristans, and choir members at length, suggesting that they be paid salaries in addition to their tribute exemption (Guaman Poma de Ayala 1980 [1615]: 624–631). For a recent, in-depth study of pastoral assistants see Charles 2003.

11. 1626 foundation document of the cofradía of Santiago in 1679 lawsuit between the parishes of Cabana and Huacaña, AAL Apelaciones de Huamanga XIV/5, f. 13–17.

12. See the documents on cofradías in Huarochirí during the 1660s in AAL Cofradías LVIII, especially documents 17 and 24.

13. Como los cantores a falta y ausencia de los dichos padres entierran los defuntos con su letanía y oraciones y rresponsos, las vísperas lo dizen con múcica cantadas y la Salve rrezan a la madre de Dios, y domingos y fiestas dizen las oraciones cantadas, rrezan todo lo dicho como cristiano, lo hazen en ausencia del dicho cura . . . Y en los días de obligación biernes y miercoles dizen la oración en maneciendo . . . y estaciones y responso a los defuntos y reza todo el pueblo y echa las festividades de las fiestas de la semana y vigilia . . . y todo lo dicho lo estorva los padres y curas de las dotrinas y castiga, diciéndole "santico ladinejo" (Guaman Poma de Ayala 1980 [1615]: 767).

14. Diminutivized forms of *santo* ('saintly') and *ladino* ('Spanish-speaking Indian').

15. Zermón del padre Varica: ancha uayllosca churicona ama pinachiuanquicho, na pinaspa poman cani na mana pinaspa caballo cinalla cabrestollamanta aysanallam cani. Deste sermón sus propios muchachos hazían farza, deziendo asi: churicona ama pinachiuanquecho na pinaspa micitom cani na mana pinaspa ucucham cani. Con esto se entretenían sus criados, no se entendía más (Guaman Poma de Ayala 1980 [1615]: 578).

16. . . . ha sido necesario, en llegando al pueblo, ver si el fiscal o muchachos que enseñan la doctrina la saben bien. Porque en algunas partes la enseñan con muchos errores, trastocando o mudando algunas palabras o letras, con que hacen muy diverso sentido, como en el credo por decir Hucllachacuininta, que es comunión o junta de santos, decir Pucllachacuininta, que es burla o trisca de santos (Arriaga 1621: 38–39).

17. Cf. 1603 carta annua, Egaña et al. eds. 1954–1986: VIII 263. A Jesuit mission report from Cotabambas, an area not far from Cuzco, described the organization of *coros* or small teams of Indians who practiced reciting the cartilla and the catechisms and prepared for confession, while the more advanced "discussed among themselves the main mysteries of our faith" (*conferían entre sí los misterios principales de nuestra fe*), 1602 carta annua, ibid.: VII 731.

18. Lo que conviene es predicarles a menudo y reprehenderles, sin consentir que se hagan tales juntas, ni que hablen entre sí otras razones que no sean oraciones de las quales son obligados a saber, y catezismos, con sus cantares divinos, que parece muy bien los canten y rezen, estorvándoles no hablen ni traten otras cosas fuera de las dichas (Pérez Bocanegra 1631: 113–114).

19. Jerónimo de Loayza, 1555 *instrucción* to Bartolomé Martínez, ACML, Liber erectionis, f. 151. A 1648 visita to the parish of San José de Chorrillos, in Huarochirí, noted that quipus were used to collect offerings from parishioners on behalf of the priest—the quipus apparently recorded what each person allegedly owed for fiesta masses, masses for the dead, and so on (AAL Visitas IX/16, f. 21, 30).

20. *Instrucción que escribió el P. Fr. Diego de Porres . . .* , Barriga ed. 1933–1954: IV 175, 181.

21. *Instrucción que escribió el P. Fr. Diego de Porres . . .* , Barriga ed. 1933–1954: IV 176.

22. 1600 carta annua, Egaña et al. eds. 1954–1986: VII 62; see other references to catechetical quipus in the 1577 carta annua, ibid.: II 276.

23. 1603 carta annua, Egaña et al. eds. 1954–1986: VIII 214.

24. 1603 carta annua, Egaña et al. eds. 1954–1986: VIII 263.

25. . . . van a tratar con estos indios lo que el Padre les dixo, y la penitencia que les dio, haziendo burla dél, diziendo que no sabe preguntar al penitente, o que no les entiende su lengua, y mofan de su manera de absolver, con otras cosas que yo e sabido dellos, harto escandalosas (Pérez Bocanegra 1631: 113).

26. Confessionariocta ricuspa, unanchaspa taripacunqui, yuyayñiiquipi aparayaspa Saçerdote Diospa rantinman confessacunqui (Prado 1641: f. 117).

27. Porres's grid system was so elaborate that it apparently allowed the supervisors to determine what part of the town an absentee lived in—i.e., the grid on the atrium reproduced the urban grid of the town (*Instrucción que escribió el P. Fr. Diego de Porres . . .* , Barriga ed. 1933–1954: IV 174).

28. 1577 carta annua, Egaña et al. eds. 1954–1986: II 280, 273–274.

29. Cf. Diego de Porres's guidelines on the subject (*Instrucción que escribió el P. Fr. Diego de Porres . . .* , Barriga ed. 1933–1954: IV 182).

30. E.g., 1602 carta annua, Egaña et al. eds. 1954–1986: VIII 716–717.

31. 1617 carta annua, Polia Meconi ed. 1999: 409.

32. Lo que se deve guardar en [las doctrinas] es primeramente que muy de mañana se ha de tañer la campana, y es señal para que los cantores se junten en el choro, y los fiscales y alguaziles de doctrina vayan por todas las casas y calles del pueblo juntando los muchachos para la doctrina. Y si fuere domingo, miércoles, o viernes, o día de fiesta, a todos los indios y indias del pueblo, que bien es menester toda esta diligencia, para que se junten a missa, a sermón, y a la doctrina. Tambien se deve tañer la campana a missa mayor, a vísperas, y a la oración, y a prima de noche se toque la campana para que se haga oración para las ánimas de purgatorio (Oré 1992 [1598]: 182–183).

33. E.g., 1609 visita of Piscobamba, Conchucos, AAL Visitas I/2.

34. . . . es muy necessario que aya escuela y maestro de ella, y cantores diputados y pagados con salario sufficiente donde sean enseñados los muchachos a rezar la doctrina, y a leer y escrivir, cantar y tañer . . . la escuela es como ánima de todo un pueblo . . . donde no la uviere faltará todo lo dicho de doctrina, música, ornato y servicio de las iglesias, altar y coro (Oré 1992 [1598]: 189).

35. 1621 testimony by Diego Sánchez, Franciscan informaciones, BNP C341, f. 55.

36. Cf. the following 1621 testimony by Oré's correligionary Buenaventura de Fuentes: *para que con más facilidad tomen la doctrina christiana le dio un tono muy a propósito y de que an gustado mucho los indios, tanto que en sus juntas quando hazen chacaras cantan la*

dicha doctrina (so that they might learn the cartilla with more ease he gave it a very suitable melody which the Indians have liked very much, so much so that in their gatherings when they cultivate their lands they sing the said cartilla) (Franciscan informaciones, BNP C341, f. 28v).

37. The Third Lima Council texts, which established the model for future editions, presented matching segments of the Spanish, Quechua, and Aymara text on each page—the Spanish original occupies the top quarter of the page and the Quechua and Aymara versions appeared in parallel columns below it, Quechua on the left and Aymara on the right. Avila and Jurado followed the same model, with the difference that their editions were bilingual rather than trilingual, so the two versions appeared in parallel columns, Spanish on the left and Quechua on the right. However, the most common solution, used by Oré, Pérez Bocanegra, Prado, Avendaño, and Molina, was to alternate segments of Spanish and Quechua text, probably because this was editorially much simpler. It also made the comparison of the Spanish and Quechua versions more difficult, a problem which Avendaño solved by making the segments very short, so there were often two matching pairs of segments on a page.

38. *Abba* was "the familiar form by which a child addressed its father" (Mohrmann 1957: 21). *Yaya* has been replaced by *tayta* (apparently of Spanish or Latin origin) as the term for "father" in Southern Quechua, and is now only used in religious contexts.

39. The term "indexical icon" was coined by Michael Silverstein to refer an array of indexical signs (signs that function via relations of contiguity) that produces an overall iconic effect.

40. Y asi sirve casca para contar nuevas, y para referir un ejemplo, o enseñar cosas del cielo, o de virtudes, o cosas ocultas, o sucesos repentinos, o cosas inauditas que no suele saber el auditorio (González Holguín 1607: f. 27).

41. The evidential suffixes are underlined in the transcription, while in the translation I have underlined the words or phrases corresponding to those that carry evidential marking in the original, indicating which suffix is used in each case.

42. One might argue that attributing information to a specific source, written or oral, constrained the author to use reportative marking in conveying the information, but this is clearly not the case—direct-witness marking is usually employed in such instances.

Conclusion

1. See Tavárez 2000 for a study of Nahuatl terms for the Trinity, and León 1611: n.p.n. and Alva 1634: f. 48–50 for discussions of terminological disagreements involving Nahuatl.

2. A Mixtec catechism printed in the Achiutla dialect in 1567 underwent a reedition the following year with modifications that adapted it to the Teposcolula dialect (Terraciano 2001: 69, 72, 74).

3. This does not mean that specific orders consistently adopted a given policy—for example, to prefer adapted terms over loan words, or vice versa. Instead, the orders seem to have responded differently to different contexts. In particular, latecomers to a missionary field tended to react conservatively to accommodationist elements in the practices of their predecessors.

4. Evidence for this hypothesis can be found in Gabriel Centeno de Osma's late colonial religious drama *El pobre más rico*. In Centeno's work we find nonstandard religious terms and tropes that also occur in the works of Pérez Bocanegra, such as *cusi quellpo* (blissful), *Cuyusmanco tiana* (roughly, "royal seat," applied to a church or altar of the Virgin), and *purun tasqui llumpac mama* (virginal and pure mother) (Centeno de Osma 1938 [n.d.]: 58, 66, 171; cf. Pérez Bocanegra 1631: 529, 704, n.p.n.). It is possible, of course, that Centeno was familiar with the *Ritual formulario*, but given that he was writing at least a couple of generations later it seems more likely that he was drawing on an independent tradition of religious speech that had been kept alive in Cuzco.

5. For an in-depth study of an ideology of this sort as reflected in a Quechua-language literature (if from a much later period), see Itier's work on the plays written by Cuzco's *indigenista* elite in the late nineteenth and early twentieth centuries (1995a and 2000a).

Pastoral Quechua Works

Note: Collections of pastoral texts as opposed to grammars and dictonaries are in bold. Reprints and reeditions are not included. Most titles are abbreviated—see bibliography for details. Full bibliographical information on all of these items, except for Castromonte's ritual, can be found in Rivet and Créqui-Montfort 1951.

1560 Domingo de Santo Tomás (Dominican), *Grammatica o arte de la lengua general* (grammar, printed in Valladolid)

1560 ——— *Lexicon o vocabulario de la lengua general* (dictionary, printed in Valladolid)

1584 Third Lima Council, *Doctrina christiana y catecismo* (cartilla and catechisms, printed in Lima)

1585 ——— *Confessionario para los curas de indios* (confesionario with other sacramental texts, printed in Lima)

1585 ——— *Tercero cathecismo* (sermonario, printed in Lima)

1586 Anonymous, *Arte y vocabulario en la lengua general* (grammar and dictionary, printed in Lima)

1598 Luis Jerónimo de Oré (Franciscan), *Symbolo catholico indiano* (breviary, printed in Lima)

1607 ——— *Rituale seu manuale peruanum* (ritual, printed in Naples)

1607 Diego González Holguín (Jesuit), *Grammatica y arte nueva de la lengua general* (grammar, printed in Lima)

1608 ——— *Vocabulario de la lengua general* (dictionary, printed in Lima)

1616 Alonso de Huerta (secular), *Arte de la lengua general* (grammar, printed in Lima)

1619 Diego de Torres Rubio (Jesuit), *Arte de la lengua quichua* (grammar and dictionary, printed in Lima)

1631 Juan Pérez Bocanegra (secular), *Ritual formulario* (ritual, printed in Lima)

1641 Pablo de Prado (Jesuit), *Directorio espiritual* (devotional manual, printed in Lima)

1647 Francisco de Avila (secular), *Tratado de los evangelios* (volume 1 of liturgical sermonario, printed in Lima)

1648 Juan Rojo Mejía y Ocón (secular), *Arte de la lengua general* (grammar, printed in Lima)

1649 Francisco de Avila (secular), *Segundo tomo de los sermones de todo el año* (volume 2 of liturgical sermonario, printed in Lima)

1649 Fernando de Avendaño (secular), *Sermones de los misterios de nuestra santa fe catolica* (sermonario, printed in Lima)

1649 Bartolomé Jurado Palomino (secular), *Declaracion copiosa* (translation of Roberto Belarmino's Italian catechism, printed in Lima)

1649 Diego de Molina (Franciscan), *Sermones de la quaresma* (liturgical sermonario, manucript volume)

ca. 1650 Juan de Castromonte (secular), *Aptaycachana* (ritual, manuscript included within a larger volume)

Bibliography

Manuscript Collections

AAA Archivo Arzobispal de Arequipa (Arequipa, Peru)
AAC Archivo Arzobispal del Cusco (Cuzco, Peru)
AAL Archivo Arzobispal de Lima (Lima, Peru)
ACML Archivo del Cabildo Metropolitano de Lima (Lima, Peru)
AGI Archivo General de Indias (Seville, Spain)
AGN Archivo General de la Nación (Lima, Peru)
ASDL Archivo de Santo Domingo de Lima (Lima, Peru)
ASFL Archivo de San Francisco de Lima (Lima, Peru)
BNP Biblioteca Nacional del Perú (Lima, Peru)

Books and Articles

Abercrombie, Thomas. 2002. La perpetuidad traducida: del "debate" al Taqui Onqoy y una rebelión comunera peruana. In *Incas e indios cristianos. Elites indígenas e identidades cristianas en los Andes coloniales*, edited by Jean-Jacques Decoster, 79–120. Cuzco: Centro de Estudios Regionales Andinos "Bartolomé de las Casas."

Abril Castelló, Vidal, ed. 1992. *Francisco de la Cruz, Inquisición, Actas I.* Madrid: Consejo Superior de Investigaciones Científicas.

Abril Castelló, Vidal, and Miguel J. Abril Stoffels, eds. 1996–1997. *Francisco de la Cruz, Inquisición, Actas II.* 2 vols. Madrid: Consejo Superior de Investigaciones Científicas.

Acosta, Antonio. 1987. Francisco de Avila, Cusco 1573(?)–Lima 1647. In *Ritos y tradiciones de Huarochirí del siglo XVII*, edited by Gerald Taylor, 551–616. Lima: Instituto de Estudios Peruanos and Instituto Francés de Estudios Andinos.

Acosta, José de. 1984–1987 [1577]. *De procuranda indorum salute,* Latin-Spanish edition by Luciano Pereña et al. 2 vols. Madrid: Consejo Superior de Investigaciones Científicas.

———. 1987 [1590]. *Historia natural y moral de las Indias,* edited by José Alcina Franch. Madrid: Historia 16.

Adelaar, Willem. 1997. Spatial Reference and Speaker Orientation in Early Colonial Quechua. In *Creating Context in Andean Cultures,* edited by Rosaleen Howard-Malverde, 135–148. Oxford: Oxford University Press.

Adelaar, Willem, and Pieter Muysken. 2004. *The Languages of the Andes.* Cambridge: Cambridge University Press.

Adorno, Rolena. 1986. *Guaman Poma: Writing and Resistance in Colonial Peru.* Austin: University of Texas Press.

Alva, Bartolomé de. 1634. *Confessionario mayor y menor en lengua mexicana.* Mexico City: Francisco Sálbago.

Anderson, Benedict. 1991 [1983]. *Imagined Communities: Reflections on the Origins and Spread of Nationalism.* London and New York: Verso.

Andrés, Melquíades. 1976. *La teología española en el siglo XVI.* 2 vols. Madrid: Biblioteca de Autores Cristianos.

Anonymous. 1603 [1586]. *Grammatica y vocabolario en la lengua general del Peru llamada quichua, y en la lengua española. El mas copioso y elegante que hasta agora se ha impresso.* Seville: Clemente Hidalgo. [Original title and imprint: *Arte, y vocabulario en la lengua general del Peru llamada quichua, y en la lengua española. El mas copioso y elegante que hasta agora se ha impresso.* Lima, 1586, Antonio Ricardo.]

Anonymous Jesuit. 1968 [n.d.]. Relación de las costumbres antiguas de los naturales del Pirú. In *Crónicas peruanas de interés indígena,* Biblioteca de Autores Españoles vol. 209, edited by Francisco Esteve Barba, 153–189. Madrid: Ediciones Atlas.

Anonymous Jesuit[2]. n.d. Photocopy of late-eighteenth-century MS on South American languages, BNP X980.564 063.

Areford, David S. 1998. The Passion Measured: A Late-Medieval Diagram of the Body of Christ. In *The Broken Body: Passion Devotion in Late-Medieval Culture,* edited by A. A. MacDonald, H. N. B. Ridderbos, and R. M. Schlusemann, 210–238. Groningen: Egbert Forster.

Arguedas, José María. 1955. Los himnos quechuas católicos cuzqueños. Colección del padre Jorge A. Lira y de J. M. B. Farfán. *Folklore Americano* 3/3: 121–232.

Armas Medina, Fernando de. 1953. *Cristianización del Perú (1532–1600).* Seville: Consejo Superior de Investigaciones Científicas.

Arriaga, Pablo José de. 1621. *Extirpacion de la idolatria del Piru.* Lima: Jerónimo de Contreras.

Augustine (St. Augustine of Hippo). 1980 [1888]. The Harmony of the Gospels. In *A Select Library of the Nicene and Post-Nicene Fathers of the Christian Church,* edited by Philip Schaff, 65–236. Grand Rapids, MI: Wm. B. Eerdmans.

Avendaño, Fernando de. [1649]. *Sermones de los misterios de nuestra santa fe catolica en lengua castellana y la general del inca.* Lima: Jorge López de Herrera.

Avila [Dávila], Francisco de. [1647]. *Tratado de los evangelios, que nuestra madre la iglesia propone en todo el año desde la primera dominica de adviento, hasta la ultima missa de difuntos, santos de España, y añadidos del nuevo rezado. Explicase el evangelio, y se pone un sermon en cada uno en las lenguas castellana, y general de los indios deste reyno del Peru, y en ellos donde da lugar la materia, se refutan los errores de la gentilidad de dichos indios . . . Tomo primero, que contiene desde la primera dominica de adviento, hasta el sabado de la octava de pentecostes.* Lima: n.p.

———. [1649]. *Segundo tomo de los sermones de todo el año en lengua indica, y castellana, para la enseñanza de los indios, y extirpación de sus idolatrias. Obra postuma del doctor Don Francisco Davila canonigo de la santa iglesia metropolitana de los Reyes.* Lima: n.p.

Bakhtin, M. M. 1981. *The Dialogic Imagination: Four Essays,* translated by Caryl Emerson and Michael Holquist. Austin: University of Texas Press.

Barnstone, Willis. 1993. *The Poetics of Translation. History, Theory, Practice.* New Haven and London: Yale University Press.

Barriga, Victor Manuel, ed. 1933–1954. *Los mercedarios en el Perú en el siglo XVI.* 5 vols. Rome: n.p., Arequipa: La Colmena.

Bartra, Enrique. 1967. Los autores del catecismo del Tercer Concilio Limense. *Mercurio Peruano* 52/470: 359–372.

Basnett, Susan, and Harish Trivedi, eds. 1999. *Postcolonial Translation: Theory and Practice.* London and New York: Routledge.

Bataillon, Marcel. 1950 [1937]. *Erasmo y España, estudios sobre la historia espiritual del siglo XVI,* translated by Antonio Alatorre. 2 vols. Mexico City: Fondo de Cultura Económica.

Bauer, Brian S. 1992. *The Development of the Inca State.* Austin: University of Texas Press.

Bauer, Brian S., and David S. P. Dearborn. 1998. *Astronomía e imperio en los Andes,* translated by Javier Flores Espinoza. Cuzco: Centro de Estudios Regionales Andinos "Bartolomé de Las Casas."

Bauman, Richard, and Charles Briggs. 1990. Poetics and Performance as Critical Perspectives on Language and Social Life. *Annual Review of Anthropology* 19: 59–88.

Bautista, Juan. 1606. *A Jesucristo N.S. ofrece este sermonario en lengua mexicana.* Mexico City: Diego López Dávalos.

Benjamin, Walter. 1968 [1955]. The Task of the Translator: An Introduction to the Translation of Baudelaire's *Tableaux Parisiens.* In *Illuminations,* edited by Hannah Arendt and translated by Harry Zohn, 69–82. New York: Schocken Books.

Bertonio, Ludovico. 1612. *Libro de la vida y milagros de nuestro señor Iesu Christo en dos lenguas, aymara y romance, traducido de el que recopiló el Licenciado Alonso de Villegas, quitadas y añadidas algunas cosas, y acomodado a la capacidad de los indios.* Juli: Francisco del Canto.

———. 1984 [1612]. *Vocabulario de la lengua aymara.* Cochabamba: Centro de Estudios de la Realidad Económica y Social.

Betanzos, Juan de. 1987 [1557]. *Summa y narración de los incas,* edited by María del Carmen Martín Rubio. Madrid: Atlas.

Beyersdorff, Margot. 1993. Rito y verbo en la poesía de Fray Luis Jerónimo de Oré. In *Mito y simbolismo en los Andes. La figura y la palabra,* edited by Henrique Urbano, 215–237. Cuzco: Centro de Estudios Regionales Andinos "Bartolomé de Las Casas."

Bloomer, W. Martin, ed. 2005. *The Contest of Language: Before and Beyond Nationalism.* Notre Dame, IN: University of Notre Dame Press.

Bossy, John. 1970. The Counter-Reformation and the People of Catholic Europe. *Past and Present* 47: 51–70.

———. 1985. *Christianity in the West, 1400–1700.* Oxford: Oxford University Press.

Briggs, Lucy T. 1981. Missionary, Patrón, and Radio Aymara. In *The Aymara Language in its Social and Cultural Context: A Collection of Essays on Aspects of Aymara Language and Culture,* edited by Martha J. Hardman, 175–185. Gainesville: University Presses of Florida.

Burke, Peter. 1993. The Social History of Language. In *The Art of Conversation,* 1–33. Ithaca, NY: Cornell University Press.

———. 2004. *Languages and Communities in Early Modern Europe.* Cambridge: Cambridge University Press.

Burkhart, Louise. 1988. The Solar Christ in Nahuatl Doctrinal Texts of Early Colonial Mexico. *Ethnohistory* 35/3: 234–256.

———. 1989. *The Slippery Earth: Nahua-Christian Moral Dialogue in Sixteenth-Century Mexico.* Tucson: University of Arizona Press.

———. 1996. *Holy Wednesday: A Nahua Drama from Early Colonial Mexico.* Philadelphia: University of Pennsylvania Press.

Cahill, David. 2000. The Inca and Inca Symbolism in Popular Festive Culture: The Religious Processions of Seventeenth-Century Cuzco. In *Habsburg Peru: Images, Imagination and Memory* by Peter T. Bradley and David Cahill, 85–150. Liverpool: Liverpool University Press.

Calancha, Antonio de la. 1974–1982 [1638]. *Crónica moralizada,* edited by Ignacio Prado Pastor. 6 vols. Lima: Universidad Nacional Mayor de San Marcos.

Calvet, Louis-Jean. 1998 [1987]. *Language Wars and Linguistic Politics,* translated by Michel Petheram. Oxford: Oxford University Press.

Castelnau-l'Estoile, Charlotte. 2000. *Les ouvriers d'une vigne stérile. Les jésuites et la conversion des Indiens au Brésil 1580–1620.* Lisbon: Fundação Calouste Gulbenkian.

Castro de Trelles, Lucila, ed. 1992 [ca. 1560]. *Relación de la religión y ritos del Perú hecha por los padres agustinos. Edición, estudio preliminar y notas de Lucila Castro de Trelles.* Lima: Pontificia Universidad Católica del Perú.

Castro Pineda, Lucio. 1945. *La cátedra de la lengua general de los indios de la catedral de Lima. Contribución para la historia pedagógica del virreynato del Peru.* Trabajo presentado para optar al grado de Doctor en Pedagogía, Pontificia Universidad Católica del Perú.

Castromonte, Juan de. [ca. 1650]. Aptaycaçhana o manual en que se contiene todo lo que los curas an de deçir y enseñar a los yndios en su lengua quando les administran los santos sacramentos de la yglesia. Sacado fielmente del Ritual Romano de la santidad de Paulo Quinto, y traducido en la lengua general Chinchaysuyo del Peru por el Bachiller Juan de Castromonte cura ynterim del beneficio de Guancabamba. MS F933 in BNP [cf. editions in Durston 2002 and Rivera Serna 1965].

Catholic Encyclopedia. Online edition at http://www.newadvent.org/cathen/ (from 1907–1914 edition).

Centeno de Osma, Gabriel. 1938 [n.d.]. *El pobre más rico. Comedia quechua del siglo XVI* (facsimile edition). Lima: Editorial Lumen SA.

Cerrón-Palomino, Rodolfo. 1987. *Lingüística quechua.* Cuzco: Centro de Estudios Regionales Andinos "Bartolomé de Las Casas."

———. 1988. Unidad y diferenciación lingüística en el mundo andino. In *Pesquisas en lingüística andina,* edited by Luis Enrique López, 121–152. Lima: Consejo Nacional de Ciencia y Tecnología [CONCYTEC], Universidad Nacional del Altiplano, and Sociedad Alemana de Cooperación Técnica [GTZ].

———. 1989. Reconsideración del llamado "Quechua costeño." In *Diglosia linguo-literaria y educación el Perú,* edited by Enrique Ballón Aguirre and Rodolfo Cerrón-Palomino, 179–240. Lima: CONCYTEC and GTZ.

———. 1991. Un texto desconocido del quechua costeño (s. XVI). *Revista Andina* 9/2: 393–413.

———. 1992. Diversidad y unificación léxica en el mundo andino. In *El quechua en debate. Ideología, normalización y enseñanza,* edited by Juan Carlos Godenzzi, 205–235. Cuzco: Centro de Estudios Regionales Andinos "Bartolomé de Las Casas."

———. 1994. *Quechumara. Estructuras paralelas de las lenguas quechua y aymara.* La Paz: Centro de Investigación y Promoción del Campesinado.

———. 1995a. Estudio introductorio. In Santo Tomás 1995 [1560], vii–lxvi.

———. 1995b. *La lengua de Naimlap. Reconstrucción y obsolescencia del mochica.* Lima: Pontificia Universidad Católica del Perú.

———. 1997. Las primeras traducciones al quechua y al aymara: Un caso de elaboración y desarrollo estilísticos. *Boletín del Instituto Riva Agüero* 24: 81–102.

———. 1999. Tras las huellas del aimara cuzqueño. *Revista Andina* 17/1: 137–161.

———. 2000. *Lingüística Aimara.* Lima: Centro de Estudios Regionales Andinos "Bartolomé de Las Casas."

———. 2005. La toponimia como fuente de usos gramaticales arcaicos y como registro cronológico de desplazamientos idiomáticos. *Lexis* 29/1: 111–124.

Charles, John Duffy. 2003. Indios Ladinos: Colonial Andean Testimony and Ecclesiastical Institutions (1583–1650). Ph.D. Dissertation, Yale University.

Cieza de León, Pedro. 1985 [n.d.]. *El señorío de los incas,* edited by Manuel Ballesteros. Madrid: Historia 16.

Clifford, James. 1982. *Person and Myth: Maurice Leenhardt in the Melanesian World.* Berkeley: University of California Press.

Cobo, Bernabé. 1956 [1653]. *Historia del nuevo mundo.* Biblioteca de Autores Españoles vols. 91 and 92. Madrid: Ediciones Atlas.

Cohn, Bernard. 1996. *Colonialism and Its Forms of Knowledge: The British in India.* Princeton: Princeton University Press.

Comaroff, Jean, and John Comaroff. 1991. *Of Revelation and Revolution: Christianity, Colonialism, and Consciousness in South Africa.* Vol. 1. Chicago: University of Chicago Press.

Congregation for Divine Worship and the Discipline of the Sacraments. 2001. Liturgiam Authenticam: On the Use of the Vernacular Languages in the Publication of the Books of the Roman Liturgy. English text at: http://www.adoremus.org/liturgiamauthenticam.html.

Cook, Noble David. 1992. Luis Jerónimo de Oré y el *Symbolo catholico indiano.* In Oré 1992 [1598]: 15–61.

Council of Trent. 1941 [1545–1563]. *Canons and Decrees of the Council of Trent. Original Text with English Translation,* translated by H. J. Schroeder. London: B. Herder Book Co.

Crickmay, Lindsey. 1999. Speaking to God: Observations on the Vocabulary of Andean Prayer and Suggestions for the Reconsideration of Its Interpretation. In *La lengua de la cristianización en Lationamérica: Catequización e instrucción en lenguas amerindias,* edited by Sabine Dedenbach-Salazar Sáenz and Lindsey Crickmay, 151–167. Bonner Amerikanistische Studien vol. 32. Bonn: Verlag Anton Saurwein.

Cummins, Tom. 1994. Representation in the Sixteenth Century and the Colonial Image of the Inca. In *Writing without Words: Alernative Literacies in Mesoamerica and the Andes,* edited by Elizabeth Hill Boone and Walter Mignolo, 188–219. Durham, NC: Duke University Press.

Cusihuamán, Antonio. 2001 [1976]. *Gramática quechua Cuzco-Collao.* 2d ed. Cuzco: Centro de Estudios Regionales Andinos "Bartolomé de Las Casas."

D'Altroy, Terence. 2002. *The Incas.* Malden (MA), Oxford (UK), and Carlton (Australia): Blackwell Publishing.

Dávila Morales, Juan Antonio. 1739. *Practica de la doctrina christiana. Obra utilissima para los curas, y confessores de indios, y de rusticos.* Lima: Francisco Sobrino.

Dean, Carolyn. 1999. *Inka Bodies and the Body of Christ: Corpus Christi in Colonial Cusco, Peru.* Durham, NC: Duke University Press.

Dedenbach-Salazar Sáenz, Sabine, ed. 1993. *Una gramática colonial del quichua del Ecuador. Transcripción e interpretación de un manuscrito del Archivo Histórico Nacional de*

Colombia. Bonn and St. Andrews: Bonner Amerikanistische Studien, Universität Bonn, and Institute of Amerindian Studies, University of St. Andrews.

———. 1997a. La descripción gramatical como reflejo e influencia de la realidad lingüística: La presentación de las relaciones hablante-enunciado e intratextuales en tres gramáticas quechuas coloniales y ejemplos de su uso en el discurso quechua de la época. In *La descripción de las lenguas amerindias en la época colonial*, edited by Klaus Zimmermann, 291–319. Frankfurt am Main and Madrid: Vervuert Verlag and Iberoamericana.

———. 1997b. La terminología cristiana en los textos quechuas de instrucción religiosa en el siglo XVI. In *Messages and Meanings: Papers from the Twelfth Annual Symposium, Latin American Indian Literatures Association / Associación de Literaturas Indígenas Latinoamericanas*, edited by Mary H. Preuss, 195–209. Lancaster, CA: Labyrinthos.

Demarest, Arthur. 1981. *Viracocha: The Nature and Antiquity of the Andean High God.* Cambridge, MA: Peabody Museum of Archaeology and Ethnology.

Dumézil, Georges. 1957. The Good Shepherd: Francisco Davila's [*sic*] Sermon to the Indians of Peru (1646). *Diogenes* 20: 68–83.

Durán, Juan Guillermo. 1982. *El catecismo del III Concilio Provincial de Lima y sus complementos pastorales (1584–1585). Estudio preliminar, textos, notas.* Buenos Aires: Facultad de Teología de la Pontificia Universidad Católica "Santa María de los Buenos Aires."

Duranti, Alessandro, and Charles Goodwin, eds. 1992. *Rethinking Context: Language as an Interactive Phenomenon.* Cambridge: Cambridge University Press.

Durston, Alan. 1994. Un régimen urbanístico en la América hispana colonial—el trazado en damero durante los siglos XVI y XVII. *Historia* 28: 59–115.

———. 2002. El *Aptaycachana* de Juan de Castromonte—un manual sacramental quechua para la sierra central del Perú (ca. 1650). *Bulletin de l'Institut Français d'Études Andines* 31/2: 219–292.

———. 2003. La escritura del quechua por indígenas en el siglo XVII—nuevas evidencias en el Archivo Arzobispal de Lima (estudio preliminar y edición de textos). *Revista Andina* 37: 207–236.

———. 2004. Pastoral Quechua: The History of Christian Translation in Colonial Peru, 1550–1650. Ph.D. Dissertation, University of Chicago.

———. n.d. Native-Language Literacy in Colonial Peru: The Question of Mundane Quechua Writing Revisited. Forthcoming, *Hispanic American Historical Review.*

Duviols, Pierre. 1977a [1971]. *La destrucción de las religiones andinas (conquista y colonia)*, translated by Albor Maluenda. Mexico City: Universidad Nacional Autónoma de México.

———. 1977b. Los nombres quechua de Viracocha, supuesto "Dios Creador" de los evangelizadores. *Allpanchis* 10: 53–63.

———. 1993. Estudio y comentario etnohistórico. In Pachacuti Yamqui Salcamaygua 1993 [n.d.], 11–126.

Egaña, Antonio de, et al., eds. 1954–1986. *Monumenta Peruana.* Monumenta Historica Societatis Iesu, 8 vols. Rome: Institutum Historicum Societatis Iesu.

Eguiguren, Luis Antonio. 1940–1951. *Diccionario histórico cronológico de la Real y Pontificia Universidad de San Marcos y sus Colegios, Crónica e Investigación.* 3 vols. Lima: Imprenta Torres Aguirre.

Eley, Geoff. 2005. *A Crooked Line: From Cultural History to the History of Society*. Ann Arbor: University of Michigan Press.

Esquivel y Navia, Diego de. 1980 [1753]. *Noticias cronológicas de la gran ciudad del Cuzco,* edited by Felix Denegri Luna. 2 vols. Lima: Fundación Wiesse.

Estenssoro Fuchs, Juan Carlos. 1992. Los bailes y el proyecto colonial. *Revista Andina* 10/2: 353–389.

———. 1994. Descubriendo los poderes de la palabra: Funciones de la prédica en la evangelización del Perú (siglos XVI–XVII). In *La venida del reino. Religión, evangelización y cultura en América, siglos XVI–XX,* edited by Gabriela Ramos, 75–101. Cuzco: Centro de Estudios Regionales Andinos "Bartolomé de Las Casas."

———. 2001. El simio de Dios. Los indígenas y la Iglesia frente a la evangelización del Perú, siglos XVI–XVII. *Bulletin de l'Institut Français d'Études Andines* 30/3: 455–474.

———. 2003. *Del paganismo a la santidad. La incorporación de los indios del Peru al catolicismo, 1532–1750.* Lima: Instituto Francés de Estudios Andinos and Pontificia Universidad Católica del Perú.

Esteve Barba, Francisco. 1968. Estudio preliminar. La historiografía peruana de interés indígena. In *Crónicas peruanas de interés indígena,* Biblioteca de Autores Españoles vol. 209, edited by Francisco Esteve Barba, v–lxxiv. Madrid: Ediciones Atlas.

Fabian, Johannes. 1986. *Language and Colonial Power: The Appropriation of Swahili in the Former Belgian Congo, 1880–1938.* Cambridge: Cambridge University Press.

Faller, Martina. 2002. Semantics and Pragmatics of Evidentials in Cuzco Quechua. Ph.D. Dissertation, Stanford University.

Fernández del Castillo, Francisco, ed. 1982 [1914]. *Libros y libreros en el siglo XVI.* Mexico City: Archivo General de la Nación and Fondo de Cultura Económica.

Flores Ochoa, Jorge, Elizabeth Kuon Arce, and Roberto Samanez Argumedo. 1993. *Pintura mural en el Sur Andino.* Lima: Banco de Crédito del Perú.

Gante, Pedro de. 1553. *Doctrina christiana en lengua mexicana.* Mexico City: Juan Pablos.

Gaona, Juan. 1582. *Colloquios de la paz, y tranquilidad christiana, en lengua mexicana.* Mexico City: Pedro Ocharte.

García, Gregorio. 1607. *Origen de los indios de el nuevo mundo e indias occidentales.* Valencia: Pedro Patricio Mey.

García-Ruiz, Jesús. 1992. El misionero, las lenguas mayas y la traducción. Nominalismo, tomismo y etnolingüística en Guatemala. *Archives de Sciences Sociales des Religions* 77: 83–110.

Garcilaso (Garcilaso Inca de la Vega). 1944 [1617]. *Historia general del Perú,* edited by Angel Rosenblat. 3 vols. Buenos Aires: Emecé Editores.

———. 1945 [1609]. *Comentarios reales de los incas,* edited by Angel Rosenblat. 2 vols. 2d ed. Buenos Aires: Emecé Editores.

Gentzler, Edwin. 2001. *Contemporary Translation Theories.* 2d ed. Clevedon and Buffalo: Multilingual Matters.

Goffman, Erving. Footing. *Semiotica* 25 (1/2): 1–29.

Godenzzi, Juan Carlos, ed. 1992. *El quechua en debate. Ideología, normalizacíon y enseñanza.* Cuzco: Centro de Estudios Regionales Andinos "Bartolomé de Las Casas."

González Holguín, Diego. 1607. *Grammatica y arte nueva de la lengua general de todo el Peru, llamada lengua qquichua, o lengua del inca. Añadida y cumplida en todo lo que le faltava de tiempos, y de la grammatica, y recogido en forma de arte lo mas necessario en los dos primeros libros. Con mas otros dos libros postreros de adiciones al arte para mas perficionarla, el uno para alcançar copia de vocablos, y el otro para la elegancia y ornato.* Lima: Francisco del Canto.

———. 1989 [1952, 1608]. *Vocabulario de la lengua general de todo el Peru llamada lengua qquichua o del inca.* Lima: Universidad Nacional Mayor de San Marcos. [Original title and imprint: *Vocabulario de la lengua general de todo el Peru llamada lengua qquichua, o del inca. Corregido y renovado conforme a la propiedad cortesana del Cuzco. Dividido en dos libros, que son dos vocabularios enteros en que salen a la luz de nuevo las cosas que faltavan al vocabulario.* Lima, 1608, Francisco del Canto.]

Gose, Peter. 1996. The Past Is a Lower Moiety: Diarchy, History, and Divine Kingship in the Inka Empire. *History and Anthropology* 9/4: 383–414.

Guaman Poma de Ayala, Felipe. 1980 [1615]. *El primer nueva corónica y buen gobierno,* edited by John V. Murra and Rolena Adorno. 3 vols. Mexico City: Siglo XXI.

Guibovich, Pedro. 1993. La carrera de un visitador de idolatrías en el siglo XVII: Fernando de Avendaño (1580?–1655). In *Catolicismo y extirpación de idolatrías. Siglos XVI–XVIII,* edited by Gabriela Ramos and Henrique Urbano, 169–240. Cuzco: Centro de Estudio Regionales Andinos "Bartolomé de Las Casas."

Hamilton, Roland. 1996. Introduction: Juan de Betanzos and Inca Traditions. In *Narrative of the Incas,* by Juan de Betanzos, translated and edited by Roland Hamilton and Dana Buchanan, ix–xiv. Austin: University of Texas Press.

Hanks, William. 1989. Text and Textuality. *Annual Review of Anthropology* 18: 95–127.

Haroldus, Franciscus. 1673. *Lima limata conciliis, constitutionibus synodalibus et aliis monumentis quibus venerabilis servus Dei Toribius Alphonsus Mogrovejus archiepisc. limanus provinciam limensem, seu peruanum imperium elimauit, & ad normam SS. Canonum composuit.* Rome: Iosepus Corvus.

Hauf i Valls, Albert G. 2001. Fray Hernando de Talavera, O.S.H., y las traducciones castellanas de la *Vita Christi* de Fr. Francesc Eiximenis, O.F.M. In *Essays on Medieval Translation in the Iberian Peninsula,* edited by Tomàs Martínez Romero and Roxana Recio, 203–250. Castelló: Publicacions de la Universitat Jaume I.

Hemming, John. 1970. *The Conquest of the Incas.* New York and London: Harcourt Brace Jovanovich.

Hermans, Theo. 1997. The Task of the Translator in the European Renaissance: Explorations in a Discursive Field. In *Translating Literature,* edited by Susan Bassnett, 14–40. Cambridge: D. S. Brewer.

———. 2002. Paradoxes and Aporias in Translation Studies. In *Translation Studies: Perspectives on an Emerging Discipline,* edited by A. Riccardi, 10–23. Cambridge: Cambridge University Press.

Hsia, R. Po-Chia. 1998. *The World of Catholic Renewal, 1540–1770.* Cambridge: Cambridge University Press.

Huamanga Synod. 1677 [1672]. *Constituciones synodales de el obispado de la ciudad de Guamanga.* Lima: Jerónimo de Contreras.

———. 1970 [1629]. *Constituciones synodales del obispado de Guamanga (Perú) 1629.* Cuernavaca: Centro Intercultural de Documentación.

Huerta, Alonso de. 1993 [1616]. *Arte breve de la lengua quechua* (facsimile edition), edited by Ruth Moya and Eduardo Villacís. Quito: Proyecto Educación Bilingüe Intercultural y Corporación Editora Nacional. [Original title and imprint: *Arte de la lengua general de los yndios deste reyno del Pirú.* Lima, 1616, Francisco del Canto.]

Hyland, Sabine. 1994. Conversion, Custom, and "Culture": Jesuit Racial Policy in Sixteenth-Century Peru. Ph.D. Dissertation, Yale University.

———. 2003. *The Jesuit and the Incas: The Extraordinary Life of Padre Blas Valera, S.J.* Ann Arbor: University of Michigan Press.

Illari, Bernardo. 2001. Polychoral Culture: Cathedral Music in La Plata (Bolivia, 1680–1730). Ph.D. Dissertation, University of Chicago.

Inca Fiestas. 1986 [1610]. Fiestas incas en el Cuzco colonial. *Boletín del Archivo Departamental del Cusco* 2: 42–47.

Irvine, Judith, and Susan Gal. 2000. Language Ideology and Linguistic Differentiation. In Kroskrity ed. 2000, 35–83.

Itier, César. 1991. Lengua general y comunicación escrita: Cinco cartas en quechua de Cotahuasi, 1616. *Revista Andina* 9/1: 65–107.

———. 1992a. La tradición oral quechua antigua en los procesos de idolatrías de Cajatambo. *Bulletin de l'Institut Français d'Études Andines* 21/3: 1009–1051.

———. 1992b. Un nuevo documento colonial escrito por indígenas en quechua general: La petición de los caciques de Uyupacha al obispo de Huamanga (hacia 1670). *Lexis* 16/1: 1–21.

———. 1992c. Un sermón desconocido en quechua general: La "Plática que se ha de hazer a los indios en la predicación de la Bulla de la Santa Cruzada" (1600). *Revista Andina* 10/1: 135–146.

———. 1992d. Commentary on Estenssoro 1992. *Revista Andina* 10/2: 395–398.

———. 1993. Estudio y comentario lingüístico. In Pachacuti Yamqui Salcamaygua 1993 [n.d.], 127–178.

———. 1995a. *El teatro quechua en el Cuzco. Dramas y comedias de Nemesio Zúñiga Cazorla: Qurichuspi (1915); T'ikahina (1934); Katacha (1930?)*. Lima: Centro de Estudios Regionales Andinos "Bartolomé de Las Casas" and Institut Français d'Études Andines.

———. 1995b. La littérature quechua d'évangelisation (XVIe et XVIIe siècles) comme source ethnolinguistique. *Amerindia* 20: 321–329.

———. 1995c. Quechua y cultura en el Cuzco del siglo XVIII: De la "lengua general" al "idioma del imperio de los incas." In *Del siglo de oro al siglo de las luces. Lenguaje y sociedad en los Andes del siglo XVIII,* edited by César Itier, 89–111. Cuzco: Centro de Estudios Regionales Andinos "Bartolomé de Las Casas."

———. 1999. Los problemas de edición, datación, autoría y filiación de *El robo de Proserpina y sueño de Endimión,* auto sacramental colonial en Quechua. In *Edición y anotación de textos coloniales hispanoamericanos,* edited by I. Arellano and J. A. Rodríguez Garrido, 213–231. Madrid and Frankfurt am Main: Iberoamericana and Vervuert.

———. 2000a. *El teatro quechua en el Cuzco. Tomo II. Indigenismo, lengua y literatura en el Perú moderno.* Lima: Institut Français d'Études Andines and Centro de Estudios Regionales Andinos "Bartolomé de Las Casas."

———. 2000b. Lengua general y quechua cuzqueño en los siglos XVI y XVII. In *Desde afuera y desde adentro. Ensayos de etnografía e historia del Cuzco y Apurímac,* edited by Luis Milliones, Hiroyasu Tomoeda, and Tatsuhiko Fujii, 47–59. Osaka: National Museum of Ethnology.

———. 2001. La propagation de la langue générale dans le sud du Pérou. In *Le savoir, pouvoir des élites dans l'empire espagnol d'Amerique,* 63–74. Centre de Recherche sur l'Amérique Espagnole Coloniale, Traxaux et Documents no. 3. Paris: Université de la Sorbonne Nouvelle Paris III.

———. 2005. Las cartas en quechua de Cotahuasi: el pensamiento político de un cacique de inicios del siglo XVII. In Bernard Lavallé ed. *Máscaras, tretas y rodeos del discurso colonial en los Andes.* Lima: Instituto Francés de Estudios Andinos, Pontificia Universidad Católica del Perú, and Instituto Riva-Agüero.

———. n.d. El *Ritual formulario* de Juan Pérez Bocanegra y el quechua cuzqueño a inicios del siglo XVII.

Jiménez de la Espada, Marcos, ed. 1881–1897. *Relaciones geográficas de Indias. Perú.* 4 vols. Madrid: Tip. de M. G. Hernández.

Jurado Palomino, Bartolomé. 1649. *Declaracion copiosa de las quatro partes mas essenciales, y necessarias de la doctrina christiana, compuesto por orden del beatissimo P. Clemente Octavo de felice memoria. Por el eminentissimo cardenal Roberto Bellarmino de la Compañía de Iesus, con las adiciones del Maestro Sebastián de Lirio . . . Traducida de la lengua castellana en la general del inga. . . .* Lima: Jorge López de Herrera.

Kamen, Henry. 1993. *The Phoenix and the Flame: Catalonia and the Counter Reformation.* New Haven and London: Yale University Press.

Keane, Webb. 1997. Religious Language. *Annual Review of Anthropology* 26: 47–71.

King James Bible. n.d. *The Holy Bible Containing the Old and New Testaments.* London: Eyre and Spottiswoode.

Kroskrity, Paul V., ed. 2000. *Regimes of Language: Ideologies, Polities, and Identities.* Santa Fe: School of American Research.

Kubler, George. 1946. The Quechua in the Colonial World. In *Handbook of South American Indians.* Volume 2. *The Andean Civilizations,* edited by Julian H. Steward, 331–410. Washington, DC: Smithsonian Institution.

Landerman, Peter. 1991. Quechua Dialects and Their Classification. Ph.D. Dissertation, University of California at Los Angeles.

Lapesa, Rafael. 1986. *Historia de la lengua castellana.* Madrid: Gredos.

Lassegue-Moleres, Juan Bautista. 1987. Sínodos diocesanos del Cuzco, 1591 y 1601. *Cuadernos para la Historia de la Evangelización en América Latina* 2: 31–72.

Lavallé, Bernard. 1993. *Las promesas ambiguas. Criollismo colonial en los Andes.* Lima: Pontificia Universidad Católica del Perú and Instituto Riva Agüero.

Lefevre, Andre, ed. 1992. *Translation—History—Culture: A Sourcebook.* London and New York: Routledge.

León, Martín de. 1611. *Camino del cielo en lengua mexicana.* Mexico City: Diego López Dávalos.

Levillier, Roberto, ed. 1921–1926. *Gobernantes del Perú. Cartas y papeles. Siglo XVI. Documentos del Archivo de Indias.* 14 vols. Madrid: Sucesores de Rivadeneyra and Juan Pueyo.

Lima Synods. 1987. *Sínodos de Lima de 1613 y 1636.* Madrid and Salamanca: Centro de Estudios Históricos del Consejo Superior de Investigaciones Científicas and Instituto de Historia de la Teología Española de la Universidad Pontificia de Salamanca.

Lissón Chaves, Emilio, ed. 1943–1946. *La iglesia de España en el Perú. Colección de documentos para la historia de la iglesia en el Perú, que se encuentran en varios archivos.* 4 vols. Sevilla: Editorial Católica Española.

Lockhart, James. Three Experiences of Culture Contact: Nahua, Maya, and Quechua. In *Native Traditions in the Postconquest World,* edited by Elizabeth Hill Boone and Tom Cummins, 31–51. Washington, DC: Dumbarton Oaks Research Library and Collection.

Lohmann Villena, Guillermo, and María Justina Sarabia Viejo, eds. 1986–1987. *Francisco de Toledo. Disposiciones gubernativas para el virreinato del Perú 1569–1574.* 2 vols. Sevilla: Consejo Superior de Investigaciones Científicas.

López Gay, Jesús. 1966. *El catecumenado en la misión del Japón del s. XVI.* Rome: Libreria dell' Università Gregoriana.

———. 1970. *La liturgia en la misión del Japón del siglo XVI.* Rome: Libreria dell' Università Gregoriana.

MacCormack, Sabine. 1984. From the Sun of the Incas to the Virgin of Copacabana. *Representations* 8: 30–60.

———. 1985. "The Heart Has Its Reasons": Predicaments of Missionary Christianity in Early Colonial Peru. *Hispanic American Historical Review* 65/3: 443–466.

———. 1988. Pachacuti: Miracles, Punishments, and Last Judgement: Visionary Past and Prophetic Future in Early Colonial Peru. *The American Historical Review* 93/4: 960–1006.

———. 1989. Atahualpa and the Book. *Dispositio* 14/36–38: 141–168.

———. 1991. *Religion in the Andes: Vision and Imagination in Early Colonial Peru.* Princeton: Princeton University Press.

———. 1994. Ubi Ecclesia? Perceptions of Medieval Europe in Spanish America. *Speculum* 69: 74–100.

Mannheim, Bruce. 1982. Person, Number, and Inclusivity in Two Andean Languages. *Acta Linguistica Hafniensia* 17: 138–154.

———. 1986a. Poetic Form in Guaman Poma's *Wariqsa Arawi. Amerindia* 11: 41–67.

———. 1986b. Popular Song and Popular Grammar, Poetry and Metalanguage. *Word* 37/1–2: 45–75.

———. 1991. *The Language of the Inka since the European Invasion.* Austin: University of Texas Press.

———. 1998a. A nation Surrounded. In *Native Traditions in the Postconquest World,* edited by Elizabeth Hill Boone and Tom Cummins, 383–420. Washington, DC: Dumbarton Oaks Research Library and Collection.

———. 1998b. "Time, not Syllables, Must Be Counted": Quechua Parallelism, Word Meaning, and Cultural Analysis. In *Linguistic Form and Social Action,* edited by Jennifer Dickinson, James Herron, et al., 238–281. Michigan Discussions in Anthropology 13. Ann Arbor: University of Michigan Press.

———. 2002. Gramática colonial, contexto religioso. In *Incas e indios cristianos. Elites indígenas e identidades cristianas en los Andes coloniales,* edited by Jean-Jacques Decoster, 209–220. Cuzco: Centro de Estudios Regionales Andinos "Bartolomé de las Casas."

Mannheim, Bruce, and Krista Van Vleet. 1998. The Dialogics of Southern Quechua Narrative. *American Anthropologist* 100/2: 330–346.

Marco, Angelo de. 1961. *Rome and the Vernacular.* Westminster, MD: Newman Press.

Marrow, James H. 1979. *Passion Iconography in Northern European Art of the Late Middle Ages and Early Renaissance: A Study of the Transformation of Sacred Metaphor into Descriptive Narrative.* Kortrijk (Belgium): Van Ghemmert.

Marzal, Manuel. 1983. *La transformación religiosa peruana.* Lima: Pontificia Universidad Católica del Perú.

Mateos, F. ed. 1954 [ca. 1600]. *Historia general de la Compañía de Jesús en la Provincia del Perú. Crónica anónima de 1600 que trata del establecimiento y misiones de la Compañía de Jesus en los paises de habla española en la América Meridional.* 2 vols. Madrid: Consejo Superior de Investigaciones Cientificas, Instituto Gonzalo Fernández de Oviedo.

Medina, José Toribio. 1904–1907. *La imprenta en Lima (1584–1824).* 4 vols. Santiago: Author.

Meléndez, Juan. 1681–1682. *Tesoros verdaderos de las yndias en la historia de la gran prouincia de San Iuan Bautista del Peru de el Orden de Predicadores.* 3 vols. Rome: Nicolas Angel Tinasso.

Melgar, Esteban Sancho de. 1691. *Arte de la lengua general del ynga llamada qquechhua.* Lima: Diego de Lyra.

Meliá, Bartomeu. 1992. *La lengua guaraní del Paraguay. Historia, sociedad y literatura.* Madrid: Editorial Mapfre.

Mendoza, Diego de. 1665. *Chronica de la Provincia de San Antonio de los Charcas.* Madrid.

Mesa, José de, and Teresa Gisbert. 1982. *Historia de la pintura cuzqueña.* 2 vols. Lima: Fundación Augusto N. Wiese.

Meyer, Birgit. 1999. *Translating the Devil: Religion and Modernity among the Ewe in Ghana.* Trenton, NJ: Africa World Press.

Middendorf, E. W., ed. 1891. *Dramatische und lyrische dichtungen der Keshua-sprache.* 1891. Leipzig: F. A. Brockhaus.

Mijangos, Juan de. 1607. *Espejo divino en lengua mexicana.* Mexico City: Diego López Dávalos.

Mills, Kenneth. 1997. *Idolatry and Its Enemies: Colonial Andean Religion and Extirpation, 1640–1750.* Princeton: Princeton University Press.

Mohrmann, Christine. 1957. *Liturgical Latin: Its Origins and Character.* Washington, DC: The Catholic University of America Press.

Molina, Cristóbal de. 1989 [1575]. Relacion de las fabulas i ritos de los ingas. In *Fábulas y mitos de los incas,* edited by Henrique Urbano and Pierre Duviols, 5–134. Madrid: Historia 16.

Molina, Diego de. [1649]. Sermones de la quaresma en lengua quechua. BNP MS B203.

Montoya, Rodrigo, Edwin Montoya, and Luis Montoya. 1987. *La sangre de los cerros. Urqukunapa yawarnin. Antología de la poesía quechua que se canta en el Perú.* Lima: Centro Peruano de Estudios Sociales, Mosca Azul Editores, and Universidad Nacional Mayor de San Marcos.

Mumford, Jeremy Ravi. 2004. Vertical Empire: The Struggle for Andean Space in the Sixteenth Century. Ph.D. Dissertation, Yale University.

Murra, John. 1962. Cloth and Its Functions in the Inca State. *American Anthropologist* 64/4: 710–727.

Murúa, Martín de. 1987 [1590]. *Historia general del Perú*, edited by Manuel Ballesteros. Madrid: Historia 16.

Nalle, Sara T. 1992. *God in La Mancha: Religious Reform and the People of Cuenca, 1500–1650*. Baltimore: Johns Hopkins University Press.

Nebrija, Antonio de. 1992 [1492]. *Gramática de la lengua castellana*, edited by Antonio Quilis. 2 vols. Madrid: Ediciones de Cultura Hispánica and Instituto de Cooperación Iberoamericana.

Oré, Luis Jerónimo de. 1607. *Rituale seu manuale peruanum, et forma brevis administrandi apud indos sacrosancta baptismi, poenitentiae, eucharistiae, matrimonii, & extremae unctionis sacramenta*. Naples: Iacobum Carlinum and Constantinum Vitalem.

———. 1992 [1598]. *Symbolo catholico indiano* (facsimile edition), edited by Antonine Tibesar. Lima: Australis. [Original title and imprint: *Symbolo catholico indiano, en el qual se declaran los mysterios de la fe contenidos en los tres symbolos catholicos, Apostolico, Niceno, y de S. Athanasio. Contiene assi mesmo una descripcion del nuevo orbe, y de los naturales del. Y un orden de enseñarles la doctrina christiana en las dos lenguas generales, quichua y aymara, con un confessionario breve y catechismo de la communion*. Lima, 1598, Antonio Ricardo.]

Pachacuti Yamqui Salcamaygua, Joan de Santacruz. 1993 [n.d.]. *Relacion de las antiguedades deste reyno del Piru. Estudio etnohistórico y lingüístico de Pierre Duviols y César Itier*, edited by Pierre Duviols and César Itier. Lima and Cuzco: Institut Français d'Études Andines and Centro de Estudios Regionales Andinos "Bartolomé de las Casas."

Pagden, Anthony. 1986. *The Fall of Natural Man: The American Indian and the Origins of Comparative Ethnology*. Cambridge: Cambridge University Press.

Parker, Gary J. 1963. La clasificación genética de los dialectos quechuas. *Revista del Museo Nacional* 32: 241–252.

Pease G. Y., Franklin. 1995. *Las crónicas y los Andes*. Lima and Mexico: Pontificia Universidad Católica del Perú, Instituto Riva-Agüero, and Fondo de Cultura Económica.

———. 1998. Garcilaso's Historical Approach to the Incas. In *Garcilaso Inca de la Vega: An American Humanist: A Tribute to José Durand*, edited by José Anadón, 32–41. Notre Dame, IN: University of Notre Dame Press.

Pello, Xavier. 2000. Los últimos días de Luis Jerónimo de Oré (1554–1630): Un nuevo documento biográfico. *Bulletin de l'Institut Français d'Études Andines* 29/2: 161–171.

Pérez Bocanegra, Juan. 1631. *Ritual formulario, e institucion de curas, para administrar a los naturales de este reyno, los santos sacramentos del baptismo, confirmacion, eucaristia, y viatico, penitencia, extremauncion, y matrimonio, con advertencias muy necessarias*. Lima: Jerónimo de Contreras.

Pérez Fernández, Isacio. 1986. *Bartolomé de Las Casas en el Perú. El espíritu lascasiano en la primera evangelización del imperio incaico (1531–1573)*. Cuzco: Centro de Estudios Regionales Andinos "Bartolomé de Las Casas."

Phelan, John Leddy. 1970 [1950]. *The Millennial Kingdom of the Franciscans in the New World.* Berkeley: University of California Press.

Polia Meconi, Mario, ed. 1999. *La cosmovisión religiosa andina en los documentos inéditos del Archivo Romano de la Compañía de Jesús (1581–1752).* Lima: Pontificia Universidad Católica del Perú.

Polo, José Toribio. 1906. Un quechuista. *Revista Histórica. Órgano del Instituto Histórico del Perú* 1: 24–38.

———. 1907. Luis Jerónimo de Oré. *Revista Histórica. Órgano del Instituto Histórico del Perú* 2: 74–91.

Prado, Pablo de. 1641. *Directorio espiritual en la lengua española, y quichua general del inga.* Lima: Jorge López de Herrera.

———. 1651 [1641]. *Directorio espiritual en la lengua española, y quichua general del inga.* Lima: Luis de Lira.

Prado, Pablo de, and Gaspar Manuel. 1705. *Selectas de el directorio espiritual en lengua española, y quichua general del inga que compusso, el P. Pablo de Prado de la Compañia . . . Reimpresso, y añadido por el P. Gaspar Manuel de la mesma Compañia. Y aora illustrado con otras de la explicacion de la doctrina del P. M. Geronymo de Ripalda de la misma Compañia, traducidas en dicha lengua en la gran ciudad del Cuzco.* Lima: Imprenta Real.

Quaderno de Directorio Espiritual. n.d. Eighteenth-century MS, BNP PR 185a.

Rafael, Vicente. 1993 [1988]. *Contracting Colonialism: Translation and Christian Conversion in Tagalog Society under Early Spanish Rule.* Durham, NC, and London: Duke University Press.

Real Academia Española. 1734. *Diccionario de la lengua española,* vol. 4. Madrid: Imprenta de la Real Academia Española.

Recopilación. 1987 [1681]. *Recopilación de leyes de los reynos de las Indias.* 4 vols. Mexico: Escuela Libre de Derecho and Miguel Angel Porrúa.

Ricard, Robert. 1966 [1933]. *The Spiritual Conquest of Mexico: An Essay on the Apostolate and the Evangelizing Methods of the Mendicant Orders in New Spain, 1523–1572,* translated by Leslie Byrd Simpson. Berkeley: University of California Press.

Richter, Federico, ed. n.d. [1600]. Información de méritos for Luis Jerónimo de Oré. *Anales de la Provincia Franciscana de los Doce Apostoles de Lima (Perú).* Lima: n.p.

Rivera Serna, Raúl. 1965. Un Ritual Romano en Lengua Chinchaysuya. *Boletín de la Biblioteca Nacional del Perú,* 18–19/35–36: 3–21.

Rivet, Paul, and Georges de Créqui-Montfort. 1951. *Bibliographie des langues aymará et kichua. Vol. I (1540–1875).* Paris: Institut d'Ethnologie.

Rodríguez, Pedro. 1998. *El Catecismo Romano ante Felipe II y la Inquisición Española.* Madrid: RIALP.

Rojo [Roxo] Mejía y Ocón, Juan. 1648. *Arte de la lengua general de los indios del Peru.* Lima: Jorge López de Herrera.

Romero, Carlos. 1928. "Un Libro interesante." *Revista Histórica* 9/1: 51–87.

Rosman, Rubel, and Abraham Rosman, eds. 2003. *Translating Cultures: Perspectives on Translation and Anthropology*. Oxford and New York: Berg.

Rostworowski, María. 1998. Pachacamac y el Señor de los Milagros. In *Native Traditions in the Postconquest World*, edited by Elizabeth Hill Boone and Tom Cummins, 345–359. Washington, DC: Dumbarton Oaks Research Library and Collection.

Salas, José Luis. 2000. *La evangelización franciscana de los guaraníes. Su apostol fray Luis Bolaños*. Asunción: n.p.

Sallnow, Michael. 1987. *Pilgrims of the Andes: Regional Cults in Cusco*. Washington, DC: Smithsonian Institution Press.

Salomon, Frank. 1991. Introductory Essay: The Huarochirí Manuscript. In Salomon and Urioste eds. 1991 [n.d.], 1–38.

———. 1994. La textualización de la memoria en la América andina: Una perspectiva etnográfica comparada. *América Indígena* 54/4: 229–261.

———. 2004. *The Cord Keepers: Khipus and Cultural Life in a Peruvian Village*. Durham, NC: Duke University Press.

Salomon, Frank, and George L. Urioste, eds. 1991 [n.d.]. *The Huarochirí Manuscript: A Testament of Ancient and Colonial Andean Religion*. Austin: University of Texas Press.

Santo Tomás, Domingo de. 1951 [1560]. *Lexicón o vocabulario de la lengua general del Perú* (facsimile edition). Lima: Instituto de Historia. [Original title and imprint: *Lexicon, o vocabulario de la lengua general del Peru*. Valladolid, 1560, Francisco Fernández de Córdova.]

———. 1995 [1560]. *Grammática o arte de la lengua general de los indios de los reynos del Perú por el maestro fray Domingo de Santo Tomás de la Orden de Santo Domingo*, edited by Rodolfo Cerrón-Palomino. Cuzco: Centro de Estudios Regionales Andinos "Bartolomé de Las Casas." [Original title and imprint: *Grammatica o arte de la lengua general de los indios de los reynos del Peru*. Valladolid, 1560, Francisco Fernández de Córdova.]

Sarmiento de Gamboa, Pedro. 1988 [1572]. *Historia de los incas*. Madrid: Miraguano Ediciones and Ediciones Polifemo.

Schieffelin, Bambi B., and Rachelle Charlier Doucet. 1998. The "Real" Haitian Creole: Ideology, Metalinguistics, and Orthographic Choice. In Schiefflin, Woolard, and Kroskrity eds. 1998, 285–316.

Schieffelin, Bambi B., Kathryn A. Woolard, and Paul V. Kroskrity, eds. 1998. *Language Ideologies: Practice and Theory*. Oxford and New York: Oxford University Press.

Seed, Patricia. 1991. "Failing to Marvel": Atahualpa's Encounter with the Word. *Latin American Research Review* 26/1: 7–22.

Sell, Barry David. 1993. Friars, Nahuas, and Books: Language and Expression in Colonial Nahuatl Publications. Ph.D. Dissertation, University of California at Los Angeles.

Shorter, Aylward. 1988. *Toward a Theology of Inculturation.* Maryknoll: Orbis Books.

Silverstein, Michael. 1997. The Improvisational Performance of Culture in Real-time Discursive Practice. In *Creativity in Performance,* edited by R. Keith Sawyer, 265–312. London: Ablex Publishing.

Silverstein, Michael, and Greg Urban. 1996. The Natural History of Discourse. In Silverstein and Urban eds. 1996, 1–17.

Silverstein, Michael, and Greg Urban, eds. 1996. *Natural Histories of Discourse.* Chicago and London: University of Chicago Press.

Simon, Sherry, and Paul St-Pierre, eds.. 2000. *Changing the Terms: Translating in the Postcolonial Era.* Ottawa: University of Ottawa Press.

Sixth Lima Council. 1772. Original del concilio provincial castellano de Lima celebrado el año de 1772 y de su version latina. MS volume in ACML.

Solano, Francisco, ed. 1991. *Documentos sobre la política lingüística en Hispanoamérica 1492–1800.* Madrid: Consejo Superior de Investigaciones Científicas.

Spalding, Karen. 1984. *Huarochirí: An Andean Society under Inca and Spanish Rule.* Stanford: Stanford University Press.

Stapper, Richard. 1935 [1931]. *Catholic Liturgics,* translated by David Baier. Paterson, NJ: St Anthony Guild Press.

Stern, Steve J. 1993 [1982]. *Peru's Indian Peoples and the Challenge of the Spanish Conquest.* 2d ed. Wisconsin: University of Wisconsin Press.

Stevenson, Robert. 1968. *Music in Aztec and Inca Territory.* Berkeley and Los Angeles: University of California Press.

Stewart, Charles. 1999. Syncretism and Its Synonyms: Reflections on Cultural Mixture. *Diacritics* 29/3: 40–62.

Stewart, Charles, and Rosalind Shaw. 1994. Introduction: Problematizing Syncretism. In *Syncretism/Anti-Syncretism: The Politics of Religious Synthesis,* edited by Charles Stewart and Rosalind Shaw, 1–26. London and New York: Routledge.

Szemiñski, Jan. 1997. *Wira Quchan y sus obras. Teología andina y lenguaje, 1550–1662.* Lima: Instituto de Estudios Peruanos and Banco de Reserva del Perú.

Tavárez, David. 2000. Naming the Trinity: From Ideologies of Translation to Dialectics of Reception in Colonial Nahua Texts, 1547–1771. *Colonial Latin American Review* 9/1: 21–47.

Taylor, Gerald. 1987. Cultos y fiestas de la comunidad de San Damián (Huarochirí) según la *carta annua* de 1609. *Bulletin de l'Institut Français d'Études Andines* 16/3–4: 86–96.

———. 1992. La normalización de la enseñanza del Quechua. In Godenzzi ed. 1992, 179–183.

———. 1999. Les sermons des religieux espagnols cités dans la chronique de Guaman Poma de Ayala. *Amerindia* 24: 213–226.

———. 2000a [1974–1976]. *Camac, camay* y *camasca* en el manuscrito quechua de Huarochirí. In Gerald Taylor, *Camac, camay y camasca y otros ensayos sobre Huaro-*

chirí y Yauyos, 1–17. Lima: Institut Français d'Études Andines and Centro de Estudios Regionales Andinos "Bartolomé de Las Casas."

———. 2000b [1995]. Dos "mapas" del pueblo de Cocha-Laraos (1595, 1597). In Gerald Taylor, *Camac, camay y camasca y otros ensayos sobre Huarochirí y Yauyos,* 89–104. Lima: Institut Français d'Études Andines and Centro de Estudios Regionales Andinos "Bartolomé de Las Casas."

———. 2000c. La Plática Breve de la *Doctrina Christiana* (1584). *Amerindia* 25: 173–188.

———. 2000d [1985]. Lengua general y lenguas particulares en la antigua provincia de Yauyos. Un documento quechua de Huarochirí – 1608. In Gerald Taylor *Camac, camay y camasca y otros ensayos sobre Huarochirí y Yauyos,* 35–69. Lima: Institut Français d'Études Andines and Centro de Estudios Regionales Andinos "Bartolomé de Las Casas."

———. 2000e [1980]. Supay. In Gerald Taylor *Camac, camay y camasca y otros ensayos sobre Huarochirí y Yauyos,* 19–34. Lima: Institut Français d'Études Andines and Centro de Estudios Regionales Andinos "Bartolomé de Las Casas."

———. 2001a. Un sermón quechua de Diego de Molina (Huánuco, 1649). *Bulletin de l'Institut Français d'Études Andines* 30/2: 211–231.

———. 2001b. La *Platica* de fray Domingo de Santo Tomás. *Bulletin de l'Institut Français d'Études Andines* 30/3: 427–453.

———. 2002. *Sermones y ejemplos. Antología bilingüe castellano-quechua. Siglo XVII.* Lima: Instituto Francés de Estudios Andinos and Lluvia Editores.

———. 2003. *El sol, la luna y las estellas no son Dios . . . La evangelización en quechua (siglo XVI).* Lima: Instituto Francés de Estudios Andinos and Pontificia Universidad Católica del Perú.

Taylor, Gerald, ed. 1999 [1987, n.d.]. *Ritos y tradiciones de Huarochirí.* 2d rev. ed. Lima: Instituto Francés de Estudios Andinos, Banco Central de Reserva del Perú, and Universidad Particular Ricardo Palma.

Tedlock, Dennis. 1983. *The Spoken Word and the Work of Interpretation.* Philadelphia: University of Pennsylvania Press.

Terraciano, Kevin. 2001. *The Mixtecs of Colonial Oaxaca: Ñudzahui History, Sixteenth through Eighteenth Centuries.* Stanford: Stanford University Press.

Third Lima Council. 1583. Originales del concilio limense de S° Toribio Mogrovejo su arçobispo. MS in ACML, Volúmenes Independientes 4.

Third Lima Council. 1985a [1584]. *Doctrina christiana y catecismo para instruccion de indios.* In *Doctrina christiana y catecismo para instrucción de indios. Facsímil del texto trilingüe,* edited by Luciano Pereña, 5–188. Madrid: Consejo Superior de Investigaciones Científicas. [Original title and imprint: *Doctrina christiana, y catecismo para instruccion de los indios, y de las demas personas, que han de ser enseñadas en nuestra sancta fe. Con un confesionario, y otras cosas necessarias para los que doctrinan . . . Compuesto por auctoridad del concilio provincial, que se celebro en la Ciudad de los Reyes, el año de 1583. Y por la misma traduzida en las dos lenguas generales, de este reyno, quichua, y aymara.* Lima, 1584, Antonio Ricardo.]

———. 1985b [1585]. *Confessionario para los curas de indios.* In *Doctrina christiana y catecismo para instrucción de indios. Facsímil del texto trilingüe,* edited by Luciano Pereña, 189–332. Madrid: Consejo Superior de Investigaciones Científicas. [Original title and imprint: *Confessionario para los curas de indios. Con la instruccion contra sus ritos: Y exhortacion para ayudar a bien morir: Y suma de privilegios: Y forma de impedimentos del matrimonio. Compuesto y traduzido en las lenguas quichua y aymara. Por autoridad del concilio provincial de Lima, del año de 1583.* Lima, 1585, Antonio Ricardo.]

———. 1985c [1585]. *Tercero cathecismo y exposicion de la doctrina christiana por sermones.* In *Doctrina christiana y catecismo para instrucción de indios. Facsímil del texto trilingüe,* edited by Luciano Pereña, 333–777. Madrid: Consejo Superior de Investigaciones Científicas. [Original title and imprint: *Tercero cathecismo y exposicion de la doctrina christiana, por sermones. Para que los curas y otros ministros prediquen y enseñen a los yndios y a las demas personas. Conforme a lo que en el sancto concilio provincial de Lima se proveyo.* Lima, 1585, Antonio Ricardo.]

Torero, Alfredo. 1964. Los dialectos quechuas. *Anales Científicos de la Universidad Agraria* 2: 446–478.

———. 1974. *El quechua y la historia social andina.* Lima: Universidad Ricardo Palma.

———. 1987. Lenguas y pueblos altiplánicos en torno al siglo XVI. *Revista Andina* 10/2: 330–405.

———. 1995. Acerca de la lengua chinchaysuyo. In *Del siglo de oro al siglo de las luces. Lenguaje y sociedad en los Andes del siglo XVIII,* edited by César Itier, 13–31. Cuzco: Centro de Estudios Regionales Andinos "Bartolomé de Las Casas."

———. 1997. Entre Roma y Lima. El *Lexicón* quichua de fray Domingo de Santo Tomás [1560]. In *La descripción de las lenguas amerindias en la época colonial,* edited by Klaus Zimmermann, 270–290. Frankfurt am Main and Madrid: Vervuert and Iberoamericana.

———. 2002. *Idiomas de los Andes: Lingüística e historia.* Lima: Instituto Francés de Estudios Andinos and Editorial Horizonte.

Torres, Julio, ed. 1970. *Sínodos diocesanos de Santo Toribio 1582–1604.* Centro Intercultural de Documentación, Fuentes 1. Cuernavaca: Centro Intercultural de Documentación.

Torres Rubio, Diego de. 1619. *Arte de la lengua quichua.* Lima: Francisco Lasso.

Torres Rubio, Diego de, and Juan de Figueredo. 1701. *Arte de la lengua quichua, por el P. Diego de Torres Rubio de la Compañia de Jesus. Y nuevamente van añadidos los romances, el cathecismo pequeño, todas las oraciones, los dias de fiesta, y ayunos de los indios, el vocabulario añadido, y otro vocabulario de la lengua Chinchaisuyo.* Lima: José de Contreras y Alvarado.

Torres Rubio, Diego de, Juan de Figueredo, et al. 1754. *Arte y vocabulario de la lengua quichua general de los indios de el Peru. Que compuso el Padre Diego de Torres de la Compañia de Jesus, y añadio el P. Juan de Figueredo de la misma Compañia. Ahora nuevamente corregido, y aumentado en muchos vocablos, y varias advertencias, notas, y observaciones, para *la mejor inteligencia del ydioma, y perfecta instrucion de los parochos, y cathequistas de indios.* Lima: Imprenta de la plazuela de San Cristóbal.

Torres Saldamando, Enrique. 1882. *Antiguos jesuitas del Perú. Biografías y apuntes para su historia.* Lima: n.p.

Toury, Gideon. 1995. *Descriptive Translation Studies and Beyond.* Amsterdam: John Benjamins.

Tupac Amaru. 1983. *Tupac Amaru y la iglesia. Antología.* Lima: Unidad de Comunicaciones del Banco Continental.

Tymoczko, Maria, and Edwin Gentzler, eds. 2002. *Translation and Power.* Amherst and Boston: University of Massachusetts Press.

Untitled Devotionary. n.d. Untitled eighteenth-century Quechua MS, Biblioteca del Convento de San Francisco de Ayacucho.

Urbano, Henrique. 1987. El escándalo de Chucuito y la primera evangelización de los Lupaqa (Perú). Nota en torno a un documento inédito de 1574. *Cuadernos para la Historia de la Evangelización en América Latina* 2: 203–228.

———. 1991. *Wiracocha y Ayar. Heroes y funciones en las sociedades andinas.* Cuzco: Centro de Estudios Rurales Andinos "Bartolomé de Las Casas."

Urteaga, Horacio, and Carlos Romero, eds. 1916. *Relación de las fábulas y ritos de los incas.* Collección de Libros y Documentos referentes a la Historia del Perú, vol. 1. Lima: Imprenta y Librería Sanmartí y Cia.

Urton, Gary. 1981. *At the Crossroads of the Earth and the Sky: An Andean Cosmology.* Austin: University of Texas Press.

———. 1990. *The History of a Myth: Pacariqtambo and the Origin of the Inkas.* Austin: University of Texas Press.

———. 2003. *Signs of the Inka Khipu: Binary Coding in the Andean Knotted-String Records.* Austin: University of Texas Press.

Van den Broeck, Raymond. 1981. The Limits of Translatability Exemplified by Metaphor Translation. *Poetics Today* 2/4: 73–87.

Vargas Ugarte, Rubén. 1956. *Historia del culto a María en Iberoamérica y de sus imágenes y santuarios más celebrados.* 3rd ed. 2 vols. Madrid.

Vargas Ugarte, Rubén, ed. 1951–1954. *Concilios limenses (1551–1772).* 3 vols. Lima: Tipografía Peruana.

Wightman, Ann. 1990. *Indigenous Migration and Social Change: The Forasteros of Cuzco, 1570–1720.* Durham and London: Duke University Press.

Winston-Allen, Anne. 1997. *Stories of the Rose: The Making of the Rosary in the Middle Ages.* Pennsylvania: Pennsylvania State University Press.

Woolard, Kathryn. 2002. Bernardo de Aldrete and the Morisco Problem: A Study in Early Modern Spanish Language Ideology. *Comparative Studies in Society and History* 44/2: 446–480.

Yates, Frances A. 1966. *The Art of Memory.* Chicago: University of Chicago Press.

Zamora, Margarita. 1988. *Language, Authority, and Indigenous History in the Comentarios reales de los incas.* Cambridge: Cambridge University Press.

Zuidema, R. T. 1982. Catachillay: The Role of the Pleiades and of the Southern Cross and α and β Centauri in the Calendar of the Incas. *Annals of the New York Academy of Sciences* 385: 203–229.

Županov, Ines. 1999. *Disputed Mission: Jesuit Experiments and Brahmanical Knowledge in Seventeenth-Century India.* New Delhi: Oxford University Press.

———. 2003. Twisting a Pagan Tongue: Portuguese and Tamil in Sixteenth-Century Jesuit Translations. In *Conversion: Old Worlds and New,* edited by Kenneth Mills and Anthony Grafton, 109–139. Rochester, NY: University of Rochester Press.

———. 2005. *Missionary Tropics: The Catholic Frontier in India (16th–17th Centuries).* Ann Arbor: University of Michigan Press.

Index

accommodation, 12–15, 63–64, 65, 85, 194, 213, 246–247, 306–307, 309
acllas: as nuns, 143, 159, 208, 218, 314
Acosta, José de: on conversion strategy, 81, 83–85; on Inca culture, 14, 83–84, 85, 143; on language competence, 82, 133; on loan words, 84; and Third Lima Council, 88; and Third Lima Council works, 91, 92, 97, 98, 101
adapted terms, 70, 207, 208, 209–210, 308, 325n21; in postcouncil works, 217, 218, 219; in Santo Tomás, 211–212; in Third Lima Council works, 215–217
Adelaar, Willem, 8
ad sensum versus *ad literam* translation, 228–229
Aguilar, Juan de, 176
Alexander VI, 262
Almaraz, Juan de, 97
alumbrados, 284, 287
Alvarez de Paz, Diego, 135–136
Amazon lowlands, 169
Andahuaylillas: baptistery entrance mural, 123–124, 294; image of Christ Child at, 252; Pérez Bocanegra at, 155, 339nn23–24
Andean languages, 40–42. *See also* Aymara; Culli; Mochica; Puquina
Andean religious terms and categories (in pastoral Quechua), 62, 67, 70, 75, 145, 150, 156, 159, 194, 208, 211–219 passim, 232–233, 246–270 passim, 307–308, 310
angels, 96, 142, 243, 250, 251, 281; Quechua terms for, 70, 84, 212, 213, 214
Anonymous Jesuit (the elder), 142–143, 314
Anonymous Jesuit (the younger), 252
Aptaycachana (Castromonte), 171, 341n42. *See also* Castromonte, Juan de
Aquaviva, Claudio, 135–136
Aramaic, 295, 297
Arequipa, 38, 39, 97, 98, 107, 160
Arequipa (diocese of), 17, 30, 131; language licensing, 117; translation, 124; synods, 124, 132, 140
Arias, Juan, 153
Arias, Miguel, 153
Arias de Saavedra, Pedro, 116
Arias de Ugarte, Fernando, 31, 132, 174

Arriaga, José de, 121, 139, 284
Arte y vocabulario (Anonymous), 91, 93, 117, 120–121, 159, 197, 329n33
Asunción (Paraguay), 160
Atahuallpa, 53, 314–315
Atienza, Juan de, 101
Augustine of Hippo, St., 295
Augustinians: early missions, 58–59; and translation, 73, 97, 106, 152–153, 332n7. *See also* Martínez, Juan
Avendaño, Fernando de, 165–166; on Chinchaysuyo Quechua, 128; on Incas, 168; linguistic features of Quechua texts, 183, 202, 203, 205, 230, 340n37, 355n37; on origins of Quechua and Aymara, 44–45; Quechua examiner, 334n30; rivalry with Avila, 340n34; rivalry with Rojo Mejía y Ocón, 130; sermons, 167
Avila, Francisco de, 30, 164–165, 340n34; on Incas, 168–169; linguistic features of Quechua texts, 202, 203, 205, 259, 300, 302; Quechua examiner, 334n30; sermons, 167, 229–230, 289; terminology and tropes, 231, 232, 259
Ayacucho. *See* Huamanga
Ayacucho Quechua, 39, 178, 191–192, 323n15, 343n14
Ayllon, Nicolás de, 175
ayllus, 175; and organization of catechesis, 82, 274, 290
Aymara, 40–41, 44–46; and Incas, 42; pastoral texts in, 82–83, 85–86, 124, 140, 147, 148, 152, 153, 161, 225; testing of clergy in, 124; in Third Lima Council works, 46, 88, 89, 97, 107, 194
Aymaraes, 153
Babel, Tower of, 42; origin of Quechua and Aymara, 44–45
Bajo, Pedro Alonso, 335n42
Bakhtin, Mikhail, 4
Balboa, Juan de, 80; on Third Lima Council Quechua translation team, 97, 99, 107, 330n42; university Quechua chair, 115, 116, 119, 120
baptism, 27, 56, 279; form for, 94, 123–124, 208–209, 272, 279; terms for, 208–209, 219
Barroeta y Angel, Pedro Antonio de, 176–177
Barzana, Alonso de, 83, 91, 98, 108, 123, 329n33
basic prayers, 19; in catechesis, 55, 56, 273, 274; First Lima Council version, 68, 69; in the mass, 55, 275; Third Lima Council version, 104. *See also* cartillas
Bedón, Pedro, 97
belief (terms for), 200, 216, 218, 220
Bellarmino, Roberto, 153, 170, 223–224
Belt of Orion, 263, 268
Berrío, Agustín, 122
Bertonio, Ludovico, 85–86, 160–161, 226, 264
Betanzos, Juan de, 66, 67, 191, 210, 306
Beyersdorff, Margot, 151, 256, 276
Bible: translation of, 33, 34, 35, 222, 231, 329n30
Bolivia, 1, 18; Quechua texts from, 178, 320n12, 342n55
Bolivian Quechua, 38, 178, 182, 342n55
Burke, Peter, 9, 31, 32
Burkhart, Louise, 65

Cabana y Guandoval, 126, 170
Cacan (language), 123, 335n40
Cahill, David, 251–252
Cajabamba, 153

Cajamarca, 126, 314, 315
Cajatambo, 245
Cajica, Juan de, 153
Calancha, Antonio de la, 58–59, 153
Camiña, 117
Campo, Gonzalo de, 30–31, 170, 174
canonical hours, 20, 59, 139; in Oré's work, 150, 151, 223, 242; performance of, 58, 274–275, 282, 283
cantors, 77, 140, 273, 282, 283, 291, 292, 352n10. *See also* choirs
Capac Yupanqui. *See* Inca Yupanqui
Carlos Inca, 332n10
Carrasco, Francisco, 97, 98, 99, 107
cartillas, 19; of diocese of Cuzco, 72–74; early, 67; of first Jesuit congregation, 82–83; of First Lima Council, 55, 68–69, 71; performance of, 55, 273–274, 281, 292; of Third Lima Council, 88–89, 103, 132, 227, 329n31
Castelnau-l'Estoile, Charlotte, 136
Castromonte, Juan de, 138, 171, 341n42, 347n7; eucharistic hymn by, 278; linguistic features of Quechua texts, 202–203, 204–205, 206; terminology and tropes, 218, 220, 278
Catachillay, 263, 264, 267, 351nn20–23
catechesis, 18–19, 54, 55, 57, 273–274, 289–290; by Jesuits, 81–82, 274, 289–290; languages of, 55, 68, 109, 124, 132
catechisms, 19; of diocese of Cuzco, 72–74; of first Jesuit congregation, 82–83; of Jurado Palomino, 170; of Oré, 140, 152; of Pérez Bocanegra, 154, 156; performance of, 81–82, 89, 273–274, 289–290; of Second Lima Council, 71; of Third Lima Council, 88, 89, 103, 173
Cejuela, Roque de, 125
Centeno de Osma, Gabriel, 356n4
Central Quechua, 38; apologetics for, 121, 127–128, 130, 313; critiques of, 93, 129, 192; and language competence system, 117, 118, 127; in linguistic works, 93, 176, 177, 201–202; in pastoral Quechua works, 128–129, 163, 171, 198, 202–206 passim, 244–245, 297; policy of archdiocese of Lima towards, 125–126, 127, 163, 201; and Standard Colonial Quechua, 109–110, 206
Cerrón-Palomino, Rodolfo, 2, 8, 42, 46, 194, 218, 322n10, 322n12
Chacana, 263, 265, 268
Chacos, 134
Charcas, 18, 107
Checacupe, 124
Chile, 135, 149
Chincha, 40, 190
Chinchaysuyo, 93
Chinchaysuyo Quechua, 93, 113, 126–127, 171, 188, 198. *See also* Central Quechua
Chiriguano (language), 123, 335n40
choirs, 58, 61, 63, 140, 155, 262, 275, 282, 283, 290, 292. *See also* cantors
Choquecasa, Cristóbal, 281, 352n8
Christ: epithets for, 62–63, 216–217, 232–233; as hamancay flower, 266; as Pachacamac, 257–258; as sacrificial llama, 232–233, 258–261; as source of irrigation waters, 254–256. *See also* Christ Child; passion; Señor de los Milagros; Señor de los Temblores
Christ Child, 225; images of, 251–252, 253, 254, 350n13

Chuquisaca, 59, 160
cislocative suffix, 297, 298–299
Citua festival, 75
coastal Quechua, 40, 48, 188, 190, 198, 322n10
Cobo, Bernabé, 170
code mixing, 294–297
cofradías, 140, 175, 279–280, 282–283
Collaguas, 148, 150, 335n42
Colla Indians, 300
Collca, 263, 265. *See also* Pleiades
college of San Martín, 166
communion: in First Lima Council, 56, 57, 278–279; promoted by Jesuits, 83; texts about, 140, 148, 150, 152, 153, 158, 227, 278–279; in Third Lima Council, 87, 94. *See also* eucharist
Conchucos, 125, 126, 170
confesionarios, 20, 277, 288; of Betanzos, 67; of first Jesuit congregation, 82–83; of Pérez Bocanegra, 154, 201, 234, 245, 284; of Second Lima Council, 71–72; of Third Lima Council, 88, 90, 121, 198 (see also *Confessionario para los curas de indios*); of Torres Rubio, 161, 218
confession, 29, 56, 84, 277–278, 294, 300; and Andean concept of *hucha*, 211–212, 287; and language skills, 82, 87, 124; terms for, 213, 214; use of quipus in, 278, 286–288
Confessionario para los curas de indios (Third Lima Council), 88, 90, 94, 95, 237, 280, 294, 315. *See also* Third Lima Council works
confirmation, 206
Copacabana, Virgin of, 262
coplas, 223, 284
Coporaque, 148, 335n42
Corbacho de Zárate, Alonso, 118, 334n30
Coricancha, 169, 253, 259
Cornejo, Luis, 155, 156
Corpus Christi, 64–65, 226, 253, 275; and Inti Raymi, 325n15; and taquis, 61, 62, 63
corregidores, 27, 102, 116, 125, 273
Cotabambas, 353n17
Council of Trent, 19, 29, 34, 36, 57, 71. *See also* Counter-Reformation
Counter-Reformation, 19, 29, 34–35, 64–65, 76, 304, 305
creation, 30, 66; terms for, 208, 213, 215–216, 239
creeds, 147; Apostles' (Credo), 19, 55, 56, 68, 69, 89, 173, 215, 275, 284; Athanasian, 150, 159, 227, 228, 248, 274; Nicene, 218, 219, 222, 346n42
Crickmay, Lindsey, 327n33
criollos, 16, 114, 117; identity politics in Cuzco, 21, 253, 310, 314; rivalry with peninsulares, 133, 336n65
Culli (language), 18, 41, 106, 125, 126, 332n7
curacas, 27, 61, 108, 144, 273, 286
Cuzco, 2, 63, 154, 160, 164, 191; under Incas, 251, 253, 259; indigenous Christianity in, 252, 284; Jesuits in, 82, 112, 116, 140; as origin point of Quechua, 37, 112–113; Quechua translation in, 72–75, 306, 309, 310
Cuzco (diocese of), 26, 56; language licensing, 115, 116, 124; pastoral works of, 72–75; reception of Third Lima Council works in, 102–103; synods, 102, 140, 148, 275
Cuzco Quechua, 37, 39, 177, 178; evidential suffixes in, 185; exaltation of, 112–113, 129, 313; in

González Holguín and Pérez Bocanegra, 199–201; and Standard Colonial Quechua, 46, 47, 49, 93, 106–107, 112–113, 191–197
Cuzqueñismo, 253, 254, 314

Dávila Morales, Juan Antonio, 342n55
Dean, Carolyn, 62
Declaracion copiosa (Jurado Palomino), 170. *See also* Jurado Palomino, Bartolomé
Dedenbach-Salazar Sáenz, Sabine, 182, 183, 209–210, 327n33
de la Carrera, Fernando, 125, 332n7
de la Cruz, Francisco (the elder), 44, 59–62
de la Cruz, Francisco (the younger), 155, 156, 173–174
del Aguila, Melchor, 72–73, 74, 196
de la Raya, Antonio, 116, 148–149
devils (terms for), 70, 92, 212
dialectology, 4, 5, 37–39, 185; in mid-seventeenth-century works, 202–206; in Oré, 198–199; in Pérez Bocanegra, 200–201; in postcouncil works, 197–206; in Santo Tomás, 188–190; in Third Lima Council works, 191–194. *See also* Central Quechua; coastal Quechua; Southern Quechua; Standard Colonial Quechua
Díaz, Alonso, 97, 98–99
dictionaries. *See* linguistic works
diglossia, 48, 109, 131
Directorio espiritual (Prado), 157–158, 222, 276; linguistic features of Quechua texts, 198, 300; manuscript versions, 177; performance guidelines in, 142, 224, 275, 277, 281–282, 288; reeditions, 157–158, 176; terminology and tropes, 218, 259, 260–261. See also *Selectas de el directorio espiritual*
disjunction, 63–64, 269–270
Doctrina christiana y catecismo (Third Lima Council), 88, 89, 92, 93, 97, 101, 103, 177; linguistic appendix of, 188, 192–197 passim, 209, 216, 227–228. *See also* Third Lima Council works
Dominicans, 59, 61, 103, 120, 141; in Mesoamerica, 211, 226, 304; and Pérez Bocanegra, 154, 155–156; and Toledo, 78–79; and translation, 68, 153, 305. *See also* Santo Tomás, Domingo de
Dumézil, Georges, 165, 229, 340n35
Duviols, Pierre, 138–139, 337n7

Ecuador, 1, 18; Quechua texts from, 178, 320n12, 342n55
Ecuadorian Quechua, 38, 126–127, 178, 342n55
encomienda, 190, 343n12
endogenous versus exogenous translation, 12, 16, 224
Enrríquez, Martín, 86, 109
epithets: for Christ, 62–63, 216–217, 232–233; for God, 96, 216–217, 247–251; for the Inca sovereign, 62–63, 247–248, 250–251; for Mary, 216–217, 233, 262–268; for Viracocha, 75, 150, 213, 248–250
Erasmus of Rotterdam, 33, 95
Espinosa Medrano, Juan, 320n15
estancias, 174–175, 282
Estenssoro Fuchs, Juan Carlos, 2, 27, 29, 58, 60, 61, 63–64, 65, 70, 83, 145, 175, 212, 226, 240, 269
eucharist, 57, 62, 140, 274, 276–277; texts about, 140, 278–279, 293, 299; tropes for, 151, 168, 250,

eucharist (*cont.*)
259–261, 265, 278–279. *See also* communion
evidential suffixes, 182, 183–185, 297, 300–302
exempla, 141, 170, 281–282, 299–300, 301
extirpation of idolatry, 16, 30–31, 138–139, 175, 232–233; and mid-seventeenth-century works, 163, 165, 166, 167, 168, 170
extreme unction, 57, 222, 279, 280. *See also* Last Rites

Fabian, Johannes, 111
Faller, Martina, 185, 300
fasting (terms for), 214, 218
feast days, 175, 275–276; terms for, 156, 218
Felipillo, 53, 315
Figueredo, Juan de, 176
First Lima Council, 54–56, 225; and Quechua translation, 67–69
First Mexican Council, 36
fiscales, 77, 273, 282, 284, 285, 291, 352n10
Foucault, Michel, 290
Franciscans: language competence, 120, 134; liturgy in early missions, 58; in Mesoamerica, 60, 211; and passion, 151, 168, 305; translation, 103, 151, 168, 254, 305. *See also* Molina, Diego de; Oré, Luis Jerónimo de

Gal, Susan, 10, 113
García, Gregorio, 44
García de Castro, Lope, 56–57
Garcilaso (Garcilaso Inca de la Vega), 37, 63–64, 143, 146, 149, 225, 250, 314–315
Gethsemane, garden of, 255, 295
gift of tongues (Pentecostal), 82, 122–123
Gilberti, Maturino, 36
God: epithets for, 96, 216–217, 247–251; identified with Inca sovereign, 247–248, 250–251; terms for, 67, 84, 142, 143, 210–211, 338n11. *See also* Pachacamac; Viracocha
Godoy, Francisco de, 173
González, Lorenzo, 97
González de Cuenca, Gregorio, 57
González Holguín, Diego, 158–161; on gift of tongues, 122; orthography, 199–200, 203; on preaching, 159, 200; on sudden-disclosure suffix, 299; terminology and tropes, 159–160, 226, 232, 250, 259
grammars. *See* linguistic works
Granada, Luis de, 147, 152, 153
Greek: code mixing with, 295, 296; as source language, 209
Gregory XIII, 80
Guaman Poma de Ayala, Felipe, 49, 75, 234; on Andean Christianity, 143–144, 145; devotional program of, 142, 283; on Jesuit *coplas*, 223, 284; pastoral Quechua texts by, 161–162; on Quechua of priests, 74, 94, 188, 283–284
Guarani (language), 89, 123, 147, 210, 224, 226, 304
Gutiérrez, Baltazar, 335n42

hamancay (flower), 265, 266, 267
Hanac pachap cussicuinin (Pérez Bocanegra), 262, 264–265, 269, 293; as dry season hymn, 267–268
harauis, 61–62, 159, 225
Haroldus, Franciscus, 95–96, 330n40
hayllis, 63–64, 226
heaven (terms for), 213, 215

Hebrew: as ancestor of Quechua, 44, 60; code mixing with, 295, 296
hell (terms for), 145, 213, 215
Hermans, Theo, 6, 228
Hispanization, 33, 36, 111, 130–133, 172–173, 177
Holy Week, 65, 276
Huacaña, 282
huacas, 56, 226, 235, 249, 281, 324n3; under Christian guise, 65, 226; identified with crucified Christ, 156, 256–258, 270; and pastoral Quechua categories, 211, 212, 215, 237, 239; term in pastoral Quechua, 211. *See also* Huanacauri; Pachacamac; Viracocha
Huamachuco: Augustinians in, 58–59, 106, 153
Huamanga, 47, 126, 148, 157, 309, 323n15
Huamanga (diocese of), 17, 30, 126; Hispanization effort, 132; language licensing, 116–117; synods, 140, 141, 148
Huanacauri, 251, 350n12
Huancabamba, 171
Huancavelica, 47, 77, 111
Huánuco, 117, 134, 166, 171, 204
Huarochirí, 62, 164; Jesuits in, 62, 108–109
Huarochirí Manuscript, 48, 141–142, 164, 235, 249, 257, 281
Huaylas, 99, 290
Huerta, Alonso de: on Central Quechua, 126–127, 201; grammar by, 118, 121, 127, 201–202; Quechua instructor and examiner, 117–118, 127
Huidobro de Miranda, Juan, 132
humanism, 31–32, 35, 146–147, 228
Hyland, Sabine, 83, 98, 337n10
hymns and songs, 223, 239–241, 293; to Mary, 262, 264–269 passim; on passion, 254–261 passim, 276; use by Jesuits, 82, 223, 284. See also *Hanac pachap cussicuinin*; Oré, Luis Jerónimo de; Pérez Bocanegra, Juan

iconicity/iconization, 10, 113, 295, 297, 355n39
iconography. *See* tropes
Illimo, 125
Immaculate Conception (doctrine of), 261
Inca empire, 2, 53, 215; expansion of, 39; language policies of, 39–40, 42, 112–113, 131; lingua franca of, 40, 46, 67, 70, 111, 188, 189–190, 191, 322n10
Incaism, 253–254, 310, 311, 314
Incarnation (doctrine of), 60, 91, 261; terms for, 346n42
Incas: multilingualism of, 42, 193, 194; their religious terms and categories in pastoral Quechua, 62, 67, 75, 145, 150, 156, 159, 194, 208, 216–217, 218, 219, 232–233, 246–270 passim, 307–308, 310
Incas (discourses about), 43–44, 66, 74–75, 81, 142–143, 144, 149–150, 306, 307, 308, 314; in mid-seventeenth-century sermons, 168–170, 308; negative, 14, 78, 83–84, 85; translation practice as expression of, 63–64, 67, 145, 159, 220, 270, 306–307, 310
Inca sovereign: as divine being, 63, 247; epithets and titles in Christian contexts, 62–63, 156, 216–217, 219, 220, 247–248, 250–251; regalia in Christian

Inca sovereign (*cont.*)
contexts, 248–249, 250, 251–252, 253 (see also *mascapaycha*)
Inca Yupanqui: monotheism of, 66, 74, 75, 149, 150
indulgences, 139, 142, 152–153, 262, 276–277, 281
Inquisition, 35, 36–37, 59, 173
instruction. *See* language competence
interpretatio christiana, 63–64, 269–270, 308
interpreters, 53, 79, 82, 109, 126, 131, 190, 315
Inti. *See* Sun god
Inti Raymi, 325n15
Irvine, Judith, 10, 113
Itier, César, 2, 21, 39, 47, 48, 128, 156, 183, 199, 200, 208, 209, 210, 213, 225, 226, 266

Jacob's ladder, 268, 301
Jauja, 148, 150
Jerome, St., 228
Jesuits: in Asia, 13–14, 85, 146; in Brazil, 136; catechesis, 81–82, 274, 289–290; conversion strategy, 81–86; *coplas*, 82, 223, 284; in Cuzco, 82, 112, 116, 140; first provincial congregation, 82–83; in Huarochirí, 62, 108–109; influence in Third Lima Council works, 91–92, 100–101; language competence, 82, 108, 114, 116, 132, 135–136; linguistic standardization, 110–111, 112; plays, 225; quipus, 284–285, 286–287; second provincial congregation, 83; translation projects, 82–83, 305, 307. *See also* Barzana, Alonso de; González Holguín, Diego; Prado, Pablo de; Santiago, Bartolomé de; Torres Rubio, Diego de
Jews: Incas compared to, 169; Indians as descendants of, 44, 60, 65, 83
John the Baptist, St., 232
Juli, 81, 161, 225, 340n32
Jurado Palomino, Bartolomé, 138, 170, 273, 300; linguistic features of Quechua texts, 202, 203, 300

Kamen, Henry, 35–36

ladino Indians, 124, 227, 273, 283
Ladrón de Guevara, Fernando, 335n42
Lambayeque, 125
Landerman, Peter, 38
language competence (Quechua requirements, instruction, and testing), 55, 57, 79, 82, 87, 114–123, 127, 177; and Central Quechua, 127, 128; decline of interest in, 172; limits of, 133–136; and Third Lima Council works, 115, 116, 120–121
language hierarchy, 312–313; in liturgy, 281–282; in pastoral Quechua editions, 230, 293–294; textual expressions of, 123–124, 294–297
language ideologies, 9–10, 23–24; in early modern Europe, 31–33; and language competence, 122–123; and perceptions of Quechua and other Andean languages, 40, 42–45, 313; and Standard Colonial Quechua, 112–114
language shift, 41, 48, 109–110, 307
La Paz, 6, 286–287
Lartaun, Sebastián de, 73–74, 86, 99, 116
Las Casas, Bartolomé de, 66, 70, 78
Last Rites, 279–280; in Third Lima Council works, 90, 95
Latin: as language of religious instruction, 55, 68, 74, 87; as

source language in translation, 227–228, 229
Lavallé, Bernard, 336n65
lengua general, 41, 46, 108–109, 110, 125–126, 323n15. *See also* Standard Colonial Quechua
lengua materna, 41, 108, 125, 126
lengua particular. See *lengua materna*
León, Luis de, 35
lexical pairing, 215–216, 234, 235, 237, 238–239; in hymns, 243–245; translinguistic, 244–245, 297
Lima, 25–26, 253; audiencia of, 17, 26, 56–57, 100, 101–102, 115; as center of Quechua studies, 114, 115, 117–119; translation in, 309–310
Lima (archdiocese of), 30–31, 57, 109; and Central Quechua, 125–130 passim, 163, 201; language licensing, 118–119, 120; Quechua chair, 79, 117–118, 172; synods, 30, 90, 101, 125, 132, 139–140, 141
lingua franca, 41; of Inca empire, 40, 46, 67, 70, 111, 188, 189–190, 191, 322n10
linguistic works (on Quechua), 20, 67, 83. See also *Arte y vocabulario;* González Holguín, Diego; Huerta, Alonso de; Santo Tomás, Domingo de; Torres Rubio, Diego de
litanies, 61, 140; of Oré, 139, 150, 262, 264, 265, 267, 268, 269, 274, 290, 350n18; Penitential, 280; of Third Lima Council, 90, 95–96
literacy (Quechua), 48–49, 107, 273, 313
liturgy, 18–20; during early period, 58–59; native agency in, 282–283; in Oré's work, 150–151; performance, 274–280, 289–293; in postcouncil period, 138–141; in Third Lima Council works, 94–96. *See also* rituals
llamas (sacrificial), 75; Christ identified with, 232–233, 258–261
loan words, 11, 14, 206–207, 293, 307, 312, 315; Acosta on, 84; in Third Lima Council works, 92, 102, 146, 214–215
Loayza, Jerónimo de, 26, 54, 55, 79, 285; *Instrucción de la orden que se a de tener doctrina de los naturales*, 54, 55, 67
Lobo Guerrero, Bartolomé, 30, 117, 118, 119
López, Luis, 108

MacCormack, Sabine, 2, 28–29, 66, 83, 149, 224, 350n12
Mamanmirco, 264, 265, 268
Mancera, Marqués de, 165
Manco Capac, 144
Manco Inca, 53
Mannheim, Bruce, 2, 37, 39, 40, 41, 46, 124, 188, 216, 233–234, 236, 238, 242, 264, 265, 268, 288, 322n10
Manuel, Gaspar, 176. See also *Selectas de el directorio espiritual*
marriage (sacrament of), 56; texts about, 90, 161
Martínez, Alonso, 97, 99, 107, 116, 121
Martínez, Juan, 103, 117, 118, 120–121, 142, 152–153
Mary, Virgin: astronomical epithets, 263–265, 268; botanical epithets, 263, 265–267; cult of, 139, 141–142, 261–262, 275–276; iconography of, 233, 263–268; key texts, 150, 154, 262, 350n18. See also *Hanac pachap cussicuinin*; rosary
mascapaycha, 251, 252, 253, 254
mass: performance of, 34, 58, 158, 275, 282; translation of, 20, 141, 156, 158, 222, 275

Maya (Kakchiquel), 211
Meléndez, Juan, 153
memorization: aids to, 274, 288, 290
mendicants, 26; and language licensing in archdiocese of Lima, 119–120; and secular clergy, 26, 28; and Third Lima Council works, 98–99, 103–104; and Toledo, 78–79; translation efforts, 152–154, 304–305. *See also* Augustinians; Dominicans; Franciscans; Mercedarians
Mendieta, Jerónimo de, 60–61
Mercado, Juan de, 153, 224
Mercedarians, 80, 134, 286
Mesoamerica, 48, 288; religious translation compared to Peru, 211, 224, 226, 230, 303–305
mestizos: in clergy, 16, 80, 83, 87–88, 97, 98, 99, 131, 164, 190
metalanguages, 271–272, 288–289; book format, 293–294; grammar, 297–302; music, 292–293; spatialization, 290–291; textual figures, 294–297
metapragmatic (context-defining) cues, 271–272, 288–302. *See also* metalanguages
meter, 233, 240–242
Mexico, 35, 36, 225, 226; religious translation compared to Peru, 211, 224, 226, 230, 303–305. *See also* Mesoamerica; Nahuatl
Meyer, Brigit, 319
Michael, St. (the Archangel): epithets, 251
mid-seventeenth-century works, 163–171, 308
Mills, Kenneth, 175
mining: linguistic consequences of, 47–48, 111–112
Mixtec (language), 304
Mochica (language), 41, 124–125, 147
Mogrovejo, Alvaro, 335n43
Mogrovejo, Toribio Alfonso de, 28, 30, 77, 86, 100, 103, 123, 125, 139
Mohrmann, Christine, 297
Molina, Cristóbal de, 74–75, 99, 116, 306; on Incas, 74–75; Quechua prayers recorded by, 75, 144, 150, 191, 194, 249, 327n33
Molina, Diego de, 103, 166–167; on Chinchaysuyo Quechua, 128, 163, 202; on language competence, 120, 134; linguistic features of Quechua texts, 128–129, 202; on orthography, 204; sermons, 168, 169–170, 230, 281; terminology and tropes, 250, 255
Mollinedo, Manuel de, 252
Moscoso, Juan, 252
Murúa, Martín de, 285–286
music, 58–59, 63, 77, 82, 154, 240, 242, 269, 282, 291–293
Muysken, Pieter, 8

Nahuatl, 18, 35, 36, 211, 225, 226, 230, 253, 303, 304, 320n13
Nebrija, Antonio de, 32
neologisms, 14, 145, 146, 207, 325n21; in postcouncil literature, 208, 217, 218; in Santo Tomás, 70, 71, 207, 213; and Third Lima Council, 207, 214, 217
Neoplatonism, 149
Nobili, Roberto, 85, 146
Nuestra Señora de Belén (parish of), 155, 338n22

Olvera, Luis de, 59
Omasuyos. *See* Umasuyos
Orcochillay, 263, 264
Oré, Luis Jerónimo de, 147–152, 229, 230, 262; on Incas, 149–150;

linguistic features of Quechua texts, 198–199, 300–301; liturgical program of, 150, 274–275, 276, 290, 291, 292; style of hymns, 151–152, 241–244, 293, 294–297; terminology and tropes, 248–250, 254–258, 259, 263, 264, 265–266, 268, 269, 270
orthography, 186–188, 312; in Cuzco's diocesan corpus, 73, 196; in González Holguín, 199–200; in mid-seventeenth-century works, 203–205; in Oré, 198–199; in Santo Tomás, 189; in Third Lima Council works, 194–197

Pachacamac, 143, 257–258; identified with God, 248, 257–258; as Inca creator god, 84, 144, 149, 150, 169, 210, 249; as name for God, 63, 64, 143, 159, 314, 315
Pachacuti. *See* Inca Yupanqui
Pachacuti Yamqui Salcamaygua, Juan de, 49, 75, 144
Pachamama, 75
Pachayachachic, 84
Padilla, Juan de, 173
Pagden, Anthony, 24
Pallasca, 126
panaca: as epithet for the pope, 251
Panofsky, Erwin, 63
Paraguay, 160, 226, 304
parallelism, 233–239; in hymns, 242–244; as metalanguage, 294
Parinacochas, 59, 132
parish assistants, 77, 140, 273, 275, 282–288, 292, 352n10. *See also* cantors; fiscales; sacristans
parish system, 27; development of, 55, 57, 77, 78, 87; weakening of, 174–175
Parker, Gary, 37
passion: iconography of, 254–261; narratives of, 151, 166, 176, 254, 260, 276; reenactment of, 276
Pasto, 153
patronato real, 22, 26, 76, 78
Paul V, 139, 251, 262
Perea, Pedro de la, 131
Pérez Bocanegra, Juan, 20, 154–157, 338n22, 339nn23–24; and Andahuaylillas baptistery mural, 123, 339n23; on baptismal form, 209; on *hermanos mayores* and quipu confession, 284–285, 287; Incaism, 254, 314; as language examiner, 116; linguistic features of Quechua texts, 156, 200–201, 299; promotion of Quechua in the liturgy, 222, 229, 275, 280; style of hymns, 154, 242, 262, 269, 293; terminology and tropes, 156, 208, 218–219, 231, 232, 250, 251, 259, 260, 263–270 passim
Pérez de Grado, Lorenzo, 156
performance, 271; catechetical, 273–274; devotional, 276–277; indigenous orchestration of, 282–283; liturgical, 274–276; and music, 291–293; sacramental, 277–280; spatialization of, 289–291
Phillip II, 35, 77, 80
Pius V (catechism of), 35, 89, 329n32
Pizarro, Francisco, 53, 314, 315
plays, 20–21, 224–225, 320nn14–16, 321n17, 356nn4–5
Pleiades, 263, 264–265, 268, 351nn20–23
poetics: textual figures, 233–245, 294–297; tropes, 231–233, 246–270 passim
Polo de Ondegardo, Juan, 258
Pomacocho, 132

Pomata, 59, 61
pope, epithets for, 251
Porres, Diego de, 139–140, 285, 286, 289, 290, 354n27
postcouncil period, 137–138, 138–162
postcouncil works, 137–138, 147–162, 307–308
Potosí, 47, 111
Prado, Pablo de, 157–158. See also *Directorio espiritual; Selectas de el directorio espiritual*
praeparatio evangelica, 65–66
prayer (powers of), 280–282
preaching, 34, 55, 74, 83, 116; González Holguín on, 159; and Gospels, 141; against idolatry, 138–139, 163; in language testing, 121; Third Lima Council style, 93–94. *See also* sermonarios
primera evangelización, 29, 53–75, 306–307
printing, 21–22, 29–30, 100–102, 293
private devotions, 141–142, 276–277
proto-evangelization, 65. *See also* Thomas, St.
psalms, 151, 177, 222
Pucarani, 153
pueblos de indios, 27, 77; as stage for pastoral performance, 289–291
Punchao, 253
Puquina, 41; as language of the Incas, 42, 194, 218, 322n12, 332n7; required for clergy, 124; translation into, 123, 124, 147, 335n43
purgatory: prayer for souls in, 139–140, 162, 274, 290; terms for, 208

Queantupa, 264
quipus, 143; in catechesis, 286; in confession, 278, 284, 285, 286–288; as liturgical calendars, 285–286; in parish administration, 285, 353n19; and rosary, 286
Quito, 18, 126–127

Rafael, Vicente, 312
Ramos, Gabriela, 155
reducción, 76, 77–78, 174, 289
requerimiento, 314, 315
Riaño, Luis de, 123, 339n23
Ricardo, Antonio, 88, 91, 100
Ricci, Matteo, 85
Rituale seu manuale peruanum (Oré), 147–148, 199. *See also* Oré, Luis Jerónimo de
Ritual formulario (Pérez Bocanegra), 154, 155–157, 262, 277. *See also* Pérez Bocanegra, Juan
rituals, 19–20, 35, 90, 137, 138, 155, 161, 222, 277, 279, 352n3. See also *Aptaycachana; Ritual formulario; Rituale seu manuale peruanum*
Robleda, Alonso de, 335n42
Rojo Mejía y Ocón, Juan, 122; on Central versus Cuzco Quechua, 129–130; grammar by, 121; as Quechua chair, 118, 222; on translation of tropes, 231
Romero, Luis Francisco, 342n55
rosary, 141–142, 276, 281; in Guaman Poma's work, 162; and quipus, 286; texts for/about, 150, 153, 158, 276
Rostworowski, María, 258

Saavedra, Francisco de, 125
sacristans, 77, 275, 282, 352n10
Sahagún, Bernardino de, 346n4
saint (terms for), 207
Salomon, Frank, 16, 235
salvation (requirements for), 27, 60, 61, 85, 96, 144

Sancho de Melgar, Esteban, 176
San José de Chorrillos, 353n19
San Martín de Reque, 125
San Pedro de Casta, 165
San Sebastián de Huaraz, 171, 175
Santa Ana, 118
Santa María del Valle, 166
Santiago, Bartolomé de, 97, 99–100, 107
Santiago del Cercado, 81
Santo Tomás, Domingo de, 28, 69–71, 91; dialectology and orthography, 188–190; on Quechua, 43–44, 106; Quechua texts reproduced by, 69, 71, 236–237; terminology, 70–71, 207, 210–214
Sarmiento Rendón, Florián, 164
satire, 283–284
Second Lima Council, 57–58, 65; and Quechua translation, 71; and taquis, 62
Selectas de el directorio espiritual, 157, 176, 178, 223
Sell, Bary David, 320n13
semantic couplets, 233, 234, 243, 244
Señor de los Milagros, 258
Señor de los Temblores, 258
sermonarios, 19, 138–139, 141, 222; historical discourse in, 168–170. See also *Sermones de la quaresma*; *Sermones de los misterios de nuestra santa fe catolica*; *Tercero cathecismo*; *Tratado de los evangelios*
Sermones de la quaresma (Molina), 166–167. *See also* Molina, Diego de
Sermones de los misterios de nuestra santa fe catolica (Avendaño), 165–166. *See also* Avendaño, Fernando de
Silverstein, Michael, 335n39
sin (terms for), 208, 211–212, 215. *See also* confession
Sixth Lima Council, 104, 177
Somorrostro, García, 125
Soras, 286
Soto, Martín de, 97
soul (terms for), 213–214, 219, 345n37
Southern Cross, 263, 351n20
Southern Quechua, 38–39, 46, 47–48, 111–112, 191–192. *See also* Cuzco Quechua; Standard Colonial Quechua
Spanish: grammatical influences in pastoral Quechua, 182–183; loan words, 206–207; translation from Quechua, 230, 347n11
Standard Colonial Quechua, 46–49; and Cuzco Quechua, 106–107, 191–194, 195, 196, 197, 307; decline, 178; effects, 312, 313; in language competence system, 121–122; spread, 107, 109–110, 307; in Third Lima Council works, 93
stem matching. *See* lexical pairing
sudden-disclosure suffix, 297, 299–300
Sun god, 63, 232–233, 247; solar symbolism in Christian contexts, 252–253
Symbolo catholico indiano (Oré), 147, 149, 150–151, 262; excerpted in later works, 157, 158, 166–167. *See also* Oré, Luis Jerónimo de
syncretism, 15, 63, 64, 246–270 passim
Syriac, 128

Tagalog, 312, 320n13
Talavera, Hernando de, 33–34
Tamil, 14, 146, 294
Tampu Toco: as epithet for Archangel Michael, 251
taqui oncoy movement, 56
taquis, 60; Christian adaptation of, 61–65, 144, 159–160, 225–226
Taraco, 335n42
Tarascan (language), 36

Tarma y Chinchaycocha, 134, 171
Taylor, Gerald, 2, 166, 168, 187, 189–190, 212, 215, 322n10, 340n37, 344n27, 347n11
Tercero cathecismo (Third Lima Council), 88, 90, 166, 167, 177. *See also* Third Lima Council works
terminology, 6, 206–210; in mid-seventeenth-century works, 219–220; in Pérez Bocanegra, 156, 218–219; in postcouncil works, 145–146, 217–219; in Santo Tomás, 70–71, 207, 210–214; in Third Lima Council works, 214–217
Third Lima Council, 28, 86–88; on language competence system, 115; language policies of, 87, 88–89, 107–108
Third Lima Council works, 3, 46, 48, 88–104; author/s, 96–97; Aymara versions, 46, 88, 89, 97, 107, 194; enforcement, 101–104; linguistic features of Quechua texts, 191–197, 300, 307; liturgy and sacraments, 94–96; model for pastoral Quechua, 92–94, 307; production and printing, 100–101; Quechua terminology, 214–217; Quechua translators, 96–100; and Standard Colonial Quechua, 93, 191–197; translated into further languages, 89, 124, 125. See also *Confessionario para los curas de indios*; *Doctrina christiana y catecismo*; *Tercero cathecismo*
Third Mexican Council, 304
Thomas, St. (the Apostle): visit to the Andes, 65, 144, 169, 300
Titicaca, 42, 59, 78, 81, 169, 300
tocapu, 248, 249, 250, 349n5
Toledo, Francisco de, 28, 76–81, 109, 115
Tonocote (language), 123, 335n40
Torero, Alfredo, 37–38, 40, 48, 111, 183–184, 206, 322n10
Torres Bollo, Diego de, 103
Torres Rubio, Diego de, 161, 176, 177, 198
Torres y Portugal, Fernando de. *See* Villar, Conde del
Tratado de los evangelios (Avila), 164–165, 340n34. *See also* Avila, Francisco de
Tree of Jesse, 266
Trinity (terms for), 214–215
tropes: Andeanization, 269–270; and disjunction, 269–270; for divine power, 247–251; and double register, 267–269; for Mary, 233, 263–267; problems in translation, 231, 233; for sacrifice of Christ, 232–233, 254–261
Trujillo (diocese of), 17–18, 30, 41; language licensing, 125
Tunupa, 169
Tupac Amaru, 78, 252, 253, 332n10, 350n12
Tupi, 123, 136, 147

Umasuyos, 153, 335n42
uncu, 249, 252
University of San Marcos, 59, 78, 155; Quechua chair at, 79, 108, 115, 117–119, 120, 130, 172, 310, 333n24
Urton, Gary, 263
Uruquilla, 332n7
Uyupacha, 282

Valera, Blas, 97, 98, 112–113, 337n10
Valignano, Alessandro, 85
Valverde, Vicente de, 53, 314, 315
Vásquez, Juan, 159
Venus, 264
Vera, Fernando de, 131, 132
Verdugo, Francisco, 132

vernacular competence. *See* language competence
viaticum, 57, 87, 279
Vilcabamba, 78
Villagómez, Pedro de, 31, 125, 132, 138, 163, 165, 166, 173, 174
Villallón, Esteban de, 99
villancicos, 33–34, 63, 242, 269, 322n6
Villar, Conde del, 109, 115–116
Viracocha, 66; epithets applied to God, 213, 248–250; as Inca creator god, 66, 75, 84, 142, 144, 213, 306; as name for God, 66, 67, 210, 306; prayers to, 74, 75, 144, 150; and textiles, 249–250
virgin/virginity (terms for), 214, 218, 345n38

worship (terms for), 212, 218

Yapuguay, Nicolás, 226
Yauri, 335n42
Yauyos, 40

Zubieta y Rojas, Bernardo de, 177
Zuidema, R. T., 264
Županov, Ines, 146, 294

ALAN DURSTON

is assistant professor of history
at York University, Toronto, Canada.